STRETCHING THE CONSTITUTION

What was the meaning of the European referendum of 23 June 2016? How far did it justify and necessitate the policies pursued in response to it? What are the implications of the vote and its prolonged aftermath for the United Kingdom (UK) constitution? This book seeks to answer these questions. They involve a specific episode that has been important to the UK and the outside world; and also engage wider challenges faced by many developed democracies internationally. Deploying methodology adapted from applied history, the work makes a virtue of being written without knowledge of the final outcomes of the tendencies it considers. The author assesses from a constitutional perspective the way in which the decision to leave the EU was taken and then pursued, discussing in particular the role of Parliament. It includes a close analysis of the referendum legislation, and parliamentary debates and publications. The book then considers the wider implications of Brexit for the UK political system. It does so through analysing a series of proposals made from 1900 onwards for constitutional reform, and discerning their contemporary applicability. Reflecting the expansive implications of Brexit, a variety of aspects of the UK system are considered, including participation in international organisations, referendums, Parliament, devolution and the Union, the executive, and the system of representative democracy itself. The book also guides readers toward issues that have gained in salience in connection with the Brexit controversy, in particular uses of the Internet and social media. Finally, the author makes proposals for constitutional reforms intended to help the democratic system of the UK to adapt to its changing environment, whatever particular conclusions the Brexit episode may reach.

Volume 9 in the series Hart Studies in Constitutional Law

Hart Studies in Constitutional Law

Volume 1 The House of Lords 1911–2011: A Century of Non-Reform
Chris Ballinger

Volume 2 Parliament and the Law
Edited by Alexander Horne, Gavin Drewry and Dawn Oliver

Volume 3 Law in Politics, Politics in Law
Edited by David Feldman

Volume 4 Parliamentary Sovereignty in the UK Constitution
Michael Gordon

Volume 5 Parliament: Legislation and Accountability
Edited by Alexander Horne and Andrew Le Sueur

Volume 6 The Codes of the Constitution
Andrew Blick

Volume 7 Essays on the History of Parliamentary Procedure:
In Honour of Thomas Erskine May
Edited by Paul Evans

Volume 8 Parliament and the Law
Edited by Alexander Horne and Gavin Drewry

Stretching the Constitution

The Brexit Shock in Historic Perspective

Andrew Blick

•HART•
OXFORD • LONDON • NEW YORK • NEW DELHI • SYDNEY

HART PUBLISHING

Bloomsbury Publishing Plc

Kemp House, Chawley Park, Cumnor Hill, Oxford, OX2 9PH, UK

HART PUBLISHING, the Hart/Stag logo, BLOOMSBURY and the Diana logo are trademarks of Bloomsbury Publishing Plc

First published in Great Britain 2019

A catalogue record for this book is available from the British Library.

Library of Congress Cataloging-in-Publication data

Names: Blick, Andrew, author.

Title: Stretching the Constitution : the Brexit shock in historic perspective / Andrew Blick.

Description: Oxford [UK] ; Chicago, Illinois : Hart Publishing, 2019. | Series: Hart studies in constitutional law ; volume 9 | Includes bibliographical references and index.

Identifiers: LCCN 2018055411 (print) | LCCN 2018055856 (ebook) | ISBN 9781509905812 (Epub) | ISBN 9781509905805 (hardback)

Subjects: LCSH: Constitutional law—Great Britain. | Referendum—Great Britain—History. | Representative government and representation—Great Britain—History. | Legislative bodies—Great Britain—History. | European Union—Great Britain—History. | Great Britain—Politics and government—History. | BISAC: LAW / Constitutional.

Classification: LCC KD3934 (ebook) | LCC KD3934 .B55 2019 (print) | DDC 342.41/0412—dc23

LC record available at https://lccn.loc.gov/2018055411

ISBN: HB: 978-1-50990-580-5
ePDF: 978-1-50990-582-9
ePub: 978-1-50990-581-2

Typeset by Compuscript Ltd, Shannon
Printed and bound in Great Britain by TJ International Ltd, Padstow, Cornwall

To find out more about our authors and books visit www.hartpublishing.co.uk. Here you will find extracts, author information, details of forthcoming events and the option to sign up for our newsletters.

For Frederick, George and Nicola

Acknowledgements

I AM FORTUNATE to be involved with a number of organisations containing within them generous colleagues who have made this book possible: at the Department of Political Economy, King's College London; The Constitution Society; History & Policy; and the Federal Trust for Education and Research.

As ever, the people to whom I owe the most are Frederick, George and Nicola Blick, and my other family members: Karen, Katharine and Robin Blick.

My excellent publisher, Hart, have once again made it possible for me to write the book that I wanted. In particular, I am grateful to Sinead Moloney, Rosamund Jubber, Linda Staniford, Rose Wood and Claire Banyard, my copy editor. Bill Asquith commissioned this work before himself being drawn into the drama that is the focus of it.

Andrew Blick
Acton, London
September 2018

Table of Contents

Introduction

I. THE POLITICAL AND THE HISTORICAL

THE POLITICAL HAS reasserted itself. In recent years, outcomes that once seemed remote possibilities in the United Kingdom (UK) have become more plausible – or have actually occurred. This trend appears to involve both the supply and demand sides of the equation. Governments and established parties have presented options to the public that previously would have been of a more marginal character; while voters have shown themselves more willing to embrace such possibilities than might have been anticipated. Forms of public participation believed to be in long-term decline have seen a revival. New methods of organisation and communication, lessening the significance of traditional channels, have become prominent. On the surface these tendencies might seem to signify the strengthening of the system of popular government. Yet they have encouraged influential observers to draw the opposite conclusion. A common theme in contemporary political analysis is the idea that liberal democracy might be under challenge, or possibly in terminal decline.[1] Authors of such assessments sometimes posit that events in the UK are a significant part of a wider tendency in the developed world.[2] In doing so, they often focus on the phenomenon known as 'Brexit'.[3] In considering – from a perspective central to its essence – this occurrence, this book, therefore, addresses an important facet of a subject of exceptional significance within the UK and internationally.

The precise point at which the reassertion of the political in the UK context began to manifest itself difficult to define. However, it is possible to identify some events that lie at its core. They include the Scottish independence referendum of 2014; the capture of the leadership of the Labour Party by Jeremy Corbyn in 2015; and the referendum on continued UK membership of the European Union (EU) of 2016. In each case, the main aspects of the wider tendency can be detected. They broadened the options presented as available to the public.[4] Radical possibilities appealed to a greater number than might have been expected at

[1] eg Yascha Mounk, *The People vs. Democracy: Why our freedom is in danger and how to save it* (Cambridge, Harvard University Press, 2018).

[2] See eg David Runciman, *How Democracy Ends* (London, Profile, 2018).

[3] See eg Roger Eatwell and Matthew Goodwin, *National populism: The revolt against liberal democracy* (London, Pelican, 2018).

[4] For instance, at the Scottish referendum of 18 September 2014, voters in Scotland were asked whether Scotland should 'become an independent country'.

the beginning of the processes involved, which were the occasion for increased popular participation.[5] Moreover, the use of emergent campaigning techniques, namely those involving the Internet and social media, has played a prominent if disputed part in each of these episodes.[6] All three occasions helped trigger chains of events wider and longer than themselves, and were interconnected. This tendency is most fully exemplified by the EU referendum, instigating as it did an episode, still ongoing at the time of writing, labelled 'Brexit'.

This word originated to describe the proposition of UK or 'British' exit from the EU. On 23 June 2016, a referendum was held across the UK and Gibraltar posing the question: 'Should the United Kingdom remain a member of the European Union or leave the European Union'. Of a total turnout of 33,578,037 (72.2 per cent of the 46,500,001 who could have voted) 17,410,742 (51.9 per cent) selected '[l]eave', while 16,141,241 (48.1 per cent) chose the '[r]emain' option. Of all those who could have voted, 37.4 per cent voted 'leave'; and 34.7 'remain'. Ever since this point (as of the end of September 2018) the UK government has interpreted this result as necessitating a commitment to departure from the EU: in other words, to 'Brexit'. But I apply the term here in a broader sense. At the time of writing – though it has set itself on a course to do so – the UK has not yet left the EU. The possibility that it will halt this process, though politically and legally complex in its implications, cannot wholly be excluded. Furthermore, the precise form that UK removal from the EU – if it occurs – will take, is difficult to predict. But it is possible to identify a period, beginning roughly during the lead-up to the EU referendum and continuing to the present. During this 'Brexit' episode, the prospect of departing has attained a dominance within UK political processes and discourse greater than any other specific concern over such a sustained period in more than a century, other than the two world wars. The scale of its impact can be assessed by considering a selection of the events it has triggered (or in the case of the 2017 General Election, at least contributed to):

- the resignation of a Prime Minister (David Cameron) in response to the 'leave' result in the referendum;
- ongoing, fundamental uncertainty and disagreement over the economic and legal impact of Brexit, its consequences for the relationship of the UK with the outside world, and its effect upon the European and international environment;

[5] See the turnouts and the level of support for the more radical option in the 2014 and 2016 referendums; and the surge in Labour membership from 2015. Voting data used in this book found in Roger Mortimore and Andrew Blick, *Butler's British Political Facts* (Basingstoke, Palgrave, 2018).

[6] See eg Andrew Whitaker, 'The truth about Scotland and online abuse: "cybernats" and "cyberbrits" are just as bad as eachother', *Herald*, 19 February 2017: https://www.heraldscotland.com/news/15102321.The_truth_about_Scotland_and_online_abuse___cybernats__and__cyberbrits__are_just_as_bad_as_each_other/ last accessed 29 September 2018; Chadwick, Andrew, and Jennifer Stromer-Galley, 'Digital media, power, and democracy in parties and election campaigns: Party decline or party renewal?' (2016) *International Journal of Press/Politics* 283–93.

- sustained disputes within the two main parties over appropriate policies;
- the holding of an early General Election, the first of this type to be instigated under the Fixed-term Parliaments Act 2011;
- public disagreements between Cabinet members;
- major disputes about serious constitutional issues, such as the meaning of the referendum result, the appropriateness of a further vote, and the respective roles of the executive and Parliament;
- disputes between devolved and central government over the handling of the response to the vote of 2016;
- renewed doubts about the future of the United Kingdom, and in particular the place of Scotland and Northern Ireland within it;
- the exposure and aggravation of deep cleavages in public opinion, cutting across more commonly accepted political divisions;
- sharp territorial variations in outlook; and
- a discrepancy in the balance of opinion on the EU issue between those involved in government and the population as a whole, with the former tending to be more favourable towards membership than the latter.

Taken together, these tendencies comprise the domestic aspect of the 'shock' referred to in the subtitle of this book. But as we will see, it is a self-inflicted shock, of the type received by someone who deliberately prods an electric socket with an unprotected finger. A number of items on this list could be defined as having a 'constitutional' aspect to them. Indeed, some of the most dramatic manifestations of Brexit are in this field. They are the subject of the present work. The term 'constitution' as employed in this book entails those institutions, rules and principles that bind together a polity. It defines the authorities and responsibilities of the various organs of governance and the way in which they interact with eachother. A constitution also specifies the nature of the relationship between those institutions and members of the public, whose rights as individuals it defines.[7] In most countries a 'written' constitution contains key provisions in this area, that is one document, or a series of interlinked documents, comprising a statement of fundamental arrangements. In democratic states such a text is seen as a central means by which the values of such a system are expressed, implemented and maintained in practice. Typically a 'written' constitution is entrenched, making it more difficult to amend than regular legislation; and is legally enforceable, by a court or other body, with all legislation and actions by public authorities invalid in as far as they conflict with its terms. The UK does not have a 'written' entity so defined. Rather, its

[7] For a revealing comparative account, see: Samuel Edward Finer, Vernon Bogdanor, and Bernard Rudden, *Comparing constitutions* (Oxford, Clarendon Press, 1995).

core constitutional arrangements are dispersed across such locations as Acts of Parliament, judicial decisions, parliamentary rules, and less formal understandings or conventions. The UK constitution is not subject to specific amendment procedures; nor is it expressly upheld by judicial review of the type practiced in other territories.[8]

Arguably its dispersed existence makes clear definition of the UK constitution a more difficult task – though it could be noted that its 'written' equivalents do not fully capture all the central elements of a system and may be subject to competing interpretations. Yet despite the degree of uncertainty, it is clear that the reassertion of the political discussed here has constitutional implications. For instance, in the case of the Scottish referendum, the future of the UK as a state was in jeopardy. Had it produced a 'yes' result the implication would have been a major reconfiguration of the system. In an effort to avoid such an outcome, leaders of the three main pro-Union parties, in the closing period of the campaign, committed themselves to significant changes within the context of the existing state, which they implemented after the vote.[9] To move to the second of the key events listed above, during the Corbyn era pronounced tensions have manifested themselves within Labour between the bulk of the parliamentary party on the one hand, and the leader, supported by wider members and other affiliates, on the other hand. This dispute is of a constitutional quality in that it pertains to the nature of the representative system. It raises questions about how far it is proper for office holders to act on their own discretion, or be subject to external forces; and the constitutional role of parties.[10] Brexit has generated systemic turmoil, and the prospect of transformative change, on a scale greater than the two previous examples, significant though they are in this regard. It arises both from the way in which the decision to leave the EU was taken, and in the implied consequences of the implementation of that policy of departure. The purpose of this book is to consider these aspects of Brexit. It does so through the use of methodology adapted from a particular discipline.

This particular focus on Brexit has considerable potential value, including through its connection to wider international concerns about the condition of democracy. For instance, it creates potential for an exploration of the possible manifestation of what is termed 'populism' in a mature democracy. If we approach populism not as a term of abuse, but as a 'thin' ideology,[11] then a

[8] Andrew Blick, *Beyond Magna Carta: a constitution for the United Kingdom* (London, Bloomsbury, 2015) 201–14.

[9] Murray Foote, 'Inside the Vow', 17 September 2015, *Daily Record*: https://www.dailyrecord.co.uk/news/politics/inside-vow-how-historic-daily-6464878 last accessed 28 September 2018.

[10] Meg Russell, 'How leadership rule changes have led to a fight for the very soul of the Labour Party', *Guardian*, 17 July 2016: https://www.theguardian.com/commentisfree/2016/jul/17/labour-leadership-battle-jeremy-corbyn-party-organisation last accessed 28 September 2018.

[11] Ben Stanley, 'The thin ideology of populism' (2008) 13(1) *Journal of political ideologies* 95–110.

fruitful consideration of this concept in the context of Brexit is possible.[12] From a constitutional perspective, the referendum and its aftermath saw populist tropes gain in salience, as chapter one in particular demonstrates. Advocates of Brexit made a classic populist case in that they presented themselves as seeking to discern and then to implement the will of the people, expressed via a referendum, and challenging the authority of a resistant domestic elite and its exploitative alliance with an external supranational agency. The desire to control inward migration – another common feature of populism – was a prominent aspect of the case for leaving.[13] Furthermore, as we will see, there was some material basis for the claim that Brexit represented the fulfilment of a mass movement of the socially or at least politically excluded, whose values differed significantly from those in authority. However, such perceptions should be qualified. It would not be possible to claim that only an elite supported continued membership of the EU, since 48.1 per cent of those who voted, making up more than 16 million people, opted for 'remain'. Some of the groups most supportive of remaining – such as Catholics in Northern Ireland – cannot realistically be dismissed as belonging to a privileged cabal. Moreover, the crucial decisions leading to the referendum and the response to it were taken within representative bodies such as Parliament, Cabinet and the parties. But regardless of whether the application of populist rhetoric would match the complex reality, this brief discussion demonstrates that the constitutional dimension to the Brexit episode can be used to explore issues of global significance, as this book seeks to do. It is in part a case study of what happens to a country seeking to leave a unique supranational organisation. I now consider the methodological approach that this work takes.

II. USES OF HISTORY

A revival of the political in the present calls in turn for a resuscitation of the study of its past. This particular branch of the historical discipline has suffered from reduced status in recent decades, or perhaps it is better to state that it has lacked 'the coherence and, frequently, the self-confidence that other scholarly enterprises seem to possess (and which political history itself once enjoyed in abundance).'[14] It should not be necessary to make a case for the research,

[12] Michael Freeden, 'After the Brexit referendum: revisiting populism as an ideology' (2017) 22(1) *Journal of Political Ideologies* 1–11; John Clarke and Janet Newman, '"People in this country have had enough of experts": Brexit and the paradoxes of populism' (2017) 11(1) *Critical Policy Studies* 101–16.

[13] For an 'ideational' definition of populism, see Cas Mudde and Cristóbal Rovira Kaltwasser, *Populism: A very short introduction* (Oxford, Oxford University Press, 2017) 1–20.

[14] David Brown, Robert Crowcroft and Gordon Pentland, 'Introduction' in Brown, Crowcroft and Pentland (eds), *The Oxford Handbook of Modern British Political History: 1800–1900* (Oxford, Oxford University Press, 2018) 1. See generally 1–9.

teaching and dissemination of political history any more than for the other variants – social, cultural and so on – that have come to emerge alongside and perhaps even challenge it.[15] There is, or there should be, space for all, and for cross-pollination between them.[16] Just as the value of political history as an academic exercise in itself is self-evident, so too is its value to the understanding of the present. This book applies history to assist the fuller perception of a particular manifestation of the contemporary political revival: Brexit, doing so specifically from a constitutional perspective. Throughout this work, I will utilise a technique central to the historical discipline: the analysis of documentary primary sources, both older and more recent, to identify and analyse the constitutional issues that Brexit has raised. My particular approach is to identify and focus on specific selected texts. There can be a temptation in history to treat groups of documents as between them explaining the arrival at given destinations. Yet on closer analysis, as we will see, matters tend to appear more complicated. Each source has its distinctive features: different from others with which it might be grouped, and possibly pointing to a path of development other than that ultimately taken. The *disaggregation* method employed in this book, therefore, is intended as a corrective to any temptation towards deterministic assumptions. It is also useful in current circumstances. Brexit, at the time of writing, consists of a dynamic set of interconnected uncertainties, and is likely to continue to do so for a significant period. A focus on the specific rather than the general from a variety of periods can help conceptualise the wide array of possible outcomes we face, and weigh their merits.

I write at a time of pronounced uncertainty. This book deliberately breaks off at the end of September 2018. At this juncture, the EU has recently responded negatively to the so-called 'Chequers' plan;[17] there is discussion of a possible second referendum;[18] and the Conservative conference is about to commence, with the Prime Minister under considerable pressure to pursue a more decisive departure than that envisaged in 'Chequers'.[19] A range of possibilities, from the UK not leaving the EU at all through to the most disruptive of exits remain in play, as does future disturbance in the security and integrity of the Union. From the point of view of an historical author, to be in this position should not be a source of regret. Rather it presents a rare opportunity: to analyse an episode

[15] For a discussion of the importance of political history, see Margaret MacMillan, *The Uses and Abuses of History* (London, Profile, 2010) 33–50.

[16] For a US perspective on the dangers of a neglect of political history, see Fredrik Logevall and Kenneth Osgood, 'Why Did We Stop Teaching Political History?', *New York Times*, 29 August 2016.

[17] Daniel Boffey and Dan Sabbagh, 'Chequers plan is dead, says Tusk as Macron calls Brexiters liars', *Guardian*, 20 September 2018: https://www.theguardian.com/politics/2018/sep/20/donald-tusk-demands-answer-to-irish-border-question-next-month last accessed 29 September 2018.

[18] Jonathan Freedland, 'We now need a people's vote on Brexit. But don't assume remain would win', *Guardian*, 21 September 2018: https://www.theguardian.com/commentisfree/2018/sep/21/peoples-vote-brexit-remain-theresa-may-salzburg-statement last accessed 29 September 2018.

[19] 'Boris Johnson sets out his "Super Canada" Brexit plan', *BBC*, 28 September 2018: https://www.bbc.co.uk/news/uk-politics-45673214 last accessed 29 September 2018.

unfettered by the knowledge of its conclusion. In a sense, this work is a time capsule. But it is intended for opening not in the distant future, but after the time that elapses between submission and publication. The latter event is intended to occur roughly at the point at which the UK is presently projected formally to leave the EU, at 11pm on Friday 29 March 2019.

A full exploitation of the possibilities this approach suggests necessitates an acknowledgement of the particularities to which it is subject. I purport neither to be wholly impartial nor, to use a term presently in vogue among those who often do not mean it, 'Brexit neutral'. The story is one in which I have played a modest part of my own in various ways, including as an historical adviser to the Welsh Government in its intervention in the Article 50 case that reached the UK Supreme Court late in 2016;[20] and as an author of articles intended to influence attitudes around the subject.[21] My views on Brexit are therefore in the public domain. I reiterate the most pertinent points here. I supported continued UK membership of the EU at the time of the referendum and continue to do so. The best future as I see it for the UK is as a fully integrated participant in the EU, eventually discarding all opt-outs, including from the single currency. The EU itself, with encouragement from the UK, should in my view continue to develop in a federal direction, including through establishing a clearer link between European elections and the composition of the leadership of the Commission. I did not agree with the holding of a referendum on continued UK membership of the EU; and judge that the particular approach taken to it meant that it was flawed as an exercise in democratic engagement. It does not form a legitimate basis in itself for departure from the EU, either along the lines pursued by the UK government, or in any other form. The decision to leave taken in response to the referendum should be reversed, without the need for a further popular vote.

I take these views openly into this book (though I accept that many will not share all or indeed any of them; and it is not my primary purpose to win others over). There is a longstanding debate among historians about partiality: whether those claiming to study the past can avoid subordinating it to their own values, derived from their relationship to social power structures of their time.[22] My approach is to upend this dilemma. Through avowedly deploying the past, I hope better to understand the present. This work considers sources as a means of understanding a sequence of events I regard as undesirable; and considering the options for the future. But how might history help?[23] To give

[20] 'Written Statement – Ground's for the Counsel General's application to intervene in the appeal of the Article 50 litigation before the Supreme Court', 21 November 2016: https://gov.wales/about/cabinet/cabinetstatements/2016-new/article50litigation/?lang=en last accessed 4 September 2018.

[21] For a selection, see: http://fedtrust.co.uk/our-work-on-europe/ last accessed 28 September 2018.

[22] Richard J Evans, *In Defence of History* (London, Granta, 2001) 191–223.

[23] For the methodology of applied history, see: John Tosh, 'In Defence of Applied History', *History and Policy*, 10 February 2006: http://www.historyandpolicy.org/policy-papers/papers/in-defence-of-applied-history-the-history-and-policy-website last accessed 29 September 2018.

some idea of its possible value, I now consider two documents that convey the capacity of this discipline for analysing, respectively, continuity and change. One provides a premonition from an earlier, 1975, European referendum of difficulties that arose in connection with its successor four decades later in 2016. It suggests that, while we should not treat history as a basis for prophecy, it can supply what Peter Hennessy has described – applying a phrase used by Fernand Braudel – as the 'thin wisps of tomorrow'.[24] The other offers an insight into significant changes that took place between the two votes of 1975 and 2016, involving the status of Northern Ireland, also with wider implications.

On 17 January 1975, the Lord President of the Council in the Labour government planning the referendum, Edward Short, circulated to Cabinet a paper drafted 'by an official working party on the practical implications of a referendum', prepared the previous November.[25] It was the work of civil servants from the Cabinet Office, Foreign and Commonwealth Office and Home Office. Their brief was '[t]o examine … all the practical implications of holding a referendum relating to European Community membership'. The working group found that this task directed it towards 'essential political questions' that it could not itself answer. It therefore 'set out the principal facts and factors which need to be taken into account'. The report commenced with a discussion of the section in the Labour Party General Election manifesto of October 1974 pertaining to the European Economic Community. It committed that Labour, if it won, would 'within 12 months of this Election … give the British people the final say, which will be binding on the Government – through the ballot box – on whether we accept the terms [of a renegotiation of membership] and stay in or reject the terms and come out'. This pledge raised various complications, pertaining for instance to when the referendum should take place, what amounted to a 'final say' on the part of the 'British people' and what it meant for that 'say' to be 'binding'.[26] To ensure the 'say' was 'final', the working group considered whether various mechanisms might be appropriate, including 'compulsory voting'; a minimum turnout requirement; or a supermajority stipulation, such as at least 51 per cent (ie: 50.1 per cent, for instance, being insufficient), 60 per cent or 75 per cent.[27] The authors recognised that, if such a rule were applied to a verdict in either direction, there was a danger of an

[24] Peter Hennessy, *Distilling the Frenzy: Writing the history of one's own times* (London, Biteback, 2012) 79.

[25] TNA PRO CAB 129/181/6, 'Practical implications of holding a referendum on European Community membership – report by official working party', Note by the Lord President of the Council, Edward Short, 17 January 1975.

[26] 'Report by officials on the practical implications of holding a referendum related to European Community members', 22 November 1974, attachment to TNA PRO CAB 129/181/6, 'Practical implications of holding a referendum on European Community membership – report by official working party', Note by the Lord President of the Council, Edward Short, 17 January 1975, p 1.

[27] ibid, 2.

inconclusive result. In such an eventuality, '[u]nless it was thought right to hold another referendum, it is for consideration whether the issue should be left to Parliament'.[28]

The paper also discussed whether there might be some means of 'taking account of the results in Scotland, Wales and Northern Ireland'. It noted that '[a] difficult situation could arise if the United Kingdom results were finely balanced, and it were known that, for example, Scotland had registered a strong majority in one direction. The Scottish Nationalists may press for a commitment that a binding majority should involve a majority in Scotland as well as the whole United Kingdom'. One option the working group considered in relation to this issue was that only the total UK voting figures be made available, with no territorial breakdown.[29] The report assessed how politicians and Parliament might respond to the outcome. If it were in favour of membership, no specific action would be required. However, a result in the opposite direction would create a need to 'negotiate our way out of the Treaty of Accession establishing by negotiation the new relationship we would wish to establish, in trade and other areas, with the Community'. It would entail a 'need to review and revise domestic policies, particularly in respect of agriculture and trade, in order to reflect the consequences of withdrawal'. Finally, having completed negotiations with the Community, it would be necessary to 'repeal the European Communities Act' and 'to make substantial legislative adjustments in the domestic sphere'.[30]

The working group judged that this combined process would require 'adequate time – perhaps up to a year' for the UK 'to complete our final withdrawal from the Community on the best conditions we could obtain and to reorient our policies'.[31] It discussed whether it might be appropriate for the Act providing for the referendum to include within it 'provision for the automatic repeal of the European Communities Act either immediately following the referendum result or after a specified period of, say, 12 months'. The working group cautioned that 'instant automatic repeal' was not practically viable. In fields such as agricultural subsidy 'there would be no satisfactory statutory provision' since they now rested on participation in the Community. 'Complicated legislation', the paper cautioned 'would have to be prepared and enacted'. The alternative would be to allow the 'Government … complete room for manoeuvre as to Parliamentary action until after the referendum result is known'.[32]

Further issues the working group addressed included the precise question to be asked, for which it offered six possible variants.[33] It dealt with organisational matters and arrangements for the count. A possibility to which it referred was the

[28] ibid, 3.
[29] ibid.
[30] ibid, 4.
[31] ibid, 5.
[32] ibid, 5.
[33] ibid, 7–14.

use of 'a computer count', but the authors took the view that 'the time needed to install and debug such a system must not be underestimated and there would be a risk of fiasco'.[34] This section also raised the concern that the publication of opinion polling could exercise 'undue influence' on voters, since in contrast to parliamentary elections 'the normal anchors of a familiar local candidate, of a range of issues and of traditional allegiances' were absent. The working group therefore suggested tentatively the consideration of the prohibition of publication of opinion poll findings for a period of perhaps four weeks leading up to the day of the referendum.[35] The paper discussed information provision and the role of the media, including the possibility of public funding for campaign groups.[36] One area of complication it identified in this respect was that of '<u>paid advertisements</u> and other forms of <u>paid</u> propaganda'. The working group noted that '[c]oncern is being expressed about the possibility of the anti-market case being swamped by massive pro-market expenditure financed largely by industry'. In the case of a General Election, restrictions were imposed through controls on local candidates, but this method was not available for a referendum.[37] The working group noted that '[a]ny control of the many organisations and individuals that might wish to pay for propaganda would raise major questions of principles about freedom of expression'. Moreover, 'it would seem impracticable to devise a fool-proof system of comprehensive control extending to all forms of paid propaganda at all levels'.[38] The paper considered further who would be responsible for organising the referendum[39] and the legislation needed to provide for it.[40] On the latter point, it expressed concern that:

> The Bill may prove contentious in Parliament and expensive in terms of Parliamentary time. Being a constitutional measure, all stages will presumably have to be taken on the floor of the House of Commons. The House of Lords could be particularly difficult, especially if they considered that the question on the ballot paper was slanted in favour of withdrawal from the EEC. Even if the Lords did not reject the Bill outright, they might insist on amendments (eg to the form of the question) which the government would find it difficult to accept.[41]

After discussing the overall timetable for action,[42] the working group then distilled its analysis into the following set of questions:

> '1.12 SHOULD VOTING BE COMPULSORY?
>
> 1.13 SHOULD A MINIMUM PROPORTION OF THE TOTAL ELECTORATE BE REQUIRED FOR A DECISIVE RESULT?

[34] ibid, 17. Entire section: 15–20.
[35] ibid, 19.
[36] ibid, 26. Entire section: 21–27.
[37] ibid, 24.
[38] ibid, 25.
[39] ibid, 28–30.
[40] ibid, 31–34.
[41] ibid, 32.
[42] ibid, 35–39.

1.14 SHOULD THE RESULT BE DECIDED BY A SIMPLE MAJORITY?

1.15 SHOULD PROVISION BE MADE FOR A FAILURE TO ACHIEVE A CONCLUSIVE RESULT?

1.16 SHOULD ANY SPECIAL PROVISION BE MADE FOR REGIONAL RESULTS?

1.17 SHOULD THE RESULT BE ENTRENCHED BY LEGISLATION?'[43]

2.18 SHOULD THE QUESTION SEEK AGREEMENT TO A COURSE RECOMMENDED BY THE GOVERNMENT?

2.19 SHOULD THE QUESTION REFER DIRECTLY TO THE RENEGOTIATED TERMS?

2.20 SHOULD THE QUESTION OFFER A CHOICE BETWEEN TWO ALTERNATIVES, OR SHOULD IT SEEK A "YES/NO" ANSWER TO A SINGLE PROPOSITION?

2.21 SHOULD SAMPLE SURVEYS BE UNDERTAKEN TO ASSESS VOTERS' REACTION TO, AND UNDERSTANDING OF, ALTERNATIVE FORMS OF QUESTIONS?

2.22 WHAT SHOULD BE THE ARRANGEMENTS FOR CONSULTATION ON THE FORM OF THE QUESTION?'[44]

3.13 SHOULD THE COUNT BE ON A LOCAL OR CENTRAL BASIS?

3.14 IF LOCAL, ON A LOCAL GOVERNMENT DISTRICT, PARLIAMENTARY OR COUNTY BASIS?

3.15 IF LOCAL, SHOULD THE INEVITABILITY OF PUBLISHING LOCAL RESULTS BE ACCEPTED FROM THE BEGINNING?

3.16 SHOULD THE PUBLICATION OF THE RESULTS OF UNOFFICIAL POLLS BE BANNED FOR A PERIOD BEFORE THE POLL?

3.17 WHAT ARRANGEMENTS SHOULD BE MADE FOR THE CHANNEL ISLES AND ISLE OF MAN? [eg: should they be able to vote in the referendum?][45]

4.19 SHOULD A LONG AND EXTENSIVE INFORMATION CAMPAIGN BE MOUNTED?

4.20 IF SO, SHOULD THE POSSIBILITY OF USING AN OUTSIDE AGENCY BE EXPLORED FURTHER?

4.21 ARE SPECIAL ARRANGMENTS NEEDED FOR TV AND RADIO TIME COMPARABLE TO ELECTION BROADCASTS?

4.22 SHOULD THE POSSIBILITY OF CONTROLLING SOME PAID PROPAGANDA ACTIVITES BE FURTHER EXPLORED?

4.23 SHOULD THE QUESTION OF GOVERNMENT FINANCE FOR DEFINED ACTIVITIES BE FURTHER EXPLORED?'[46]

[43] ibid, 6.
[44] ibid, 13–14.
[45] ibid, 19–20.
[46] ibid, 27.

5.8 WOULD MINISTERS WISH FURTHER WORK TO BE UNDERTAKEN ON THE POSSIBILITY OF USING AN AGENCY OR AGENCIES TO:

- DISSEMINATE INFORMATION;
- CONTROL PR ACTIVITIES
- ORGANISE THE REFERENDUM?[47]

6.12 WHICH MINISTER IS TO BE IN CHARGE OF THE [referendum] BILL?

6.13 ARE SPECIAL ARRANGEMENTS NEEDED FOR OFFICIAL SUPPORT?'[48]

7.7 IS THE WORKING ASSUMPTION TO BE THAT THE BILL WILL BE INTRODUCED AT THE END OF APRIL (OPTION A) OR AS SOON AS POSSIBLE IN THE NEW YEAR (OPTION B)?

7.8 DO MINISTERS WISH TO RETAIN THE OPTION OF A REFERENDUM IN JUNE (RATHER THAN IN OCTOBER)?'[49]

As we will see, the prescience of this document became fully apparent long after it was written. We cannot be sure how extensive was the briefing that David Cameron, the Conservative Prime Minister who brought about the 2016 vote, received regarding the complications his decision implied. However this text would have been a useful reference point for any such advice. But circumstances surrounding the 2016 vote were not simply a replication of those of 1975. Not only the result differed. While some concerns recurred, others developed in the interim, as is illustrated by a consideration of the Belfast or 'Good Friday' Agreement of 1998, to which the governments of the UK and Republic of Ireland, as well as various parties in Northern Ireland, were signatories.

The Agreement was a crucial stage in the peace process in the region. The parties to it noted their view that it 'offers a truly historic opportunity for a new beginning'. They were 'committed to partnership, equality and mutual respect as the basis of relationships within Northern Ireland, between North and South, and between these islands'. Crucially they pledged to 'recognise the legitimacy of whatever choice is freely exercised by a majority of the people of Northern Ireland with regard to its status, whether they prefer to continue to support the Union with Great Britain or a sovereign united Ireland'. This principle suggested that the population of Northern Ireland possessed self-determination overriding their absorption within the UK (or any attachment some might feel to the Republic). Furthermore, the Agreement posited 'that it is for the people of the island of Ireland alone, by agreement between the two parts respectively and without external impediment, to exercise their right of self-determination on the basis of consent, freely and concurrently given … to bring about a united Ireland',

[47] ibid, 30.
[48] ibid, 34.
[49] Ibid, p.39.

provided there was majority support in Northern Ireland. While qualified by consent stipulations, this statement accepted the existence of a special association between Northern Ireland and the Republic. The Agreement provided for the introduction of democratic institutions for Northern Ireland, with an elected Assembly; and various mechanisms for North-South cooperation. The reintroduction of devolution to Northern Ireland (it had previously operated from the 1920s to the early 1970s, followed by failed attempts at a revival) was part of a wider pattern of the late 1990s, whereby devolved institutions were established for the first time in Wales and Scotland. By the time of the EU referendum of 2016, devolution in Northern Ireland was not functioning, but it was operative in the two other territories, adding immense complications that did not pertain in 1975.

The two governments, of the Republic and of the UK, noted their strong support for the Agreement in its text, referring to the 'opportunity for a new beginning in relationships within Northern Ireland, within the island of Ireland and between the peoples of these islands'. Among their listed aspirations were 'to develop still further the unique relationship between their peoples and the close co-operation between their countries as friendly neighbours and as partners in the European Union'. The agreement did not expressly make guarantees regarding the continued presence of the UK – and within it Northern Ireland – in the EU. In a sense, both the UK and Republic remaining within the EU was so fundamental to the text that it did not require specific expression within it. For the UK to withdraw from the EU would clearly be a challenge to the spirit of the Agreement. The UK government, nearly two decades later, decided that the referendum of 23 June 2016 necessitated the adoption of such a policy. Issues connected to the Agreement would become a major obstacle to realisation of this objective in a way UK ministers deemed satisfactory.[50]

The two documents discussed above represent history that was perhaps not sufficiently taken into account in advance of the Brexit episode. Other learning from the past did take place – but seems to have led to difficulties. It is reasonable to speculate that, in adopting a commitment to a referendum in 2013,[51] David Cameron hoped to emulate Harold Wilson, who was the Labour Prime Minister in 1975. Wilson had used a popular vote on Europe as a device through which he might manage an internal dispute within the party he led.[52] He was successful, at least in the short-to-medium term. Ultimately the clearest difference between the two efforts was, from the point of view of both prime ministers, the most important aspect of them: the outcome. Unlike Cameron, Wilson achieved a comfortable vote in favour of continued membership of the European

[50] See ch 1.
[51] See ch 1.
[52] 'The reluctant European', *Economist*, 17 October 2015: https://www.economist.com/leaders/2015/10/17/the-reluctant-european last accessed 29 September 2018.

Economic Community. Though he brought about in 1975 what was the first ever UK-wide referendum, Wilson protested at the time that he did not intend to set an example for anyone; or seek to instigate and encourage further use of referendums. As he put it to the House of Commons in January 1975 'it is right that we should … use the word "unique". It is a very special situation which I do not think anybody will take as a precedent'.[53] It is clear from National Archive files that arrangements made in 1975 for the establishment and funding of officially recognised umbrella groups campaigning on either side of the vote were driven to a significant extent by political contingencies and sensitivities of the time, rather than an attempt to discern general principles.[54] Yet the process that began in the late 1990s leading to the establishment of the contemporary legislative framework for legislations, created by the Political Parties, Elections and Referendums Act 2000, treated the 1975 case as a model to be followed and built upon.[55]

Seeking to transfer the past directly into the present, or seizing upon some components of it while neglecting others, can be as misguided as a complete rejection of the importance of previous events. It is important to cast widely in the search both for relevant material and possible interpretations of it. Taking into account this need, this book deploys some of the techniques of the historian – in particular the analysis of documentary sources – to help to conceptualise present circumstances, and identify, in a time of flux, possibilities for the future. It seeks to demonstrate how this process would work, through presenting both accounts of the contents of particular sources and an analysis of their significance.

Part one of the book draws on a selection of texts from the Brexit period itself, setting out to convey the chaos and complexity that has characterised it, while also distilling certain key themes. Chapter one provides an overview of the constitutional issues raised by Brexit; while chapter two addresses the legislation that provided for the 2016 referendum. Part two considers a series of aspects of the UK constitution through the prism of proposals for reform of the UK constitution and related matters published in the period since 1900. The themes addressed are: the UK and multi-state organisations (chapter three); referendums (chapter four); the system of representative democracy (chapter five); Parliament (chapter six); the territorial constitution (chapter seven); the UK executive (chapter eight); and the digital constitution (chapter nine). The sources used in this part are selected either because they provide a view of paths not taken, that might merit further consideration; or because they can broaden understanding of the present, or both. Mainly they are the works of individual

[53] Hansard, House of Commons Debates, 23 January 1975, col 1747.

[54] TNA PRO CAB 129-181-25, 'Referendum: outstanding issues', Memorandum by the Lord President of the Council, Edward Short, 7 March 1975.

[55] See: Fifth Report of the Committee on Standards in Public Life, *The Funding of Political Parties in the United Kingdom* (October 1998) 156–59.

named authors or groups of writers, selected because they provide a particular line of analysis leading to concrete recommendations. My special interest is in considering the free development of ideas, outside of official structures, and the rationales they seek to convey. For this reason, I have not used reports issued by public bodies; and have largely avoided statements of party policy. I portray the key contents of these documents, before proceeding to reflect on their significance from a contemporary experience. The main purpose is not to place them in the context of their time or explain their influence or otherwise (though I give attention to such concerns as appropriate), but to extract value from them for the purposes of today. The book then concludes with an assessment of the 2016 referendum and its legitimacy, as well as making some reform recommendations for the future of the UK constitution. This closing chapter addresses concerns specific to the UK that are, as discussed above, also of international relevance, and can be taken as a contribution to a global debate. A postscript sets out in memorandum form some key constitutional lessons that another country contemplating exit from the EU might wish to take into account; and reproduces legal advice on the possibility for challenging a referendum result in the courts.

On the point of possible reforms, a further caveat is needed, that again can be derived from a study of history. Proposals intended to facilitate or improve democracy, however admirable in themselves, can generate difficulties. As will be shown, restricting – in 1911 – the ability of an hereditary parliamentary chamber, the House of Lords, to veto legislation produced by the elected House, the Commons, though it was clearly necessary, also produced a problematic imbalance in the constitution. More recent events are also instructive. The present supposed democratic and constitutional malaise in the UK presents a particular challenge to reform campaigners. It calls into question many of their previously established precepts and objectives. A text that serves to illustrate this platform and the challenges it now faces was produced by the Power Inquiry, a large-scale civil society initiative that reported in 2006.[56] It bemoaned 'plummeting turnout' in elections.[57] Alongside this trend, it noted that participation among less privileged social groups tended to be far lower.[58] It called for more 'direct' involvement of the public in 'decisions and policies'.[59] The public, the report argued, tended to regard the parties as 'too similar and lacking in principle'.[60] It advocated a loosening of 'the power of the whips' in Parliament, which 'should have greater powers to initiate legislation … and to act on public petitions'.[61]

[56] Power Inquiry, *Power to the People* (York, Power Inquiry, 2006).
[57] ibid, 14.
[58] ibid, 33–34.
[59] ibid, 20.
[60] ibid, 17.
[61] ibid, 21.

The inquiry advocated that the House of Lords become 70 per cent elected;[62] and made recommendations intended to ensure that MPs were more accountable to their constituents.[63] It proposed measures to secure greater activist involvement in parties.[64] In the report, the Internet was presented as a potential means of attaining more meaningful public involvement in politics. It wrote:

> [a] big part of the appeal of the internet as a tool is the way…it gives today's citizens a chance to exercise their intelligence as freely as possible on a matter that concerns them. It also offers them a direct and immediate route to others who may or may not share their opinion and opens up opportunities for debate. Where it offers a possible route to influencing those in power internet politics provides a freedom and a respect for the citizen's intelligence which from the overwhelming evidence most people do not believe exists in parties or through the process of simply voting.[65]

I have highlighted those aspects of the Power Inquiry programme that have a special piquancy from the perspective of Brexit and the more general reassertion of politics identified here. Higher turnout has been achieved in referendums and general elections (in fact, it had already risen slightly from the 2001 to the 2005 general elections), and there has lately been evidence of increased political engagement among social groups that had tended previously to be excluded.[66] The referendums of 2014 and 2016 were a type of 'direct' participation (though the form they took did not necessarily accord with the recommendations of the inquiry[67]). The two main parties have arguably disagreed increasingly on key matters (though in some senses they have converged over the EU). Both Conservative and Labour whips have struggled to impose discipline over the EU issue (though the increase of rebelliousness was a long-term tendency that long predated the Power Inquiry). The holding of the referendum of 2016 was driven to a large extent by a group of Conservative backbenchers, encouraged in part by a public petition of 2011.[68] Members and activists on both sides have by various means achieved greater influence over the direction of their parties; and MPs have become subject to pronounced pressure from their constituencies over the EU issue. Finally, the Internet has taken on an increasingly prominent role in political processes.

In some ways, then, these aspects of the Power Inquiry agenda – and by extension those of the reform community of which it was broadly reflective – were attained. Yet the subjects of concern raised in democratic analysis today tend to involve consequences arising from these very changes. Wider and more

[62] ibid, 21–22.
[63] ibid, 25.
[64] ibid, 24.
[65] ibid, 107.
[66] Hansard Society, *Audit of Political Engagement 15: The 2018 Report* (Hansard Society, London, 2018) 4.
[67] See eg Power Inquiry, *Power to the People* 239–40.
[68] See Conclusion.

inclusive public engagement has encouraged concern about a rise of populism. Direct involvement of the public through referendums has prompted concerns about a threat to representative democracy, as has activist pressure in constituencies. The House of Lords has for some been reconceived as a defender of, rather than affront to, democratic principles (while, on the other side of the Brexit argument, others have displayed a new distaste for its unelected composition). Moreover, the Internet is now far less likely to be presented as a means by which individuals can engage in political issues and expose themselves to a range of views, including those that differ from their own, fostering healthy debate. Nor, in the current climate, does the online environment tend to be depicted as conducive to people being able to influence authority and attain 'freedom and a respect for' their 'intelligence'. More constitutional changes are likely today. Those who advocate them should be aware that one of the greatest dangers reformers face is that they might be successful.

Part 1

Brexit and the Constitution

1

The Constitutional Connotations

BREXIT IS CONSTITUTIONALLY significant in two interconnected senses. The first involves the way in which the Brexit decision was taken, centring on the referendum of 23 June 2016. The second derives from the consequences of that course of action. Whatever the outcomes may prove to be, both these aspects of Brexit provide a fruitful basis for the study of a contemporary democratic system. In this chapter, discussion of a series of selected sources provides an overview and introduction to key constitutional issues that have arisen from Brexit, that are considered from an historical perspective in later chapters. As throughout this book, there is a focus on specific texts that appeared at precise moments. History unfolds in an uneven way. This technique is adopted to reflect rather than conceal this characteristic. Brexit has been chaotic. At any given time, multiple tendencies have manifested themselves and will continue to do so beyond the cut-off point for this book (end of September 2018). Though there were links between them, no one player or institution could possibly have a complete overview. The purpose here is both to convey the turbulence of the period, but also ultimately to transcend episodic impressions and discover underlying patterns, connections and tensions.

For Brexit, even assembling an itinerary of the basic constitutional issues is a challenging task. Late in 2017, I produced (but did not at the time publish) the following list. It was inevitably partial. Parts of it already seem dated, and some might quibble with aspects of the content, but it provides a snapshot of the impression of one observer at the time:

> **Brexit: the constitutional connotations**
>
> **Dr. Andrew Blick**
>
> 24 November 2017
>
> It is often said that the referendum on European Union membership of June 2016 and its aftermath have enormous constitutional implications. The following is an attempt to encapsulate in alphabetical list form what these 'implications' are.
>
> It has been compiled primarily through a survey of reports issued by parliamentary committees since the referendum. Issues identified in those publications connected to the referendum and prospective UK departure from the EU are included if they are judged to be constitutional in nature, or at least arguably to fit such a description. The definition of constitutional used here is that it engages:
>
> (a) values, rules or operational practices that are fundamental to the operation of governance, including in a legal, legislative and executive sense; or

(b) the relationship between different organs of governance; or
(c) the relationship between those organs of governance and the public they serve.

Some of the issues identified engage more than one of these aspects of the definition of 'constitutional' set out above. Each subject is listed with a brief explanation as appropriate.

Balance of power between UK government and UK Parliament: does the European Union (Withdrawal) Bill as drafted imply an inappropriate transfer of legislative power away from the legislature and to ministers?

Balance of power between UK and devolved governance: the allocation of repatriated powers between them.

Balance of power between UK and local governance (especially in England).

Balance of power between devolved and local governance.

British Overseas Territories: The UK has special responsibility for the governance of these Territories. While Gibraltar is the only British Overseas Territory within the EU, the prospect of UK departure from the EU raises complexes issues for them all.

Campaign funding: whether the rules were circumvented for the referendum.

Citizenship and the prospects for acquired rights: uncertainties about the future status of EU citizens present in the UK; and UK citizens in the EU, and the extent to which existing citizenship rights can be preserved for both groups as acquired rights post UK exit.

The Civil Service: its impartiality during the referendum campaign given the official government support for 'remain'; the accountability during the referendum campaign of the Civil Service to dissenting ministers who supported the 'leave' side; the capacity of the Civil Service to negotiate and plan for exit from the EU; its capacity to cope with enhanced demands during and beyond the process of leaving the EU.

Collective responsibility: its suspension during the referendum campaign to allow for ministerial dissent; the subsequent tendency for Cabinet members publicly to promote apparently divergent views regarding policy on departure from the EU.

Confidence: the potential for the Fixed-Term Parliaments Act 2011 to have created confusion about the meaning of House of Commons confidence in the government; whether this concept might be tested at some point.

Conventions: the role of understandings such as Sewel and Salisbury-Addison could become important. Sewel entails a commitment that the UK government will not normally seek to legislate with respect to devolved matters without the consent of the devolved legislature or legislatures concerned. Salisbury-Addison requires the House of Lords not to attempt to block legislation enacting commitments in the manifesto of the party that won the previous General Election (and possibly now extends to the government programme as a whole, whether a particular item was included in a manifesto or not). In January 2017, the Supreme Court in the *Miller* case dampened expectations about the justiciability of conventions, even if they were, as with Sewel, included in an Act of Parliament.

Court of Justice of the European Union: what will be its impact upon the UK after leaving the EU; how plausible is it that the UK can completely remove itself from the jurisdiction of this Court.

Crown Dependencies: the UK has special responsibilities for the Crown Dependencies comprising the various Channel Islands and the Isle of Man, that differ from those that apply to the British Overseas Territories. As it does for the Territories, Brexit raises complex issues for the Dependencies.

Delegated legislation: the European Union (Withdrawal) Bill has raised various concerns over the breadth of secondary law-making powers it proposes to provide to ministers; the mechanisms for their parliamentary oversight; the alleged lack of clarity and its implications for the rule of law; and the scope to impact significantly upon the devolved institutions.

Devolution: where should policy areas currently not reserved to the centre be placed post-exit – at central or devolved level; by what means should decisions about their location after UK departure from the EU be made; how can the autonomy of the devolved territories be reconciled with the perceived need to retain an integrated UK market; is some kind of quasi-federal; federal; or even confederal arrangement desirable or necessary for the UK?

Digital/online issues; whether the existing regulatory framework for referendums requires updating to take into account the increased importance of the Internet and social media; complaints about the government referendum website; the malfunctioning of the voter registration site; suspicions of violation of rules and external interference via social media; uncertainties about the impact of EU data protection rules post-departure.

Direct democracy: the use of referendums and their status within a broader system of democracy traditionally regarded as representative.

European law: the complexities inherent in transposing it into UK law; the potential for it to continue to impact upon the UK post-departure from the EU; the future role of the European Court of Justice; the significance of European law to the Article 50 process.

Finance: principles underpinning the allocation of funding, in particular on a territorial basis, after departure from the EU.

The **Fixed-term Parliaments Act 2011**: the ability of a government, perhaps prompted by EU-related issues, to trigger an early General Election, as Theresa May did in April 2017.

Franchise: whether the franchise used for the referendum was appropriate.

Gibraltar: the only British Overseas Territory that is (for the time being) inside the EU; after voting overwhelmingly to 'remain', it faces uncertainties post exit from the EU.

'Good Friday' (Belfast) Agreement: continued UK participation in the EU is an underlying assumption of this key component of the peace process.

Henry VIII powers: the ability to alter primary legislation through delegated law-making power; whether the government has included sufficient protections applying to its use in the European Union (Withdrawal) Bill.

House of Commons primacy: its meaning in the context of departure from the EU; how far could the House of Lords seek to assert itself against the Commons?

Human Rights: while departure from the EU will not entail exit from the European Convention on Human Rights, it implies the end of human rights requirements contained within European law, including the Charter of Fundamental Rights.

Individual ministerial responsibility: restrictions were introduced on the support that civil servants could provide to ministers who chose to dissent from the official government recommendation and support 'leave' during the referendum campaign, arguably compromising the crucial relationship between official and minister.

International agreements: how will they be negotiated in future; what will be the constitutional implications of their content; the role Parliament will play in them; the implications for devolution.

Joint Ministerial Committee: whether it is an adequate mechanism for managing UK intergovernmental relations in the context of UK departure from the EU.

Legal system: numerous uncertainties, for instance over the future of the European Arrest Warrant. Judicial cooperation over civil matters, within what is known as the 'Brussels Regime', is in doubt.

Legislative Consent Motions: (used as a means of attaining consent from devolved legislatures to Acts of the UK Parliament that impact upon devolved spheres of responsibility) whether they are required for Brexit-related legislation; what happens if consent is withheld; the possible use of delegated legislation to circumvent the legislative consent motion process.

Local government: what will be its role in determining the use of repatriated powers that impact upon its spheres of operation.

Mandates: eg: the status of a referendum vote; or of a General Election result. What is the constitutional status of a referendum result if Parliament has given it no express legal force in advance; can a referendum result be reversed only by a further referendum; is the mandate of an MP subordinate to that of a referendum; for how long does a referendum mandate last; what is the relationship between a General Election mandate and a referendum mandate; what is the nature of a mandate following a General Election that produced no overall winner (as in June 2017)?

Minority government: the position of the UK government since June 2017 and its dependence upon the support of the Democratic Unionist Party.

Northern Ireland: uncertainty about its status and that of the border after UK departure from the EU; possible difficulties for the peace process.

Parliamentary privilege: including the right of Parliament to obtain papers from the government.

Parliamentary sovereignty: the importance of a reassertion of this doctrine in narratives promoted by supporters of 'leave'; the implications of the use of referendums for this doctrine; the decision of the Supreme Court in *Miller* that the government had to seek express statutory authorisation to activate Article 50 of the Treaty on European Union, formally commencing the exit process.

The Political Parties, Elections and Referendums Act 2000: whether it requires review and amendment for such purposes as updating it to a changed campaign environment. The possibility of extending the 28-day restricted period during which the government could not issue material pertaining to the referendum to cover the entire referendum period; whether a generic order to cover regulation of all referendum campaigns should be devised; whether the law was circumvented with respect to finance by referendum campaigners.

Referendums: the appropriate way in which they should be used within a representative democracy (eg: over what issues, if any, should they be held; should they be pre- or post-legislative), what should be the status of their results (ie: binding or advisory); the preparations or lack thereof made by the government for the eventuality of a 'leave' vote; whether the rules in existence are appropriate and sufficiently consistent.

Representative democracy: the role that the referendum, an instrument of direct democracy, plays within this wider system; whether a government should hold a referendum when it does not support the radical change that could arise from it; whether the referendum result should have led to the resignation of the Prime Minister.

The Royal Prerogative: the limitations upon it as explored in the *Miller* case; the role of Parliament in relation to it, including the ability of the House of Commons potentially to block the ratification of a treaty under the Constitutional Reform and Governance Act 2010.

Rule of law: whether media criticism and scrutiny of the judiciary in relation to the *Miller* case constituted a threat to this principle, and whether the government was sufficiently robust in its response; whether the alleged ambiguity and indeterminacy of the European Union (Withdrawal) Bill creates such doubt as to potentially compromise the rule of law.

Salisbury-Addison doctrine (traditionally involving the House of Lords not seeking to obstruct a Bill that delivers a component of a party election programme, perhaps extending to all government legislation): what does it mean in practice; does it apply when no single party has a majority in the Commons and there is a minority government; under what circumstances can it be ignored?

Select and other parliamentary committees: their reconfiguration and refocusing to exercise oversight of government post-EU referendum; the form they might take after exit; their rights of access to papers and witnesses.

Sovereignty: various forms, including national, popular and (as noted above) parliamentary.

Sunset clauses: their desirability and effectiveness as a means of limiting statutory powers provided to ministers.

Supreme Court: its role as a constitutional arbitrator, as demonstrated in the *Miller* case; whether it will be tested further; complexities around the role it might come to play in interpreting 'retained law' in the post-EU environment.

The Union: territorial divergence in voting patterns across different parts of the UK and their implications; varied proposals for post-Brexit arrangements emerging from different parts of the UK; cooperation between Wales and Scotland in seeking to alter the European Union (Withdrawal) Bill and the overall approach of the UK government; destabilisation of the Union and possible secession, especially for Northern Ireland and Scotland.

Votes on exit deal in both Houses of Parliament: what will be their status; what options will be on offer; what will be the arrangement in event of no deal.

I. SELECT COMMITTEE PERSPECTIVES ON BREXIT

Whatever view taken on the exact content of the list above, it is clear that Brexit is both sprawling and powerful in its constitutional implications. The issues it raises are both individually complex and often connected to one another. Consideration of two particular parliamentary select committee reports among the many that have appeared in the period since the EU referendum demonstrates this point. Though focusing on specific subjects, they engage a network of wider themes. The first I have selected for consideration – issued in April 2017, nearly 10 months after the vote – is the House of Commons Public Administration and Constitutional Affairs Committee (PACAC) publication, *Lessons learned from the EU referendum*.[1] Commons select committees, made up of MPs, have cross-party membership (as do their equivalents in the Lords), balanced roughly in proportion to the representation of the different groups in the Commons. They seek to proceed by consensus, providing their findings with a significance that more partisan statements would lack. The credibility of this particular report was heightened further because PACAC included members who had been on either side of the referendum campaign. Its chair, Bernard Jenkin MP, was a prominent 'leave' supporter,[2] and that its report could reach firm conclusions on such sensitive matters was to his credit, as well as that of the other members and staff. I have had some experience of the internal workings of a Commons select committee. It suggests to me that we should avoid over-idealising their processes. As with any such group, their outputs involve various trade-offs between competing agendas. Nonetheless, for the purposes of this book, it is important that we cannot dismiss the PACAC report merely as the work of an elite pro-EU cabal, or of rabid opponents of membership.

The PACAC report identified a variety of serious constitutional issues raised by the poll of June 2016, perceiving problems in the way the government had approached it. The Committee noted the existence of a view that referendums posed a threat to the established form of government of the UK.[3] Under this prevailing system, known as representative democracy, central governments derive from voters, via parliamentary elections, a general authority to pursue programmes and take decisions, subject to various forms of parliamentary oversight, judicial control and public scrutiny.[4] The principal role of the voter is to

[1] House of Commons Public Administration and Constitutional Affairs Committee, *Lessons learned from the EU referendum* (London, House of Commons, 2017).

[2] See ch 3.

[3] See further: House of Lords Select Committee on the Constitution, *Referendums in the United Kingdom* (London, Stationery Office, 2010), esp 16; 20.

[4] For a discussion of this principle in the context of the use of referendum, see eg: Matt Qvortrup, *Direct democracy: A comparative study of the theory and practice of government by the people* (Manchester, Manchester University Press, 2013) 12–25.

play a part in determining who will act on their behalf. By contrast, referendums entail direct involvement of the electorate in specific decisions.[5] The implication for government is that the policy area involved is not subject to the same form of general authorisation as the other activities in which ministers are engaged, and involves a more precise popular input.[6] Furthermore, as PACAC recognised, referendums raise another connected issue. A distinctive feature of the UK system of representative democracy is a principle known as 'parliamentary sovereignty'. According to this doctrine, the Westminster Parliament is the ultimate source of authority within the UK constitution.[7] In many other systems, so-called 'written' constitutions occupy this position of primacy, setting out the fundamental principles and rules applying to governmental institutions, and their relationships with eachother and the public.[8] However, in the UK, no such text expressly labelled the 'constitution', possessing this special status, and that might thereby restrain the UK legislature, exists.[9] Yet, if the public is invited directly to vote on a particular question in a way that seems to supplant the authority of Parliament at least in the given area, the implication might be that voters, rather than Parliament, are 'sovereign'.

Because of such tensions, as PACAC noted, critics of the idea of using the referendum in the UK have tended to depict it as 'alien' to the UK system. Clement Attlee, the Labour leader, used this term when responding negatively to the proposal from Winston Churchill in 1945 for a popular vote on the extension of the life of the wartime coalition government, in which Churchill and Attlee were both participants. But, PACAC concluded, there had been 13 major referendums in the UK since 1973, and the device could be considered to have obtained an established place within UK political processes. Indeed, discussion about the possible use of this mechanism had long preceded 1973, dating back as far as the 1880s.[10] Nonetheless, PACAC recognised that '[t]he relationship between the direct democracy of a referendum and the established expectations of representative democracy requires careful management'.[11] Agreeing with an earlier report, from 2010, issued by the House of Lords Select Committee on the

[5] See ch 4. See also Independent Commission on Referendums, *Report of the Independent Commission on Referendums* (London, Constitution Unit, 2018) 62–63.

[6] For historic and contemporary discussion of the referendum, see: Lucy Atkinson, Andrew Blick and Matt Qvortrup, *The People's Veto: the history of referendums in the United Kingdom* (Oxford, Oxford University Press, 2019 forthcoming).

[7] Jeffrey Goldsworthy, *Parliamentary sovereignty: contemporary debates* (Cambridge, Cambridge University Press, 2010) 14.

[8] See Samuel Edward Finer, Vernon Bogdanor and Bernard Rudden, *Comparing constitutions* (Oxford, Clarendon Press, 1995).

[9] See Andrew Blick, *Beyond Magna Carta: a constitution for the United Kingdom* (Oxford, Hart Publishing, 2015) 287–89.

[10] Lucy Atkinson, Andrew Blick and Matt Qvortrup, *The People's Veto: the history of referendums in the United Kingdom* (Oxford, Oxford University Press, 2019 forthcoming), esp ch 2.

[11] House of Commons Public Administration and Constitutional Affairs Committee, *Lessons learned from the EU referendum* (London, House of Commons, 2017) 13.

Constitution,[12] PACAC argued that, if they were used, referendums were best applied to questions of a constitutional nature. It also held that they were appropriate in circumstances where the regular party political system seemingly could not resolve a particular matter.[13] Both these conditions applied to the EU vote. It certainly had major systemic connotations, as this book explains; and pertained to an issue, European integration, that had divided both the main two parties over time.[14] However, while EU membership might have fulfilled the criteria PACAC endorsed as making an issue the suitable subject of a referendum, the Committee had reservations regarding the particular approach the government had taken to the process.

Central to the PACAC objections was the idea that the referendum was, as the report put it, a 'bluff call'.[15] Technically, the referendum offered a choice between two different changes: remaining within the EU on renegotiated terms, or leaving. The second of the two options, if taken, would seemingly be far more radical than the first in impact (in as far as what it meant could be ascertained). Yet the government, in officially advocating a 'remain' vote, opposed the transformation it was offering.[16] In the judgment of the Committee, the referendum was therefore an exercise in manipulation, rather than meaningful democratic decision making. As the report put it: '[t]he UK Government initiated the process which led to the referendum, despite being against the suggested proposal, and with the aim of using a negative result to shut down the debate about the question at issue'.[17] The Committee found this 'bluff call' approach to a referendum 'questionable'.[18]

On this interpretation, since the referendum was – from the perspective of the government that facilitated it – a means of ensuring continued membership of the EU, insufficient attention was given to the meaning of a 'leave' vote. The Committee noted that it had received evidence stressing that there were many different possible outcomes that Brexit might take, involving, for instance, variations in the degree of regulatory alignment after departure between the UK and the EU.[19] Yet the referendum offered only a binary choice. The Committee complained:

> If the results of referendums are to command the maximum of public support, acceptance and legitimacy, then they must be held on questions and issues which are

[12] House of Lords Select Committee on the Constitution, *Referendums in the United Kingdom* (London, Stationery Office, 2010) 27.

[13] House of Commons Public Administration and Constitutional Affairs Committee, *Lessons learned from the EU referendum* (London, House of Commons, 2017) 12.

[14] See Anthony Forster, *Euroscepticism in contemporary British politics: opposition to Europe in the Conservative and Labour parties since 1945* (London, Routledge, 2003).

[15] House of Commons Public Administration and Constitutional Affairs Committee, *Lessons learned from the EU referendum* (London, House of Commons, 2017) 12.

[16] See further ch 3.

[17] House of Commons Public Administration and Constitutional Affairs Committee, *Lessons learned from the EU referendum* (London, House of Commons 2017) 12.

[18] ibid, 13.

[19] ibid, 11.

> as clear as possible. Voters should be presented with a choice, where the consequences of either outcome are clear … the referendum was confined to a tight question, on the basis of a clear binary choice. There could, however, have been more positive efforts to explain, and therefore to plan for, the consequences for voters in the event of either outcome. This would have required providing impartial consideration of the outcome which the Government clearly did not want.[20]

Since the result was contrary to that sought by the government, the question of whether it had to be acted upon was significant. The legislation providing for the vote did not contain any provision compelling its implementation. Anyway, given the doctrine of parliamentary sovereignty, a legally binding referendum was not technically possible, since Parliament could if it wished alter the law after the vote to remove any obligations for which it had previously provided. Yet PACAC judged that 'in reality, referendums are seen by the public as conferring an obligation on parliamentarians to deliver the result'.[21] It can reasonably be concluded that if, in practice, the idea of an advisory referendum is not viable, the need to give careful consideration to both possible outcomes is heightened, because the result, even if the government dislikes it, cannot be evaded.

One consequence of the 'bluff call' approach to the referendum, PACAC judged, was that it led to the resignation of the Prime Minister, despite his previously insisting that he would remain in post regardless of the outcome. The Committee argued that '[a] more responsible conduct of the Government's case in the run up to the referendum, and proper planning for a Leave vote, would not have opened up so much new controversy nor left the Prime Minister's authority and credibility undermined.'[22] A further manifestation of the lack of preparation for a 'leave' result, PACAC found, came with the legal challenge that was mounted against the government in the wake of the referendum. The government believed that it could trigger Article 50 of the Treaty on European Union, commencing the process that would lead to UK exit on a two-year schedule, under the collection of ancient non-statutory authorities it possessed known as the Royal Prerogative (for the text of Article 50, see appendix A). Yet, on 24 January 2017, the Supreme Court confirmed finally that the prerogative could not be used to activate Article 50, and that the government would need to obtain specific statutory authority from Parliament for this purpose.[23] The Committee noted that 'few, if any, anticipated' this turn of events in advance of the referendum.[24] The Committee took the view that referendums should be held on issues that could be properly expressed in the form of a 'binary question'. To do otherwise, it held, was to risk exacerbating 'the potential tensions between

[20] ibid, 12.
[21] ibid, 13.
[22] ibid, 13.
[23] For further discussion see below.
[24] House of Commons Public Administration and Constitutional Affairs Committee, *Lessons learned from the EU referendum* (London, House of Commons, 2017) 13.

referendums and representative democracy and risks increasing the public's disenchantment with politics'.[25] If referendums were to attain the 'acceptance and legitimacy' required of them, they needed 'to be designed in such a way as to provide the utmost clarity for parliamentarians, campaigners and, above all, the electorate'.[26]

Given the problems the Committee had identified with the coherence of the choice offered to voters, it might be held that the result was not necessarily valid as a genuine expression of popular will. By extension, the idea that the referendum had created a democratic obligation to depart from the EU, however implemented, could be called into question. However, the report did not address this issue. This omission is not surprising. The membership of PACAC, as already discussed, combined supporters both of leaving and remaining. Furthermore, there was a more general reluctance within Parliament on both sides of the argument to seek to revisit the result of the vote.[27] The Committee focused instead on possible referendums to come, concluding that it was 'incumbent on future Parliaments and governments to consider the potential consequences of promising referendums, particularly when, as a result, they may be expected to implement an outcome that they opposed'.[28] The Committee reemphasised the point subsequently stating that:

> Referendums are the creations of Parliament and the Government. Parliament and the Government are therefore accountable and must take responsibility for the conduct of referendums, and the fairness of the question, and there should be proper information about, and planning for, either outcome.[29]

The Committee, therefore, implied that there had been a failure on the part of both the executive and the legislature to ensure that the referendum was a satisfactory exercise. A purpose of this book is to consider whether such a defect did manifest itself, and if so why, and what were the implications. It does so in particular from the perspective of Parliament, which is in theory the ultimate locus of authority within the UK constitutional and legal system.

Other recommendations contained in the PACAC report included the consolidation of referendum law.[30] It also proposed that the period in advance of a referendum during which central and local government bodies were prohibited from issuing promotional material should be extended from 28 days to the full statutory referendum period of 10 weeks. The reasoning behind this proposal was that it would provide better protection for the fairness of the contest

[25] ibid, 13.
[26] ibid, 13–14.
[27] See ch 3.
[28] House of Commons Public Administration and Constitutional Affairs Committee, *Lessons learned from the EU referendum* (London, House of Commons, 2017) 13.
[29] ibid, 14.
[30] ibid, 22.

by limiting the opportunity for the government to campaign for its favoured outcome.[31] These restrictions were contained in section 125 of the Political Parties, Elections and Referendums Act 2000 (PPERA). Commenting further on section 125 of PPERA, PACAC noted that since it was passed at the beginning of the previous decade 'campaigning and publishing have both become increasingly digital in nature. As a result, terminology and provisions that may have been appropriate in 2000, may be less effective at regulating campaign activity in 2017.' The Committee called on the government to propose alterations to PPERA to reflect these developments.[32] (Appendix B of this chapter reproduces sections 125–127 of PPERA, that seem anachronistic in the context of online campaigning via social media.) PACAC recommended further that section 125 be subject to a more general review to assess its effectiveness;[33] and that the clarity of PPERA as it applied to organisations seeking to campaign jointly be investigated.[34]

Further underlining the importance that online technology had acquired in the context of referendums and more generally, PACAC commented on the incident that occurred on 7 June 2016, when the website for voter registration for the referendum crashed.[35] It stated that it could not exclude that the failure was the outcome of a deliberate hostile intervention or 'distributed denial of service' (DDOS). Developing this theme PACAC went on:

> The US and UK understanding of 'cyber' is predominantly technical and computer-network based. For example, Russia and China use a cognitive approach based on understanding of mass psychology and of how to exploit individuals. The implications of this different understanding of cyber-attack, as purely technical or as reaching beyond the digital to influence public opinion, for the interference in elections and referendums are clear. PACAC is deeply concerned about these allegations about foreign interference.[36]

The Committee urged concerted government action to respond to this threat.[37] Other official bodies would subsequently corroborate and augment the concerns of PACAC. In June 2018, reflecting rising salience for the subject, the Electoral Commission published *Digital Campaigning: Increasing transparency for voters*.[38] It noted that reported spending in this field was rapidly increasing; and that there was other related activity difficult precisely to quantify, but

[31] ibid, 22–24.
[32] ibid, 26.
[33] ibid, 27.
[34] ibid, 28–29. See further Independent Commission on Referendums, *Report of the Independent Commission on Referendums* (London, Constitution Unit, 2018) 124–33.
[35] House of Commons Public Administration and Constitutional Affairs Committee, *Lessons learned from the EU referendum* (London, House of Commons, 2017) 31–35.
[36] ibid, 35.
[37] ibid, 35.
[38] Electoral Commission, *Digital campaigning: increasing transparency for voters* (London, Electoral Commission, 2018).

that seemed to be significant and expanding.[39] By this time, online political promotion had acquired an exceptional level of negative publicity, partly as a consequence of campaign methods associated with the EU referendum, some of which were the subject of allegations of criminal activity.[40] In July 2018, following an investigation into conduct that involved the use of social media, the Electoral Commission found that Vote Leave, the nominated lead campaign on the 'leave' side in the referendum, and the founder of another pro-leave group, BeLeave, had broken the law on spending limits. The Commission issued a fine to the individual concerned and reported the matter to the police.[41] Its publication of June had identified broader democratic concerns arising from online campaigning beyond the issue of controlling expenditure. They included the creation of the potential for foreign interference in democratic processes. There were dangers of the misuse of personal data for the purposes of targeting voters.[42] False information could be spread.[43] The sources of political advertising were not clear; and it was possible for groups to 'micro-target' individual voters with messages specially tailored to appeal to them on a basis of their digital personal profiles.[44] These latter two tendencies could be seen as problematic from the point of view of accountability. They implied that a particular group could send out contradictory messages in pursuit of the same cause, without a clear awareness in the outside world that it had done so.[45] The idea of voters choosing between clearly defined, coherent programmes, in which contemporary democracy rests, might thereby be compromised.[46]

Aside from its concerns about online activity, the PACAC report noted that witnesses had praised much of the administrative organisation of the referendum and found it in compliance with the law. However, it argued that 'greater

[39] Electoral Commission, *Digital campaigning: increasing transparency for voters* (London, Electoral Commission, 2018) 3–4.

[40] Stephanie Hankey, Julianne Kerr and Ravi Naik, *Data and Democracy in the Digital Age* (London, The Constitution Society, 2018) 14–18: https://consoc.org.uk/wp-content/uploads/2018/07/Stephanie-Hankey-Julianne-Kerr-Morrison-Ravi-Naik-Data-and-Democracy-in-the-Digital-Age.pdf last accessed 11 September 2018.

[41] Electoral Commission, *Report of an investigation in respect of – Vote Leave Limited – Mr Darren Grimes – BeLeave – Veterans for Britain* (London, Electoral Commission, 2018): http://www.electoralcommission.org.uk/__data/assets/pdf_file/0019/244900/Report-of-an-investigation-in-respect-of-Vote-Leave-Limited-Mr-Darren-Grimes-BeLeave-and-Veterans-for-Britain.pdf last accessed 13 September 2018.

[42] See also Information Commissioner's Office, *Democracy disrupted? Personal information and political influence* (London, Information Commissioner's Office, 2018).

[43] See also Digital, Culture, Media and Sport Committee, *Disinformation and 'fake news': Interim Report* (London, House of Commons, 2018).

[44] Electoral Commission, *Digital campaigning: increasing transparency for voters* (London, Electoral Commission, 2018).

[45] Julia Carrie Wong, '"It might work too well": the dark art of political advertising online' *Guardian*, 19 March 2018: https://www.theguardian.com/technology/2018/mar/19/facebook-political-ads-social-media-history-online-democracy last accessed 18 September 2018.

[46] Jamie Bartlett, *The People Vs Tech: How the internet is killing democracy (and how we save it)* (London, Ebury, 2018) 84–85.

transparency and clarity' could be sought for the process by which the Electoral Commission designated official lead campaign groups on each side of the contest.[47] The Committee held, furthermore, that Civil Service impartiality had been compromised during the referendum campaign, into which officials had inappropriately been publicly drawn.[48] It noted that ministers had been allowed to opt out of collective responsibility in relation to the EU vote, publicly dissenting for a limited period from the government support for a 'remain' outcome. While endorsing this decision, PACAC objected to the introduction of a ruling that civil servants could not support dissenting ministers by providing them with briefings with respect to their involvement in the referendum.[49] The Committee also criticised the use of public resources for the publication, in the lead up to the referendum, of documents that it regarded as clearly forming part of a campaign for a 'remain' outcome.[50] It questioned the extent to which the Civil Service had planned for a 'leave' result, and indeed to which officials had been able to do so given the reluctance of pro-'remain' ministers to countenance an outcome they sought to avoid.[51]

While PACAC dealt with the mechanism that led to the decision to leave the EU, another report discussed here focused on some of the consequences of that decision. Within Parliament the House of Lords Select Committee on the Constitution is responsible for assessing bills from a constitutional perspective, and considering constitutional issues more generally. On 7 September 2017 it published *European Union (Withdrawal) Bill: interim report*.[52] As the title suggested, it was a preliminary assessment, also building on earlier work, of the legislation the government had introduced to Parliament to attain, as the Committee put it: 'legal certainty after the UK leaves the European Union'.[53] The purpose of the Bill, as the government defined it, was to repeal the *European Communities Act 1972*; to 'convert EU law as it stands at the moment of exit into UK law before we leave the EU'; and 'create powers to make secondary legislation', facilitating the making of 'corrections ... to the laws that would otherwise no longer operate appropriately once we left the EU', and to ensure that UK law could be altered to give effect to 'any withdrawal agreement'.[54] To achieve its stated purpose of legal certainty, the Bill provided

[47] House of Commons Public Administration and Constitutional Affairs Committee, *Lessons learned from the EU referendum* (London, House of Commons, 2017) 42.

[48] ibid, 44–47.

[49] ibid, 35.

[50] ibid, 47–49.

[51] ibid, 49–52.

[52] House of Lords Select Committee on the Constitution, *European Union (Withdrawal) Bill: interim report* (London, House of Lords, 2017).

[53] ibid, 4.

[54] Department for Exiting the European Union, *Legislating for the United Kingdom's Withdrawal from the European Union* (London, Department for Exiting the European Union, 2017) 12: https://assets.publishing.service.gov.uk/government/uploads/system/uploads/attachment_data/file/604516/Great_repeal_bill_white_paper_accessible.pdf last accessed 13 September 2018.

for a wholly new class of legislation known as 'retained EU law'.[55] (However, as is discussed later in this book, the commitment to continuity did not extend to the EU Charter of Fundamental Rights, which, the government insisted, would 'not be converted into UK law'[56]).

The Bill, the Select Committee on the Constitution found, was 'likely to be the most important legislation that this Parliament will consider'. The task it set out to perform was essential in the context of UK departure from the EU. Yet 'the practicalities of delivering' the objective of post-exit clarity were 'not straightforward and the Government will need to be realistic about the complexity of the challenges involved in achieving it'.[57] This premise was important. It implied that, however problematic the task, it had to be pursued. Lurking behind this assumption were two principles: first, and longer-established, that the Lords was limited in the extent to which it could challenge the legislative programme of the government; secondly that the referendum result produced a binding obligation. Whether the former rule ought to apply in present circumstances was debatable, since the General Election of June 2017 had not produced a single-party majority, and the government could not therefore claim for its manifesto pledges the authority imbued in them by victory.[58] Whether the second dictum should exist at all, or if it should, whether it applied in present circumstances were also questionable propositions, that this book considers in closer detail.[59]

The Bill performed a twin function: repealing the European Communities Act 1972 that gave domestic legal expression to UK membership of the EU, while managing the consequences of the disappearance of this legal source. Under the Act, European law was supreme within the UK domestic hierarchy; and covered an extensive range of subject matter. Therefore, the committee noted, were Parliament simply to abolish the 1972 Act 'the degree of legal chaos that would result would be unmanageable'. Consequently, after providing for the repeal of the European Communities Act, the rest of the European Union (Withdrawal) Bill focused on 'attempting to ameliorate such consequences'. It sought to do so 'by preserving EU-derived domestic legislation and domesticating directly effective EU law, while assigning extremely broad executive powers for the purpose of amending such law'.[60]

[55] Graham Cowie, *The Status of 'Retained EU Law'* (London, House of Commons Library, 2018).

[56] Department for Exiting the European Union, *Legislating for the United Kingdom's Withdrawal from the European Union* (London, Department for Exiting the European Union, 2017) 18: https://assets.publishing.service.gov.uk/government/uploads/system/uploads/attachment_data/file/604516/Great_repeal_bill_white_paper_accessible.pdf last accessed 13 September 2018.

[57] House of Lords Select Committee on the Constitution, *European Union (Withdrawal) Bill: interim report* (London, House of Lords, 2017) 4.

[58] See Richard Reid, *The House of Lords: conventions and Brexit* (London, The Constitution Society, 2017): https://consoc.org.uk/wp-content/uploads/2017/12/HoL-Brexit-A4-web.pdf last accessed 23 September 2018.

[59] See, especially, chs 2 and 3.

[60] House of Lords Select Committee on the Constitution, *European Union (Withdrawal) Bill: interim report* (London, House of Lords, 2017) 6.

The Committee summarised its view of the legislation by stating that it:

> raises a series of profound, wide- ranging and interlocking constitutional concerns. Indeed, it is difficult to think of areas of constitutional concern that are not deeply engaged by the Bill. In this report, we draw attention to three broad constitutional themes that emerge from our analysis. Those themes respectively concern the relationship between Parliament and the executive, the rule of law and legal certainty, and the stability of the UK's territorial constitution.[61]

A central concern raised by the Committee was the authorities it would vest in the executive, providing it with the ability to issue delegated legislation in order to transpose European into UK law. The report, describing these powers as 'unprecedented and extraordinary' in their reach, noted the extent of the 'deep legislative competence' involved, creating the ability to introduce 'any provision that could be made by an Act of Parliament'. Furthermore, 'the Bill contains multiple such powers, which overlap to a very considerable extent' and would not be subject to an appropriate degree of parliamentary control. The Committee concluded that 'the Bill weaves a tapestry of delegated powers that are breath-taking in terms of both their scope and potency'.[62] The effect would be 'fundamentally [to] challenge the constitutional balance of powers between Parliament and Government' through 'a significant – and unacceptable – transfer of legal competence'.[63] A particular concern for the Committee was the extent to which the Bill proposed to create 'Henry VIII' powers (that enable the amendment of primary legislation through delegated powers), subject to insufficient parliamentary control.[64]

With regard to its second category of concern, the rule of law, the committee noted that the Bill had 'considerable' potential to 'undermine legal certainty'. A lack of legislative clarity, it held, was detrimental to the 'rule of law' in any circumstance. This concern magnified when it involved 'a constitutional Bill such as this'. The withdrawal legislation was 'fundamental to the content and application of the legal system post- exit since it determines both the content of large parts of the law ("retained EU law") and the rules of priority and interaction as between retained EU law and other parts of domestic law'. Precision was vital, meaning that 'the apparent multiple ambiguities in the Bill are deeply problematic. Individuals, organisations and the government need to know what exactly the law is, and what their rights and responsibilities are'.[65] Finally, 'ambiguities and uncertainties' that characterised the legislation also engaged 'issues of devolved competence', with 'implications for the balance of power within the Union and the future of the devolution settlements'.[66] The Bill would

[61] ibid, 2.
[62] ibid.
[63] ibid, 14.
[64] ibid, 14–15.
[65] ibid, 2.
[66] ibid, 2.

facilitate potential alterations to European law falling within the spheres of operation of the devolved legislatures. The UK Parliament was 'sovereign', the Committee noted, and therefore able to pass the withdrawal legislation unilaterally if it wished. However, to press ahead without securing 'legislative consent' at devolved level 'would be significant and potentially damaging'.[67]

This report was an example of the extensive efforts that the Select Committee on the Constitution made thoroughly to assess the government approach to Brexit and its consequences. Its engagement helped bring about changes in the Bill that took into account some of the constitutional concerns raised.[68] However, such work was always predicated on the assumption that major changes of some kind were unavoidable following the result of the 2016 referendum. Knowledge of the consequences of Brexit would have been more valuable at an earlier stage, when the apparent range of options was wider. Yet in advance of Parliament legislating for the referendum, or of it taking place, the Committee proved less effective at assessing what might be the constitutional impacts of a decision to leave. In October 2015 it reported on the European Union Referendum Bill.[69] The Committee found that, in accordance with previous recommendations it had made, the possibility of leaving the EU was an appropriate subject for a referendum, as a matter of pronounced constitutional significance. It stated that: 'If the United Kingdom were to leave the European Union it would be the most significant change to the United Kingdom's constitutional arrangements in decades, with far-reaching effects on every part of our constitutional framework.' Yet the Committee declined 'to comment on the Bill in detail'. The reasoning it offered for this abstention was that '[a]lthough the referendum it institutes will be of the utmost constitutional importance, the Bill itself simply provides for the holding of a referendum'.[70] In a report that was only nine paragraphs in total, the Committee then made recommendations of second-order significance regarding the timing of the referendum, the designation of lead organisations and the application of legislation.[71]

Evidence of detailed prior parliamentary consideration of a 'leave' result is generally difficult to find. A limited exception came in May 2017, shortly before the referendum, when the House of Lords European Union Committee issued a report on *The process of withdrawing from the European Union*.[72] As the

[67] ibid, 22. See also Richard Rawlings, *Brexit and the Territorial Constitution: Devolution, Re-regulation and Intergovernmental Relations* (London, The Constitution Society, 2017): https://consoc.org.uk/wp-content/uploads/2017/10/Brexit-and-devolution-final.pdf last accessed 23 September 2018.

[68] For a text showing the changes made to the final Act as compared with the Bill originally introduced, see: https://publications.parliament.uk/pa/bills/cbill/2017-2019/0229/CompleteCMP-BilltoAct.pdf last accessed 23 September 2018.

[69] House of Lords Select Committee on the Constitution, *European Union Referendum Bill* (London, House of Lords, 2015).

[70] ibid, 3.

[71] ibid, 3–4.

[72] House of Lords Select Committee on the Constitution, *The process of withdrawing from the European Union* (London, House of Lords, 2016).

title suggested, and in keeping with the remit of the Committee, the publication focused more on the Article 50 process than on the domestic constitutional aspects of a possible departure. The Committee inquiry was a response to a recently published government document of the same name. The subject of criticism from supporters of exit for supposedly being misleading, it argued that negotiating departure and related agreements 'on any terms that would be acceptable to the UK' would require an 'extended period', and that 'a vote to leave the EU would be the start, not the end, of a process. It could lead to up to a decade or more of uncertainty'.[73] The House of Lords report did not address the issue dealt with in the *Miller* case, that is whether the government needed specific statutory authorisation to instigate Article 50, or could do so under the Royal Prerogative (nor had the government text addressed this matter). However, it did draw a number of conclusions on the general subject that were significant from the point of view of the referendum as a device of democratic decision making. The Committee held that the Article 50 process was the only means by which the UK (or any member state) could leave the EU if wishing to remain compliant with both European and international law. It took the view that, having activated Article 50, it was technically possible for a member state unilaterally to revoke it.[74] The report concluded that, at the EU end, alongside the Commission, member states and the European Parliament (that had the power to veto agreements reached) would play a prominent part in the process.[75] It noted that as well as fixing the terms of withdrawal, it would be necessary to establish a future relationship between the UK and the EU.[76] The Committee expressed doubt as to whether the two-year time period envisaged under Article 50 would prove of sufficient duration for the business that needed to be conducted, and concluded that an extension would be necessary. If the unanimous consent of the European Council to a delay were not obtained, the UK would be forced to leave with no deal in place and operate on World Trade Organisation (WTO) terms.[77]

Though it did not overtly make this point, issues raised by the report were significant to the nature of the choice about to be presented to voters. The referendum presented a binary selection between 'remain' and 'leave'. But if they selected the second of the two, what it might mean in practice was uncertain, in number of senses. First, a range of end outcomes was possible, including various types of exit arrangement and of post-Brexit relationship with the EU, or even no agreement at all and perhaps a WTO framework. Secondly, though

[73] Secretary of State for Foreign and Commonwealth Affairs, *The process of withdrawing from the European Union* (London, HM Government, 2016) 8.

[74] House of Lords Select Committee on the Constitution, *The process of withdrawing from the European Union* (London, House of Lords, 2016) 5.

[75] ibid, 9.

[76] ibid, 10.

[77] ibid, 14–15.

the committee did not favour this option, it was in theory possible that leaving might be pursued without reference to Article 50, perhaps by a government that was not concerned that it might be perceived as having violated European and international law. Thirdly, whatever outcome a government seeking to implement a 'leave' result might favour, and whether it sought to do so through Article 50 or some other means, it involved outside players. As highlighted by the Committee, the EU Commission, member states and the European Parliament would all have a part to play. The UK would be entering a negotiation with another party that itself comprised sub-components each with its own agenda and influence. The outcome of such a process was hard to predict, and certainly not wholly within the power of a UK government (much less UK voters) to determine.

The European Union Committee report also contained a relatively circumscribed but nonetheless prescient discussion of matters with a clear internal dimension. The Committee anticipated complications involving the rights of EU citizens resident in the UK (and for UK nationals in the EU).[78] It judged that unpicking UK and European law would also be an immensely challenging task, and that the UK would wish to retain a significant portion of the latter after departure. This handling of the legal consequences of Brexit, the Committee discerned, would involve legislation that would be subject to approval from the devolved legislatures. Finally, the Committee formed the view that, should the UK seek to leave the EU, then 'the UK Parliament should have advanced oversight of the negotiations on the withdrawal and the new relationship, beyond existing ratification procedures'. The report stated that the Committee would 'consider best how to achieve that, should the need arise'.[79] These observations were useful and preceded the actual referendum. However, at the time they were brought to the attention of Parliament, the legislation providing for the vote had already been passed, setting in chain the events that followed.

II. THE MAY DOCTRINE

The parliamentary select committee reports cited above illustrate well the two constitutional dimensions to Brexit: that it was a decision, with implications. Binding together these two aspects was a government: choosing – or feeling obliged – to interpret and apply a referendum result in a particular way. When giving her first speech to a Conservative conference as party leader and Prime Minister on 2 October 2016, Theresa May presented a set of principles pertaining to Brexit that at the time I collectively labelled the 'May Doctrine'.[80]

[78] ibid, 9.

[79] ibid, 19.

[80] See Andrew Blick, *Taking back control? The EU referendum, Parliament and the 'May Doctrine'* (London, Federal Trust for Education and Research, 2016). The following passages draw on this publication.

May had supported, if not in a notably enthusiastic manner,[81] the 'remain' side in the referendum. Its defeat had brought her to No 10; an uncomfortable basis on which to arrive. May seems to have perceived a need to establish her credentials as the appropriate person to implement leaving. In doing so, she made a series of claims of a constitutional character that, despite their contestable nature, she presented as manifest. The first was that 'Brexit' was an outcome 'the country voted for'. Obliquely confirming that some disputed this view, she bemoaned the fact that 'politicians – democratically-elected politicians' were holding that the referendum was not sufficient in itself and that another was needed. May, furthermore, alluded to individuals who 'don't like the result' who were attempting through legal means to frustrate Brexit. She was disdainful of such resistance and determined that the 'result was clear' and 'legitimate'; and 'was the biggest vote for change this country has ever known'. Uttering a mantra she had already made famous, May said: 'Brexit means Brexit – and we're going to make a success of it'. She acknowledged that the referendum had taken place thanks to her predecessor as Conservative leader and Prime Minister, David Cameron. In doing so, though it was not a perception she intended to promote, May highlighted the importance of the internal considerations of a specific political party to the occurrence of this popular vote, and the response to it.

May made a further assertion of constitutional importance when averring that her government would 'not be able to give a running commentary or a blow-by-blow account of the negotiations'. As well as downplaying the idea of openness around the process of leaving, she also insisted that the instigation of this process, through activation of Article 50 of the Treaty on European Union, was purely a matter for the executive. Stating that it would do so by the end of March 2017, May insisted that 'it is not up to the House of Commons to invoke Article Fifty, and it is not up to the House of Lords'. There was no place for the legislature in this act since it had created the statutory basis on which the referendum was held, passing to voters the opportunity to decide whether to remain within or leave the EU. They had answered 'with emphatic clarity'. The consequent task of the government was 'not to question, quibble or backslide on what we have been instructed to do, but to get on with the job'. Those who questioned this approach were 'not standing up for democracy', May held. They were 'trying to subvert it. They're not trying to get Brexit right, they're trying to kill it by delaying it'. Furthermore, 'the negotiations between the United Kingdom and the European Union are the responsibility of the Government and nobody else'. She did, however, commit that her government would 'consult and work with the devolved administrations for Scotland, Wales and

[81] Asa Bennett, 'Theresa May wants you to stay in the EU. Has she blown her chances of ever being Tory leader', *Telegraph*, 25 April 2016: https://www.telegraph.co.uk/news/2016/04/25/theresa-may-wants-you-to-stay-in-the-eu-has-she-blown-her-chance/ last accessed 26 August 2018.

Northern Ireland', in an effort to guarantee that 'Brexit' could 'work in the interests of the whole country'. It also intended to cooperate with local authorities and business representatives. Yet responsibility for the actual negotiations would fall to the UK government. In her perception the UK had voted as a whole and would depart from the UK in the same way. As she put it:

> Because we voted in the referendum as one United Kingdom, we will negotiate as one United Kingdom, and we will leave the European Union as one United Kingdom. There is no opt-out from Brexit. And I will never allow divisive nationalists to undermine the precious Union between the four nations of our United Kingdom.

May set out plans for a 'Great Repeal Bill' intended to 'remove from the statute book … the European Communities Act', and then described the 'Government's vision of Britain after Brexit'. She insisted that there would not be 'a relationship anything like the one we have had for the last forty years or more'. Moreover, the UK would not set out to obtain a relationship with the EU similar to those of Norway or Switzerland. It would instead secure 'an agreement between an independent, sovereign United Kingdom and the European Union'. May ruled out the idea that there must be a '"trade-off" between controlling immigration and trading with Europe'. She insisted that the UK had 'voted to leave the European Union and become a fully-independent, sovereign country'. Consequently it would act in this way. She explained that '[w]e will decide for ourselves how we control immigration. And we will be free to pass our own laws'.

May, then, contended that the vote of 23 June 2016 had created a mandate – or rather compulsion to act – of which the executive was the sole custodian and interpreter. Other constitutional branches – the courts, Parliament, and the legislatures in the devolved territories – had no direct part to play. Yet unnamed internal enemies might seek to use the cumbersome procedures of the representative system to frustrate the popular will, which, among other requirements, demanded a reassertion of domestic political control, partly for the purposes of controlling foreign entry into the country. In that it gave rise to a Prime Minister expressing such views, the Brexit episode had a populist aspect to it. In practice, as we will see, the power of the executive was exercised subject to constraints and pressures, including from forces external to the UK and from within the Conservative Party itself. Moreover, though she presented her constitutional perception as axiomatic, it was open to question. The member of her own Cabinet specifically entrusted at the time with implementing the Brexit policy had once provided an exemplary account of a different position. David Davis, who served as Secretary of State for Exiting the European Union from 2016–18, had offered this perspective in November 2002, when speaking for the Opposition during the Second Reading debate of the Regional Assemblies (Preparations) Bill 2002–03.[82]

[82] Hansard, House of Commons (HC) Debates, 26 November 2002, cols 201–04.

The legislation was designed to allow for referendums to be held on the establishment of devolved assemblies at regional level across England. Davis advanced a series of propositions regarding the proper constitutional role of such popular votes. First, he stressed that 'in a democracy, voters have to know what they are voting for. They need to know what the choice is … For that to happen, the proposition has to come before the vote'. Yet the Bill being discussed that day 'proposes that referendums should be held without voters knowing the structure or powers of the assemblies for which they are asked to vote'. Davis accepted that '[t]here is a proper role for referendums in constitutional change, but only if done properly. If it is not done properly, it can be a dangerous tool'. Recalling the celebrated comment by the Labour leader Clement Attlee in 1945 that such public votes were 'the device of demagogues and dictators' (to which the PACAC report cited above would also refer), Davis suggested that '[w]e may not always go as far as [Attlee] did, but what is certain is that pre-legislative referendums … are the worst type of all'. Davis cautioned that '[r]eferendums should be held when the electorate are in the best possible position to make a judgment. They should be held when people can view all the arguments for and against and when those arguments have been rigorously tested. In short, referendums should be held when people know exactly what they are getting. So legislation should be debated by Members of Parliament on the Floor of the House, and then put to the electorate for the voters to judge'.

A chief concern for Davis was that a referendum could vest inordinate discretionary authority in the government of the day. As he put it: 'We should not ask people to vote on a blank sheet of paper and tell them to trust us to fill in the details afterwards.' For a popular vote 'to be fair and compatible with our parliamentary process, we need the electors to be as well informed as possible and to know exactly what they are voting for'. Davis insisted that '[r]eferendums need to be treated as an addition to the parliamentary process, not as a substitute for it'. He suspected that the government did not wish to set out the framework for devolution prior to the vote because of a disinclination to 'debate the details'.

Davis recognised that '[m]ajor constitutional changes justify the use of referendums because the constitutional rights of our citizens are owned by the people and not by politicians'. Yet these exercises in popular participation were problematic if they provided only 'a snapshot of volatile changes of opinion'. The objective should be to establish what was the 'settled will' of the people. With this objective in mind, Davis advocated that thresholds be applied. In the case of English regional devolution, his view was that if there was a 'yes' majority, with at least a quarter of those who could have taken part supporting this outcome, then a sufficient quota of public support would have been reached to implement a change. However, he argued that such minimums should vary in accordance with 'the level of constitutional change' envisaged. For instance, if a more substantial body with powers equivalent to those of the Scottish were planned, then he 'would set the threshold a little higher'. The 'Davis criteria' for judging the appropriateness of a referendum, then, are: clear prior knowledge for voters of the implications of a change; a central role for Parliament rather than the executive, with substantive legislation passed before the referendum; and a threshold commensurate with the constitutional significance of the issue, to discern a 'settled will' on the part of the public. They are used to assess the 2016 vote in chapter two.

Whatever force May felt that the vote of 23 June 2016 had, by spring 2017 she seems to have come to the view that her Brexit policy (as well as her leadership and government more widely) required additional democratic authorisation. Moreover, she apparently regarded the exact settlement that she was going to obtain on behalf of the public as characterised by greater fluidity than she had previously suggested, and that her government should reserve for itself significant discretion in its approach to Brexit. These considerations seem to have been crucial to her decision to seek an early General Election. With the necessary level of assent from the House of Commons under the Fixed-term Parliaments Act 2011, it took place on 8 June 2017 (the next regular General Election was not scheduled under the 2011 Act until nearly three years after this point). A possible indication of May's motives can be found in the following excerpt from the manifesto on which her party contested this poll.

> LEAVING THE EUROPEAN UNION
>
> Following the historic referendum on 23rd June 2016, the United Kingdom is leaving the European Union. Only the Conservative Party, under Theresa May's strong and stable leadership, can negotiate the best possible deal for our country …
>
> We want to agree a deep and special partnership with the European Union …
>
> The negotiations will undoubtedly be tough, and there will be give and take on both sides, but we continue to believe that no deal is better than a bad deal for the UK. But we will enter the negotiations in a spirit of sincere cooperation and committed to getting the best deal for Britain. We will make sure we have certainty and clarity over our future, control of our own laws, and a more unified, strengthened United Kingdom. We will control immigration and secure the entitlements of EU nationals in Britain and British nationals in the EU. We will maintain the Common Travel Area and maintain as frictionless a border as possible for people, goods and services between Northern Ireland and the Republic of Ireland … we will protect the democratic freedom of the people of Gibraltar and our overseas territories to remain British, for as long as that is their wish. The final agreement will be subject to a vote in both houses of parliament. As we leave the European Union, we will no longer be members of the single market or customs union but we will seek a deep and special partnership including a comprehensive free trade and customs agreement. There may be specific European programmes in which we might want to participate and if so, it will be reasonable that we make a contribution. We will determine a fair settlement of the UK's rights and obligations as a departing member state, in accordance with the law and in the spirit of the UK's continuing partnership with the EU. The principle, however, is clear: the days of Britain making vast annual contributions to the European Union will end …

> We believe it is necessary to agree the terms of our future partnership alongside our withdrawal, reaching agreement on both within the two years allowed by Article 50 of the Treaty on European Union.[83]

There was significant ambiguity, presumably intentional, in these passages, crafted to maximise flexibility for May and her government following the anticipated expansion in the Conservative Party majority in the House of Commons. The reference to parliamentary votes is an example of how her initial stance on executive control had softened under political pressure (as well as legal defeat in the Article 50 case), but in a vague way. It was not clear from this commitment when consent would be sought, how the decision would be framed, or what would be the consequence of either one or both Houses of Parliament rejecting what was offered. The expression of an intention to secure a 'deep and special partnership with the European Union' created room for interpretation: what precisely did 'deep and special' mean? Possibly of greater importance was the observation that '[t]he negotiations will undoubtedly be tough, and there will be give and take on both sides'. This statement implied concessions by the UK (as well as the EU). But what might it have been willing or required to 'give' and how would doing so effect the promises made elsewhere in the manifesto? The document then reminded the reader that 'we continue to believe that no deal is better than a bad deal for the UK'. However, it did not indicate how the UK government would determine that a possible arrangement was so 'bad' as to make 'no deal' a better option. The commitment to 'control immigration' was another example of vagueness. The manifesto seemed to attempt to create yet more space for manoeuvre through its statement of a desire to 'maintain as frictionless a border as possible for people goods and services between Northern Ireland and the Republic of Ireland'.

The manifesto also dealt with matters over which the UK government did not have direct control, for instance when stating that '[w]e believe it is necessary to agree the terms of our future partnership alongside our withdrawal, reaching agreement on both within the two years allowed by Article 50 of the Treaty on European Union'. Attainment of this objective was dependent both upon the cooperation of the remaining EU and the constraints of the practical. One commitment that was seemingly both definite and possible for the UK unilaterally to insist upon involved the intention to 'no longer be members of the single market or customs union'. However, objectives that were less clear were then iterated. The manifesto described the plan to achieve a 'deep and special partnership including a comprehensive free trade and customs agreement'. Furthermore, the drafters of the text seemed to strive for discretion with the statement that the UK might want to take part in 'specific European programmes' that would require a contribution from the UK. This delicate financial theme led on to the insistence

[83] *Forward Together: Our Plan for a Stronger Britain and a Prosperous Future, The Conservative and Unionist Party Manifesto 2017* (London, Conservative Party, 2017), 35–36.

that '[w]e will determine a fair settlement of the UK's rights and obligations as a departing member state, in accordance with the law and in the spirit of the UK's continuing partnership with the EU'. Yet another vague assertion was that 'the days of Britain making vast annual contributions to the European Union will end'.

This passage from the manifesto provided confirmation that translation of the vote of 23 June 2016 into precise action was not a straightforward task. Creative intermediation was required. May sought through the election to legitimise the discretion that the executive would need to exercise in performing this task. The referendum, as a direct democratic device, was nested within a wider representative system within the context of which its outcome was interpreted and implemented. That May had resorted to a parliamentary poll to strengthen her hand raised complex questions regarding the nature of democratic authority. What was the relationship between a (supposed) referendum obligation and a General Election mandate? The implication of the Conservative manifesto appeared to be that the latter could clarify the means by which the former was to be implemented. But could a General Election be used to reverse a referendum result – and if not, was there any way in which it could be overturned? May failed to win the General Election outright, but sought to proceed with the programme that had been set out anyway, suggesting that she and her government were not operating within a clearly defined set of constitutional understandings. The referendum result had instigated a period of fluidity in which it was more possible – and necessary – than normal to imply or assert the existence of norms to suit political circumstances and objectives. May advanced one set of novel propositions with her October 2016 speech, that by the time of the 2017 General Election she had modified. In 1979 JA Griffith wrote that: '[t]he constitution of the United Kingdom lives on, changing from day to day for the constitution is no more and no less than what happens. Everything that happens is constitutional. And if nothing happened that would be constitutional also.'[84] In the period from June 2016 this description became increasingly apt.

III. VOTING PATTERNS AND TERRITORIAL PERSPECTIVES

One possible critique of the EU referendum as a basis for leaving the EU could be derived from the arguments Davis advanced in a different context in 2002. They turned on provisions made – or neglected – in advance of the vote. Another ground for questioning the idea that the vote should have the effect that May held it must came from the result itself. The margin of the 'leave' victory, at least measured in percentage terms, was narrow: 51.9 per cent 'leave' to 48.1 per cent

[84] John A Griffith, 'The political constitution' (1979) 42(1) *The Modern Law Review* 1–21, at 19.

'remain'.[85] In this sense, the vote was divisive because it suggested a fairly even split around a binary choice. Moreover, while 51.9 per cent was a bare majority of those who voted, it only represented slightly over 37 per cent of those who were registered to take part. Furthermore, behind these global figures, rather than relatively close results, there were a variety of sharp subdivisions. The overall impression was of two groups of voters, one nearly four per cent larger than the other, possessed of distinctly different profiles.

For example, as revealed by Ipsos-MORI in its survey work, older voters were generally more disposed towards 'leave'. For those between 65 and 74, 34 per cent were remain while 66 were leave. Of those who were 75 and above, 37 were remain, with 63 leave. On the other hand, the age group of 18–24 year olds was 75 per cent committed to 'remain', and only 25 per cent to 'leave'. Another cleavage involved ethnicity. Among whites, 46 per cent were remain and 54 per cent were leave; but for the BME (Black and Minority Ethnic) group, 69 per cent voted remain with 31 per cent leave. Social class provided another perspective suggestive of polarisation. The AB category split in favour of remain by 59 to 41 per cent. The DE group supported leave by 64 to 36 per cent. Among those who had no formal educational qualifications, 70 per cent were leave and 30 remain. Within the category of those with a degree or higher, 68 per cent favoured remain to 32 per cent leave.[86] These figures are important from a constitutional viewpoint. Those who hold office in various governmental institutions – parliamentarians, officials, judges and so on – are overwhelmingly university educated. It was reasonable to assume, therefore, that the referendum result was contrary to the wishes of the majority of the personnel of the representative system. Yet they would be in different ways responsible for responding to and even implementing it. Perhaps this aspect of the Brexit cleavage will continue in the future when a new generation comes to occupy such posts, since students split 80 per cent remain to 20 per cent leave.[87]

When these several divisions are considered, the referendum, rather than producing the decisive result May claimed, appears to have revealed and exacerbated a complex social partition. Some analysis suggests the existence of two groups who were bound together not as much by factors such as class as by shared cultural values, attachment to which could cut across other divisions.[88]

[85] There were 33,577,342 voters, representing 72.2% of those who were eligible to take part. Of them, 16,141,241 – 48.1% – opted for 'remain', while 17,410, 742 – 51.9% – voted 'leave' (23,359 ballot papers were rejected). Electoral Commission, *The 2016 EU Referendum* (London, Electoral Commission, 2016) 17.

[86] Ipsos-MORI, *The 2016 EU Referendum – who was in and who was out? How Britain voted in the 2016 referendum* (2016) at: https://www.ipsos-mori.com/researchpublications/researcharchive/3774/The-2016-EU-referendum-who-was-in-and-who-was-out.aspx last accessed 19 March 2017.

[87] ibid.

[88] Brian Salter, 'When intellectuals fail? Brexit and hegemonic challenge' 6–7, available at: https://www.kcl.ac.uk/sspp/departments/politicaleconomy/research/biopolitics/publications/workingpapers/Brexit-hegemony-and-intellectuals3.pdf last accessed 23 September 2018.

Those who found favour with environmentalism, feminism, inward migration and a multicultural society, for instance, were likely to vote 'remain'; while those who disliked such movements and tendencies were prone to be supporters of 'leave'.[89] Membership of the EU was the particular subject that had served to expose and amplify this division; but it appeared to pertain to a deeper lying set of issues.[90] One possible response to this observation, not necessarily made by those who describe such tendencies, might be to question how far the vote could truly be seen as a precise and definitive answer from the public regarding the exact subject of continued participation in the continental integration project. Were voters expressing a general disposition more than passing judgement on the question of UK membership of a complex supranational entity?

From the standpoint of the UK system of government, a particularly important variation in voting patterns was territorial. England favoured leave by 53.4 per cent to 46.4 per cent; though London produced a 59.9 per cent remain vote, as against 40.1 per cent leave. In Wales there was a vote of 52.5 to 47.5 in favour of leaving. In Scotland, the outcome was remain, by 62 to 38. Northern Ireland too saw a remain victory, with a margin of 55.8 to 44.2.[91] It also produced a division within a divergence.[92] Among those of a Catholic background, there was 85 per cent support for remain and 15 per cent in favour of leave. For Protestants, there was a 60 leave vote and 40 per cent remain. An associated division existed reflecting preferred constitutional arrangement for Northern Ireland. Of those who wished to maintain Northern Ireland as part of the UK under direct rule, 60 per cent were leave and 40 per cent remain. Advocates of a devolved Northern Ireland within the UK were 58 per cent remain and 42 per cent leave Those who supported making Northern Ireland part of the Republic of Ireland were 85 per cent remain and 15 per cent leave. In the words of John Garry, who carried out this analysis, '[t]he referendum divided leavers from remainers; equally it divided Protestant unionists from Catholic nationalists'.[93]

This territorial differentiation pertained to the system of devolution, the status of the Union, and the Northern Ireland peace process, all matters of fundamental systemic importance. Furthermore, the referendum revealed and

[89] Lord Ashcroft, 'How the United Kingdom voted on Thursday … and why' *Lord Ashcroft Polls*, 24 June 2016: http://lordashcroftpolls.com/2016/06/how-the-united-kingdom-voted-and-why/ last accessed 23 September 2018.

[90] For the importance of migration, see also eg Matthew Goodwin, 'Why Britain backed Brexit' *The UK in a Changing Europe*, 4 July 2016 http://ukandeu.ac.uk/why-britain-backed-brexit%E2%80%8F/ last accessed 23 July 2018.

[91] BBC News, *EU Referendum results: UK votes to leave EU*: http://www.bbc.co.uk/news/politics/eu_referendum/results last accessed 26 August 2018.

[92] John Garry, *The EU Referendum Vote in Northern Ireland: Implications for our understanding of citizens' political view and behavior*: https://www.qub.ac.uk/home/EUReferendum/Brexitfilestore/Filetoupload,728121,en.pdf last accessed 26 August 2018.

[93] ibid.

produced not only diverse public attitudes regarding EU membership, but also divergent perceptions of the UK constitution across different tiers of governance. It was illustrated by three Brexit white papers issued at the turn of 2016–17 by the Scottish, Welsh and UK executives (there was no equivalent Northern Ireland publication since devolution was not functioning in this territory at the time).

On 20 December 2016 the Scottish government, composed of the pro-independence Scottish National Party (SNP), issued *Scotland's Place in Europe*.[94] The foreword by the First Minister, Nicola Sturgeon, noted the advent of a 'remain' majority in Scotland and that – while there was an outcome in the same direction in Northern Ireland – England and Wales had produced 'leave' results. She judged that '[t]he stark divergence in the democratic will between the different nations of the United Kingdom … demands a reappraisal of how political power in the UK is exercised'. While the Scottish government preferred the idea of Scotland as an independent country and member state of the EU, Sturgeon stated that it was prepared to seek means by which it could safeguard Scottish interests within the UK as it left the EU. She saw the coming period as one in which the idea of the UK as a true 'partnership of equals' could be assessed.[95] The Scottish government would judge developments purely from the point of view of their impact upon Scotland. It believed it was entitled to be engaged fully in the Brexit process and that it should be able to make a contribution to the objectives pursued. It held that, if a satisfactory outcome could not be achieved for Scotland, there should be an independence referendum.[96]

The Scottish government wanted to continue participation in the European Single Market and Customs Union. But given that the UK administration had appeared to rule out these options, the Scottish executive wanted an exception for Scotland, allowing it to retain membership of these entities irrespective of the overall position of the UK. It also wished to avoid the introduction of any trade barriers between it and the rest of the UK. Such an arrangement, the Scottish government held, would be in keeping with the traditions of the UK constitution, that had been defined by a 'principle of differentiation' from its outset, and that devolution had served to accentuate.[97]

The text made further recommendations of significance to the UK constitution. It proposed that Brexit required 'a fundamental reconsideration of the nature of the UK state, with different relationships between its constituent parts as well as changes to the detail of their powers'. At the centre of this realignment

[94] Scottish government, *Scotland's Place in Europe* (Edinburgh, Scottish government, 2016).
[95] ibid, v.
[96] ibid, viii.
[97] ibid, 24–27.

was the allotment of various policy responsibilities between devolved and UK tiers after departure. First, the Scottish government dealt with the issue that lay at the core of arguments about Brexit and the territorial constitution. Some powers that fell within policy areas that were devolved were not actually under the control of the devolved institutions since, while the UK was part of the EU, they were handled at European level. A question that arose involved whether, following UK departure from the EU, those technically devolved responsibilities should, when returned from the EU to the UK, automatically come to rest at devolved level, or should be held centrally. The Scottish government argued that such patriated functions ought all to come within the remit of the Scottish Parliament. Secondly, the paper held that relevant authorities that presently resided at UK level should be reassigned to Scotland to allow for the guarantee of citizens' rights following Brexit. The Scottish government stated, thirdly, that there were further powers that it might be appropriate to devolve in the future and that should be subject to review.[98] The text allowed that it might be necessary for responsibilities contained within the first category to be exercised within the context of a 'crossborder framework' to ensure that they were aligned as necessary. However, it stressed that any such mechanism would involve agreement between the different tiers as opposed to 'imposition from Westminster'.[99] While this stipulation implied a new arrangement for the whole UK, the Scottish executive stressed that 'the governance and constitutional arrangements of England, Wales and Northern Ireland are matters for the people of those countries'.[100] In other words, the Scottish government did not wish to engage in promoting a comprehensive constitutional overhaul for the whole UK, a state which after all it ultimately sought to leave.

The Welsh government, Labour in complexion, issued a paper agreed with the Welsh nationalist party, Plaid Cymru, on 23 January 2017. Both had supported remain. But the document, *Securing Wales' Future: Transition from the European Union to a new relationship with Europe*, was founded in the premise that Brexit of some kind was necessitated by the referendum, in which Wales had voted leave.[101] However, the text contained proposals that diverged from the approach taken by the UK government. It insisted that '[t]he case for continuing Single Market participation is overwhelming and we can agree to no other position'.[102] The document also supported, less enthusiastically, a sustained presence within the Customs Union.[103]

In tandem with a particular programme for exit, the *Securing Wales's Future* paper recommended the introduction of new decision-taking structures for the

[98] ibid, 41–44.
[99] ibid, 41.
[100] ibid, 40.
[101] Welsh government, *Securing Wales' Future: Transition from the European Union to a new relationship with Europe* (Cardiff, Welsh government, 2017) 4.
[102] ibid, 9.
[103] ibid, 14.

UK. The period since the UK had first participated in European integration in 1973, it held, had seen, in devolution, constitutional change on such a scale as to preclude a simple reversion to the pre-1973 position. The text therefore supported the formation of a UK constitutional convention to consider new arrangements for the governance of the UK. The outcome the paper favoured from such a process was a transition towards a 'more federal' polity. Like the Scottish government publication, the Welsh equivalent addressed the handling of powers transferred from the EU post-Brexit. It held that those functions that fell within devolved areas would come to rest at that level. Other powers, though they did not fit within the devolved category, concerned matters in which Wales held an 'active interest', that could at some point be shifted to its purview. Satisfactory management of all these responsibilities would necessitate 'a new approach to the UK's governance structure that reflects the interdependencies and interests between devolved and non-devolved' levels. Such a system, the paper noted, would be designed to ensure the maintenance of such regulatory harmonisation across the UK as was required for the preservation of a single UK market. However, it had to rest on participation between the devolved and UK institutions 'on equal terms'.[104] To resolve possible demarcation disputes, 'robust, and genuinely independent arbitration mechanisms' were needed. The text also advocated 'wholly new intergovernmental machinery'. The Joint Ministerial Committee, an entity without statutory basis that allowed for discussions between the UK and devolved executives, could become a 'UK Council of Ministers', for addressing issues over which action required unanimous agreement between the executives.[105]

The UK government issued *The United Kingdom's exit from and new partnership with the European Union* on 2 February 2017. In her foreword May referred to 'the strength of our identity as one nation'[106] and the paper proper insisted that the JMC would have an input into Brexit policy, as would its sub-committee specially convened for this purpose.[107] In discussing the return of regulatory powers from Brussels post-Brexit, it stated that 'these rules will be set here in the UK by democratically elected representatives'. However, it did not place the same emphasis on devolution as the Scottish or Welsh executives. It referred to the importance of 'ensuring power sits closer to the people of the UK than ever before'. The UK government also iterated 'that no decisions currently taken by the devolved administrations will be removed from them'; and that it would seek 'to ensure that more decisions are devolved'.[108] However, the UK executive stressed the importance of preserving the UK single market

[104] ibid, 26.
[105] ibid, 28.
[106] HM Government, *The United Kingdom's exit from and new partnership with the European Union* (London, Stationery Office, 2017) 3.
[107] ibid, 10–11.
[108] ibid, 18.

and ensuring that 'no new barriers to living and doing business within our own Union' were established. To this end it was necessary to sustain 'common standards and frameworks for our own domestic market', assisting the UK in reaching new international trade agreements.[109]

Each of the three executives could find, in the referendum and its aftermath, evidence to support their propositions, but the interpretations they placed upon it were clearly driven by their political motivations. The UK government wished to maximise its control over the process of leaving, and avoid what it saw as excessive regulatory divergence in the post-Brexit environment. For the Welsh, an important concern was to promote a new UK governmental framework within which there was increased status and influence afforded to the devolved institutions. For the Scottish executive, the possibility of being able to claim unfair treatment from the UK government, thereby strengthening the case for independence, must have figured prominently in political calculations. But this divergence of outlook, revealed and encouraged by Brexit, could not be explained purely in terms political imperatives and opportunism. It suggested a polity that was characterised not only by territorial divergence, but – increasingly – a lack of consensus about what its fundamental principles were.

A protracted period of manoeuvring and negotiation – centring on the contents of the European Union (Withdrawal) Bill – followed. On 16 October 2017, a 'Communique' from the Joint Ministerial Committee (EU Negotiations)[110] iterated that the UK and devolved governments (a senior official from the Northern Ireland Executive, which was not functioning, had attended as an observer) intended 'to work together to establish common approaches in some areas that are currently governed by EU law, but that are otherwise within areas of competence of the devolved administrations or legislatures'. The principles embodied in the communique had been established partly as a consequence of the Welsh and Scottish administrations jointly applying pressure for a greater role in the process of leaving the EU and the arrangements that followed.[111] In this sense they were working together for a different whole-UK approach, rather than dealing bilaterally with London. However, this Cardiff-Edinburgh axis did not endure.

The document explained that '[a] framework will set out a common UK, or GB, approach and how it will be operated and governed'. It signalled a shared

[109] ibid, 19.

[110] Available at: https://assets.publishing.service.gov.uk/government/uploads/system/uploads/attachment_data/file/652285/Joint_Ministerial_Committee_communique.pdf last accessed 26 August 2018.

[111] See Nicola Sturgeon, First Minister of Scotland and Carwyn Jones, First Minister of Wales, to Theresa May, Prime Minister of the United Kingdom, 19 September 2017: https://beta.gov.scot/publications/eu-withdrawal-bill-joint-letter-to-prime-minister/FMs%20letter%20to%20Theresa%20May.pdf?inline=true last accessed 5 August 2018; *The Proposed Amendments to the European Union (Withdrawal) Bill*: https://beta.gov.scot/publications/eu-withdrawal-bill-joint-letter-to-prime-minister/Proposed%20amendments%20to%20EU%20(Withdrawal)%20Bill.pdf?inline=true last accessed 5 August 2018.

acceptance that '[c]ommon frameworks' were required to: 'enable the functioning of the UK internal market' (though 'acknowledging policy divergence'); to 'ensure compliance with international obligations'; to 'ensure the UK can negotiate, enter into and implement new trade agreements and international treaties'; to 'enable the management of common resources'; to 'administer and provide access to justice in cases with a cross-border element'; and to 'safeguard the security of the UK'. These arrangements would 'respect the devolution settlements and the democratic accountability of the devolved legislatures'. Consequently they would 'be based on established conventions and practices, including that the competence of the devolved institutions will not normally be adjusted without their consent'. Frameworks would 'maintain, as a minimum, equivalent flexibility for tailoring policies to the specific needs of each territory as is afforded by current EU rules'. They would, moreover, 'lead to a significant increase in decision-making powers for the devolved administrations'. There would also be 'recognition of the economic and social linkages between Northern Ireland and Ireland and that Northern Ireland will be the only part of the UK that shares a land frontier with the EU'. Finally, new mechanisms would 'adhere to the Belfast Agreement'.

Part of the significance of the communique was derived from its being an assessment – shared between UK and devolved administrations – of aspects of the post-Brexit territorial constitution. In particular, it proposed areas of operation that should be regarded as applying to the whole UK, but into which the devolved tiers would have an input, via specified processes that recognised their legitimate democratic status within the system. This type of thought had similarities to that underpinning a federal system, in which sub-components or 'states' may be given a role in determining certain federal-level decisions. It could admittedly be argued that since the proposed frameworks related to areas of operation that were technically devolved, it represented a centralisation of power. Yet, the powers concerned had been subject to EU, not devolved control. Moreover, the communique also stipulated that there would 'be close working between the UK Government and the devolved administrations on reserved and excepted matters that impact significantly on devolved responsibilities'. This aspect of the statement suggested to some extent a sharing of power with the devolved territories that had previously been held centrally (or subject to EU authority) – again redolent of a federal approach.

Though it was an important text, the communique was subject to certain limitations. It did not propose new legally enforceable constitutional rights for the devolved institutions. Furthermore, England, in which there was no devolution as extensive as that implemented in other parts of the UK, and that did not have its own Parliament or executive, was not specifically represented. Northern Ireland, moreover, was unable to be fully party to the agreement. Finally, the translation of this broad statement of principle into a detailed settlement acceptable to all was a challenging task. Ultimately, though the Welsh and UK executive were able to issue the terms of an agreement pertaining to the European Union (Withdrawal) Bill and its operation, the Scottish administration held back (though the text issued deliberately left open the possibility of both Northern Ireland and Scotland participating, if circumstances changed).[112]

On 24 April 2018, the Welsh and UK governments reached a statement of terms regarding the European Union (Withdrawal) Bill and its operation.[113] The purpose of the negotiations had been to ensure that the Bill was altered in such a way, accompanied by suitable undertakings, that the devolved administrations were able to recommend that their legislatures voted to express their consent to it. In the case of Scotland, this outcome had not proved possible. According to the so-called 'Sewel Convention', the UK government will not normally seek to legislate with respect to devolved policy areas without the approval of the devolved legislatures in the territories concerned.[114] As we will see, the UK Supreme Court had already taken the view that the Sewel Convention was not justiciable, despite its having received statutory recognition for Scotland, through the Scotland Act 2016 (and subsequently Wales, under the Wales Act 2017). Nonetheless, the withholding of legislative consent by Scotland was a politically and constitutionally significant episode, since it entailed the passing of a UK Act of Parliament notwithstanding the express denial of approval by a devolved legislature. With no court or other independent adjudicator to issue a ruling, whether or not the UK government had violated the Sewel rule was a matter of opinion. But the intergovernmental agreement of April 2018 was important not only for the government that was not party to it, but for its contents, through which the government made undertakings about how it would proceed by consultation in future (though it included three uses of the words 'not normally').[115]

IV. THE CONSTITUTIONAL ROLE OF THE SUPREME COURT

If disagreements arose between the UK and devolved administrations, ultimately the Westminster Parliament could impose a solution. The UK government wished to avoid the deployment of this power, but was willing to use it – and did so in the case of Scotland. In a federal system, such disputes might well

[112] See: *Intergovernmental Agreement on the European Union (Withdrawal) Bill and the Establishment of Common Frameworks*, 24 April 2018: https://assets.publishing.service.gov.uk/government/uploads/system/uploads/attachment_data/file/702623/2018-04-24_UKG-DA_IGA_and_Memorandum.pdf last accessed 26 August 2018.

[113] ibid.

[114] Gordon Anthony, *Devolution, Brexit and the Sewel Convention* (London, The Constitution Society, 2018) 2–5: https://consoc.org.uk/wp-content/uploads/2018/04/Gordon-Anthony-Devolution-Brexit-and-the-Sewel-Convention-1.pdf last accessed 24 September 2018.

[115] *Intergovernmental Agreement on the European Union (Withdrawal) Bill and the Establishment of Common Frameworks*, 24 April 2018, Memorandum on the European Union (Withdrawal) Bill and the Establishment of Common Frameworks.

be resolved not unilaterally by one of the parties to them, but by the courts, interpreting a written constitution. However, the UK Parliament was not subject to any such restraint. Indeed, the Supreme Court, in January 2017, had been careful to discount the idea that it might have such a role in this area. The exclusion of this possibility, however, was a peripheral aspect to a judgment in which the Supreme Court confirmed an assertion of judicial authority with respect to Brexit.

The *Miller* case is in itself the worthy subject of the articles and books being written about it.[116] I cannot cover all its aspects in detail here. But it is worth considering some features of the judgment given by a majority (eight to three) of Supreme Court members on 24 January 2017 in as far as they engage key aspects of this work. An irony of the Brexit process arises in connection to the concept of parliamentary sovereignty. This doctrine entails the UK Parliament being legally subordinate to no other authority when passing Acts.[117] Objections to UK participation in European integration have often rested on the proposition that it – undesirably – compromises parliamentary sovereignty through making Acts of Parliament subject to the supremacy of European law.[118] The merits or otherwise of parliamentary sovereignty, whether it is an intellectually coherent concept at all, and if EU membership undermined it, are all complex and heated subjects of debate.[119] For the purposes of the present discussion, it is important to note that Brexit produced ambiguous attitudes towards the doctrine. The UK government, for instance, in its Brexit white paper of February 2017, stated that '[t]he sovereignty of Parliament is a fundamental principle of the UK constitution. Whilst Parliament has remained sovereign throughout our membership of the EU, it has not always felt like that'.[120] This statement suggests a series of propositions. First, that EU membership did not in reality violate the doctrine of parliamentary sovereignty. Secondly, that it was such an important component of the UK system, that even for it to 'feel' undermined was a problem. Thirdly, that membership of the EU created this feeling. Fourthly, that its creation of such a feeling was a motive for leaving the EU, and for executing this departure in a way that allayed the unwanted feeling.

[116] eg Mark Elliott, 'The Supreme Court's Judgment in Miller: In Search of Constitutional Principle' (2017) 76(2) *The Cambridge Law Journal* 257–88; Pavlos Eleftheriadis, 'Two Doctrines of the Unwritten Constitution' (2017) 13(3) *European Constitutional Law Review* 525–50; Mark Elliott, Jack Williams and Alison L Young (eds), *The UK Constitution after Miller: Brexit and Beyond* (Oxford, Hart Publishing, 2018).

[117] For an historic and contemporary analysis of this doctrine, see Jeffrey Goldsworthy, *The sovereignty of parliament: history and philosophy* (Oxford, Oxford University Press, 2001).

[118] Andrew Blick, *Beyond Magna Carta: a constitution for the United Kingdom* (Oxford, Hart Publishing, 2015).

[119] Vernon Bogdanor, 'Imprisoned by a doctrine: The modern defence of parliamentary sovereignty' (2011) 32(1) *Oxford Journal of Legal Studies* 179–95.

[120] *The United Kingdom's exit from and new partnership with the European Union* (London, Stationery Office, 2017) 13.

This platform for departure from the EU suggested that it amounted to a conscious rejection of the rational in favour of the emotional. Given this perspective on the process, the wider approach to parliamentary sovereignty taken in pursuit of Brexit becomes easier to comprehend. Those who pursued Brexit often presented themselves as propelled by veneration for the doctrine, as the white paper quoted above demonstrates. The concept of taking back control of law-making power could imply reassertion of parliamentary sovereignty.[121] Yet at other times advocates of Brexit appeared hostile towards this principle and the idea that Parliament should be the preeminent institution within the UK constitution. The desire to achieve Brexit could override a supposed key motive for the project itself. We have seen how the 'May Doctrine' entailed assertion of executive primacy in the interpretation and implementation of the 2016 referendum result, rejecting a central role for Parliament (along with other institutions and interests). Moreover, some variants on the post-Brexit relationship between the UK and EU seemed to entail significant constraints upon the Westminster Parliament. The government white paper published in July 2018 setting out the so-called Chequers agreement proposed that the UK share a 'common rulebook for goods', to facilitate trade after exit.[122] The arrangement would be overseen by a Joint Committee between the two parties.[123] In those areas in which continuity was maintained, the UK legislature would be notified, consulted and able to offer opinions, but no more.[124] The Article 50 case provided further evidence of how those seeking to bring about Brexit, though supposedly motivated by a desire to promote parliamentary sovereignty, were ready to minimise or evade this principle if it appeared to represent an encumbrance to the achievement of their purpose.

The finding of the Supreme Court, upholding an earlier conclusion reached by the Divisional Court of England and Wales, was that the government did not have the power to activate Article 50 of the Treaty on European Union, the means by which it sought to leave the European Union in response to the result of the referendum of 23 June 2016. The government had intended to instigate the Article 50 process using an ancient source of non-statutory executive authority known as the Royal Prerogative. However, the Supreme Court judgment meant that it had to obtain further specific authorisation through an Act of Parliament to do so. The logic underlying this conclusion was that to withdraw from the EU would be to remove the UK from a central source of its own law, as opposed to

[121] See eg Dave Richards, Kinglsey Purdham, Liz Richardson and Oliver James, 'Brexit and the Meaning of "Taking Back Control" Great State Expectations?', *Manchester Policy Blogs*, 27 March 2017: http://blog.policy.manchester.ac.uk/posts/2017/03/brexit-and-the-meaning-of-taking-back-control-great-state-expectations/ last accessed 24 September 2018. See further ch 3.

[122] HM Government, *The future relationship between the United Kingdom and the European Union* (London, HM Government, 2018) 8.

[123] ibid, 88.

[124] ibid, 95–96.

an alteration of the position within the existing framework.[125] As the Supreme Court majority put it: '[w]e cannot accept that a major change to UK constitutional arrangements can be achieved by ministers alone; it must be effected in the only way that the UK constitution recognises, namely by Parliamentary legislation'.[126] Furthermore, in addition to entailing the 'loss of a source of law', activation of Article 50 would lead to 'changes in domestic rights', another circumstance that could not be brought about by the prerogative.[127]

The Supreme Court majority drew specific conclusions of a constitutional character regarding the role of referendums in general and the 2016 referendum in particular. This aspect of the argument presented by the Court was important in that the reason the government wanted to leave the EU, and by extension that the case existed at all, was the holding of a particular referendum and the result it had produced. The Court noted that, on behalf of the government, the Attorney General had held that the usual constraints upon the Royal Prerogative, preventing it from being used to alter statute law or alter rights, should be set aside in circumstances where voters had supported a particular course of action in a popular vote.[128] One of the arguments made in the written evidence submission on behalf of the government was that 'the legality of the use of the prerogative in the present case, to implement the outcome of a referendum' could not be dealt with by standard historically-based arguments. There was, it held, a requirement for a 'recognition that the usual democratic objections to use of the prerogative do not apply in the circumstances of the present case'.[129] Tension between the prerogative and 'Parliamentary sovereignty' could not 'be resolved in a vacuum, without regard to the outcome of the referendum'.[130] The implication was that the particular result produced by the referendum should have legal consequences. Yet the legislation providing for the vote had not dealt with the issue of what the outcome would mean.[131]

Here we can detect a manifestation of the May doctrine and its populist dimension. The model advanced by the government was one in which the executive was empowered directly by the people on whose behalf it could act, without further reference to representative institutions. The idea that the Article 50 case involved a clash between differing concepts of governance was heightened by the intense public interest it generated, with some sections of the media questioning the legitimacy of judicial involvement in this area.[132] A *Daily Mail* headline, for

[125] *R (on the application of Miller and another) (Respondents) v Secretary of State for Exiting the European Union (Appellant)* [2017] UKSC 5, 24 January 2017, para 80, p 27.

[126] ibid, para 82, p 28.

[127] ibid, para 83, p 28.

[128] ibid, para 116, p 38.

[129] *Appellant's case*, para 83, p 45.

[130] ibid, para 85, p 46.

[131] See further ch 3.

[132] Claire Phipps, 'British newspapers react to judges' Brexit ruling: "Enemies of the People"', *Guardian*, 4 November 2016: https://www.theguardian.com/politics/2016/nov/04/enemies-of-the-people-british-newspapers-react-judges-brexit-ruling last accessed 24 September 2018.

instance, famously described the three judges who gave the Divisional Court ruling as 'Enemies of the people'.[133]

It is important in this context that the Court rejected the government view. Referendums were, it held, 'a relatively new feature of UK constitutional practice', though, the Court observed, one provided with a statutory framework in 2000 (through the Political Parties, Elections and Referendums Act 2000).[134] The majority judgment stressed that '[t]he effect of any particular referendum must depend on the terms of the statute which authorises it'.[135] It noted previous occasions on which legislation providing for the holding of referendums had also stipulated the consequences of the outcome. Popular votes conducted on these terms had included those held on Scottish devolution in 1979 and on the UK parliamentary voting system in 2011.[136] They demonstrated the existence of the option for referendum legislation to set out 'what should happen in response to the referendum result, and what changes in the law were to follow, and how they were to be effected'. The Court then reflected that, conversely, the statute authorising the 2016 EU referendum (also like that, it noted, for the 1975 European vote) did not make 'provision for any consequences of either possible outcome'. It 'provided only that the referendum should be held'.[137]

The Court also dealt with the significance of political statements of intent regarding the referendum. It observed that:

> the 2016 referendum was described as advisory by some ministers and as decisive by others, but nothing hangs on that for present purposes. Whether or not they are clear and consistent, such public observations, wherever they are made, are not law: they are statements of political intention. Further, such statements are, at least normally, made by ministers on behalf of the UK government, not on behalf of Parliament.[138]

The conclusion was that if 'as in this case, implementation of a referendum result requires a change in the law of the land, and statute has not provided for that change, the change in the law must be made in the only way in which the UK constitution permits, namely through Parliamentary legislation'.[139] The precise content and length of such a provision was the business of Parliament. However, 'if, as we consider, what would otherwise be a prerogative act would result in a change in domestic law, the act can only lawfully be carried out with the sanction of primary legislation enacted by the Queen in Parliament'.[140]

[133] James Slack, 'Enemies of the people', *Mail*, 3 November 2016: https://www.dailymail.co.uk/news/article-3903436/Enemies-people-Fury-touch-judges-defied-17-4m-Brexit-voters-trigger-constitutional-crisis.html last accessed 24 September 2018.

[134] *R (on the application of Miller and another) (Respondents) v Secretary of State for Exiting the European Union (Appellant)* [2017] UKSC 5, 24 January 2017, para 117, p 38.

[135] ibid, para 118, p 38.

[136] ibid, para 118, pp 38–39.

[137] ibid, para 119, p 39.

[138] ibid, para 119, p 39.

[139] ibid, para 121, pp 39–40.

[140] ibid, para 122, p 40.

The majority judgment also made significant points with respect to the territorial constitution and devolution. One such conclusion concerned the right of the people of Northern Ireland, expressed in section 1 of the Northern Ireland Act 1998, to determine whether to remain part of the UK or join with the Republic of Ireland. The majority of the Supreme Court took the view that section 1 'neither regulated any other change in the constitutional status of Northern Ireland nor required the consent of a majority of the people of Northern Ireland to the withdrawal of the United Kingdom from the European Union'.[141]

Another view taken by the Court concerned the position of the three devolved legislatures of the UK. It involved the so-called 'Sewel Convention'. As the majority judgment noted, '[i]n each of the devolution settlements the UK Parliament has preserved its right to legislate on matters which are within the competence of the devolved legislature'.[142] However, it was balanced by a convention binding the UK government 'not to seek or support relevant legislation in the UK Parliament without the prior consent of the devolved legislature. That consent is given by a legislative consent motion which the devolved government introduces into the legislature'.[143] But 'Judges … are neither the parents nor the guardians of political conventions; they are merely observers.' While courts could 'recognise the operation of a political convention in the context of deciding a legal question … they cannot give legal rulings on its operation or scope, because those matters are determined within the political world'.[144]

The Court noted that this convention had recently been recognised through section 2(8) of the Scotland Act 2016, which contained the statement that it was 'recognised that the Parliament of the United Kingdom will not normally legislate with regard to devolved matters without the consent of the Scottish Parliament'. (Similar provision was about to be made through the Wales Act 2017).[145] However, the Court held that:

> by such provisions, the UK Parliament is not seeking to convert the Sewel Convention into a rule which can be interpreted, let alone enforced, by the courts; rather, it is recognising the convention for what it is, namely a political convention, and is effectively declaring that it is a permanent feature of the relevant devolution settlement.[146]

Therefore, by extension, the court believed that were departure from the EU judged to engage the Sewel Convention and consequently to require legislative consent at devolved level, the courts could not be called upon to enforce this view.[147]

[141] ibid, para 135, p 44.
[142] ibid, para 136, p 44.
[143] ibid, para 139, p 45.
[144] ibid, para 146, pp 47–48.
[145] ibid, para 147, p 48.
[146] ibid, para 148, p 48.
[147] ibid, para 150, p 49.

V. CITIZENS' RIGHTS AND THE STATUS OF NORTHERN IRELAND

The UK government, in as far as it could secure the compliance of the Commons and Parliament as a whole, was the most powerful player within the domestic political institutional environment of the UK. But the internal constitutional pressures discussed in this chapter were a by-product of a policy pertaining to the external relations of the UK. As a state it was conducting negotiations with an organisation that had a stronger bargaining position than its own, the outcome of which would in turn have implications for the UK constitution. An example of the kind of impact that could arise in this regard came on 8 December 2017. The two parties to the Brexit negotiations issued a *Joint Report from the Negotiators of the European Union and the United Kingdom Government on Progress During Phase 1 of Negotiations Under Article 50 TEU on the United Kingdom's Orderly Withdrawal from the European Union.* It dealt with certain preliminary issues that the EU had insisted be addressed before proceeding to dealing with wider issues related to Brexit. They included Citizens' Rights and Northern Ireland.

In the first category the text described its 'overall objective' as being 'to provide reciprocal protection for Union and UK citizens, to enable the effective exercise of rights derived from Union law and based on past life choices, where those citizens have exercised free movement rights by the specified date'.[148] In the UK context, it applied to those 'who in accordance with Union law legally reside in the UK' by the point at which the UK exited the EU.[149] The rights in question would be 'interpreted in line with the case law of the' European Court of Justice as it stood at the point of departure.[150] The implication of this aspect of the agreement was that a group of individuals within the UK (citizens' from the remaining 27 EU member states) would possess legally enforceable rights that others in the UK would not. This prospect prompted protest on the grounds that it was an inequitable arrangement. (A fact that tended to escape attention was that reciprocal arrangements would apply to people from the UK living in the EU.)[151] Moreover, it meant that the European Court of Justice would continue to exert influence on the UK after departure. Not only would the decisions be made 'in line' with existing case law on exit, but courts in the UK would 'have due regard to relevant decisions of the' European Court of Justice 'after the specified date'. Furthermore, a 'mechanism' would be created 'enabling UK

[148] *Joint Report from the Negotiators of the European Union and the United Kingdom Government on Progress During Phase 1 of Negotiations Under Article 50 TEU on the United Kingdom's Orderly Withdrawal from the European Union*, 8 December 2017, p 1.

[149] Ibid, p 2.

[150] ibid, p 2.

[151] Professor Steve Peers, 'Beginning of the End? Citizens' Rights in the Brexit "Sufficient Progress" Deal', *EU Law Analysis*, 9 December 2017: http://eulawanalysis.blogspot.com/2017/12/the-beginning-of-end-citizens-rights-in.html last accessed 13 September 2018.

courts or tribunals to decide, having had due regard to whether relevant case-law exists, to ask the CJEU questions of interpretation of those rights'. This 'mechanism' would 'be available for UK courts or tribunals for litigation brought within 8 years' of the citizens' rights agreement being applied. The joint report, moreover, contained specifications regarding the means by which the UK would provide for the domestic implementation of citizens' rights. It required the UK government to 'bring forward a Bill, the Withdrawal Agreement & Implementation Bill' for this purpose.[152]

The joint report had important implications not only for the operation of the UK legal system, but also for its territorial governance. The document iterated that '[c]ooperation between Ireland and Northern Ireland' was critical to the 1998 Belfast or 'Good Friday' Agreement and was 'essential for achieving reconciliation and the normalisation of relationships on the island of Ireland'.[153] 'North-South cooperation', moreover, was dependent 'to a significant extent on a common European Union legal and policy framework. Therefore, the United Kingdom's departure from the European Union gives rise to substantial challenges to the maintenance and development of North-South cooperation'. As well as supporting 'North-South cooperation', the UK had made a 'guarantee of avoiding a hard border'. It hoped 'to achieve these objectives through the overall EU-UK relationship'. However, were it unable to do so, it would 'maintain full alignment with those rules of the Internal Market and the Customs Union which, now or in the future, support North-South cooperation, the all-island economy and the protection of the 1998 Agreement'. However, in parallel it would also 'ensure that no new regulatory barriers develop between Northern Ireland and the rest of the United Kingdom, unless, consistent with the 1998 Agreement, the Northern Ireland Executive and Assembly agree that distinct arrangements are appropriate for Northern Ireland. In all circumstances, the United Kingdom will continue to ensure the same unfettered access for Northern Ireland's businesses to the whole of the United Kingdom internal market'.[154] The UK government appeared to have committed itself to the reconciliation of the irreconcilable. While it remained determined not to be part of the Customs Union and Single Market, unless self-such exclusion was to be purely cosmetic, it was not clear how a 'hard border' and regulatory divergence could be avoided – unless Northern Ireland were to be provided with a special status for these purposes within the UK.[155] Yet this solution was also

[152] *Joint Report from the Negotiators of the European Union and the United Kingdom Government on Progress During Phase 1 of Negotiations Under Article 50 TEU on the United Kingdom's Orderly Withdrawal from the European Union*, 8 December 2017, p 6.

[153] ibid, p 7.

[154] ibid, p 7.

[155] Jonathan Lis, 'Free movement of people or a sea border: the indissoluble Brexit dilemma', 7 May 2018: https://www.prospectmagazine.co.uk/politics/free-movement-of-people-or-a-sea-border-the-insoluble-brexit-dilemma last accessed 24 September 2018.

specifically precluded – moreover, the dependence of the UK government on the parliamentary support of the Democratic Unionist Party made it politically untenable.[156]

In this instance, the act of seeking to leave the EU had led directly to a serious constitutional dilemma that would torture the UK government as it negotiated exit – continuing to do so at the time of writing – and creating a serious possibility that talks would fail and lead to the most disruptive of exits from the EU.[157] In other cases, such tensions arose in a more tangential fashion, involving changes designed to accommodate anticipated features and consequences of Brexit. But whether a specific factor in negotiations or a secondary outcome of the overall process, it was apparent that a decision presented primarily as involving membership or otherwise of an external organisation had simultaneously opened up a range of constitutional disputes and uncertainties of unsurpassed scale. The basis for the referendum that triggered this upheaval is the subject of the next chapter.

APPENDICES

Appendix A: Text of Article 50 of the Treaty on European Union (Lisbon Treaty) 2007 (Entering into Force 2009)

1. Any Member State may decide to withdraw from the Union in accordance with its own constitutional requirements.
2. A Member State which decides to withdraw shall notify the European Council of its intention. In the light of the guidelines provided by the European Council, the Union shall negotiate and conclude an agreement with that State, setting out the arrangements for its withdrawal, taking account of the framework for its future relationship with the Union. That agreement shall be negotiated in accordance with Article 218(3) of the Treaty on the Functioning of the European Union. It shall be concluded on behalf of the Union by the Council, acting by a qualified majority, after obtaining the consent of the European Parliament.
3. The Treaties shall cease to apply to the State in question from the date of entry into force of the withdrawal agreement or, failing that, two years after the notification referred to in paragraph 2, unless the European Council,

[156] For the text of the confidence and supply agreement between the Conservative Party and the Democratic Unionist Party, see: https://assets.publishing.service.gov.uk/government/uploads/system/uploads/attachment_data/file/621794/Confidence_and_Supply_Agreement_between_the_Conservative_Party_and_the_DUP.pdf last accessed 24 September 2018.

[157] Brendan Donnelly, 'Brexit: Salzburg makes a People's Vote more likely', *Federal Trust* blog, 24 September 2018: http://fedtrust.co.uk/brexit-salzburg-makes-a-peoples-vote-more-likely/ last accessed 24 September 2018.

in agreement with the Member State concerned, unanimously decides to extend this period.

4. For the purposes of paragraphs 2 and 3, the member of the European Council or of the Council representing the withdrawing Member State shall not participate in the discussions of the European Council or Council or in decisions concerning it.

   A qualified majority shall be defined in accordance with Article 238(3)(b) of the Treaty on the Functioning of the European Union.

5. If a State which has withdrawn from the Union asks to rejoin, its request shall be subject to the procedure referred to in Article 49.

Appendix B: Excerpts from Political Parties, Elections and Referendums Act 2000

Part VII, Chapter III Controls on Publications

Restriction on publication etc. of promotional material by central and local government etc.

125. – (1) This section applies to any material which—

(a) provides general information about a referendum to which this Part applies;
(b) deals with any of the issues raised by any question on which such a referendum is being held;
(c) puts any arguments for or against any particular answer to any such question; or
(d) is designed to encourage voting at such a referendum.

(2) Subject to subsection (3), no material to which this section applies shall be published during the relevant period by or on behalf of—

(a) any Minister of the Crown, government department or local authority; or
(b) any other person or body whose expenses are defrayed wholly or mainly out of public funds or by any local authority.

(3) Subsection (2) does not apply to—

(a) material made available to persons in response to specific requests for information or to persons specifically seeking access to it;
(b) anything done by or on behalf of the Commission or a person or body designated under section 108 (designation of organisations to whom assistance is available);
(c) the publication of information relating to the holding of the poll; or
(d) the issue of press notices;
and subsection (2)(b) shall not be taken as applying to the British Broadcasting Corporation or Sianel Pedwar Cymru.

(4) In this section—

(a) "publish" means make available to the public at large, or any section of the public, in whatever form and by whatever means (and "publication" shall be construed accordingly);
(b) "the relevant period", in relation to a referendum, means the period of 28 days ending with the date of the poll.

Details to appear on referendum material.

126. – (1) No material wholly or mainly relating to a referendum to which this Part applies shall be published during the referendum period unless—

(a) in the case of material which is, or is contained in, such a printed document as is mentioned in subsection (3), (4) or (5), the requirements of that subsection are complied with; or
(b) in the case of any other material, any requirements falling to be complied with in relation to the material by virtue of regulations under subsection (6) are complied with.

(2) For the purposes of subsections (3) to (5) the following details are "the relevant details" in the case of any material falling within subsection (1)(a), namely—

(a) the name and address of the printer of the document;
(b) the name and address of the promoter of the material; and
(c) the name and address of any person on behalf of whom the material is being published (and who is not the promoter).

(3) Where the material is a document consisting (or consisting principally) of a single side of printed matter, the relevant details must appear on the face of the document.

(4) Where the material is a printed document other than one to which subsection (3) applies, the relevant details must appear either on the first or the last page of the document.

(5) Where the material is an advertisement contained in a newspaper or periodical—

(a) the name and address of the printer of the newspaper or periodical must appear either on its first or last page; and
(b) the relevant details specified in subsection (2) (b) and (c) must be included in the advertisement.

(6) The Secretary of State may, after consulting the Commission, by regulations make provision for and in connection with the imposition of requirements as

to the inclusion in material falling within subsection (1)(b) of the following details, namely—

(a) the name and address of the promoter of the material; and
(b) the name and address of any person on behalf of whom the material is being published (and who is not the promoter).

(7) Regulations under subsection (6) may in particular specify—

(a) the manner and form in which such details must be included in any such material for the purpose of complying with any such requirement;
(b) circumstances in which—

- (i) any such requirement does not have to be complied with by a person of any description specified in the regulations, or
- (ii) a breach of any such requirement by a person of any description so specified is not to result in the commission of an offence under this section by that person or by a person of any other such description;

(c) circumstances in which material is, or is not, to be taken for the purposes of the regulations to be published or (as the case may be) published by a person of any description so specified.

(8) Where during the referendum period any material falling within subsection (1)(a) is published in contravention of subsection (1), then (subject to subsection (10))—

(a) the promoter of the material,
(b) any other person by whom the material is so published, and (c) the printer of the document, shall be guilty of an offence.

(9) Where during the referendum period any material falling within subsection (1)(b) is published in contravention of subsection (1), then (subject to regulations made by virtue of subsection (7)(b) and to subsection (10))—

(a) the promoter of the material, and
(b) any other person by whom the material is so published, shall be guilty of an offence.

(10) It shall be a defence for a person charged with an offence under this section to prove—

(a) that the contravention of subsection (1) arose from circumstances beyond his control; and
(b) that he took all reasonable steps, and exercised all due diligence, to ensure that that contravention would not arise.

Referendum campaign broadcasts.

127. – (1) A broadcaster shall not include in its broadcasting services any referendum campaign broadcast made on behalf of any person or body other than one designated in respect of the referendum in question under section 108.

(2) In this section "referendum campaign broadcast" means any broadcast whose purpose (or main purpose) is or may reasonably be assumed to be—

(a) to further any campaign conducted with a view to promoting or procuring a particular outcome in relation to any question asked in a referendum to which this Part applies, or
(b) otherwise to promote or procure any such outcome.

2

The Basis for the 2016 Referendum: Law, Politics and the Constitution

On 27 June 2016 the House of Commons discussed for the first time the outcome of the EU referendum that had taken place four days previously. The Conservative Prime Minister, David Cameron, who – in response to the 'leave' result – had already announced his attention to stand down told the House that:

> [t]he British people have voted to leave the European Union. It was not the result that I wanted, or the outcome that I believe is best for the country I love, but there can be no doubt about the result. Of course, I do not take back what I said about the risks. It is going to be difficult. We have already seen that there are going to be adjustments within our economy, complex constitutional issues, and a challenging new negotiation to undertake with Europe. However, I am clear – and the Cabinet agreed this morning – that the decision must be accepted, and the process of implementing the decision in the best possible way must now begin.[1]

The Labour Leader of the Opposition, Jeremy Corbyn, agreed with this basic premise, stating that: '[t]he Opposition Benches put forward a positive case to remain part of the European Union and convinced more than two thirds of our own supporters, but the majority of people voted to leave and we have listened to and accepted what they have said'.[2] The leaders of the two largest groupings in the Commons, then, while professing their regret at the outcome of the vote, were accepting that it bound them. Their acquiescence was representative of a mood that prevailed in both Houses of Parliament and other governmental institutions. A good example of this compliance on the part of the primary chamber of Parliament came with the Resolution the House of Commons passed by 448 votes to 75 on 7 December 2016, including in it the statement that it 'recognises that this House should respect the wishes of the United Kingdom as expressed in the referendum on 23 June; and further calls on the Government to invoke Article 50 by 31 March 2017'. (See appendix A for the full text of resolution.) Even those who might privately have hoped for a chance to

[1] House of Commons (HC) Debates, 27 June 2016, col 22.
[2] ibid, col 24.

reverse it at a later stage tended publicly at this point to concur with the proposition that Cameron and Corbyn advanced. The referendum result, they agreed, had to be implemented.[3]

But the precise way in which the vote of June 2016 should be put into effect and the process that should be followed in doing so were less clear. Arguments over these subjects – which could be a proxy for continued disagreement about leaving or remaining – were a source of division from the highest level of government downwards. Cabinet might, on the morning of 27 June 2016, have agreed on the necessity of departure, but beyond this basic point consensus was harder to reach. Nonetheless, the consequences for the UK of this broad acceptance of the referendum outcome – whatever, precisely it meant – were immense, both internally and externally; the preceding discussion of the sprawling constitutional issues that arose dealt with just one segment of the whole. There were also important implications for the European Union, and the wider world beyond. This chapter considers the nature of this obligation, so important in its consequences, that the referendum was perceived as creating, and to which politicians in Parliament were willing to subordinate themselves. It asks what was the basis for this requirement, how it came about, and what it meant. In accordance with the methodology of the book, it does so by focusing on two main sources: the European Union Referendum Act 2015, which provided the legal basis for the vote; and the debate that took place in the House of Commons on the Second Reading of the Bill that became this Act. The chapter considers what conclusions might be drawn, from a constitutional and democratic perspective, regarding the Brexit episode as a whole.

I. THE EUROPEAN UNION REFERENDUM ACT 2015

The bare text of the European Union Referendum Act 2015 provides only slight indication of the momentous sequence of occurrences it helped instigate. It describes itself as 'An Act to make provision for the holding of a referendum in the United Kingdom and Gibraltar on whether the United Kingdom should remain a member of the European Union'. This title is accurate in as far as the content of the legislation fits within this description. But the popular vote for which it provided, and the result it produced when held on 23 June 2016, extended in their consequences far beyond the strict terms of this remit.

Section 1, 'The referendum', tells us that '[a] referendum is to be held on whether the United Kingdom should remain a member of the European Union' (s 1[1]). The vote was not optional – it was a legal requirement. However, the precise day on which it would take place was to be fixed by the Foreign

[3] See eg the position adopted by the Welsh and Scottish governments, discussed in ch 1.

Secretary ('[t]he Secretary of State') 'by regulations'. This statement reveals the importance of secondary powers conferred upon the executive to the practical functioning of government – a subject that would gain heightened controversy in the wake of the EU referendum. It demonstrates, furthermore, that, while referendums are held to be justified as means of ensuring popular engagement in decision making, not only do they rest upon statutory authorisation by one representative institution, Parliament, but their practical implementation falls to another such body, the executive. Matters such as timing are important. They present a variety of different options, that can have implications for the outcome, and that must be resolved by some means.

Potentially ministers who wield such powers possess a significant degree of freedom of manoeuvre: in this instance, to set the date of the vote at a time deemed suitable to securing the desired result. However, any advantage this authority might have conferred did not lead to victory in the referendum for the side endorsed by the government (though with some ministers taking up an option openly to disagree). Furthermore, the Act imposed a specific time restriction. It stated that the referendum would take place 'no later than 31 December 2017' (s 1[3(a)]). In fact, the vote took place well ahead of the final cut-off point. By the time the 31 December 2017 deadline was reached, the referendum had been held, the Prime Minister under whom it had taken place had resigned, Article 50 of the Treaty on European Union had been triggered, and EU and UK negotiators had reached an initial agreement on their first subjects of discussion. Yet much, externally and domestically for the UK, remained to be resolved.

The Act also prohibited the referendum from taking place on 5 May 2016 and 4 May 2017 (s 1[3(b)]; s 1[3(c)]). The reason for this restriction, not stated in the legislation, was the desire to avoid clashes with various elections taking place on these dates including to devolved legislatures (on 5 May 2016) and local councils. These limitations draw attention to an important aspect of the use of referendums in the UK. They are a device of direct democracy, seeking the views of a defined population on a specific issue. Yet they are utilised within a representative system, in which voters are normally asked to choose not whether to endorse a particular course of action, but who should hold public office, making decisions and acting in other ways on their behalf. The insistence that the referendum take place on a day separate from elections does not necessarily indicate a clash between the two approaches. It is better to perceive it as arising from a desire to avoid distractions from the important decision embodied in the referendum, and to ensure that the referendum did not detract from those elections. However, following the vote, difficulties in reconciling direct and representative democracy would become apparent. A Prime Minister resigned; Cabinet and the two main parties divided internally; members of the House of Lords sought to resist the government; devolved and central executives entered into disputes; and a further General Election was held, partly in an effort by the Prime Minister to lessen some of the disagreements that had arisen.[4] It is wrong to assume that referendums, as mechanisms of direct democracy, have no proper place in or cannot be reconciled with the representative system. But their use can present challenges to it, and did so in the context of EU referendum held in 2016. While politicians might largely purport to wish to act upon the referendum result, doing so in practice proved immensely divisive.

This exclusion of certain days also provided a reminder of the diversity of the UK polity. Potential or actual systemic stresses associated with the referendum extended beyond timetabling clashes or the counterposition of direct with representative democracy. They could also involve different territorial layers within the representative system itself. While the 2015 Act was passed by the UK Parliament, there were other levels of governance within the UK, in possession of their own electoral mandates and democratic legitimacy. Though they were not involved in authorising the referendum, it could (and did) have substantial implications for them, and they would seek to exert influence over the response to the result, insisting that they had a right to do so.[5]

Having dealt with the timing of the referendum, the Act then addressed the primary issue with which it was intended to deal. It stated that the question put to voters would be '[s]hould the United Kingdom remain a member of the European Union or leave the European Union?' (s 1[4]). The options offered would be '[r]emain a member of the European Union' or '[l]eave the European Union' (s 1[5]). The government had initially intended that voters would be asked to answer 'Yes' or 'No' to the proposition 'Should the United Kingdom remain a member of the European Union?' However, the Electoral Commission recommended that it be changed to the version eventually included in the Act on the grounds that some people – especially supporters of leaving – might regard the previous wording as loaded in favour of continued membership. Consequently the government introduced an amendment to the legislation at Report Stage in the Commons.[6] The advent of this modification reveals once again that ascertaining the will of the people through a referendum is not a simple task. It involves decisions of significance to the overall process that are taken within representative institutions, demonstrating the difficulties of achieving exercises in pure popular decision making. Furthermore, that the executive was successfully prevailed upon to change the envisaged wording shows that, while it had discretionary power deposited within it, it was subject to outside influences.

A consideration of the question arrived at itself is central to an understanding of the constitutional issues surrounding Brexit. The proposition that

[4] See Introduction and ch 1.

[5] See ch 1.

[6] *European Union Referendum Bill 2015–16: Progress of the bill* (London, House of Commons Library, 2015) 16.

referendums involve the public meaningfully in the taking of specific decisions is crucial to the supposed democratic value of these devices. If the 2015 Act failed to deliver on this count, then the legitimacy of the decision to leave the EU, founded as it was in the referendum result, was compromised. On the surface it might appear to have offered a straightforward choice to voters. However, closer analysis of this question suggests complexities. It was both expansive and restrictive. The question fit the former definition because it asked voters to choose between options both of which were characterised by uncertainty. To 'remain' within the EU was the more knowable of the outcomes, implying more continuity than 'leave'. However – as we will see – it involved membership on new terms negotiated by the UK government as a prelude to the referendum. Moreover, it entailed sustained presence within an organisation the future development of which was hard to predict. Indeed one of the arguments offered in favour of holding this referendum had been that, following a similar vote in 1975 that supported continued participation in continental integration, the European project had developed in ways that voters in this earlier referendum might not have anticipated.[7] According to this school of thought, the transformation that had taken place required further direct authorisation from the public, based on knowledge of the contemporary EU. This logic was deployed in support of a further referendum. Yet it might also be seen as calling into to question the validity of referendums as devices for the making of decisions – or at least those of a lasting nature, which is held to be their special source of value.

While the 'remain' option had a degree of indeterminacy, 'leave' was far more nebulous still. It could not be clear to voters what departure from the EU might mean. There were no useful examples of other member states exiting the organisation to draw upon. The question itself gave no clues as to the basis on which the UK would seek to withdraw, and what the internal and external consequences for the UK would be. Furthermore, final outcomes were beyond the immediate control of the UK, since they involved the reactions of and negotiations with outside entities, in particular the EU, with input from the 27 remaining member states. In this sense, the referendum fell short when judged against one of the 'Davis criteria' discerned in chapter two: that voters should be given a clear idea of the meaning of the possibilities that face them in a referendum.

It should be noted that post-referendum polling conducted for the Electoral Commission found that 62 per cent of those asked felt they had sufficient knowledge of both sides of the argument to be able to make an informed decision, while 28 per cent did not. When they were asked specifically about the possible consequences of a 'remain' result, 65 per cent said they had been provided with sufficient information, and 26 per cent not. However, when asked

[7] See below.

the same question about the 'leave' outcome, 45 per cent believed they knew enough, while 46 per cent did not.[8] But what precisely respondents defined as 'enough information' is not clear. No-one was able to predict on 23 June 2016 all the ramifications of the result, that remain uncertain at the time of writing (the end of September 2018). In any case, this survey was completed within a few weeks of the vote. The full range of possibilities manifested themselves over a longer time frame. Furthermore, as we will see, though a substantial proportion of those who took part may have believed that they had access to sufficient information, the same research showed a majority demurring from the proposition 'that the conduct of the campaigns was fair and balanced'.[9]

The referendum sought to compress a complex range of possibilities into a binary choice.[10] There were consequences for the coherence of the result. While we know that 51.9 per cent of those taking part selected 'leave', we cannot discern the precise way in which they wished this course of action to be put into effect. Different voters are likely to have had varied opinions on the subject; and some may not have had definitely formed views at all. The referendum had the effect of corralling together all versions of 'leave'. Yet some possible outcomes coming under this general heading may have had more in common with remaining inside the EU than they did with other variants on departure from it.

Equally, a 'remain' vote did not allow for the offering of a view on what the UK stance within the EU should be in future. Should, for instance, it adopt a more enthusiastic approach to accelerated integration? Should the UK reverse its stance of reluctance regarding the prospect of membership of the single currency? Or should it persist with a more resistant approach on such matters? The referendum question legislated for in 2015 did not help discern attitudes in these specific areas. Neither, more generally, can a referendum of this sort, in offering a choice between two options, provide a guide as to the strength of feeling that individuals attach to the issue addressed, and the degree of priority that they afford to it relative to other matters.[11]

Continuing with a reading of the text of the Act, it also contained provision for a bilingual ballot paper in Wales (s 1[6]). This stipulation further underlined the diverse nature of the UK state, discussed above. The UK is characterised by territorial diversity. Each geographical component has a particular perspective of its own and – in turn – its own internal differentiations. No state is entirely homogenous in this sense. But the UK arguably stands out in this regard, especially because of its multinational composition, encompassing Wales, Scotland, Northern Ireland and England. This quality expressed itself in the

[8] Electoral Commission, *The 2016 EU referendum* (London, Electoral Commission, 2016) 46.

[9] ibid, 47.

[10] See ch 1.

[11] For arguments for and against the use of the referendum, see eg House of Lords Select Committee on the Constitution, *Referendums in the United Kingdom* (London, Stationery Office, 2010) 13–20.

referendum result. As we have seen, there was a significant territorial discrepancy in voting patterns, with the balance between 'leave' and 'remain' votes varying substantially across different parts of the UK.[12] Perhaps one source of this outcome was another, prior, difference: in the way the question was perceived. In Northern Ireland, for instance, it might for some appear to have important connotations for the specific relationship with the Republic of Ireland and for the peace process; while this issue was far less likely to be in the minds of voters in other parts of the UK.

It is possible to extend this interpretation further. The referendum revealed other sharp differentials. Those who were younger, with more formal education, and who were middle class, were more likely to choose the 'remain' than the 'leave' option, and vice versa. It is possible that two voters can interpret the question in broadly the same way, but reach opposite conclusions for other reasons. However, it might also be that their conceptions of the question differ substantially, even though they could potentially give the same answer. If voters interpret the question differently, the potential for a referendum to deliver on its purpose of providing a definite answer on a specific question is compromised. Different voters may understand – or perhaps fail to understand – the question in diverse ways. Or they may wilfully use their votes for a purpose other than simply expressing a view on the subject matter, for instance, registering a protest of some kind, or following a partisan instinct.

But who exactly would comprise the group of individuals whose views would be sought in the referendum? Section 2 of the Act, 'Entitlement to vote in the referendum' dealt with this matter. Clearly, the franchise used in any vote is crucial to its legitimacy. If too exclusive or too inclusive, the democratic appropriateness of the process can be questioned. The basic principle set out in the Act was that those who could 'vote as electors at a parliamentary election' could take part (s 2[1][a]). An additional allowance was made for members of the House of Lords (who are not allowed to participate in general elections) (s 2[1][b]). Voters in Gibraltar were also included within the franchise for the EU referendum (s 2[1][c]). This latter provision was an indicator of some of the complications that would become more apparent following the 'leave' result of 23 June. If the UK left the EU, Gibraltar would depart with it, but executing this change while protecting the interests of this territory raised particular concerns, especially given its proximity to Spain, an EU member state.[13]

Section 3 deals with the relationship between the 2015 Act and the Political Parties, Elections and Referendums Act 2000. The 2000 Act provides the overall legal framework within which referendums are held, supplemented by

[12] See ch 1.

[13] For issues pertaining to Gibraltar, see: Alastair Sutton, *Relics of Empire or Full Partners of a New Global United Kingdom? The Impact of Brexit on the Crown Dependencies and Overseas Territories* (London, The Constitution Society, 2018).

specific Acts (such as the European Union Referendum Act) as well as further subordinate legislation (for the 2016 vote, 'the European Union Referendum (Conduct) Regulations 2016, the European Union Referendum (Date of Referendum) Regulations 2016 and the European Union Referendum (Voter Registration) Regulations 2016'.)[14] The 2000 Act establishes the Electoral Commission, among the functions of which are to produce reports on the administration of referendums and on the intelligibility of the proposed referendum question. The key focuses of the 2000 Act are on the registration and public financing of campaigning groups; regulation of their expenditure and donations to them; controls on the activities of public authorities during the campaign; and the administration of the vote. The 2000 Act does not, however, deal with higher level constitutional issues, such as on what subjects referendums should be held, can be held, or ought not to be held; whether referendum results should be made legally binding; or whether a bare majority of those voting should always be regarded as settling the matter, or whether higher requirements such as thresholds or supermajorities might be appropriate.

Section 4 of the European Union Referendum Act, entitled '[c]onduct regulations, etc' vested in the minister the ability to issue regulations pertaining to the referendum, subject to consultation with the Electoral Commission. It demonstrated once again that, though a referendum is in theory a direct empowerment of the people, it also involves, like many aspects of government, the delegation of authority by one organ of representative democracy, Parliament, to another – the executive. This general practice, long a source of unease, would become a subject of pronounced controversy in the wake of the referendum. Section 5 dealt with the application of such powers to Gibraltar.

The contents of section 6 of the 2015 Act arose from the political context within which the referendum was being held. David Cameron had first committed himself (in January 2013)[15] to a policy of a popular vote on continued membership of the EU under pressure within his own party and subject to the perceived external threat of the United Kingdom Independence Party (UKIP). But his plan was not simply to hold a referendum. Before calling it, he would engage in a negotiation with the EU. Initially, he presented his intention as being to achieve an overall reform of the EU, but with an objective of changed terms of membership specific to the UK if this primary approach failed. However, by the time he began the process in 2016, the emphasis was firmly upon attaining special arrangements for the UK rather than the wider EU. Cameron held that after negotiations had concluded, depending on their outcome, his government would decide whether the terms were

[14] House of Commons Public Administration and Constitutional Affairs Committee, *Lessons learned from the EU referendum* (London, House of Commons, 2017) 15–16.

[15] The Rt Hon David Cameron, 'EU speech at Bloomberg', 23 January 2013: https://www.gov.uk/government/speeches/eu-speech-at-bloomberg last accessed 24 August 2018.

sufficiently satisfactory to recommend a vote to remain. The referendum would then take place.

Section 6, therefore, required the secretary of state to issue 'information on outcome of negotiations between member states'. It would include an account of the agreement reached 'following negotiations relating to the United Kingdom's request for reforms to address concerns over its membership of the European Union' and state 'the opinion of the Government of the United Kingdom on what has been agreed'. (s 6[1]). Publication had to take place more than 10 weeks before the vote (s 6[2]). The Secretary of State was required to lay the document before Parliament (s 6[5]). The approach Cameron took – to hold a referendum, but only after a negotiation with the EU – can be seen as attempt to shape the context in which the vote occurred, maintaining some control over the agenda and achieving an outcome that suited him. Political engineering of this type was evidence of the way in which the referendum, while supposedly a means of ensuring the primacy of the popular will, is vulnerable to manipulation from above. However, while section 6 draws attention to the efforts of Cameron to shape the political environment to serve his interests, the actual effect of this part of the Act was to constrain his discretion in so doing, in that it placed a reporting requirement with a deadline upon his government.

Further such imposition came in section 7, entitled '[d]uty to publish information about membership of the European Union etc'. It required the Secretary of State to issue, again more than 10 weeks before the referendum (s 7[2]), details of the 'rights, and obligations, that arise under European Union law as a result of the United Kingdom's membership of the European Union' (s 7[1][a]). This statement would also provide 'examples of countries that do not have membership of the European Union but do have other arrangements with the European Union' (s 7[1][b]). On the surface, the reports required by sections 6 and 7 might provide valuable information to voters about the decision that they faced, helping them to form a judgement. However, as already noted, the extent to which those who participate in referendums form their opinions through interpreting a shared body of information pertaining specifically to the subject addressed in the referendum question is debatable. Moreover, such publications were always likely to be vulnerable to the claim that they were in some way partial, particularly given that the government took an official stance over which way to vote (in favour of continued EU membership).[16]

The difficulties involved in achieving the public perception that an honest debate has taken place over a divisive issue were illustrated by some of the findings of the Electoral Commission post-referendum opinion survey. It revealed that 52 per cent of people disagreed with the statement 'that the conduct of the referendum campaigns was fair and balanced.' Only 34 per cent agreed.

[16] See below and ch 1.

Overall, those on the losing, 'remain', side, unsurprisingly, were more prone to objecting in this way: 63 per cent of them opposed the statement that the campaigns were 'fair and balanced', while 47 per cent of leave voters shared this negative view. Voters on the remain side who disagreed with the statement were more likely to attribute their opinion to 'inaccurate/misleading information' (38 per cent); while supporters of 'leave' who were of this outlook tended to hold that they had formed it because 'the campaign was "one-sided"'.[17]

Section 8 also addressed the issue of information made available to the public. It allowed the minister to alter section 125 of the 2000 Act. This section of the 2000 Act, entitled '[r]estriction on publication etc. of promotional material by central and local government etc.' applies during the 28 days leading up to the vote (see chapter one Appendix B). It means that central and local government, or other publicly funded entities, cannot publicly disseminate 'in whatever form and by whatever means' (s 125[4][a]) material pertaining to the referendum. Organisations exempt from this rule include the Electoral Commission and the British Broadcasting Corporation (BBC) and Welsh language television. The role of the media in referendums, especially that of the BBC but also of non-public sector outlets, is always potentially controversial, and once again points to the complications involved in exercises in direct democracy. It is necessary to inform the public about the vote, but difficult to achieve presentation of the issues involved in ways that are widely accepted as neutral, truthful and comprehensive.

Section 125 applied to 'general information about a referendum' (s 125[1][a]); 'any of the issues raised by any question in which such a referendum is being held' (s 125[1][b]); and efforts to 'encourage' participation (s 125[1][d]). Crucially, it also prevented the promotion of 'any arguments for or against any particular question on which such a referendum is being held' (s 125[1][c]). This particular provision can be read as intended to prevent the use of public resources for what it treats as improper purposes, including the encouragement of a particular outcome in the vote. It also attempts to protect the fairness of the process as an exercise in democracy, by preventing activity by public authorities that that might give an advantage to a particular side. More broadly, section 125 can be seen as setting out to create a partial quarantine for a referendum, isolating it from governmental interference (the term 'purdah' was once used to describe the application of such rules in Whitehall, though it is now considered culturally inappropriate).

Yet this insulation of direct democracy is limited in its extent and duration. The representative system is always present. A referendum takes place because a government wants or feels obliged to bring it about; and it is able to shape the overall context of the vote (though, as we know, it may not succeed). Parliament

[17] Electoral Commission, *The 2016 EU referendum* (London, Electoral Commission, 2016) 47.

provides the regulatory framework for the referendum, the enforcement of which falls to various organs associated with the system of representative democracy. Furthermore, the parties, and individual politicians, can take part – on both sides. Taking this perspective, a referendum appears as a simulation of direct democracy, designed, run and subject to intervention by agents of representative democracy who are also responsible for deciding how to respond to the result of the vote (or prescribing in advance how they should do so). For reasons that will be discussed below, section 8 of the 2015 Act allowed for further relaxation of the restrictions imposed by section 125 of the 2000 Act. The Minister could, in particular, issue regulations permitting defined forms of 'oral communications and communications with the media' about the referendum, subject to consultation with the Electoral Commission (s 125[3]; [4]). However, the government had initially intended to allow a full exemption for itself from this rule. Under political pressure it heavily diluted its plans as the 2015 legislation proceeded through Parliament; and provided a commitment that it did not intend to introduce the power it had created to disapply section 125 of the 2000 Act.[18]

Section 9 returned to the issue of delegated powers. It stipulated that all regulations issued under the Act take the form of statutory instruments (s 9[1]). It also required most such legislation to be approved in draft by both Houses of Parliament (s 9[2]). This practice – known as the affirmative procedure – represents the more rigorous form of parliamentary control available for delegated legislation.[19] It means that, though Parliament has vested powers in ministers, it retains the ability to veto their exercise. Section 10 dealt with the financing of the referendum; while section 11 defined terms for the purposes of the Act. Sections 12 and 13 addressed respectively the territorial extent of the Act (UK and Gibraltar); and when it came into force – sections 9–14 as soon as it was passed, but with the remainder implemented, once again, on days determined by the relevant minister, using delegated powers. Section 14 described the '[s]hort title' of the Act as being 'the European Union Referendum Act 2015'. The Act closed with three detailed schedules, dealing with '[c]ampaigning and financial controls' (Sch 1); '[c]ontrol of loans etc. to permitted participants' (Sch 2); and '[f]urther provision about the referendum' (Sch 3). These schedules totalled 77 paragraphs between them. They demonstrated the inescapable complexity of government, and the attention to detail required from officials attached to representative institutions. This necessity was always present, even – or especially – for the purposes of an exercise presented as transferring political responsibility away from official sites of authority and to the people.

[18] House of Commons Public Administration and Constitutional Affairs Committee, *Lessons learned from the EU referendum* (London, House of Commons, 2017) 16–20; Electoral Commission, *The 2016 EU referendum* (London, Electoral Commission, 2016) 25–26.

[19] Simon Patrick, *Scrutiny of Delegated Legislation in Relation to the UK's Withdrawal from the European Union* (London, The Constitution Society, 2017) 7–11: https://consoc.org.uk/wp-content/uploads/2017/10/delegated-legislation-and-brexit-2.pdf last accessed 24 September 2018.

The final subheading in the Act, above Schedule 3(19), had the intriguing title 'Restriction on challenge to referendum result'. The existence of a restriction could imply that there was a possibility of a challenge, subject to certain conditions. The legislation allowed for the possibility of review provided:

(a) the proceedings are brought by a claim for judicial review; and
(b) the claim form is filed before the end of the permitted period.

The 'permitted period' was one of six weeks (s 19 [2][2]). By the time concerns about illegal activity in relation to the referendum began fully to surface, this period had long since lapsed. Moreover, the activities that the Electoral Commission found in violation of the law, referring them on to the police, did not fall within the definition of the basis for a challenge described in the Act. It referred to (s 19 [1]) 'procedures for questioning the number of ballot papers counted or votes cast in the referendum as certified by the Chief Counting Officer or a Regional Counting Officer or counting officer'. No-one has claimed that the kind of irregularity envisaged in the Act as possibly engaging judicial review had occurred. The UK is genuinely fortunate as regards the integrity of its electoral administration. The chief problems with the referendum lay elsewhere, and most of them involved actions entirely within the law.

A. The Limits of the Act

Alongside all the rules regarding campaign regulation and funding, the appointment of counting officers and so on, the Act is as notable for its omissions as its inclusions. While it provided for a referendum the result of which triggered political and constitutional disruption on an historic scale, it did not address the possible consequences of the exercise for which it provided the statutory basis. Issues *not* dealt with in the 2015 Act included (I lean here more towards preparations for the 'leave' scenario, since it was the more in need of special arrangements, and transpired to be actual the result of the referendum):

- The status of the vote – in other words, whether it was to be binding or advisory (by implication, as the Supreme Court found, it was therefore the latter, at least in strict legal terms).
- Whether the response to the vote by government and Parliament should take into account matters such as turnout, size of the overall majority in either direction; and territorial voting patterns. In this sense, the Act allowed the referendum to fail to match another of the 'Davis criteria': that referendums should include a threshold provision. Moreover, Davis had suggested in his 2002 speech that the threshold should be set at a level commensurate with the significance of the decision. Given the exceptional importance of the issue at stake, the lack of such a provision was, from the point of view of this criterion, a severe omission. It is interesting to speculate on what might

have been the consequences of the application of a threshold in 2016. In 1979, referendums were held on the introduction of devolution to Wales and Scotland. In each case, the automatic implementation of the new system required not only a 'yes' result, but for 40 per cent of those who could have voted to support this outcome. The vote in Wales produced a straightforward 'no'. For Scotland, there was a narrow 'yes' majority, but it fell short of the 40 per cent threshold. Devolution was not introduced on this occasion. If one accepts the argument in favour of a 40 per cent rule for devolved institutions of the sort proposed in 1979, then to apply the Davis criteria, a higher minimum might have been appropriate over the EU in 2016, since it was arguably a decision of greater gravity. Yet even if only the 40 per cent stipulation were applied in 2016, the 'leave' vote, supported by 37.4 per cent of registered electors, would not have met the necessary level.

- The meaning both of a 'remain' and a 'leave' vote. In particular, on what terms the UK might attempt to depart from the UK; how it would seek to structure its subsequent relationship with the EU and the rest of the world; what might be the consequences for the internal governance of the UK; and what would be UK policy in areas such as the position of EU citizens' from other member states within the UK; the same for UK citizens in the EU; and how to handle issues involving Northern Ireland and the border with the Republic of Ireland. (In this sense, two 'Davis criteria' were failed: providing a clear view to the public of the possible outcomes, and allowing Parliament a central role through legislating for the potential consequences of the referendum in advance of its taking place.)
- Who would implement leaving, under what authority, according to what processes and on what timetable.
- In the event that the UK pursued a policy of exit from the EU, whether there would be further occasion for democratic approval of this course of action, such as a further referendum, voting in Parliament, or perhaps another General Election. (Arguably, this absence meant that the need Davis once identified to establish the 'settled will' of the people was overlooked.)

Perhaps not all of these contingencies could have been dealt with in an Act of Parliament. Some would have been more appropriate as statements of government policy. But as the analysis of the Act above has shown, it did impose reporting requirements upon the Secretary of State. Their particular purpose was to create greater clarity about the meaning of the vote, the lack of which was a serious problem with the referendum. One difficulty in this area was that, in discussing what arrangements might be for the UK outside the EU, rather than suggesting a preferred model, the government presented them all as undesirable in comparison to membership (see Appendix B and Appendix C). This approach was unsatisfactory from the point of view of informed voting. It arose because, through the referendum, the government was offering the possibility of a dramatic change while seeking to persuade the public to reject it. This 'bluff call'[20] aspect of the vote was the central defect of the entire exercise.

Moreover, there was no unified 'leave' movement with a single programme for which to vote. Different groups and individuals with varied priorities occupied the field. Perhaps the closest equivalent to an official statement of what exit meant from the 'leave' side was the leaflet produced and mailed to every UK household by the Electoral Commission on behalf of the nominated lead 'leave' campaign, Vote Leave (as part of its information pamphlet that also included a remain leaflet).[21] Yet, even given the space constraints, it was vague about objectives (see Appendix D). Indeed, even though it was in a sense a single entity, Vote Leave was deliberately conceived of as a disparate movement. The legislative framework for the referendum and the way in which it was applied (by the Electoral Commission) overtly encouraged this approach. Designation as the lead campaign group on either side within the terms of the 2000 Act allowed the organisation concerned 'a spending limit of £7m, one free postal distribution of information to voters, the use of certain public rooms, referendum campaign broadcasts and a grant of up to £600,000'.[22] When deciding whether an organisation was suitable to be designated, the Electoral Commission was required by section 109 of PPERA to judge whether it 'adequately represents those campaigning for that outcome'. If it had identified multiple applicants meeting this test, the Act stipulated that the Commission should choose the entity that matched this requirement to the greatest extent. In seeking applicants for designated lead status, the Board of the Electoral Commission decided to set out 'criteria' that included 'how the applicant's objectives' matched the result it advocated; 'the level and type of support for the application'; the plans of the organisation concerned to 'engage with other campaigners'; and its 'capacity to deliver' its 'campaign.'[23]

The Electoral Commission, therefore, did not include an express requirement that designated lead groups should convey a single consistent message about the reasons that voting in the direction they advocated was desirable, or about what the outcome might be. Nor did it refer to a need to support a well-informed, honest and meaningful public deliberation process. Such prescriptions, if they were made, would no doubt be difficult to enforce in a way that was appropriate. But the terms of reference the Commission and the 2000 Act proposed seemed to encourage the opposite forms of behaviour. The requirement to represent campaigners on a particular side entailed incorporating a wide range of opinion

[20] The label subsequently attached to it by the Public Administration and Constitutional Affairs Committee. See ch 1.

[21] Electoral Commission, *The 2016 EU referendum* (London, Electoral Commission, 2016) 94.

[22] Electoral Commission, 'EU Referendum: designation of lead campaigners' (London, Electoral Commission, 2016) 3. See further: Independent Commission on Referendums, *Report of the Independent Commission on Referendums* (London, Constitution Unit, 2018) 134–44.

[23] Electoral Commission, 'EU Referendum: designation of lead campaigners' (London, Electoral Commission, 2016) 4.

that might be contradictory. In its selection of a 'leave' lead campaign group, the Commission chose 'Vote Leave Ltd' over 'Go Movement Ltd' stressing the 'depth of representation' the former had demonstrated.[24]

The breadth of orientation of the supporting organisations 'Vote Leave' listed in its application was such that it was hard to imagine they could have agreed about much other than their desire – each for their own reasons – for a 'leave' result. But this disparity was the very point Vote Leave was asserting for the benefit of the Electoral Commission selection process. Associated participants included: Conservatives for Britain; Conservatives for Liberty; Conservative Voice; Democratic Unionist Party; Green Leaves; Liberal Leave; Bangladesh Caterers Association; Business for Britain; The City for Britain; Farmers for Britain; Lawyers for Britain; Africans for Britain; Americans for Britain; BeLeave (a youth group); Christians for Britain; Kiwis for Britain; Muslims for Britain; Out & Proud (an LGBT+ group); Vapers for Britain; Veterans for Britain; Women for Britain; Economists for Britain; Historians for Britain; and Students for Britain.[25] The array of groups was a model of contemporary diversity; a curious proposition given the evidence that 'leave' voters were less likely to approve of such a quality than supporters of 'remain' (and the organisations on the list were perhaps at variance with one-another on this point).[26]

The Electoral Commission noted that Vote Leave would not make 'support' for 'other campaigning organisations … conditional on … agreeing to deliver messages or activity on behalf of Vote Leave Ltd'. Go Movement, by contrast, took an 'approach … based on other organisations signing formalized agreements as "affiliates"'.[27] A reason Vote Leave was favoured over Go Movement, therefore, was precisely because it seemed to allow for a greater variety of presentation. The criteria, then, promoted the idea of a campaign that maximised its connections within a given cause rather than striving to present a unified coherent case to inform public decision making. They also stated that the ability to 'deliver' this inclusive but potentially nebulous campaign was important. In this sense, a campaign that used any available method to win, regardless of ethical considerations (provided it remained within the law), was adhering to the requirements of the 2000 Act and the Commission. It is notable in this regard that Vote Leave presented an aspect of its campaigning that would subsequently attract significant controversy as part of its case to the Commission. Under the heading 'Online advertising' it stated that:

> [w]e will aim to raise awareness of the referendum and our campaign by using sophisticated analysis of data to get our message to as many voters as possible … Our data

[24] ibid, 8.

[25] 'Application to register as a designated lead campaigner – referendum on the United Kingdom's membership of the European Union', p 18: https://www.electoralcommission.org.uk/__data/assets/pdf_file/0008/199934/Vote-Leave-ltd-designation-application.pdf last accessed 30 September 2018.

[26] See ch 1.

[27] Electoral Commission, 'EU Referendum: designation of lead campaigners' (London, Electoral Commission, 2016), 9.

> science team will work with social media experts to optimize these campaigns. One of the great things about platforms such as Facebook and Google Ads is that one can measure various metrics precisely and see exactly who is engaged by what. Using this data allows us to spread the word more effectively.[28]

Even had they been more unified in their cause, campaigners for leaving, whether part of the lead group or otherwise, were not primarily seeking to form a government (though some were within it already, and others, who possibly had aspirations in this direction, went on to join it). They were attempting to win a referendum. It was for the UK administration to respond to the result; and it was disparaging regarding the options that would follow a 'leave' outcome, despite committing to abide by it if it occurred.

It is not clear whether the 2015 Act alone could, if differently drafted, have dealt with the lack of clarity. Had legislation sought to bind the government expressly to stating what would be its approach to departure from the EU, there might have been objections that this degree of transparency undermined the UK bargaining position in such a circumstance. But if this argument is decisive, it could call into question the entire concept of a referendum on EU membership, since it would not be possible to provide the public with clear information about what they might be voting for, for fear of weakening the UK in negotiations.

Other concerns omitted from the Act could straightforwardly have been provided for (though I do not necessarily endorse all of the following possibilities). For instance, the Act could have contained a stipulation that, were a simple majority – or perhaps a defined supermajority, or a majority also reaching a threshold of percentage of registered voters – to support 'leave', then the Secretary of State was required to trigger Article 50 of the Treaty on European Union by a specified date. The Act could also have clearly vested in the Secretary of State the power to instigate the Article. It might also have established firm principles regarding reporting to Parliament, and what role it would have – if any – in authorising the approach to departure from the EU. Parliament could, through the Act, have provided for itself (either the Commons or both chambers) the right to a binding vote on whether to approve any final deal, and also defined the options that would be on offer at this point, and whether they would have included seeking to revoke Article 50 and remaining within the EU (though the revocability of Article 50 is a subject of debate). Parliament might also have provided in the 2015 Act for a further referendum at some point in the process, and again specified the choices it would have presented to voters.

But none of these options was taken. The Act had a guarded quality about it. It provided for a referendum but failed to clarify important issues connected to it. Both the meaning of the vote and the means of acting upon it, were, to a

[28] 'Application to register as a designated lead campaigner – referendum on the United Kingdom's membership of the European Union', p 47 https://www.electoralcommission.org.uk/__data/assets/pdf_file/0008/199934/Vote-Leave-ltd-designation-application.pdf last accessed 30 September 2018.

significant extent, retrospective inventions. That an Act could create the potential for such momentous events in the UK and beyond, yet be so indeterminate as to the consequences, raises difficult questions about the Brexit process – both from the point of view of its democratic legitimacy and the preparedness of government. In addition to the content of the Act, then, the process by which it was passed is also an important area of constitutional study, addressed in the following sections.

As a postscript, following the Supreme Court judgment in the Miller case,[29] Parliament was, almost despite itself, given the opportunity to create a more comprehensive statutory basis for the response to the referendum than it had for the vote itself. It could, in theory, have denied the government the authority to activate Article 50. Perhaps more realistically, it could have imposed conditions regarding negotiating positions, provision of information, further parliamentary consultation, or even another referendum. Seemingly embarrassed by the sovereignty the courts had upheld on its behalf, it passed – in the European Union (Notification of Withdrawal) Act 2017 – a law only two sections in length, reproduced here:

> European Union (Notification of Withdrawal) Act 2017.
>
> An Act to confer power on the Prime Minister to notify, under Article 50(2) of the Treaty on European Union, the United Kingdom's intention to withdraw from the EU.
>
> 1 Power to notify withdrawal from the EU
>
> (1) The Prime Minister may notify, under Article 50(2) of the Treaty on European Union, the United Kingdom's intention to withdraw from the EU.
> (2) This section has effect despite any provision made by or under the European Communities Act 1972 or any other enactment.
>
> 2 Short title
>
> This Act may be cited as the European Union (Notification of Withdrawal) Act 2017.

With the European Union Referendum Act, Parliament surrendered itself to a flawed referendum process; with the European Union (Notification of Withdrawal) Act, it once again chose to renounce power, in this instance to the executive.

II. THE PARLIAMENTARY PERSPECTIVE: SECOND READING DEBATE IN THE HOUSE OF COMMONS

Through the European Union Referendum Act, Parliament subjected itself to a supposedly irresistible, far reaching but vague obligation. As a consequence, many members of both Houses felt obliged to follow a course of action to which

[29] See ch 1.

they were opposed. To understand this outcome, and assess its implications, it is worth considering the process by which this legislation was produced. If seeking to discern the key impulses lying behind a measure and the dynamics surrounding it, a valuable source to consider is the Second Reading debate in the House of Commons. It provides the opportunity for the discussion of the general principles of a Bill in the primary parliamentary chamber. At this point in its passage through Parliament, the European Union Referendum Bill was agreed to by a substantial majority of 544 to 53. A consideration of the debate leading to this firm endorsement – the rationales offered, the exchanges that occurred and the issues that were and were not addressed – can help us to appreciate, from a constitutional perspective, the Brexit episode and its implications.

The task of moving for a Second Reading of the European Union Referendum Bill in the Commons on 9 June 2015 fell to the Foreign Secretary, Philip Hammond. As Chancellor of the Exchequer in the May government, Hammond – who supported 'remain' in June 2016 – would become the most powerful advocate inside Cabinet of a form of Brexit that retained as much continuity as possible in the relationship between the UK and the EU.[30] In a sense he was seeking to minimise the impact of the very referendum the legislative basis for which he had shepherded through Parliament. Analysis of the speech he gave in June 2015 helps to expand upon and understand this tension, connected to political dynamics of the time, that in turn had consequences of a constitutional nature.

Hammond, though among the more well-disposed towards it within his party, presented the EU in negative terms. The EU was, in his account, a failing organisation, in need of reform for all its members, and from which the UK must seek some degree of disengagement, even if not leaving altogether. It might seem odd that a government contemplating recommending a 'remain' vote in the referendum (though reserving the possibility that it would take a different stance) should depict the EU in this way. This circumstance had arisen because, since the early 1990s, Euroscepticism had become an increasingly powerful force within the Conservative Party, influencing the way in which successive leaders presented and approached the EU.[31]

During this time, opinion among the more vigorous Eurosceptics had increasingly shifted towards the idea of exiting the EU altogether. The holding

[30] eg Chris Giles, 'Hammond calls for soft Brexit to safeguard economy', *Financial Times*, 25 January 2018: https://www.ft.com/content/cb08996a-01d3-11e8-9650-9c0ad2d7c5b5 last accessed 25 September 2018.

[31] See eg Philip Lynch and Richard Whitaker, 'Where there is discord, can they bring harmony? Managing intra-party dissent on European integration in the Conservative Party' (2013) 15(3) *The British Journal of Politics and International Relations* 317–39; Brendan Donnelly, 'On the edge: Britain and the European Union' (2012) 11(1) *European View* 31–37.

of the referendum represented the latest in a succession of attempts to conciliate the firmly Eurosceptic wing of the party.[32] The referendum, from this point of view, rather than a neutral exercise in democratic engagement, was intrinsically an expression of the movement to achieve UK departure from the EU. Some supporters of membership (in the Conservative Party and elsewhere) formed the view that such a vote could resolve the dispute about membership in favour – they hoped – of continued participation; and the government that provided for the referendum officially supported remaining (though with ministers allowed publicly to dissent from this position).[33] But the referendum came about not because of pressure from those who wished to retain membership of the EU, but from those who wished to end it. The vote was judged necessary to achieve exit – hence those who wanted to attain this outcome, both inside and outside the Conservative Party, were the main drivers of it.[34] Euroscepticism had been the dominant viewpoint among Conservative members for some time,[35] and a referendum had been promoted determinedly by an organised minority of Conservative MPs.[36] The perceived electoral threat posed by the UK Independence Party had advanced this cause.[37] Reflecting these tendencies – that had led to the commitment to a referendum that Cameron first made in January 2013 – the Conservative government began preparation for the vote with an outward posture of negativity regarding the EU. Yet senior figures in the party were also seeking to create conditions within which they might achieve a 'remain' victory. This dual stance, and the complexities inherent within it, helps to explain some of the decisions about the content of the European Union Referendum Act 2015 and associated issues.

Hammond opened by describing the bill as 'a simple, but vital piece of legislation' with 'one clear purpose: to deliver on our promise to give the British people the final say on our EU membership in an in/out referendum by the end of 2017'.[38] The 'promise' he referred to had been included in the Conservative manifesto for the General Election that had taken place just over a month previously, on 7 May (see Appendix E). From the perspective of the UK constitution, that the Conservatives had won the election on such a pledge invested the bill introduced to implement it with a special status, sometimes encapsulated by

[32] eg Nathaniel Copsey and Tim Haughton, 'Farewell Britannia? "Issue Capture" and the Politics of David Cameron's 2013 EU Referendum Pledge' (2014) 52 *JCMS: Journal of Common Market Studies* 74–89.

[33] This attitude can be found eg: in Tony Blair, *A Journey* (London, Arrow, 2011) ch 16.

[34] See eg Ian McAllister, and Donley T Studlar, 'Conservative Euroscepticism and the Referendum Party in the 1997 British general election' (2000) 6(3) *Party Politics* 359–71.

[35] eg Tim Bale, 'Between a soft and a hard place? The Conservative Party, valence politics and the need for a new "Eurorealism"' (2006) 59(3) *Parliamentary Affairs* 385–400.

[36] For further analysis see Conclusion.

[37] For UKIP see eg Philip Lynch and Richard Whitaker 'Rivalry on the right: The Conservatives, the UK Independence Party (UKIP) and the EU issue' (2013) 8(3) *British Politics* 285–312.

[38] HC Debates, 9 June 2015, col 1047.

the label 'Salisbury-Addison convention'.[39] It meant that, though the House of Lords did not contain a government majority within it, the Lords would in practice not block its passage. Peers might, however, seek to amend the legislation, though subject to the understanding that they would not do so in a way that negated its core purpose.[40] Ultimately, the Lords passed various relatively minor amendments that were retained, but its most radical alteration – to extend the vote to 16 and 17-year-olds – was rejected.[41] The Lords can do much to modify legislation. But the decisive political drive over major issues comes from the Commons.

Hammond sought to explain why, given that a referendum was held on EEC membership in 1975, a further vote was needed now. Speaking as someone who had 'cast my vote in favour of our membership of the European Communities' on that earlier occasion, he claimed that in doing so he 'believed I was voting for an economic community that would bring significant economic benefits to Britain, but without undermining our national sovereignty. I do not remember anyone saying anything about ever-closer union or a single currency'. Yet in the intervening period 'the institution that the clear majority of the British people voted to join has changed almost beyond recognition'. This statement suggested a fine balance. Referendums had to be recognised as having force, otherwise the use of the device now anticipated would lack purpose. But at the same time, Hammond needed to demonstrate that the mandate of the previous vote had expired, justifying a further such exercise.

To challenge this argument, therefore, was to call into question the premise for the referendum as presented by the government. Kenneth Clarke, a senior Conservative who was now a backbencher, and a longstanding supporter of UK participation in European integration, immediately mounted such a criticism. Recalling the 1975 campaign, in which he was 'active', he said that '[m]ost of the debates I took part in were about the pooling of sovereignty and the direct applicability of European legislation without parliamentary intervention, which was a very controversial subject, and, besides, ever-closer union was in the treaty to which we were acceding'.[42] Hammond responded that 'as an 18-year-old voter in that election, I did not actually read the treaty before I cast my vote'.[43] This remark inadvertently highlighted a possible criticism of referendums: that they seek the views of the public on issues the complexity of which they are not fully aware. If Hammond – who was in fact 19 by the date

[39] Andrew Blick, *The Codes of the Constitution* (London, Hart Publishing, 2016) 175–76.

[40] See Richard Reid, *The House of Lords: conventions and Brexit* (London, The Constitution Society, 2017) 11–12: https://consoc.org.uk/wp-content/uploads/2017/12/HoL-Brexit-A4-web.pdf last accessed 23 September 2018.

[41] *European Union Referendum Bill 2015–16: Progress of the bill* (London, House of Commons Library, 2015) 22–26.

[42] HC Debates, 9 June 2015, col 1047.

[43] ibid, col 1048.

of the EEC vote (which took place on 5 June 1975) and had been studying Politics, Philosophy and Economics at Oxford since the previous October[44] – was unfamiliar with the contents of the Treaty of Rome, how many participants in the referendum he was now advocating might be expected to be aware of the existence let alone the details of such documents as the Treaty on European Union?

Hammond then listed a succession of treaties – 'the Single European Act, Maastricht, Amsterdam, Nice and Lisbon' – that had 'added hugely to the' authority of the EU in spheres 'unthinkable in 1975'. Such developments, Hammond concluded, had 'eroded the democratic mandate for our membership to the point where it is wafer-thin and demands to be renewed'.[45] As we will see in chapter three, transformations Hammond seems to have held as being 'unthinkable' at the time of the previous referendum had in fact been conceived of, in the UK, long before 1975. Alongside claims about the implications of change in the EU, the Foreign Secretary offered a second set of justifications for the holding of a referendum. It rested in the observation of such votes being held on EU-related matters in various other member states; and on issues other than the EU within the UK. As he put it:

> Since our referendum in 1975, citizens across Europe from Denmark and Ireland to France and Spain have been asked their views on crucial aspects of their country's relationships with the EU in more than 30 different national referendums – but not in the UK.
>
> We have had referendums on Scottish devolution, Welsh devolution, our electoral system and a regional assembly for the north-east, but an entire generation of British voters has been denied the chance to have a say on our relationship with the European Union. Today we are putting that right.[46]

None of the European states to which Hammond referred, having joined the EU or predecessor organisations, had held a referendum expressly on whether to leave or remain within it.[47] The UK already stood out among them in this regard following the 1975 vote, and was about to repeat the exercise. But Hammond was correct to portray referendums as a cross-European phenomenon.[48] In using them since 1973 the UK had in some ways demonstrated that it was a European polity, even if, for some, the purpose of the referendums on EEC and EU membership was to assert divergence from the continent. Hammond was also correct to recognise that referendums had become, since 1975, a relatively

[44] Information derived from the Conservative Party website: https://www.conservatives.com/OurTeam/Members_of_Parliament/Hammond_Philip last accessed 3 March 2018.

[45] HC Debates, 9 June 2015, col 1048.

[46] ibid.

[47] For referendums internationally, see Matt Qvortrup, *A comparative study of referendums: Government by the people* (Manchester, Manchester University Press, 2005).

[48] See eg Matt Qvortrup, 'The three referendums on the European constitution treaty in 2005' (2006) 77(1) *The Political Quarterly* 89–97.

familiar part of the UK political system (notwithstanding an 18-year gap under the Conservative governments of 1979–97).[49] Hammond then introduced a third strand in his case for the referendum. He described the Conservatives, in May 2015, as 'fighting and winning the general election as the only major party committed to an in/out referendum, in the face of relentless opposition from the other parties'.[50]

Hammond set out the plan for a negotiation with the EU that would precede the referendum. It was his intention both to reduce the concentration of powers at EU level in general, and to achieve a special arrangement for the UK.[51] He presented reform as essential for the whole EU, but also argued that the UK had special requirements:

> For the good of all 28 countries, there are things that need to be done to reform the way in which the European Union works to make it more competitive, effective and democratically accountable. However, the British people have particular concerns, borne of our history and circumstances. For example, we are not part of the single currency and, so long as there is a Conservative Government, we never will be. We made that decision because we will not accept the further integration of our fiscal, economic, financial and social policy …[52]

The Labour MP, Andrew Gwynne, inquired if the Foreign Secretary would 'tell the House which powers affecting the United Kingdom Brussels has too much of?' Hammond protested that he was being asked 'to set out a list of powers for repatriation, then … to say that the Prime Minister would have failed if we did not achieve the repatriation of every single one of them. No sensible person with any negotiating experience would approach a complex negotiation in that way.'[53] While this response was sensible, it highlighted the difficulties in holding referendums in connection to a diplomatic process. If members of the public were being asked to endorse the outcome of a negotiation, how were they to judge whether it was successful without an original set of objectives against which to measure it? This fault was a source of problematic ambiguity for the 'remain' option. But, from this perspective, the 'leave' outcome was more difficult to assess still. If selected by voters, its precise form would depend upon negotiations taking place after the referendum was held, and therefore could not be known at the time of the referendum. Hammond was in effect asking Parliament to legislate for a vote that offered a choice between what were at that point two unknown quantities.

Another Labour MP, David Hanson, raised a question that pertained to two features of the referendum: that the government sought to premise it on

[49] Lucy Atkinson, Andrew Blick and Matt Qvortrup, *The People's Veto: the history of referendums in the United Kingdom* (Oxford, Oxford University Press, 2019 forthcoming).

[50] HC Debates, 9 June 2015, col 1048.

[51] ibid.

[52] ibid, col 1049.

[53] ibid, col 1050.

a negotiation; and that it was binary in nature. Voters would be able to choose between two possible changes, but not to retain the existing position. They could select either the new arrangement the government planned to obtain, or to leave the EU altogether. Hanson asked: '[s]hould we not have a specific vote on the Prime Minister's recommendations as well as on the retention of membership of the European Union?' In response, Hammond fell back on the argument that the Conservatives had 'made a proposal to the British people, it was put to the test in the general election and we have received an overwhelming mandate to progress'.[54] This argument was significant not only to the particular point Hanson raised, but also in demonstrating the necessary and complex relationship between referendums and the overall system of representative democracy. It implied that the authority to hold a referendum on a particular subject in a given way derived from victory in a General Election, attained while winning well under 50 per cent of total votes cast for Conservative candidates in individual constituencies (36.9 per cent on a 66.2 per cent turnout). In this contest, the referendum pledge was one of a number contained in a manifesto, that that most voters anyway had surely not read (though it is fair to say that this particular policy was more widely publicised than most). The term 'overwhelming mandate' employed by Hammond was difficult to justify. Advocacy of the use of referendums is often founded in criticism of the idea that general elections can resolve particular issues.[55] Yet the justification for a referendum, Hammond argued, rested in just such a process. The concept subsequently advanced – and accepted by many in Westminster – that the EU referendum had a moral force superior to the authority of Parliament is curious given that the supposed initial basis for holding it, and the particular way in which it was framed, rested in a parliamentary election.

A central argument in favour of referendums is that they are a means of soliciting the views of the people on a given issue.[56] But who 'the people' are is open to interpretation in each particular instance. The definition arrived at can have implications for the result and for the perceived fairness of the exercise. It is a topic that has generated controversy in the past. For instance, there have been disagreements over whether referendums on home rule or devolution for parts of the UK should be held only in the specific territory concerned, or – because of the wider constitutional implications – across the whole UK. To date, the narrower, territory-specific electorate has been used for such votes. Similar discussions have taken place – resolved in the same direction – over referendums on possible secession from the UK, which have been held in Northern Ireland in 1973 and Scotland in 2014.[57] In the late nineteenth and

[54] ibid, col 1052.

[55] See ch 4.

[56] See ch 4.

[57] Lucy Atkinson, Andrew Blick and Matt Qvortrup, *The People's Veto: the history of referendums in the United Kingdom* (Oxford, Oxford University Press, 2019 forthcoming) chs 2–3.

early twentieth centuries in the UK, the idea of holding a referendum on the right of women to vote was sometimes proposed. It raised difficult questions about who should take part. To limit participation to men would be objectionable to supporters of female suffrage, who could argue it was unjust for men to be able to deny the vote to women, and would entail acceptance of the principle that women were unfit for such engagement. To allow women to vote might appear as acceptance in advance of a principle that it was the purpose of the referendum to decide (A further problem beyond who could participate, was the question of whether it should be possible for a majority voting in a referendum to deny any group the ability to vote).[58]

In introducing the Bill, when discussing the envisaged electorate, Hammond explained that '[s]ince this is an issue of national importance, the parliamentary franchise is the right starting point. It means that British citizens in the UK or resident abroad for less than 15 years and resident Commonwealth and Irish citizens can take part'. Added to this regular list of potential voters in a General Election for the purposes of the referendum would be members of the House of Lords and Commonwealth citizens who resided in Gibraltar (to facilitate the arrangement, the government of Gibraltar would bring forward referendum legislation of its own).[59] Hammond acknowledged the existence of a view that 16 and 17-year-olds should be able to vote in the EU referendum. He rejected this outlook on the grounds that '[t]his is an issue of national importance about Britain's relationship with the European Union and it is right that the Westminster parliamentary franchise should be the basis for consulting the British people'. While there was also support for the idea of extending the franchise for elections to the House of Commons down from 18 to 16, it should be kept separate from the present discussion, Hammond held.

The Foreign Secretary also overtly dismissed any notion that EU citizens who lived inside the UK should be permitted a vote. He insisted that: '[t]he referendum is about delivering a pledge to the British people to consult them about the future of their country. It would be a travesty to seek to include EU nationals whose interests might be very different from those of the British people.'[60] A possible response to this point might have been that all elections and referendums involve people with different interests taking part – indeed that is their essence in a democracy. To exclude a group on the grounds that its 'interests might be very different' could seem puzzling. Moreover, the inclusion of people living in Gibraltar in the vote was difficult to reconcile with the case Hammond presented. They had no part in the UK General Election at which the Conservative Party made a commitment to a referendum. Moreover, they surely would have fitted within the category Hammond proposed of those whose

[58] ibid, ch 2.
[59] HC Debates, 9 June 2015, col 1052.
[60] ibid.

'interests' were 'very different' from British people, as reflected in the result in Gibraltar – just under 96 per cent supported 'remain' (compared to 48.1 per cent in the UK).

However, as with proposals for a referendum on female suffrage, there was a connection between the question of who should be able to take part and the subject of contention towards which the vote would be directed. Those who saw the EU as an undesirable external imposition upon the UK and therefore wished to leave (and were the main source of pressure for the holding of a referendum) would naturally reject the idea of EU citizens from other member states participating as equals alongside British citizens. So too could others who might favour continued membership on pragmatic grounds (the position of the Conservative government during the referendum) but who did not view the EU as a genuine supranational polity.[61] Those who were more convinced of the EU ideal might believe that all EU citizens residing in the UK, whether British or otherwise, should share in the decision over the future position of the UK (though they might also prefer that there was not a vote on this subject at all). Since the occurrence of the referendum itself largely represented a capitulation to forces hostile to the EU, it was logical that the selection of a franchise should be in accordance with a Eurosceptic frame of thought. The decision had obvious material implications, making a remain victory less likely.

The approach Hammond advocated to the franchise was challenged in debate. The sole Green Party MP, Caroline Lucas, referring to 'the question of extending the franchise to 16 and 17-year-olds' suggested that '[t]he answer he gave about why we should not do it – because it is an issue of national importance – is the main reason he should do it …Why not let young people have a say on their future, which is what this Bill is about'. On the exclusion of EU citizens from other member states, a point offered in support of the bill as drafted was that, elsewhere in Europe, it was not the practice to let individuals from elsewhere in the EU vote in referendums. Hammond also noted that Luxembourg had recently opted not to allow citizens from other EU states to vote in parliamentary elections.[62] But as Angus MacNeil of the Scottish National Party noted, the Scottish independence referendum in 2014 had been more inclusive, allowing EU citizens resident in Scotland to take part. MacNeil asked why his constituent from Germany who had 'lived in North Uist for 25 years' had been able to vote 'in the Scottish referendum, but … cannot vote in this referendum.'[63]

Moving on to the contents of the bill that dealt with regulatory matters, Hammond observed that 'running a referendum is not straightforward'.[64]

[61] ibid.
[62] ibid.
[63] ibid, col 1048.
[64] ibid, col 1054.

This comment reflected an important quality of referendums that we have already noted (though Hammond did not expressly make this elaboration). On the surface they might seem a means of directly connecting voters with given decisions, bypassing representative processes. But in practice they are subject to the very system they might appear intended to circumvent. Moreover, decisions about the precise application of rules presented as intended to achieve a fair contest can generate controversy, especially because they might have implications for the outcome. Introducing the regulatory aspects of the European Union Referendum Bill, Hammond noted that while some of the content was more technical, there was a contentious aspect. As he put it 'some media attention' had been devoted to the plan to disapply section 125 of the Political Parties, Elections and Referendums Act 2000. As discussed above, it prevented central and local government and other public agencies from publishing material pertaining to the referendum, including the advocacy of a particular side. Hammond held that there were 'operational and political' justifications for the relaxation of this rule. Section 125, were it to remain fully intact, would prohibit the government from carrying out regular ongoing interactions with the EU. This point related to the 'operational' justification. The 'political' aspect to the proposed amendment of section 125 involved 'a clear manifesto commitment and a mandate won at the general election.'[65]

Hammond argued that the 'mandate' attained at the recent poll had been 'to renegotiate the terms of the UK's relationship with the European Union' and to then ask the public to vote on them. The government anticipated that it would 'take a position' in the referendum, and 'if we have been successful, as we expect to be', it would wish to set out the arrangement secured and how it dealt with the needs of the UK population: in other words, make the case for remaining on a basis of the deal. It would 'want to make a recommendation on where the national interest lies, and Ministers will want to be able to continue making the case, up to referendum day, without being constrained by fears that, for example, the posting of comments on Twitter accounts could constitute publication'.[66] In presenting this case, Hammond demonstrated how discerning what, precisely, people had voted for in a democratic contest could involve a degree of inference or even creative interpretation. The Conservative manifesto had made no express reference to the possibility that the government would campaign on a particular side. Yet Hammond claimed that to do so was somehow implicit in the mandate it had won, assuming it achieved goals it regarded as satisfactory (which were themselves not precisely described in the manifesto) from the EU negotiations, an outcome he anticipated would be achieved. Following the referendum itself, further efforts to read from the result of a vote more than was contained in the exact words put to the electorate would take place. The reference Hammond made to Twitter was also significant. It was a

[65] ibid.
[66] ibid, col 1055.

reminder that communications technology and its application to campaigning and politics in general had developed significantly since the 2000 Act was passed.[67]

At this point, Peter Bone, a Conservative Member and a prominent Eurosceptic, intervened, asking: '[i]s that not what a lot of people are concerned about – that the Government will use the apparatus of state to push a case, rather than letting the two sides have equal and fair access?' Hammond addressed his point by emphasising that the nominated campaigns on either side, as selected by the Electoral Commission, would 'lead the debate'. They would 'receive a number of benefits, including a public grant and eligibility to make a referendum broadcast and send a free mailshot to voters'. The government had 'no intention of undermining these campaigns' or of incurring substantial expenses 'during the purdah period' set out in the 2000 Act. He insisted that '[a] vibrant, robust debate in the best traditions of British democracy is in all our interests'. The government would display 'proper restraint' and provide for 'balanced debate during the campaign'.

Another Conservative, Dominic Grieve, a former Attorney General, then entered the debate. After the referendum, at which he supported the remain side, he would become the leading figure of a dissident group of Conservative MPs who sought to enhance the role of Parliament in the process rather than allowing the government to dominate proceedings; and who sought to avoid a highly disruptive Brexit, as well as possibly keeping open the option of not leaving at all. Its members were depicted by their opponents as in practice setting out to frustrate the will of the public.[68] But when taking part in the debate on the legislation providing for the EU vote, Grieve did not address matters pertaining to the force that the referendum result would have, how a vote to leave might be implemented, or what would be the proper role of Parliament, on this occasion. Rather, he dealt with the same subject as Bone. Grieve recalled that, during the passing of the 2000 Act, the Conservative position, for which he had been spokesperson, had been that the 'purdah' phase should be made longer. He said he anticipated that, subject to the outcome of the forthcoming diplomacy, he would support continued membership of the EU in the popular vote on the subject. Yet he held it was important to 'provide a level playing field and make it clear that the Government will not abuse their position'.[69] To loosen further a control included in the 2000 Act that the Conservatives had previously criticised as excessively lax might 'convey an impression that the Government will come in and try to load the dice' – a perception Grieve regarded as undesirable.[70]

[67] See: Electoral Commission, *Digital campaigning* (London, Electoral Commission, 2018) esp 4–6.

[68] 'Leading Remainer Dominic Grieve insists he is not part of anti-Brexit conspiracy', *Daily Mail* online, 14 June 2018: http://www.dailymail.co.uk/wires/pa/article-5843191/Leading-Remainer-Dominic-Grieve-insists-not-anti-Brexit-conspiracy.html last accessed 5 July 2018.

[69] HC Debates, 9 June 2015, col 1055.

[70] ibid, cols 1055–56.

These exchanges involving Hammond, Bone and Grieve were revealing regarding their attitudes towards the purpose of the referendum. For Hammond, and presumably for others within the government (though some members of it would later exercise the option granted to them publicly to dissent over this issue), the referendum was a means of settling the debate over membership of the EU, in favour of its continuation. They had decided in advance that there was a least a strong chance they would be able to secure a package that they could present to the electorate as satisfactory, and sought to avoid certain problematic regulatory restrictions on their ability to do so. This attitude connected directly to one of the most important characteristics of the EU referendum, and the most significant source of its defects: that it was a 'bluff call'.

Bone and Grieve both registered concerns about the relaxation of restrictions that the Bill entailed. Yet, beneath this apparent similarity, their motivations differed. Bone sought to convey the idea of a government using its position to advantage the side it supported. It might seem that his main motive was to secure a change in the legislation, thereby removing an advantage for his opponents, and increasing his chances of victory. But equally he could be seen as promoting the idea that the referendum was somehow held on a flawed basis. This concept could be rhetorically useful to the Eurosceptic side, both during a campaign and afterwards. Indeed, if the referendum produced a vote in favour of remaining, the idea that this outcome had somehow been manipulated could be useful to those planning to continue to promote the objective of leaving in future. If the government did not amend the bill and retained the relaxation of pre-election rules, such claims would be strengthened. Even if the plan was removed from the legislation, the opportunity to create an impression that this provision was a symptom of a broader desire on the part of the government to skew the contest in favour of continued EU membership was useful to advocates of exit.

Grieve seems to have opposed this relaxation of the rule set out in the 2000 Act precisely because he did not want Bone and others to be provided with such ammunition. It can be assumed that his hope was that the referendum would settle for some time arguments, especially within his own party, about the EU. (Indeed, Hammond confirmed the intra-party nature of the issue when telling Grieve that he shared his basic desire to avoid the impression of unfairness and that he had made efforts to 'reassure colleagues who have such concerns, and that the Government will continue to seek to reassure colleagues.')[71] Grieve seemingly suspected winning the vote might not be enough. Challenges to its legitimacy had to be, as far as possible, pre-empted. The use Grieve made of phrases such as 'make it clear' and 'an impression' suggests a focus on appearances: that the primary requirement was being able to claim that the process was equitable, as much as ensuring that it actually was fair (though perhaps

[71] ibid, col 1056.

he perceived fulfilment of the latter requirement as the means of securing the former). It may well have been for Bone that perception was of equal importance, though in an inverted sense: the ability to assert that the contest was in some way flawed was perhaps as important as achieving an amendment to the Bill.

A further aspect of this particular discussion was that, in the way it addressed referendum campaigning, it focused on the attainment of balance as between the two sides rather than how to ensure that the public was properly informed about the options being presented to it and their implications. How fully politicians themselves were assessing the possibilities is also open to question. Hammond, speaking for the government, had expressed the view that the government anticipated it would be able to recommend a vote to continue EU membership. It was focused, therefore, on securing this outcome. By implication, it was neglecting the possibility of a vote to leave. The intervention from Grieve was motivated by a desire to ensure that a result in favour of EU membership could be presented as the product of a fair contest. Even Bone appeared to be seeking partly to establish grounds on which he could query the appropriateness of the process, suggesting that the possibility of a vote in favour of remaining in the EU was prominent in his thinking. The Second Reading debate on the Bill seems to have been conducted to a significant extent on the premise that it was a reasonable proposition that voters might choose to remain in the EU, and even that this outcome was the more likely of the two (though opinions on the probability must have differed among participants). This foundation for discussions was connected to the general phenomenon of the government not desiring the more radical option of the two it was offering, and believing that it could win. It seems to have mitigated against discussion of the force that a referendum vote might have (since an outcome in favour of continued membership would not raise the possibility of further specific action by government and Parliament); and what exit from the EU, if adopted as a policy, would entail.

Hammond then concluded his speech by asserting that:

> whether we favour Britain being in or out, we surely should all be able to agree on the simple principle that the decision about our membership should be taken by the British people, not by Whitehall bureaucrats, certainly not by Brussels Eurocrats; not even by Government Ministers or parliamentarians in this Chamber. The decision must be for the common sense of the British people. That is what we pledged, and that is what we have a mandate to deliver. For too long, the people of Britain have been denied their say. For too long, powers have been handed to Brussels over their heads. For too long, their voice on Europe has not been heard. This Bill puts that right. It delivers the simple in/out referendum that we promised, and I commend it to the House.[72]

[72] ibid.

The use of such negative rhetoric regarding the EU, its democratic legitimacy and UK participation within it by a minister who hoped to advocate continued membership was indicative of the nature of the referendum project from the Conservative point of view. To express enthusiasm in this regard was difficult from inside a party within which hostility to continental integration was such a powerful force that it had led to the policy of holding a public vote. This stance of criticism was not the ideal place from which to mount a campaign for a vote to remain within.

This closing statement was also significant in that it appeared to endorse the idea that the referendum would produce a popular verdict superseding all other authority, including even that of the House of Commons. Yet it did not resolve ambiguities, involving various matters such as the nature of the 'mandate to deliver' such a vote; and the franchise that appropriately represented the 'British people'. Moreover, what might appear to be a 'simple in/out referendum' would, when it delivered an 'out' verdict, lead to political and policy challenges of unsurpassed complexity. Though the 'British people', however defined, were the participants in the referendum, they had no direct role in the process that followed, the nature of which few of them (voting on either side, and including the present author) could have anticipated. 'Whitehall bureaucrats' acting under the instruction of 'Government Ministers' were responsible for devising and implementing policy; while the Commons (and Lords) came to play a part, although its members were often reluctant to act upon their own opinions. Furthermore, 'Brussels Eurocrats' were important players in the negotiations that would determine the way in which the UK exited the EU and the relationship between the UK and the outside world that followed. Indeed, given the relative balance of power between the UK and the EU, it could be held that the 'British people', through voting (by a majority of those who took part in the referendum) for 'leave', had placed their future to a significant extent in the hands of officials acting on behalf of the EU, rather than escaping their supposed dominance.

A. The Labour Response

Responding for Labour was the Shadow Foreign Secretary, Hilary Benn. His father, Tony Benn, had been a primary instigator of the previous European referendum, held almost exactly four decades previously, on 5 June 1975. In many ways, circumstances of 2016 would be similar to those of 1975, though it was the Conservatives rather than Labour that held office – and, crucially, the result was different.[73] During the 1975 campaign Benn senior, then a member of the

[73] Robert Saunders, 'A tale of two referendums: 1975 and 2016' (2016) 87(3) *The Political Quarterly* 318–22.

Labour Harold Wilson Cabinet, campaigned for exit. In doing so Benn made use of the allowance provided for ministerial dissent from the official stance of the government, which – like that of Cameron in 2016 – had recommended a vote to remain on a basis of the renegotiated terms of membership it had secured.[74] In the Second Reading debate in 2015 Benn senior was referred to as an influence both by Labour[75] and Conservative advocates of departure from the EU. Almost immediately after Hilary had finished his speech, for instance, the Conservative Bernard Jenkin described Tony as one of his 'mentors' on the European subject when he had first joined the House.[76] Tony Benn was a key influence on Jeremy Corbyn,[77] who secured the Labour leadership in September 2015. While technically Corbyn supported 'remain' at the referendum, he seemed at most lukewarm about the EU.[78] Tony Benn had first advocated a referendum on membership before the UK joined the European Communities, not from a position of hostility, but as a means of securing genuine popular consent, if it could be obtained, prior to such a major constitutional change.[79] His son promoted a similar view when speaking on the Bill in 2015. Hilary Benn argued that it would serve to 'set before the British people a clear and simple question'. Yet the answer reached would have 'profound consequences' for the UK. Seemingly referring to the 1975 vote, he described the forthcoming referendum as entailing the public making 'the most important decision on our place in the world for 40 years'. In describing the significance of the choice, Benn used the phrase 'our proud and great islands'.[80] In using the plural of island, he avoided an error often made. Though he did not elaborate on this point, it was not only Great Britain, but also Northern Ireland (along with various other smaller islands) that was involved – and that would come to be an immensely complicating factor in the Brexit process.[81]

Having emphasised the importance of the decision, Benn confirmed that his party supported the Bill, while also favouring continued UK participation in the EU. Previously Labour had not supported a public vote on this subject. In deciding to acquiesce in the referendum legislation, and stating an intention to participate in the campaign, Labour was contributing to the authority

[74] Lucy Atkinson, Andrew Blick and Matt Qvortrup, *The People's Veto: the history of referendums in the United Kingdom* (Oxford, Oxford University Press, 2019 forthcoming), ch 3.

[75] HC Debates, 9 June 2015, col 1118.

[76] ibid, col 1065.

[77] Daniel Boffey, 'Jeremy Corbyn's world: his friends, supporters, mentors and influences', *Guardian*, 15 August 2015: https://www.theguardian.com/politics/2015/aug/15/jeremy-corbyn-world-supporters-mentors-influences last accessed 25 September 2018.

[78] 'Corbyn: I'm "seven out of ten" on EU', 11 June 2016, *BBC*: https://www.bbc.co.uk/news/av/uk-politics-eu-referendum-36506163/corbyn-i-m-seven-out-of-10-on-eu last accessed 25 September 2018.

[79] For the early views of Tony Benn on referendums, see ch 9. For his later opinion on European integration, see ch 3.

[80] HC Debates, 9 June 2015, col 1056.

[81] See ch 1.

of the process. Regardless of whether it supported 'leave' or 'remain' when the time came, in agreeing to the legislation and treating the vote for which it provided as a proper occasion for pursuit of a particular end, Labour could be seen as having enhanced the credibility of the referendum. It would certainly make any efforts from within the party to block leaving after the outcome more problematic.[82] John Redwood, a Conservative and firm Eurosceptic, then intervened to insist that 'the British people want a very substantial reduction in migration into this country', an objective necessitating that 'Parliament … regain control of our borders from Brussels'.[83] In response, Benn contrasted Labour support for membership with the position of some 'hon. Members on the Conservative Benches'. He nonetheless went on to list areas in which Labour wanted the EU to function differently: over 'benefits, transitional controls, the way the EU works and how it relates to national Parliaments. We also want to see the completion of the single market in services to boost jobs and economic growth here in the United Kingdom'. While attainment of those objectives required more integration, at the same time, Benn held, there existed rising support within different member states 'for greater devolution of power'.[84]

Jim Cunningham, a Labour MP, though engaging in partisan rhetoric, drew attention to the arbitrary aspect to the holding of the referendum. He complained that '[t]he Conservatives criticised us when we were in office for taking the people further into Europe'. Yet, Cunningham went on, 'let us remind them when they complain about the free movement of labour that they signed up to the single market and the British people never got a referendum then; they signed up to Maastricht and the British people never got a referendum then'. In response Benn agreed that Cunningham was 'entirely right'. Moreover, Benn went on '[t]here are lots of people who have changed their minds on Europe. I remind the House that as recently as June 2012 the Prime Minister told a press conference in Brussels: "I completely understand why some people want an in/out referendum … I don't share that view. That is not the right thing to do."'[85] The implication that this exchange encouraged was that the referendum was being instigated at a time when there was no obvious substantive reason related to the EU itself to do so – especially in comparison to previous moments of genuine transformation in the continental integration project over which no popular vote was held in the UK. The Prime Minister could be viewed as having taken the decision in contradiction of his earlier claimed principled opposition, for reasons of political convenience.

The Labour Member, Diane Abbott, then asked Benn whether he agreed 'that those of us who were in the House for John Major's Administration watched the Government party fall apart under the pressure of their rows on Europe,

[82] HC Debates, 9 June 2015, col 1056.
[83] ibid.
[84] ibid.
[85] ibid.

and that we look forward cheerfully to it happening again?'[86] This intervention demonstrated how the referendum could be seen from all sides as a component in the party political contest, involving the management of problems, the promotion of factional causes, or an opportunity to enjoy the spectacle of an enemy inflicting self-harm, rather than a means of consulting the people on a major decision. The prominence of such attitudes helps explain why consideration of the full implications of the referendum – and what 'leave', if it were the result, actually meant – was neglected.

Benn responded to Abbott by remarking that it was 'clear that my hon. Friend takes great pleasure from the discomfort that is already evident on the Government Benches'. Delving partly into his own family history he then noted that 'it is interesting that here we are, 40 years on from 1975, and the same thing is happening, but in mirror image. It is the Conservative party that has agreed to a referendum in order to try to deal with splits.'[87] The implication was that he and his party were accepting or even welcoming the holding of a popular vote the primary driver of which was a struggle between Conservatives. Benn and others in Labour might criticise Cameron for placing partisan interest ahead of principle. Yet, it could be observed, a plausible explanation for the reversal of Labour policy since the recent General Election was political calculation. To oppose the vote might expose the party to criticism for seeking to deny the public the chance to pass a verdict on UK membership of the EU. It would be harder for Labour to campaign credibly in a referendum that they had voted against in Parliament. Aside from a desire to avoid such problems, some in Labour – such as Abbott – saw in the vote the opportunity to inflict damage on the Conservatives. Sectional interest seemed to be crucial. The perception that Brexit was chiefly a problem for the Conservative Party would persist within Labour. It encouraged an irresponsible attitude – shared at senior level during the Corbyn leadership – that it was better for Labour to allow the government to persist with ill-advised policy if to do so might lead the Conservatives to suffer, regardless of the wider consequences.[88]

Douglas Carswell, the sole UKIP MP, alluding to the intention to create an exemption from section 125 of the Political Parties, Elections and Referendums Act 2000, asked Benn if he concurred 'that if this referendum is to be considered free and fair it would be wise to ensure the neutrality of the civil service and the machinery of government' and whether he would 'look sympathetically at any amendments to try to enshrine in the legislation an appropriate period of purdah'. This question showed a politician in the vanguard of the drive for departure focused not on the meaning of leaving, but on process surrounding

[86] Ibid, cols 1057–58.
[87] ibid, col 1058.
[88] Stephen Bush, Barry Gardiner's Brexit tweet is unwise, damaging to Labour – but right', *New Statesman*, 22 September 2018: https://www.newstatesman.com/politics/staggers/2018/09/barry-gardiners-brexit-tweet-unwise-damaging-labour-right last accessed 25 September 2018.

the vote. Benn responded that he agreed with Hammond that 'once the Government eventually reach a view, they are entitled to explain it to the British people.' Perhaps foreseeing the coming suspension of collective responsibility, he went on to remark that the government 'will have to explain their view to some of the members of the Cabinet.'[89] Bernard Jenkin then maintained the pro-leave concentration on process and the suspension of section 125 by asking Benn 'what he thinks Ministers will have to be able to do that they were not doing during the Scottish referendum or the AV referendum? I seem to remember Ministers giving lots of explanations of their view.' Jenkin suggested a hidden agenda, with the Bill as drafted creating 'an opportunity for the Government to call the referendum so soon after the deal has been concluded that the British people do not have a chance to digest what has occurred – a snap referendum designed to get a certain result?'[90]

Continuing the theme, Ian Austin, a Labour MP, insisted that:

> for the result to be accepted and for it to be long lasting and settle the question for a generation, it is very important that the process is seen to be fair on all sides. Ministers are perfectly at liberty to say what they like in interviews and as they go round the country making speeches, but there is a big difference between that and public money being used to send out leaflets and promote one side of the debate. It is very important that the spending limits are designed to ensure that spending is equal on both sides and both sides have a fair say.[91]

Benn responded that there was universal agreement in the Commons 'that the referendum must be fair and must be seen to be fair, but at the same time the Government – any Government – are entitled to argue their case'.[92] This exchange served to emphasise the difficulties of conducting a pure exercise in direct democracy, into which representative institutions and their agendas do not intrude. Governments in the UK have not held referendums solely – if at all – to discern the views of voters. The motivations that drive them to bring about the vote will impact on the way in which they frame it and conduct themselves during campaigns. It also shows that the Commons was focused on the way in which the vote was to be regulated to a greater extent than what the result might mean.

There followed discussion of the wording of the question, which at this point was drafted with possible answers of 'yes' or 'no', rather than 'remain' or 'leave'.[93] Benn continued his speech, advocating that 16 and 17-year-olds be allowed to take part.[94] Expanding on this view in some detail, he received a range of supportive comments, including from Sarah Wollaston, Conservative

[89] HC Debates, 9 June 2015, col 1058.
[90] ibid, cols 1058–59.
[91] ibid, col 1059.
[92] ibid.
[93] ibid, cols 1058–59.
[94] ibid, col 1061.

Member for Totness, who suggested that 'since nearly one in four 16-year-olds can expect to live to 100 years of age and will be living with the consequences of this decision for far longer than Members of this or the other House, and given that they have the mental capacity to weigh up these decisions and the enthusiasm to take part, we should extend the franchise'.[95] Benn proposed that the vote take place 'on a separate day' from any other poll.[96]

He also held that 'the Government have a responsibility to ensure that voters have enough information to be able to make an informed decision'. It 'should include an independent assessment of the economic consequences of leaving the European Union and what that would mean compared with our remaining a member'.[97]

This superficially reasonable and straightforward request, when examined more closely, was complex. The basis on which the UK would seek to leave was not made clear in advance of the referendum. Later in the debate, the Conservative, Damian Green, would draw attention to this indeterminacy when insisting that '[t]hose who argue that we should pull out of the EU need to set out what Britain would look like – what our economy and country would look like – in their alternative, because there are many alternatives'.[98] However, it was not a collective of those who had campaigned for exit that would take on the task. It was a Conservative government – of which Green would for a time be a senior member – composed of people who had taken both sides in the referendum. As already discussed, the UK administration (with dissenters) had supported remaining and had not set out a specific programme for departure that could provide a basis for an assessment of the type Benn advocated.

Even had the government indicated the basis on which it wished to leave, achieving its goals would depend on a successful negotiation with the EU. Discussion of the EU-defined process by which the UK would depart was largely absent. Cheryl Gillan, a Conservative, held that it was 'important that the necessary intricacies of article 50 of the treaty on European Union be spelt out to people. On both sides of the argument, we need to know what would govern the processes and negotiations of unilateral withdrawal.'[99] But the Second Reading debate did not properly address such important matters as the difference between an exit agreement and a post-departure Free Trade Agreement between the EU and the UK; or the distinction between the Single Market and the Customs Union, and how the UK attitude towards each might affect negotiations. In any case, even were circumstances more certain, economic forecasting cannot guarantee accuracy, and is always open to challenge, as is the independence of those who produce it, and the very premise of the activity in

[95] ibid, col 1062.
[96] ibid.
[97] ibid, cols 1062–63.
[98] ibid, col 1086.
[99] ibid, col 1104.

which they are engaged.[100] It is not clear how a process for the prediction of 'economic consequences' that Benn envisaged which satisfied both sides could have been devised. Finally, while Benn identified a need for public awareness as to the economic context in advance of voting, there were many other areas in which a 'leave' result in particular would impact, including of a constitutional character, as became apparent – though largely after the referendum had taken place.

B. Other Contributions

More fundamental interrogation of the referendum bill on a constitutional basis came from beyond the two main parties. Unlike Labour, the SNP, since the General Election of the previous month the third largest party in the Commons, opposed the Second Reading. The amendment it moved held that the Bill was unsatisfactory 'in terms of inclusivity and democratic participation, in particular because the Bill does not give the right to vote to 16 and 17 year olds or most EU nationals living in the UK'. It also registered objection to the absence of 'a double majority provision to ensure that no nation or jurisdiction of the UK can be taken out of the EU against its will'. Finally, the Bill lacked 'provision to ensure that the referendum vote cannot be held on the same day as the Scottish, Welsh or Northern Ireland elections'.[101]

Speaking for the SNP, Alex Salmond referred to what he described as 'the essential nonsense of this referendum'. He argued that:

> [w]hen someone proposes a referendum, it should be because they are proposing a significant constitutional change, whether it be the alternative vote, Scottish independence, Scottish devolution or Welsh devolution, and they are looking for democratic sanction – the sovereignty of the people – to back that change. That is not the position of the Prime Minister. Nobody seriously believes that he wants to take this country out of the European Union. The referendum is a tactic that is being deployed as a means of deflecting support from UKIP and as a sop to Back Benchers. Nobody believes that the Prime Minister wants to take the country out of the European Union.[102]

Salmond queried the way in which the Labour Party had reversed its position on the subject, professing to be 'surprised by its argument, "We lost an election, and we therefore have to change our policy", as the acting Leader of the Opposition said just the other day. Does that apply to all the policies that Labour fought the election on, or just to the policy on the referendum?'[103] On the matter of the voting rights of European citizens, Salmond criticised

[100] See ch 3.
[101] ibid, col 1067.
[102] ibid, col 1069.
[103] ibid, col 1070.

the Conservatives for 'their narrow-minded nationalism and narrow view of people's interests'. The SNP, he held, took 'a broad view of the matter. We believe in civic nationalism – we believe that if someone engages in a country, lives in a country, works in a country and pays tax in a country, they are entitled to vote on the future of the country'.[104] Regarding what he described as 'the double majority or quad lock', Salmond asked 'why should it be the case that Scotland, Wales or Northern Ireland – or, for that matter, England – should be taken out of the European Union against the will of that nation?'[105]

Perhaps the fullest exposition of potential constitutional difficulties came from Mark Durkan of the Social Democratic and Labour Party. Noting that his was 'a border constituency in Northern Ireland' he observed that 'the implications of the UK leaving the EU would be pretty fundamental, not just for my constituency but for the political institutions in Northern Ireland'. Durkan held that '[t]he common experience of EU membership provided the very context in which there were changed British and Irish relations, which in turn provided the context for the peace process'.[106] He cautioned that 'the institutions of the Good Friday agreement' took as 'givens' not only 'the human rights provisions of the Human Rights Act and the European convention on human rights, but the common EU membership of the UK and Ireland'. Indeed, 'some of the cross-border institutions that were set up as a result of the Good Friday agreement directly address and reflect our common membership of the EU. Fundamental damage and change may be done when serious questions are raised about our commitment to human rights and to our membership of the EU. If we are facing a referendum, we will have to address those issues and carry forward the arguments responsibly'.[107]

Durkan also argued that 'people have more questions about the sovereignty of this Parliament than just where it stands vis-à-vis the European institutions'. He observed 'clear tensions and ambiguities around what the notion of parliamentary sovereignty means for this Parliament, and around the implications for devolved institutions and the rightful authority that they should have'. He would preferred 'to have had something like a constitutional convention before the referendum'. Such an initiative could have fulfilled two basic functions. The first was to consider 'the longer-term democratic relations within the UK and create a new democratic charter between this Parliament and the other elected institutions in different parts of the UK'. The second was to produce 'a new democratic charter that clearly creates a delineation between this Parliament and the various EU institutions'. Durkan concluded by warning of:

> a danger that we will end up with a referendum campaign in which the yes side includes people who want to be both half in and half out, and a no side that is also confused because it includes some people who want to be totally out, as well as

[104] ibid, col 1071.
[105] ibid, col 1073.
[106] ibid, col 1103.
[107] ibid, col 1104.

> people who say that if we reject it, we can be half out and renegotiate in the way that Ireland did. The danger is that we will end up with a referendum that does not settle the question at all in the terms in which Members believe it will.[108]

The two most concerted constitutional critiques of the referendum policy, then, came from MPs (Salmond and Durkan) whose parties (the SNP and SDLP) and territorial bases (Scotland and Northern Ireland) gave them a special perspective from which to view the matter. The UK-wide parties did not grasp, or wish to recognise, the problems that might await. Even those who might have been expected to have been more critical of the way in which the referendum was being handled conveyed the impression of resignation. Kenneth Clarke professed 'fundamental doubts about referendums'. He explained that '[l]ike every politician of my generation, I prefer parliamentary democracy'. However, Clarke went on, 'we are where we are and it is obvious that we will have a referendum. I probably will not vote in favour of the Bill tonight, but I shall do nothing to stop it going ahead in principle'. Contrary to the optimism of others, who hoped to resolve the EU controversy for a lasting period, however, Clarke warned that popular votes in the UK had not proved successfully to 'settle any question'.[109] He also counselled against a belief 'that we can somehow have all the advantages of the European Union and the market without complying with any of the obligations. I know of no trading bloc that allows anybody entry to its markets on the basis that they will decide whether to comply with its rules'.[110] In this sense he was calling into question a premise on which he felt leaving might be based.

Of issues that might be termed constitutional, those that were most prominent in the debate pertained to the fairness of the process, in a relatively narrow administrative sense, and focusing on the period of the campaign. Concerns in this area – raised both by advocates of leaving and of remaining, with different motives – tended to turn on the possibility of perceived or actual skewing of the contest in favour of continued membership. Alongside the UK government itself, a variety of other potential culprits were identified. Gillan, for instance, asked whether:

> the Front-Bench team know what plans any of the devolved Governments within the UK have for spending money on this referendum, or indeed what plans the European Commission or other European institutions have? I think we might find money being spent from other directions that will slant the results of the referendum.[111]

Another institution identified as a possible source of unfairness in the contest was a perennial target for allegations of bias: the British Broadcasting Corporation.[112] While the use of social media by the government was touched

[108] ibid, col 1082.
[109] ibid, col 1074.
[110] ibid, col 1075.
[111] ibid, col 1104.
[112] ibid, col 1086.

upon, the debate did not fully foreshadow the role that the Internet might play (or be construed as doing) as a source of information and persuasion. Some have argued, as is discussed elsewhere in this book, that the overall impact of online campaigning was to favour the 'leave' rather than 'remain' side.[113] Given hindsight, this omission from the Second Reading debate is conspicuous. But it would be fair to hold that controversies in this area would have been harder to predict than in others – such as the impact of Brexit on Northern Ireland. Ultimately, even if the contest was slanted against it, the 'leave' side won and did not need to account for defeat, in these terms or any other. Supporters of 'remain', following this reverse, had an interest in explaining it as in some way improper and illegitimate, and found helpful material in the form of revelations about data and social media.[114] Concerns about the fairness of referendums and other democratic processes can, of course, be proper, and many reasonable points were raised on both sides. But political imperatives, hiding behind arguments about process, often provide the primary motivation in such discussions. Moreover, regardless of the integrity or otherwise of the campaign, there was a more fundamental problem with the vote of 23 June 2016. It offered an option of radical change that was not and could not be clearly defined in advance; but which the UK government then insisted had to be pursued, in a way that it discerned, and that involved radical and controversial change, including of a constitutional nature, that had not been prefigured. That the vote was close in percentage terms, and that there were sharp divisions on territorial and other lines, served to aggravate the problems inherent in the referendum.

Beyond a bare stipulation of the wording, the legislation providing for the referendum offered no guidance as to what the result might mean; and what should follow it. Legally, it had no force. Only politics, shaped by various forces, calculations and understandings (and subject to basic legal principles), could fill this gap. Leading politicians, however, fell short in considering some of the most important aspects. They proved more willing to suggest that the vote would bind them than they did to give attention to what it would bind them to. Analysis of the Second Reading debate in the Commons shows that MPs did not sufficiently acknowledge the ambiguity of the decision that they agreed to ask voters to make. They did not fully recognise the way in which this uncertainty was intrinsic to the choice (especially the 'leave' option) and could not simply be dispelled by expert forecasting or position statements. Moreover, their discussion suggested a lack of insight into how far this uncertainty extended, reaching into multifarious policy areas and the configuration of the system itself, or how complex were the implications of the doubt created. Nor, given

[113] See ch 9.

[114] See eg Rob Merrick, 'Brexit result has been thrown into question by the Cambridge Analytica data scandal, says Tory MP', *Independent*: 30 April 2018 https://www.independent.co.uk/news/uk/politics/brexit-vote-result-second-referendum-cambridge-analytica-antoinette-sandbach-mp-a8325636.html last accessed 24 August 2018.

this failure to recognise how much the referendum could leave unresolved, did they deal with the issues of who and by what process the necessary answers might be provided.

Politicians created a vacuum. At the time of writing, more than three years later, and more than two years after the referendum, desperate and conflicting efforts to fill it continue. In the process, the UK courts diplomatic and economic disaster, the promotion of regional instability in Europe, and a wider undermining of structures of international cooperation. Those who object to the country having found itself in this position might ask how it came about. The reasons were largely of a tactical nature. A consensus had formed – taking in major parties and both sides of the argument about EU membership – around the holding of a referendum. The motives of those who shared this outlook, as well as their private degree of enthusiasm for the vote, might differ. But the coalescence that existed was sufficiently broad to ensure not only that the referendum was provided for, but it was authorised without sufficient attention being devoted to its constitutional aspects. Some amendments were made, most notably involving the intended disapplication of section 125. But more difficult issues were overlooked. Labour could not alone have stopped the Bill from passing. But it might have forced more scrutiny of its problematic features, perhaps working with the Lords and members of other parties. In the adversarial system of the UK, a principal role of the Opposition is to oppose. If it fails to do so, problems can follow. Had Labour offered resistance to the Bill, the questionable claims subsequently made regarding the obligation the referendum created would have been less credible. It is an irony that two non-Unionist parties – the SNP and SDLP – offered advice, overlooked by supporters of the continuation of the Union – that might have helped protect the integrity of the UK and served its interests more generally.

While the behaviour of politicians contributed to the outcome, it is necessary to consider the framework within which they operated: the constitution. It allowed the instigation of a process whereby a major decision was taken first and its meaning was worked out – in a non-consensual way – afterwards. Such a process is difficult to reconcile with basic democratic requirements, for instance the need to provide voters with the possibility of grasping satisfactorily decisions they face; and that constitutional change should ideally involve a higher than normal level of agreement. These principles found expression in what I have labelled the 'Davis criteria', derived from the parliamentary speech David Davis gave on the subject of referendums in 2002.[115] (On the occasion of the Second Reading of the European Union Referendum Bill, Davis, who voted in favour of it, did not assert these principles. His only contribution to the debate was to raise an unrelated point of order about the publication of a report by the Independent Review of Terrorism Legislation[116]).

[115] See ch 1.
[116] HC Debates, 9 June 2015, col 1132.

The system failed to prevent this approach to the referendum from being followed. Though representatives of the SNP and SDLP sought to raise important systemic issues, there was no mechanism to ensure their territorial perspective was taken into account: they were simply minorities in a House of Commons set upon a referendum. Now, as a consequence, the system is being forced to change, to accommodate the consequences of the decision arrived at. But this stretching of the constitution could present an opportunity. It could be the occasion for reform that prevents the future reoccurrence of the very problems that made it necessary.

APPENDICES

Appendix A

Opposition Motion, as amended by the government, passed by the House of Commons on 7 December 2016 (Division number 103, Ayes 448, Noes 75)

That this House recognises that leaving the EU is the defining issue facing the UK; notes the resolution on parliamentary scrutiny of the UK leaving the EU agreed by the House on 12 October 2016; recognises that it is Parliament's responsibility to properly scrutinise the Government while respecting the decision of the British people to leave the European Union; confirms that there should be no disclosure of material that could be reasonably judged to damage the UK in any negotiations to depart from the European Union after Article 50 has been triggered; and calls on the Prime Minister to commit to publishing the Government's plan for leaving the EU before Article 50 is invoked, consistently with the principles agreed without division by this House on 12 October; recognises that this House should respect the wishes of the United Kingdom as expressed in the referendum on 23 June; and further calls on the Government to invoke Article 50 by 31 March 2017.

Appendix B

Excerpts from *Why the Government believes that voting to remain in the European Union is the best decision for the UK* (London, HM Government, 2016)

[p 8] What happens if we leave?

Voting to leave the EU would create years of uncertainty and potential economic disruption. This would reduce investment and cost jobs.

The Government judges it could result in 10 years or more of uncertainty as the UK unpicks our relationship with the EU and renegotiates new arrangements with the EU and over 50 other countries around the world.

Some argue that we could strike a good deal quickly with the EU because they want to keep access to our market.

But the Government's judgement is that it would be much harder than that – less than 8% of EU exports come to the UK while 44% of UK exports go to the EU.

No other country has managed to secure significant access to the Single Market, without having to:

- follow EU rules over which they have no real say
- pay into the EU
- accept EU citizens living and working in their country

A more limited trade deal with the EU would give the UK less access to the Single Market than we have now – including for services, which make up almost 80% of the UK economy. For example, Canada's deal with the EU will give limited access for services, it has so far been seven years in the making and is still not in force.

[p 14] This is your decision. The Government will implement what you decide.

If you're aged 18 or over by 23rd June and are entitled to vote, this is your chance to decide.

Appendix C

Excerpts from *Alternatives to membership: possible models for the United Kingdom outside the European Union*, 2016 ('Presented to Parliament pursuant to section 7 of the European Union Referendum Act 2015')

[p 41] Chapter 4 – conclusion

4.1 If the UK voted to leave the EU, the Government would do all it could to secure a positive outcome for the country. We would seek the agreement of the remaining 27 EU Member States for the best access for UK companies and consumers to the Single Market. We would start the slow process of agreeing Free Trade Agreements with countries outside of the EU. We would aim to keep those elements of non-economic cooperation that serve our national interest, enhance UK power in the world and increase our ability to get our way. And we would use all the levers at our disposal to achieve such an outcome.

4.2 It would, however, be hard even to come close to replicating the level of access and influence from which the UK currently benefits as a result of our special status in the EU.

In addition to the pressure imposed on the UK by the Article 50 process to secure a deal quickly, reaching agreement on a wide range of issues with 27 Member States, each of which would seek to fight for their own interests, is likely to be challenging and involve difficult trade-offs. If we failed to reach agreement within two years under the Article 50 process, our membership of the EU – including our access to the Single Market and to Free Trade Agreements with 53 markets around the world – would lapse automatically, unless all 27 other Member States agreed to an extension.

4.3 The UK would therefore have to make some difficult decisions about its priorities. Each possible approach would involve a balance between securing access to the EU's Single Market, accepting costs and obligations and maintaining the UK's influence.

4.4 In particular, we would need to decide if we wanted full access for UK companies to the EU's free-trade Single Market. If we did, we would have to accept the rules of the Single Market. But outside the EU, we would not have a vote on those rules. And full access to the Single Market would almost certainly require us to accept many of the costs and obligations of EU membership, including the free movement of people and substantial contributions to EU budgets and programmes (but without the UK rebate, which we would lose upon leaving the EU).

4.5 Alternatively, we could seek a relationship based on a Free Trade Agreement. Even the most advanced of these agreements offers less access to the Single Market. In particular, they offer less access for services, which make up almost 80 per cent of the UK economy.

4.6 In the absence of any agreement, we would have a relationship based on WTO membership alone. This would provide the most definitive break with the EU. It would mean we did not have to follow EU rules when exporting outside the EU (though UK companies exporting to the EU would still have to comply with EU Single Market rules, such as on [p.42] the environment or safety, in order to trade with the EU). We would not have to accept the free movement of people and we would not have to contribute to the EU's budgets and programmes. But this would come at a serious price for UK businesses and jobs.

4.7 Every alternative to membership would involve the UK losing its vote and vetoes over how EU laws are written. And regardless of our preferences and choices, the EU will continue to be the UK's biggest export market (at present, UK exports to the EU are worth more than two and half times UK exports to the United States – our next largest overseas market).

So those EU laws will continue to be of fundamental importance to UK companies. At the moment, the UK has a significant voice in how these rules are written…

4.9 Despite our negotiating advantages, the UK would not get a free choice on its future relationship with the EU. Any model except a basic WTO arrangement would need to be agreed with the other Member States and approved by the European Parliament. Some of the models described in the paper could also require unanimous agreement by the remaining 27 Member States and ratification by their national parliaments. Reaching agreement on such a wide range of issues with a large number of negotiating partners, each of which would seek to defend their individual interests, is likely to be difficult and could involve potentially unpalatable trade-offs.

4.10 It would not be quick or straightforward to establish a new relationship.... We should expect this process to take up to a decade or more to complete.

...

4.12...It is the assessment of the UK Government that no existing model outside the EU comes close to providing the same balance of advantages and influence that we get from the UK's current special status inside the EU.'

Appendix D

Text of leaflet by 'Vote Leave', designated lead campaign for the 'leave' side in the 2016 EU referendum, distributed by Electoral Commission. Text produced by Vote Leave with no control over content exercised by the Electoral Commission.

OUR LAST CHANCE TO TAKE BACK CONTROL

Some facts

EU law controls UK migration policy. More than a quarter of a million people came to the UK from the EU in the last 12 months – the equivalent of a city the size of Newcastle. If this continues for a decade, there will be over two million extra people. EU law means all members must accept 'free movement of people'. Many migrants contribute to society. They also affect public services.

The EU is growing. When we joined, there were 9 member states. Now there are 28, the most recent being Romania, Bulgaria and Croatia. Five more countries are in the process of joining, including Turkey. When they join, they will have the same rights as other members.

We pay about £350 million a week to the EU budget. That's about the same as the cost of building a new NHS hospital every week or hiring 600,000 nurses. We get less than half of this back and have no control over how it's spent.

[inset] The EU costs us £350 million a week. Let's take back control and spend our money on our priorities like our NHS

If we vote 'remain'... The EU will continue to control migration, trade, VAT, and vital security policies such as counterterrorism. EU law will carry on having ultimate authority over British law. The European Court will continue to overrule our laws and will keep taking powers over how our intelligence services fight terrorism. We will not be in control of who comes in to our country, on what terms, and who we can remove. We will keep handing over £350 million of your taxes to Brussels every week.

If we Vote Leave... We will take back control. We will stop sending £350 million of our money to Brussels every week and instead spend it on our priorities like the NHS. We will control our borders. We will trade with Europe without handing over permanent control to people we cannot vote out. We will control our own economy and trade. We will retake our seats on international bodies. We will have more international influence and use it to encourage more friendly international cooperation.

We pay about £350 million a week to the EU budget. That's about the same as the cost of building a new NHS hospital every week or hiring 600,000 nurses. We get less than half of this back and have no control over how it's spent.

It's safer to take back control than to keep giving away power and money every year to the EU.

Appendix E

Excerpts from the Conservative Party 2015 General Election manifesto, *Strong Leadership, A Clear Economic Plan, A Brighter More Secure Future*

[pp 29–30] ['Controlled immigration that benefits Britain'] We will negotiate new rules with the EU, so that people will have to be earning here for a number of years before they can claim benefits, including the tax credits that top up low wages. Instead of something-for-nothing, we will build a system based on the principle of something-for-something. We will then put these changes to the British people in a straight in-out referendum on our membership of the European Union by the end of 2017...

[p 49] ['Making government work better for you'] We will respect the will of the British people, as expressed in the 2011 referendum, and keep First Past the Post for elections to the House of Commons...

[p 69] ['Stronger together: a Union for the 21st century'] [W]e held the referendum on Scottish independence. It was the right thing to do, and the question of Scotland's place in the United Kingdom is now settled...

[p 72] ['Real change in our relationship with the European Union']

For too long, your voice has been ignored on Europe. We will: give you a say over whether we should stay in or leave the EU, with an in-out referendum by the end of 2017...

We believe in letting the people decide: so we will hold an in-out referendum on our membership of the EU before the end of 2017...

The EU needs to change. And it is time for the British people – not politicians – to have their say. Only the Conservative Party will deliver real change and real choice on Europe, with an in-out referendum by the end of 2017...

The EU is too bureaucratic and too undemocratic. It interferes too much in our daily lives, and the scale of migration triggered by new members joining in recent years has had a real impact on local communities. We are clear about what we want from Europe. We say: yes to the Single Market. Yes to turbocharging free trade. Yes to working together where we are stronger together than alone. Yes to a family of nation states, all part of a European Union – but whose interests, crucially, are guaranteed whether inside the Euro or out. No to 'ever closer union.' No to a constant flow of power to Brussels. No to unnecessary interference. And no, of course, to the Euro, to participation in Eurozone bail-outs or notions like a European Army.

It will be a fundamental principle of a future Conservative Government that membership of the European Union depends on the consent of the British people – and in recent years that consent has worn wafer-thin. That's why, after the election, we will negotiate a new settlement for Britain in Europe, and then ask the British people whether they want to stay in the EU on this reformed basis or leave. David Cameron has committed that he will only lead a government that offers an in-out referendum. We will hold that in-out referendum before the end of 2017 and respect the outcome.

So the choice at this election is clear: Labour and the Liberal Democrats won't give you a say over the EU. UKIP can't give you a say. Only the Conservative Party will deliver real change in Europe – and only the Conservatives can and will deliver an in-out referendum.

Our plan of action:

[pp 73–73] We will let you decide whether to stay in or leave the EU We will legislate in the first session of the next Parliament for an in-out referendum to be held on Britain's membership of the EU before the end of 2017. We will negotiate a new settlement for Britain in the EU. And then we will ask the British people whether they want to stay in on this basis, or leave. We will honour the result of the referendum, whatever the outcome.

Part 2

The Past and the Future

3

Multi-state Organisations

In this book, the term 'Brexit' is used to describe a period in UK politics during which certain concerns became predominant in the domestic political environment. However, the term 'Brexit' originated as a description of a more specific proposition: UK exit from the EU. The origins of the Brexit episode, therefore, lay in UK membership of, and projected departure from, this supranational organisation. An attempt to understand from history Brexit and the possibilities it creates can usefully begin with a consideration of proposals relating to organisations comprising multiple states. This chapter discusses a range of views and models that have emerged in the UK over the period since 1900. It considers their motives, the nature of the projects they advocated, and the particular value they attached to their plans. The chapters asks what can be learnt from this analysis regarding attitudes within the UK towards participation in the EU, including its internal and external significance; the process of leaving; and future possibilities post-Brexit.

I. INTERNATIONAL GOVERNMENT

July 1916 saw the publication by the Labour Party-affiliated Fabian Society, in a single volume entitled *International Government*, of two reports written by LS (Leonard) Woolf. Written in the context of the ongoing World War I, it was accompanied by a scheme produced by a committee of the Fabian Research Department 'for a supranational authority' to ensure the avoidance of armed conflict in future.[1] The committee noted that its task was 'limited and practical'. It set out to construct an outline proposal for an 'international treaty', drawing on observations of past practices and events, that would ensure 'future wars may be as far as possible prevented'. The hope lying behind the publication was that it would stimulate dialogue across the world about the possibility of such an agreement; and that the current appalling experience would provide a powerful incentive to such efforts. The committee noted the practical challenges involved in securing the agreement of the numerous states to agree to any such arrangement. The text stressed that, in the interests of realism, it did not

[1] LS Woolf, *International Government* (London, Fabian Society, 1916).

propose 'merging of independent national units into a "world-State," though to this Utopia future ages may well come'. There would be no restriction of 'sovereignty' or 'sacrifice of independence'. Indeed, every country that was party to the agreement could, ultimately, engage in armed combat if it perceived no other option. The envisaged agreement did not seek to achieve 'disarmament'. The committee anticipated this objective would come about spontaneously once some form of international order was established, just as the establishment of 'the rule of law' within a given state might lead to a decline in the possession of personal weaponry.[2]

The committee proposed proceeding with the introduction of a 'new world' by beginning with 'the ruins of the old'. To this end, it advocated 'a more systematic development of the rapidly multiplying Arbitration Treaties ... and the conclusions of the two Conventions of The Hague'. States could not, it reasoned, be pressed to adopt anything more radical. The essential challenge was to ensure that countries could resolve disputes between them without conflict. As the committee put it '[t]he alternative to war is law'. The objective was to establish a means of international arbitration between governments, akin to the legal mechanisms which operated within states for settling differences between people. The chief means of achieving this goal would be the formation of 'a Supernational Authority'. One component of this entity would be an 'International High Court'. This body would deal only with those disagreements deemed resolvable by judicial means, rather than every conceivable area of controversy. The committee argued that parties to a decision made in these defined areas made by such an institution would generally be willing to abide by them. If they did not, the scheme allowed for the application of non-military pressure by the other participants in the agreement, that is 'sanctions' that were 'principally economic and social in character'. Existing in parallel to, rather than exercising control over, the International High Court would be an International Council. It would comprise all the participating countries ('forty or fifty independent sovereign States of the world'). This body would have two distinct functions. First would be to operate 'as a World Legislature for codifying and amending international law, and for dealing with questions interesting only America or Europe respectively'. Second would be to arbitrate in differences that it was not appropriate to bring to the International High Court. The 'enactments or ... decisions' it issued would not generally 'be binding', however.[3] An International Secretariat, permanently sitting, would provide administrative support to the International Council. An International Official Gazette would provide for the prompt publication of 'all treaties or agreements', which would only be valid if included in the journal.[4]

[2] ibid, 231.
[3] ibid, 232.
[4] ibid, 233.

All parties to the system reserved 'the right to go to war'. However, they were obliged to take all disputes as appropriate either to the International High Court or the International Council (unless another suitable mechanism existed); and not to engage in armed conflict 'or commit any act of aggression' less than a year after the disagreement had been sent either to the Court or the Council (or other body). Participants were also bound to take part in the implementation of non-violent 'sanctions' determined by the Court; and 'to make common cause, even to the extent of war, against any constituent State which violates this fundamental agreement'.[5] The committee then proceeded to set out a draft of the text it envisaged being adopted, comprising 16 articles in total.[6]

This proposal was indicative of a willingness among thinkers in the UK to contemplate the creation of and participation in international organisations. The particular driver of this proposal was war and the desire to prevent it from taking place in future. The committee was careful to limit the extent of the authority of the body it envisaged: formal impairments on 'sovereignty' were eschewed. The creation of a single world state – while expressly not ruled out – was deemed unrealistic. Nonetheless, the recommendation for the establishment of a court and a council, along with a permanent secretariat, pointed to the establishment of institutions similar to those associated with a full system of governance, promoting the goal of rule of law on an international rather than country specific basis. It was intended as more than a treaty: it would be a continuously functioning organisation. Furthermore, the proposal was significant since it represented a willingness to subordinate practical authority to an external body in the interests of peace.

The proposal was a manifestation of a lasting tradition in UK thought. Alfred Tennyson had described in his poem 'Locksley Hall', published in 1842, a vision of a future in which 'the war-drum throbb'd no longer, and the battle-flags were furl'd/In the Parliament of man, the Federation of the world'.[7] From the late nineteenth century some within the UK advocated incorporation or federation not of the whole world, but of the British Empire, with a view to enhancing and preserving its coherence.[8] This idea was not realised. But the international (as opposed to Imperial) model advocated by the Fabian committee in 1916 is credited as an influence on the establishment of the League of Nations after the conclusion of World War I.[9] The UK, then, was capable of

[5] ibid, 233.

[6] ibid, 234–55.

[7] The poem provided a title for Paul Kennedy, *The parliament of man: the United Nations and the quest for world government* (London, Allen Lane, 2006).

[8] See eg Duncan Bell, *The idea of Greater Britain: Empire and the future of world order, 1860–1900* (Princeton, Princeton University Press, 2009); John Kendle, *Federal Britain: a history* (London, Routledge, 1997), chs 3 and 5. For Tennyson and Imperial federation, see Robert Inglesfield, 'Tennyson and the Imperial Federation League' (1998) 7(2) *Tennyson Research Bulletin.*

[9] Mark Mazower, *Governing the world: The history of an idea, 1815 to the present* (Penguin, 2012) ch 5; Peter Wilson, *The international theory of Leonard Woolf: A study in twentieth-century idealism* (Basingstoke, Palgrave Macmillan, 2003).

producing momentum towards the founding of international organisations. But, as we will see, its commitment to them seems to have been significantly greater at times of military threat or crisis than in less perilous circumstances.

II. FRIEDRICH A HAYEK AND 'INTER-STATE FEDERALISM'

World War I had prompted the *International Government* proposal; and the threat of renewed conflict in Europe stimulated interest in more extensive collaboration between states.[10] In September 1939, coinciding with the outbreak of World War II, the economist Friedrich A Hayek, resident in the UK, published an article in *New Commonwealth Quarterly* entitled 'The Economic Conditions of Inter-state Federalism'.[11] He was active at the time within a discussion and campaign group called Federal Union. It was formed in 1938 to promote supranational federation in the face of threats to peace and democracy of the time.[12] Its objectives were more far reaching than those advocated in *International Government* in that they entailed consolidation of states into a single entity.[13] Federal Union recruited prominent politicians and intellectuals of the time, soon generating extensive public interest.[14] This impact subsided following the Nazi conquest of Western Europe, that rendered the prospect of integration more distant.[15] Yet Federal Union ideas attained substantial influence, after some of its literature came to the attention of Alterio Spinelli, an Italian political prisoner detained by the Mussolini regime. As co-author of the *Ventotene Manifesto* of 1941 and through his campaigning over the years and decades that followed, Spinelli – who acknowledged the inspiration he had derived from Federal Union – became an instigator and driver of the European federalist movement. Spinelli and others aligned with this cause helped supply some of the ideological content for the European integration project, the contemporary culmination of which is the EU.[16] A dispassionate analysis of the EU today

[10] Richard Mayne and John Pinder, *Federal Union: the pioneers: a history of Federal Union* (London, Macmillan, 1990). See eg Clarence Streit, *Union Now: A Proposal for a Federal Union of the Leading Democracies* (New York, Harper, 1938).

[11] Reproduced in Friedrich A Hayek, *Individualism and Economic Order* (London, Routledge & Kegan Paul Ltd, 1949) 255–71.

[12] For the origins of Federal Union, see Richard Mayne and John Pinder, *Federal Union: the pioneers: a history of Federal Union* (London, Macmillan, 1990) 5–12.

[13] For an account of these underlying principles see eg WB Curry, *The Case for Federal Union* (Harmondsworth, Penguin, 1939).

[14] For the influence of Federal Union, see Andrea Bosco, *Federal Union and the Origins of the 'Churchill Proposal': The Federalist Debate in the United Kingdom from Munich to the Fall of France, 1938–1940* (London, Lothian Foundation Press, 1992).

[15] For the origins of Federal Union, see Richard Mayne and John Pinder, *Federal Union: the pioneers: a history of Federal Union* (London, Macmillan, 1990) 29–33.

[16] John Pinder, 'Introduction' in John Pinder (ed), *Alterio Spinelli and the British Federalists* (London, Federal Trust, 1998) 1–16.

reveals that it contains some of the features of a federation, both in terms of structure and powers.[17] Given the provenance of some of the ideas that led to its instigation, this realisation should not be an immense surprise. The consideration of avowedly federal proposals by Hayek and others makes it possible to focus on some of the federal qualities of the EU of today, and what they mean from the perspective of the UK and the project of leaving.

It is important not to overstate the extent to which Federal Union was a unified movement with an agreed and exact model. There was some debate within the organisation, for instance, about the precise territorial form that the federation should take: should it, for example, focus on Europe – and if so, which parts of Europe – or should it have an Atlantic dimension?[18] In his article Hayek was not clear on the geographical scope of the system he discussed, simply referring to 'interstate federation'.[19] But he was precise about the particular value he saw in such a system. Hayek acknowledged that:

> the main purpose of interstate federation is to secure peace: to prevent war between the parts of the federation by eliminating causes of friction between them and by providing effective machinery for the settlement of any disputes which may arise between them and to prevent war between the federation and any independent states by making the former so strong as to eliminate any danger of attack from without.[20]

But while Hayek shared with the authors of *International Government* the motive of averting war, his proposal differed from that of the Fabian committee both in advocating a full merger into a federal polity, and in envisaging further benefits beyond the prevention of conflict. Hayek argued that the system he supported 'would do away with the impediments as to the movement of men, goods, and capital between the states and that it would render possible the creation of common rules of law, a uniform monetary system, and common control of communication'. Hayek anticipated immense 'material benefits' potentially arising from such a system. Furthermore, he took the view that this 'economic union' would be essential if the 'political union' intended to preclude military conflict were to succeed.[21] The federation could not function internally and as an actor on the international stage were this combination not achieved.[22]

Free movement of 'goods, men and money' would entail the establishment of a 'single market'. This system, Hayek held, would have 'important consequences which are frequently overlooked'. It would 'limit to a great extent the scope of

[17] See eg NW Barber, *The Constitutional State* (Oxford, Oxford University Press, 2010) ch 10.

[18] Andrea Bosco, 'Lothian, Curtis, Kimber and the Federal Union Movement 1938–40' (1988) 23(3) *Journal of Contemporary History* 465–505.

[19] Friedrich A Hayek 'The Economic Conditions of Interstate Federalism' reproduced in Friedrich A Hayek, *Individualism and Economic Order* (London, Routledge & Kegan Paul Ltd, 1949) 255.

[20] ibid.

[21] ibid.

[22] ibid, 255–58.

the economic policy of the individual states' that made up the federation.[23] They would lose the ability to manipulate prices, the main device of protectionism. Moreover, given the existence of 'a common monetary unit', distinctive monetary management at state level would no longer be possible.[24] Other means of economic intervention would remain available to individual components of the federation, such as the use of regulations. But those states that utilised approaches of this type would suffer a loss of competitiveness within the federation, discouraging the pursuit of such policies.[25] At the federal level, given the varied conditions and interests across the whole territory, securing agreement between the different diverse components over the adoption of particular economic planning policies would be an exceptionally challenging task. Hayek observed that 'in the national sense, the submission to the will of a majority will be facilitated by the myth of nationality'. But, 'people will be reluctant to submit to any interference in their daily affairs when the majority which directs the government is composed of people of different nationalities and different traditions'.[26]

Yet Hayek stressed that there would 'be ample scope for economic policy in a federation and … no need for extreme laissez faire in economic matters'. His analysis suggested 'only that planning in a federation cannot assume the forms which today are pre-eminently known under this term; that there must be no substitution of day-to-day interference and regulation for the impersonal forces of the market'.[27] Nonetheless, Hayek suspected that, for many, the limitation he identified would be unpalatable and therefore a possible barrier to a shift towards federalism. However, he felt it necessary to draw attention to this tension, since 'if we do not admit [these difficulties] from the beginning, they may at a later date form the rock on which all the hopes for international organizations may founder'.[28]

Other associates of Federal Union did not emphasise a free market aspect to the same extent as Hayek, and some federalists took an opposite view to his.[29] But it is significant that it was possible to conceive of 'interstate federalism', as Hayek called it, in the way he did. It was not necessarily a movement of the interventionist left. With his federal blueprint, Hayek anticipated some of the features of the European integration project that developed in the post-World War II era, underscoring that it is reasonable in some senses to depict the EU and its predecessors as federal in nature. In referring to the free movement of

[23] ibid, 258.
[24] ibid, 259.
[25] ibid, 260.
[26] ibid, 264.
[27] ibid, 268.
[28] ibid, 272.
[29] Or Rosenboim, 'Barbara Wootton, Friedrich Hayek and the debate on democratic federalism in the 1940s' (2014) 36(5) *The International History Review* 894–918.

'goods, men and money' as the basis for a 'single market', Hayek identified all but one of the so-called 'four freedoms' of the EU of today: goods, people, services and capital.[30] The idea of a market as comprising a package of freedoms is important from the perspective of Brexit. Any effort to opt out of some but not others would run counter to the overarching logic of the scheme. From the point of view of those fully committed to the union, it might appear as an effort to maximise benefits while avoiding responsibilities, undermining the integrity of the market as a whole.[31] The UK has expressed during the Brexit process a desire to withdraw from some of the freedoms but not others. For instance, the Chequers Agreement announced on 6 July 2018 committed to common rules on goods, but not services or the free movement of people.[32]

There was an important political dimension to the Hayek scheme. For him the establishment of an economic and political union would involve the liberalisation of trade across all the components making up the federation, preventing or deterring the use of internal barriers for protectionist purposes. Either at state or federal level, economic planning as construed at that time would in practice be excluded as an option, though some forms of interventionism might be possible. As we will see, opponents of the European integration project from the political left in the UK would subsequently criticise it precisely because they saw it is a vehicle for free market agendas. Yet the supposedly 'free market' right in the UK also became one of the most prominent sources of opposition to the EU. Though Hayek influenced the doctrine labelled 'Thatcherism'[33] and the many on the right have venerated his work, they seem largely to have failed to imbibe this particular 1939 article.[34] Indeed, a number of the propositions he presented as desirable would come to form key components of the case against integration advanced from the right (and other parts of the spectrum). The concept of a political union was depicted as objectionable;[35]

[30] Catherine Barnard, *The Substantive Law of the EU: The Four Freedoms* (Oxford, Oxford University Press, 2013).

[31] See eg Anushka Asthana, Heather Stewart and Daniel Boffey, 'May "double cherry-picking" on Brexit, says leaked EU report', *Guardian*, 6 March 2018: https://www.theguardian.com/politics/2018/mar/06/theresa-may-conservative-politics-brexit-solutions-leaked-eu-report last accessed 6 September 2018.

[32] 'Statement from HM Government', Chequers, 6 July 2018: https://assets.publishing.service.gov.uk/government/uploads/system/uploads/attachment_data/file/723460/CHEQUERS_STATEMENT_-_FINAL.PDF last accessed 6 September 2018; HM Government, *The Future Relationship between the United Kingdom and the European Union* (London, HM Government, 2018) Cm 9593, p 14.

[33] See Mark Garnett, 'An unheard voice in the squabbles of mankind' (1993) 64(3) *The Political Quarterly* 336–43.

[34] Diego Zuluaga, 'Hayek would have voted to remain', *Institute of Economic Affairs*, 17 March 2016: https://iea.org.uk/blog/hayek-would-have-voted-to-remain, last accessed 6 September 2018. See also Ryan Bourne, 'Hayek would have been a Brexiteer', *Institute of Economic Affairs*, 18 March 2016: https://iea.org.uk/blog/hayek-would-have-been-a-brexiteer last accessed 6 September 2018.

[35] For a conspiratorial version of this viewpoint, see Christopher Booker and Richard North, *The Great Deception: Can the European Union Survive?* (London, Bloomsbury, 2016).

as was a single defence and external policy (which appeared to be part of the project as Hayek envisaged it).[36] A single monetary policy and 'common monetary unit', again as advocated by Hayek, were anathema to Eurosceptics.[37] While Hayek saw the free movement of people as essential, opposition to it became central to the campaign to secure UK exit from the EU during the twenty-first century.[38] Furthermore, the method by which regulatory barriers to trade were eliminated created objections to European integration.[39] Hayek seemed in 1939 to envisage the market mechanism creating an inbuilt disincentive to such measures without a need for federally enforced harmonisation. However, the framers of the 1986 Single European Act sought to attain the goal to which Hayek aspired of a single market through creating powers at the centre to introduce uniform regulatory measures, overriding the differing arrangements across Europe, and reducing protectionist distortions.[40]

In this sense the European project differed from the model Hayek proposed in 1939 in means if not objectives. The support of Margaret Thatcher, as UK Prime Minister, for a European single market was important in securing the 1986 Act within the European Economic Community.[41] She hoped to achieve an ideal in keeping with that advanced by Hayek nearly half a century previously, that of free trade on a continental scale. However, she soon came to resent the mechanisms she had helped instigate, presenting them as instruments for socio-economic interference from a growing Brussels bureaucracy.[42] Hayek in 1939 saw federal integration as means of reducing the possibility of centralised intervention. Thatcher eventually perceived what became the EU as an instrument for such activity. The ideas and imagery she advanced proved influential, and were taken to greater extremes in the process. Thatcher, who lost office in 1990 partly as a consequence of disagreements with other Cabinet members over the

[36] See eg Harvey Gavin, 'EU Army: The 5 countries that REFUSED to sign up to France and Germany's defence force', *Express*, 15 November 2017: https://www.express.co.uk/news/world/879322/eu-army-latest-5-countries-refuse-sign-up-france-germany-defence-force last accessed 6 September 2018.

[37] See eg the Conservative Party 2001 General Election manifesto, *Time for Common Sense* (London, Conservative Party, 2001). It used the phrase 'keep the pound' or 'keeping the pound' five times.

[38] Senior Conservatives made up the largest body of prominent politicians in the leave campaign. For an emphasis on migration and control of borders, see: 'Why Vote Leave': http://www.voteleavetakecontrol.org/why_vote_leave.html, last accessed 6 September 2018.

[39] See eg Margaret Thatcher, 'Speech to the College of Europe' ('The Bruges Speech'), 20 September 1988: https://www.margaretthatcher.org/document/107332 last accessed 7 August 2018.

[40] Claus-Dieter Ehlermann, 'The Internal Market following the Single European Act' (1987) *Common Market L. Rev* 24; Andrew Moravcsik, 'Negotiating the Single European Act: national interests and conventional statecraft in the European Community' (1991) 45(1) *International organization* 19–56.

[41] John W Young, *Britain and European Unity, 1945–1992* (Basingstoke, Macmillan, 1993) 151.

[42] See Margaret Thatcher, 'Speech to the College of Europe' ('The Bruges Speech'), 20 September 1988: https://www.margaretthatcher.org/document/107332 last accessed 7 August 2018. The argument presented in this speech, however, was more balanced than is sometimes assumed.

European issue, became an inspiration for a rising Eurosceptic movement on the political right within and beyond the Conservative Party.[43] Within such circles, the term 'federalism', that Hayek had used as descriptive of a system to which he was attracted, became a term of abuse; and those who viewed it in this pejorative sense achieved a degree of success in contaminating the word and concept in public discourse.[44] Yet the application of the federal label to the EU was (and is) to some extent correct, and some of the areas in which it matched this description arose in as far as it adhered to the ideas Hayek advanced in 1939. Certain EU institutions – a court, a Parliament, an executive, a council of ministers of member states and so-on – had a federal dimension to them, as did the existence of a single external tariff, and a single market.[45]

Hayek was surely correct to caution against perceiving federalism as a means of implementing interventionist planning on a continental scale; arguing that it was better to disabuse in advance than disappoint later. However, at some point, the pre-emptive debunking of certain other illusions might also have been beneficial. Principally they involved the means necessary to the attainment of a continental single market. For instance, as Hayek observed, it could not properly be attained without provision for free movement of people. Furthermore, it is reasonable to conclude, in keeping with the Hayek 1939 model, that a single market would be part of a package also including political integration that would have at least some federal characteristics. There was always likely to be pressure, again in line with Hayek, in the direction of a single monetary policy, and 'monetary unit' – though the UK, with some domestic vacillation on the subject, first delayed and then exempted itself from participation in such a project.[46] Furthermore – and here is to engage an error to which Hayek himself seems to have been committed – the idea that barriers other than tariffs would wither away without central governmental action, when there are strong local incentives in the opposite direction, was questionable. The historic experience of European integration encourages such scepticism.[47]

Regulations are integral to any economic system. The only area of uncertainty involves how far these rules diverge from those of other territories. The extent to which a functioning market can be attained depends to a significant

[43] Hugo Young, *This Blessed Plot: Britain and Europe from Churchill to Blair* (Basingstoke, Macmillan, 1998) 384–85; Richard Whitman, 'On Europe: Margaret Thatcher's Lasting Legacy', 9 April 2013: https://www.chathamhouse.org/media/comment/view/190655 last accessed 9 August 2018.

[44] Charles Kennedy, 'European federalism isn't what you've been told it is', *Guardian*, 2 July 2014: https://www.theguardian.com/commentisfree/2014/jul/02/european-federalism-eu-debate-super-state last accessed 7 August 2018.

[45] Andrew Blick, *Beyond Magna Carta: a constitution for the United Kingdom* (Oxford, Hart Publishing, 2015) 145.

[46] James Igoe Walsh, 'How and why Britain might join the single currency: The role of policy failure' (2007) 14(5) *Review of International Political Economy* 868–92.

[47] See Neil Fligstein, and Iona Mara-Drita, 'How to make a market: Reflections on the attempt to create a single market in the European Union' (1996) 102(1) *American journal of sociology* 1–33.

extent on the degree of regulatory harmonisation that can be secured within it. This task is often regarded as being best pursued through uniform rules set centrally.[48] If properly handled, rather than amounting to problematic interference, such an approach is a means of creating a framework within which the 'impersonal forces' that Hayek sought to foster can operate. However, in his estimation that 'people will be reluctant to submit to any interference in their daily affairs when the majority which directs the government is composed of people of different nationalities and different traditions', Hayek was perceptive, capturing a key aspect of Euroscepticism as it would develop in the UK.

III. IVOR JENNINGS AND WESTERN EUROPEAN FEDERATION

In 1940, the constitutional lawyer, Ivor Jennings, published his book *A Federation For Western Europe*, inspired by his participation in discussions arranged under the auspices of Federal Union.[49] Jennings wrote his monograph in response to criticism that the group had not considered the practical aspects involved in realising its principled objectives. As Jennings put it '[a]dvocates of a federal solution of our immediate post-war problems have been accused of favouring a vague Utopian ideal without giving adequate consideration to the many difficulties involved'. Jennings sought to demonstrate, as he knew from first-hand experience of internal Federal Union discussions, that it had devoted attention to the details.[50] He produced his plan as a 'personal and tentative' statement, rather than a finished, official Federal Union output. But it came from the perspective the organisation provided, with participants in it providing useful advice.[51]

The primary motive for Jennings in the scheme he advocated was the desire to prevent war from reoccurring. As he wrote '[t]he desirability of replacing international anarchy by international government is so generally recognised in Great Britain that it needs no demonstration'. But the experience of the League of Nations demonstrated the difficulties even in establishing a relatively loose 'world government'. While an international arrangement, therefore, might be desirable, its attainment in the near future was unlikely. A focus on more pressing concerns was necessary.[52] Consequently, as Jennings put it '[t]he proposition on which this book is founded is that a large number of the difficulties that

[48] For the European perspective, see Peter Holmes, 'Non-Tariff Barriers' in George McKenzie and Anthony J Venables (eds), *The Economics of the Single European Act* (Basingstoke, Macmillan, 1991) 27–50.

[49] W Ivor Jennings, *A Federation For Western Europe* (Cambridge, Cambridge University Press, 1940).

[50] ibid, vii.

[51] ibid, ix.

[52] ibid, 1.

vex the world can be solved by the establishment of a democratic federation in Western Europe'.[53] Jennings stated that '[t]he primary purpose of federation, then, is the perpetuation of European peace'.[54] Describing Europe as 'the cauldron in which most wars are brewed', he saw his federation as a means not only of preventing European conflict, but also creating a bloc so powerful that it could prevent other wars also.[55] In a projected scenario in which a post-conflict Germany had abandoned dictatorship, Jennings envisaged a 'federation of democracies'. It would comprise 'a solid block of democratic States stretching from the Pyrenees, the Mediterranean and the Swiss and Austrian Alps to the Arctic Circle', made up of 'France, Germany, Switzerland, Luxembourg, Belgium, Holland, the United Kingdom, Eire, Denmark, Sweden, Finland, Norway and Iceland'.[56] While focusing on this group initially, Jennings hoped that a full global federation would be attained eventually.[57]

While the states Jennings proposed for inclusion were democratic in nature he eschewed specific ideological content for his model. He wrote that '[t]he constitutional scheme in this book is not suggested as a means for protecting capitalism or hindering socialism. Nor, on the other hand, is it suggested as a means for attaining socialism. These are questions that the people of the Federation and of the several States may be asked to answer by political parties'.[58] Nonetheless he subscribed to free trade in the sense of commercial transactions within the federation being, within certain limitations, unhindered. Jennings took that view that '[n]o one, I think, has successfully contested the economists' argument that, at least where it is mutual, free trade provides the highest standard of living within the area that enjoys it'.[59]

Attaining this end was a more complex task than it might seem, entailing the overcoming of a wide range of obstacles. Jennings noted that successful 'inter-state free trade' necessitated 'more … than a mere prevention of State tariffs. Tariffs are one only of the many methods now adopted to achieve exclusionist policies. Exchange control, restrictions on the movement of capital, control of investments and banking, quotas of imports and production, subsidies for exports, marketing monopolies, discriminatory transport facilities, and many more weapons are in the armoury of "aurtarky"'.[60] An expansion of 'federal powers' was the most effective means of preventing this 'concealed protection'[61] (and might avoid the creation of a 'lawyer's paradise').[62]

[53] ibid, 1–2.
[54] ibid, 12.
[55] ibid, 6.
[56] ibid, 23.
[57] ibid, 28.
[58] ibid, 122.
[59] ibid, 115.
[60] ibid, 124.
[61] ibid, 125.
[62] ibid, 121.

Action on internal trade, however, would not be sufficient. Jennings argued that:

> 'free trade within the Federation implies federal control of trade outside the Federation. One could not have, say, a 25 per cent tariff on motor cars in Great Britain and a 50 per cent tariff on such motor cars in France but no tariff between Britain and France, because the result would be that all American motor cars would be imported into Great Britain even when they were intended for France ... Obviously, if there is to be an external tariff, it must be uniform – which means in practice that it must be federal.'[63]

Another measure necessitated by free trade within the system he depicted was federal responsibility for monetary policy. While it did not inevitably entail a single currency, it could lead to such an outcome through stages: first, 'stabilisation of exchange rates through a Federal Bank', secondly, the introduction of a 'federal currency' in parallel to individual state currencies, and thirdly, the abolition of those 'separate state currencies'.[64] Jennings also held that the federation might adopt the metric system of weights and measures.[65] He advocated freedom of movement within the federation. While a single national identity might not be attainable, Jennings expressed the view that he would 'not feel myself to be a truly federal citizen unless I could travel as freely to France or Germany as I can travel to Scotland'.[66] He concluded that '[f]ree trade requires free migration because it assumes some mobility of labour. The language bar is sufficiently strong to prevent any large scale flooding of a country by cheap labour'.[67]

Jennings included as an appendix to his book a 'Rough Draft of a Proposed Constitution for a Federation of Western Europe'.[68] Comprising 23 articles, it included features commonly associated with the constitution of a state. Important aspects included a specification that the constitution was the 'supreme law' of the federation taking precedence over all other law (Article II). The political system was parliamentary rather than presidential. His reasoning was that '[a] constitution should be as simple as the conditions of the time permit, and there is nothing simpler than the essential principle of responsible government'.[69] The constitution created a Federal Legislature (Article VII), composed of a directly elected 'People's House' (Article IX) and a 'State's House', the membership of which would be determined by each state concerned (Article X). Both chambers would between them elect a President of the Federation (Article V), who would in turn appoint a Prime Minister, who was

[63] ibid, 125.
[64] ibid, 128.
[65] ibid, 128–29.
[66] ibid, 129.
[67] ibid, 129–30.
[68] ibid, 159–88.
[69] ibid, 1.

required to sit in one of the two Houses (Article VI). The Federal Legislature would exercise those powers expressly allotted to it, with all others falling to the states. However, laws produced at the federal level would have priority over state legislation (Article XI). Jennings underlined the importance of this point in his commentary when stating that: '[a]ny state law which is inconsistent with [the constitution] will be invalid ... Similarly, if a State law is inconsistent with a valid federal law, the latter prevails over the former and the former is invalid'.[70]

Federal responsibilities would include 'External Relations' (Article XIII) and Defence (Article XV). The allocation of these powers to the centre was vital to the primary purpose of the Jennings federation: the prevention of war within Europe, and beyond.[71] Article XVI provided for the management of the colonies of the member states, through the creation of a 'Colonial Commission'. A 'Federal Supreme Court' would uphold the constitution (Article XXII). Jennings expressly acknowledged the substantial power that would be vested in this entity, while also stressing that the function it fulfilled would be integral to the purpose of the federation as he conceived it. As he put it: '[a] federal Constitution implies a division of powers between States and Federation according to law; and he who decides the law inevitably decides also the precise division of authority. This result is in large degree unavoidable; government according to law implies in large measure government by judges'. While 'government by law' had been attained at domestic level, the present conflict was taking place 'because government by law has never been established internationally on the same kind of foundation. We are fighting ... in order to re-establish the rule of law in Europe'. This end could only be achieved and made secure if 'all disputes are determined by judicial decisions'.[72]

Finally, amendments to the constitution would require consent by a two thirds majority in each House of the Federal Legislature and perhaps – though here Jennings was uncertain – assent from legislatures in two thirds of the states comprising the federation (Article XXIII). He saw a need to strike a fine balance. On the one hand, Jennings judged, the constitution was likely to have faults, the correction of which should not be made excessively difficult through elaborate and demanding procedural requirements. Yet on the other hand, smaller units within the federation would find reassurance in the knowledge that alterations in the system that impacted on them in a way they found undesirable would be difficult to secure.[73]

The Jennings constitution provided clear evidence of the depth of federal thought taking place in this period in the UK, and that it was far from a

[70] ibid, 146.
[71] ibid, 6; 101.
[72] ibid, 144.
[73] ibid, 150–52.

fringe outlook, encompassing many prominent opinion formers. Like Hayek, Jennings is regarded as a preeminent figure of his time in his given field. He became a leading international adviser on constitutional matters, affording this earlier experiment an added significance as a precursor to later activities.[74] A number of observations can be made regarding the rationale and content of the programme Jennings advanced. Like the two previous publications considered in this chapter, the desire to prevent war was the foremost motivation. It approached the task in a highly constructive fashion, seeking to create a fully embracing polity encompassing the region that was the site and source of repeated conflict. Given his starting point, it was natural that Jennings should propose that defence and foreign policy be placed under federal control. This approach is frequently followed in federal systems worldwide, such as that of the US.[75] However, the European integration project that developed after 1945 did not accord with this model. Even in the contemporary EU, external and military policy (despite such initiatives as the formation of a European External Action Service led by a High Representative for Foreign Affairs and Security Policy)[76] is more dispersed than certain other functions, such as external trade policy. In this sense the EU is not fully federal.

Yet Jennings was more prescient in other respects. While he did not precisely identify the original six founders of the European Economic Community (Belgium, France, Italy, Luxembourg, The Netherlands, West Germany), his focus on Western Europe as the embryo for a supranational project was broadly correct. So too was his emphasis on democratic states as suitable participants. In this respect, the openness to participation from a post-Nazi Germany was of especial importance. The idea of European integration as an inherently democratic mission, intended to promote this system of government and the values associated with it on the international stage would become central to the project and its public presentation. Indeed international relations analysts have described the EU as a 'normative power', seeking through encouragement, negotiation and setting an example – but not 'hard' coercion – peacefully to spread its principles (though how well it performs this task or lives up to these ideals in every instance is another matter).[77]

Moreover, many of the organisational criteria Jennings identified as essential to such a union became part of the European integration programme and are visible in the EU of today. The similarities between the avowedly federal Jennings model and the EU help elucidate the federal characteristics of the latter.

[74] H Kumarasingham (ed), *Constitution-Maker: Selected writings of Sir Ivor Jennings* (Cambridge, Cambridge University Press, 2014) 3.

[75] See Articles I and II of the Constitution of the United States.

[76] See Articles 18 and 27 of the Treaty on European Union.

[77] Ian Manners, 'Normative power Europe: a contradiction in terms?' (2002) 40(2) *JCMS: Journal of common market studies* 235–58.

They involve in particular the single market concept he advanced. Like Hayek, Jennings favoured the creation of such an entity, and recognised that the inhibitions to it were more than simply tariffs, extending to what are today known as 'non-tariff barriers'. But Jennings differed from Hayek in that he was clear that special powers should be created at the federal level to override protectionist measures. Jennings also iterated that, alongside the dissolution of internal customs, a single external tariff was necessary. He provided a cogent account of the difficulties that would arise were a state within a federation able to import items at lower tariff rates than those applied elsewhere within that system. The implication of this logic for a post-Brexit UK was important: an ability to negotiate new trade deals could have negative implications for the degree of access that the UK retained to the European market.

Other features of the Eurosceptic agenda have involved objections to qualities of the EU that Jennings had identified as necessary to his Western European federation. The very idea that there should be an EU constitution generated controversy within the UK early in the twenty-first century.[78] The possibility of a movement towards a single currency, that Jennings discerned as likely to develop in his Western European polity, became a reality in the EU, creating disagreement within the UK. He saw it as essential that the constitution and federal law should take priority over legislation issued at state level. The supremacy of European law, including even over Acts of Parliament, raised questions about whether UK participation in the integration project entailed violation of the sovereignty of the Westminster Parliament.[79] Jennings envisaged that a court created under his constitution would be the ultimate resolver of legal disputes, a role he recognised would make it in practice a powerful body. In UK Eurosceptic narratives the European Court of Justice has figured as a threat to the democratic integrity of the UK. Objections to the Court figured in the 'leave' campaign, and in the Brexit agenda that followed.[80] Another target was EU freedom of movement. While Jennings identified the need for such a system in his federation, his prediction that, for linguistic reasons, it would not entail large scale migration, did not apply to the EU by the time of the 2016 referendum. Nonetheless, many of the functions over which the designated lead 'leave' campaign demanded that the UK 'take back control'[81] were envisaged by Jennings as coming within the remit of his federation.

[78] 'Blair confirms EU constitution poll', 20 April 2004, *BBC*: http://news.bbc.co.uk/1/hi/uk_politics/3640949.stm last accessed 6 September 2018.

[79] HWR Wade, 'Sovereignty-Revolution or Evolution?' (1996) 112(4) *Law Quarterly Review* 568–75.

[80] Michael Howard and Richard Aikens, 'The EU's court is picking apart our laws', *Telegraph*, 22 June 2016: https://www.telegraph.co.uk/news/2016/06/22/the-eus-court-is-picking-apart-our-laws/ last accessed 6 September 2018.

[81] 'Why Vote Leave': http://www.voteleavetakecontrol.org/why_vote_leave.html, last accessed 6 September 2018.

IV. WILLIAM BEVERIDGE AND WORLD GOVERNMENT

In 1948 Lord (William) Beveridge published his pamphlet *for World Government*.[82] The Foreword comprised a statement by the National Executive Council of the Crusade for World Government, of which Beveridge was a member and of whom a group of backbench MPs formed the nucleus. They held that 'the world is in mortal danger of self-destruction through war', necessitating 'the establishment by peaceful means of a World Government, capable of enforcing world law'. They intended that this goal would be attained through the formation in 1950 of an elected People's World Constituent Assembly, that would meet possibly in Geneva or New Delhi, with the objective of devising a Charter of World Government.[83] They envisaged that the Charter would provide for its coming into force once it had been ratified by 50 per cent or more of states in the world.[84]

Beveridge held that 'secure peace is the greatest interest of all ordinary men of all nations throughout the world', and that it was plainly absent 'in the world today'. He noted that World War II had 'ended with the atomic bomb. Now the atomic bomb not only makes war incredibly more destructive than anything that we have had even in World War II, but it puts a premium on unannounced attack'.[85] Beveridge proposed that the same methods used for achieving security within a given state should be applied to international relations. He envisaged a system that ensured 'that when two nations have a difference, which they cannot settle by agreement in a friendly way, they should be compelled to accept an impartial decision – to arbitrate instead of fighting upon it'. Such a mechanism required 'an authority above all nations – a Court of Justice, and a Police-man, that is to say international force to enforce the decisions of that Court of Justice'.[86] The establishment of this 'World Authority' called for the 'abrogation of what in the past has been called the absolute sovereignty of nations', but not the 'loss of national self-government or national freedom'.[87] It would need to have 'power over armaments' as well as 'boundaries' and to be responsible for supervising colonies.[88]

Beveridge rejected the possible view that the 'World Authority need have powers over currency, over trade, over such questions as migration, education, social security or the kind of economic system that each country prefers', though there would 'as part of the international structure of the world, be Councils and Boards for systematic consultation on such topics'. However, he

[82] Lord Beveridge, *for World Government* (London, Crusade for World Government, 1948).
[83] ibid, 2.
[84] ibid, 3.
[85] ibid, 6.
[86] ibid, 7.
[87] ibid, 8.
[88] ibid, 11.

recognised that other supporters of world government held its proper sphere of operation to be more extensive. Beveridge held that a World Authority was preferable to the League of Nations model, which allowed members ultimately to follow their own path if determined to do so.[89] He also argued that the World Authority would be more effective than the existing United Nations (UN). While the UN could use 'actual force' to impose peace, such action was subject to veto by individual members of the Security Council.[90] Beveridge saw a campaign for European integration as compatible with his objectives, 'though, of course, for world peace one must have something wider in scope than Western Europe'.[91] He recognised a possible debate about whether a World Authority should be directly elected, or rest on the governments of member states.[92] However, whatever precise model was adopted, he insisted that '[i]f you want lasting peace … you must learn to be world citizens as well as national citizens. You must have a World Authority above your National Government, for purposes essential to the prevention of war'.[93]

Beveridge, like Hayek and Jennings (alongside whom he had been active in Federal Union in its early period), provides another example of how proposals for supranational governance could emerge from the UK, voiced by figures of substance. Beveridge was by this time a venerated social scientist, most notably for his report of 1942 that provided the basis for post-war welfare reforms.[94] Like the previous authors considered here, the desire to prevent destructive conflict drove on the part of Beveridge an interest in the formation of a multi-state organisation. For the purpose he had in mind, a global rather than European focus was necessary. Yet while the plan was more expansive in its proposed geographical reach than that of Jennings, it was less extensive in its remit, concentrating primarily on control of the use of force and on dispute resolution. The Beveridge World Government was nonetheless intended to have genuine power over its constituent members, to a greater extent than the League of Nations or even the United Nations. When measured against the *International Government*, Hayek and Jennings proposals, however, the Beveridge model has, so far, proved the least prophetic, with the basic UN model that he found too limited remaining in place. The most effective outlet for UK thought in this area has proved to be Europe. If in future, the UK seeks for some reason to achieve more effective supranational integration than presently exists, it will either have to re-engage with Europe, or attempt to be more successful on an international landscape than it has previously.

[89] ibid, 10.
[90] ibid.
[91] ibid, 15.
[92] ibid, 15.
[93] ibid, 16.
[94] For the life of Beveridge, see: Jose Harris, *William Beveridge* (Oxford, Clarendon Press, 1997).

V. UNITED STATES OF EUROPE

John Pinder and Roy Pryce were advocates of European federalism connected to the Federal Trust for Education and Research, the research branch of Federal Union. They published as a Penguin Special *Europe After De Gaulle: Towards the United States of Europe* in 1969. When they commenced writing the book, Charles De Gaulle, to whom the title referred, had been, since 1958, the inaugural and only President of the French Fifth Republic. From this post he had resisted UK efforts to join the European Economic Community (EEC). Formed in 1957, the UK had declined to participate initially, but subsequently decided that that to do so was in its interests. De Gaulle vetoed the first two UK bids for membership, in 1963 and 1967.[95] Then in April 1969 he resigned following the loss of a referendum on constitutional reform, potentially opening the path to UK accession to the Community, and in the view of Pinder and Pryce, enhancements to the integration project itself. They wrote how: '[t]here is a new opportunity for Europe to unite, not only economically but also politically'.[96]

Writing in the context of a Cold War that had divided the European continent between western and Soviet blocs, the authors advocated the establishment of 'a United States of Europe, organised on federal lines' as a means of addressing a number of challenges facing multiple European states.[97] They included pressure for sub-state autonomy by groups such as the Bretons in France, Basques in Spain, and Welsh and Scots in the UK; and student protest movements across the continent. Federalism, in the view of the authors, was a suitable response to such tensions since it could enable centralisation of authority in those areas where common action was needed, alongside a dispersal of power in other fields.[98] Pinder and Pryce advocated both widening and deepening of the EEC. The membership, they held, should expand to countries including the UK that had already applied (though they seem not to have seen it as realistic that it would encompass what was then known as Eastern Europe). At the same time the Community should enhance its economic role and widen its remit to take in foreign affairs and defence policy. They also saw institutional reform as a necessity.[99] The authors hoped that the UK as a new participant would promote such an outcome. They wrote: '[m]uch depends on Britain. Having waited so long in the wings, Britain now has an opportunity to play a major part in the next stages of construction of a new Europe'.[100]

[95] See David Gowland, Arthur Turner, and Alex Wright, *Britain and European integration since 1945: on the sidelines* (London, Routledge, 2009) 42–76.

[96] John Pinder and Roy Pryce, *Europe After De Gaulle: Towards a United States of Europe* (Harmondsworth, Penguin, 1969) 7.

[97] ibid, 24.

[98] ibid, 24–26.

[99] ibid, 26.

[100] ibid, 27.

Pinder and Pryce judged that, to date, the progress of the EEC had taken the form of 'negative integration' entailing 'the removal of barriers and distortions to economic transactions between member states'. Though they saw this process as worthwhile, they advocated the pursuit of 'positive integration' in pursuit of ends including 'economic growth, social welfare, and the ability to bargain on broad terms with the super powers'.[101] A first area they highlighted as in need of group action was science and technology policy.[102] Secondly they promoted the idea of a European currency. The authors felt that the completion of such a project would be achieved only some distance in the future.[103] However, they argued that it would be possible to take two intermediate steps in the shorter-term. The first was the creation of a 'reserve pool' of European currencies, followed by the introduction of a 'European reserve unit', that they labelled the 'Europa'.[104] In establishing these forms of positive integration, the authors felt, a consolidated Europe could address its present inability to 'compete with America in advanced technology or in the international monetary field'. But they also supported policies 'to ensure that there is social justice as well as economic efficiency, and that the unfortunate or the weak are not trampled underfoot in the rush of general economic and technological progress'.[105] Pinder and Pryce saw a need to counter the perception that other continental states were 'socially reactionary' compared to the UK, and insisted that these countries might in fact be disposed towards such an interventionist programme.[106] They considered that 'a United States of Europe with a new, modern economic and social system would be a beacon to that great majority of peoples throughout the world who reject both private capitalism and state collectivism in their most uncompromising form'.[107]

Europe After De Gaulle advocated the development of European defence capacity within the broader context of the western military alliance, as convened through the North Atlantic Treaty Organisation (NATO).[108] Alongside defence, a coordinated foreign policy, including aid, would be necessary.[109] These aspects of a federal Europe would enable it to 'counterbalance the Russian super-power' without a need for reliance on the US.[110] The authors hoped that an improvement in relations with the Eastern Bloc could be attained in such circumstances.[111] With this global outlook in mind, they promoted an

[101] ibid, 96.
[102] ibid, 97–102.
[103] ibid, 107.
[104] ibid, 107–08.
[105] ibid, 109–10.
[106] ibid, 113–14.
[107] ibid, 115.
[108] ibid, 124–31.
[109] ibid, 131–32.
[110] ibid, 142.
[111] ibid, 147.

adjustment in the international orientation of the UK. The state had 'set great store by its ... special relationship with a large part of the less-developed South, namely the Commonwealth'. Yet 'the British have been bitterly disappointed by the results'.[112] A federal Europe could be a more successful means of exerting international impact, in particular through promoting international cooperation. The authors addressed a particular debate within the federalist movement, over whether there was tension between support for regional, European unity, on the one hand, and global integration on the other hand.[113] Pinder and Pryce rejected this dichotomy. They believed that a United States of Europe could, over a period of perhaps four decades, stimulate 'a tendency towards "convergence" between different systems ... in the creation of a world community'. The development of a series of regional blocs could facilitate the formation of '[s]trong world institutions ... sufficiently federal to succeed where the United Nations, based as it is on the jealously guarded national sovereignty of the member states, has inevitably failed'.[114]

After considering these long-term, wide objectives, *Europe After De Gaulle* focused on more immediate prospects for the internal arrangements of a federal Europe. Attainment of the various goals they had set for a United States of Europe urgently required 'a transfer of some important powers from the member states to European institutions acting on behalf of all the members'.[115] The end point of this reform programme would be a system in which authority shifted from a Council of Ministers composed of the member states to European institutions with their own democratic legitimacy.[116] Pinder and Pryce thought this objective could be achieved through the establishment of a directly elected European Parliament and an executive the head of which they thought should be elected separately from the Parliament, to ensure that the maintenance of European governments was not subject to shifting alliances within the Parliament.[117] Related developments would include the emergence of pan-European political parties.[118]

As with the Hayek and Jennings texts, the extent to which the recommendations of *Europe After De Gaulle* have been fulfilled varies. The UK and numerous other additional states joined what is now the EU from 1973 onwards, as Pinder and Pryce hoped. However, the UK never became the consistent and powerful driving force for integration that they envisaged. While, as we will see, some of the 'positive integration' they advocated for Europe would take place, the UK was not always in the vanguard, often opposing more radical change,

[112] ibid, 149.
[113] ibid, 160.
[114] ibid, 159.
[115] ibid, 161.
[116] ibid, 166–67.
[117] ibid, 176–77.
[118] ibid, 170–71.

or seeking individual opt-outs, and even questioning its own membership.[119] One significant wave of accessions came as a consequence of the collapse of the Soviet Union in 1991. This turn of events might be seen as an historic success for European integration. Yet in the longer term it could prove to have been hugely destabilising. Post-Communist expansion has arguably led to the incorporation of member states incompatible with the democratic principles of the EU.[120] Furthermore, from the UK perspective, it produced mass inward migration that served eventually to strengthen the domestic Eurosceptic movement.[121]

The EU, as already discussed, has not yet developed the central control over foreign and defence policy the authors hoped would enable it to become a third pole in the Cold War of their time. Moreover, the project of driving global integration through a federation of Europe is far from complete, though there are a number of organisations worldwide that share some similarities with the EU model. They include the African Union, ASEAN (Association of Southeast Asian Nations) and in South America, Mercosur.[122] The EU today, in keeping with the hopes of Pinder and Pryce, has extensive science and technology programmes and a single currency in which most members participate (19 of 28 at the time of writing, with the UK being the most significant of the self-excluders). It also became a guarantor of social minimums, for instance through the Social Chapter of 1997. To a significant extent the political left in the UK, especially from the late 1980s, became more enamoured with European integration and the 'socially reactionary' image was dispelled[123] (though some on the left, including the present Labour leadership, seem to have retained this negative perception).[124] However, accompanying this transition was a turn against Europe on the UK right, with its own caricature of an excessively interventionist Brussels bureaucracy. The extent to which the EU is an international 'beacon' through attaining a combination of social justice and market economies, especially in the wake of the eurozone crisis and the period of austerity that followed, is questionable.[125]

[119] See eg Stephen George, *An awkward partner: Britain in the European Community* (Oxford, Oxford University Press, 1998).

[120] See eg Frank Schimmelfennig, 'The community trap: Liberal norms, rhetorical action, and the Eastern enlargement of the European Union' (2001) 55(1) *International organization* 47–80; Ulrich Sedelmeier, 'After conditionality: post-accession compliance with EU law in East Central Europe' (2008) 15(6) *Journal of European public policy* 806–25.

[121] Jonathan Portes, 'Immigration, free movement and the EU referendum' (2016) 236(1) *National Institute Economic Review* 14–22.

[122] Mark Corner, *Towards a Global Sharing of Sovereignty* (London, Federal Trust for Education and Research, 2008) 12–22.

[123] Philip Daniels, 'From hostility to "constructive engagement": The Europeanisation of the Labour Party' (1998) 21(1) *West European Politics* 72–96.

[124] Oliver Wright, 'Jeremy Corbyn "would be campaigning for Brexit if he was not Labour leader", says long-time ally Tariq Ali', *Independent*, 16 May 2016: https://www.independent.co.uk/news/uk/politics/jeremy-corbyn-would-be-campaigning-for-brexit-if-he-was-not-labour-leader-says-long-time-ally-tariq-a7032736.html.

[125] See eg Walter Laqueur, *After the Fall: The end of the European dream and the decline of a continent* (New York, Thomas Dunne Books, 2012).

An important feature of the federal model stressed by Pinder and Pryce was that rather than simply entailing centralisation, it involved managing matters at an appropriate level of governance. For them, this approach was a potential means of addressing the concerns driving the student protests and rising regional movements of their time. In the contemporary era, it may seem that the EU is a target of, rather than constructive channel for, social unrest. However, though the powers of the Committee of the Regions are limited, the EU has been effective at fostering links with sub-member state territorial units.[126] This multi-tiered aspect of European integration was not fully considered in the UK in advance of the referendum of 2016; and the handling of devolution issues, as we have seen, has proved to be one of the most complex and contentious aspects of Brexit. For some in Scotland in particular, it is more appropriate that the European Union should legislate within policy areas that are devolved than the UK Parliament should do so. However, the idea of the EU as a democratically legitimate force was clearly not shared by all in the UK. This lack of support came about notwithstanding the implementation of perhaps the most important of the recommendations contained in *Europe After De Gaulle*: for the introduction (from 1979) of a European Parliament the membership of which was determined by direct election. While steps were made in the direction of forming European political parties (another hope of the authors), the Conservative Party in particular struggled to find or form a credible grouping with which it could align itself.[127] Moreover, rather than being incorporated into a European polity, a tendency developed for voters in the UK to use elections to the European Parliament as an opportunity to support parties sceptical regarding or hostile towards the EU.[128] A democratic shortcoming in the EU has been that elections do not determine who forms the executive. The Pinder and Pryce proposal, for separate elections for this purpose, would have been one method of addressing this weakness.

VI. COMMONWEALTH OF EUROPE

Within four years of the Pinder and Pryce work appearing, the UK joined the EEC. Tony Benn, as we have seen, was an influential proponent of the holding of a referendum on UK membership, both before accession and then afterwards. Initially he took this stance as a supporter of UK participation in the continental integration project, for which he hoped to secure legitimacy,

[126] John Loughlin, 'Representing regions in Europe: the Committee of the Regions' (1996) 6(2) *Regional & Federal Studies* 147–65.

[127] Philip Lynch and Richard Whitaker, 'A loveless marriage: The Conservatives and the European People's Party' (2007) 61(1) *Parliamentary Affairs* 31–51.

[128] See eg Richard Hayton, 'Towards the Mainstream? UKIP and the 2009 Elections to the European Parliament' (2010) 30(1) *Politics* 26–35.

and then as an opponent of it, hoping to invoke a popular rejection of the policy. In the 1975 referendum, as a member of the Labour Cabinet, he made use of the specially introduced exemption from collective responsibility to campaign against the government recommendation for a vote to remain within the EEC.[129] Nearly 20 years later Benn maintained his stance, arguing against UK membership of the EEC successor organisation, the EU. Writing with Andrew Hood, he proposed a new form of continental institution, set out in a 'Commonwealth of Europe Bill', to be introduced alongside a 'written' constitution for Great Britain, included in a 'Commonwealth of Britain Bill' (under which Northern Ireland would cease to be part of what had been the UK).[130]

Explaining the need for the twin transition they advocated, Benn and Hood wrote that 'Britain has for centuries accepted the absurd notion that the nation is glued together by common loyalty, as subjects, to a hereditary sovereign … Now, under the Maastricht Treaty of European Union, all British subjects are to be magically transformed into citizens of this new union'. They held that '[t]hese two completely contradictory constitutional arrangements have one thing in common – neither of them has been put to the people of this country for endorsement and therefore neither can be said to carry the democratic legitimacy that such an endorsement alone could provide'.[131] Benn and Hood depicted their Commonwealth of Britain Bill as setting out 'a new constitution for this country'. It 'proposes a democratic, secular, federal Commonwealth comprising the nations of England, Scotland and Wales dedicated to the maintenance of the welfare of all its citizens'. The accompanying Commonwealth of Europe Bill 'suggests a looser and wider form of cooperation across the continent as a whole'.[132] In discussing the background to the latter text, Benn and Hood depicted the EEC and NATO as 'committed to preserving capitalism and defending it from external attack'. They observed swift 'progress towards a federal Europe', that would eventually have 'a common currency and an independent central bank' to 'remove economic policy effectively from the constituent governments'. The authors expected that many states would remain excluded from the integration project, perpetuating divisions that had characterised Europe for much of the twentieth century.[133] Benn and Hood opposed 'insularity' within Europe, but suggested that more 'traditional' intergovernmental forms of cooperation might be preferable.[134]

They accepted that a 'Union of Europe' with directly elected central institutions, like those of the US federal government, would be democratically

[129] See Lucy Atkinson, Andrew Blick and Matt Qvortrup, *The People's Veto: The history of the referendum in the United Kingdom* (Oxford, Oxford University Press, 2019 forthcoming) ch 2.

[130] Tony Benn and Andrew Hood, *Common Sense: A New Constitution for Britain* (London, Random House, 1993) App 1 and App 2.

[131] ibid, 90–91.

[132] ibid, 91–92.

[133] ibid, 112–13.

[134] ibid, 113.

legitimate. But 'the advocates of European political union do not want, or believe in, this alternative'. The existing model was 'bureaucratic' and 'centralised'.[135] Benn and Hood suspected that a direct transposition of the US constitutional system to Europe was 'unlikely'. The model they proposed, therefore, 'sought to harmonise the policies of the continent on the basis of consent, at the pace chosen by each country adhering to the Commonwealth'. They advocated a wide membership of approximately 50 member states, comprising any European country that wished to join. While the Commonwealth would have institutions such as an Assembly, a council of ministers, and a court of justice, 'they would have no power to take action that would prejudice the democratic decisions of the member states, although membership of the Commonwealth could be suspended'.[136] The Assembly would produce 'conventions' aimed at attaining regulatory convergence in fields such as defence, energy, the environment, food, social policy and trade. But, unlike in a 'Union ... law making would remain the exclusive function of the member states, which would be obliged to try to comply with these conventions, subject to the consent of their own Parliaments and electors'.[137]

Benn and Hood warned that the existing European integration project risked replicating the then-recent demise of the Soviet Union: 'Communism run from Moscow broke down because it was bureaucratic, inefficient and inflexible; and there is a real risk that capitalism run from Brussels or Frankfurt might reproduce the same sense of frustration and anger, as undemocratic institutions become more powerful and less responsive.'[138] The Commonwealth of Europe Bill itself was 9 pages and 20 articles in length. Notable features included provision for a Human Rights Commission (Article 15) and a Secretariat (Article 16). Amendments to the system were made subject to approval by a referendum in every member state and the recommendation of a majority of participants in the Council of Ministers (Article 20). The Annex contained a Charter of Rights, providing for 'political', 'legal', 'social' and economic rights.

The Benn and Hood scheme was founded in a left case against participation in European integration. As noted above, the 'socially reactionary' reputation that Pinder and Pryce identified had been to a significant extent counteracted by the early 1990s. but some, including Benn and Hood, were not persuaded. They viewed the existing project as fulfilling some of the free market objectives that Hayek had attached to his federal proposal, though, unlike Hayek, Benn and Hood were opposed to such outcomes. Yet they also chose to criticise the EU by way of analogy with Soviet communism, presenting an image of an overcentralised, unresponsive monolith. While they accepted in principle the idea of a

[135] ibid, 113.
[136] ibid, 114.
[137] ibid, 114–15.
[138] ibid, 115.

continental federation, looking to the US, they did not believe such a model was realistic for Europe. The Benn and Hood proposal envisaged exit from the EU as more than a self-contained change. It would, as they conceived it, be part of a wider programme of transformation, including the introduction of a 'written' constitution, the end of UK jurisdiction over Northern Ireland, and a general re-orientation away from free market economics. While they favoured national level democracy and sovereignty, there was also an internationalist dimension to their programme, involving the establishment of a larger, looser multi-state organisation.

VII. THE PLAN

In 2008, Douglas Carswell and Daniel Hannan published *The Plan: Twelve Months to renew Britain*.[139] Both the authors were then Conservative politicians (though Carswell would subsequently defect to UKIP) and would play a prominent role in events leading to the referendum and 'leave' vote of 2016. In *The Plan*, they set out a connected set of political and constitutional proposals, of which departure from the EU was an important, but not the only, component. They explained their motivation in the following terms:

> The British state is failing. It can't deliver even the most basic services competently. We have the highest prisoner population in Europe, and one of the highest crime rates. Our schoolchildren compare dismally with similarly aged pupils in other countries and in previous generations. Our healthcare system is more likely to kill its charges than any other in the developed world. Our roads are choked, our railways crumbling, our airports unbearable. Our borders are, to all intents and purposes, wide open.[140]

In response to these perceived difficulties Carswell and Hannan set out what they described as 'a plan to make the state accountable once more to the people'. Avowing the influence of the 1994 US Republican Party congressional election programme, *Contract with America*,[141] their equivalent consisted of:

> a number of related initiatives: placing the criminal justice system under locally elected Sheriffs; making local councils self-financing; making healthcare answerable to patients, and education to parents; returning social security to counties and cities; withdrawing from the European Union; replacing prime ministerial patronage with open parliamentary hearings; tackling judicial activism; introducing local and national referendums.[142]

[139] Douglas Carswell and Daniel Hannan, *The Plan: Twelve months to renew Britain* (Douglas Carswell and Daniel Hannan, 2008).
[140] ibid, 7.
[141] ibid, 36–39.
[142] ibid, 9.

Common themes running through the book and the programme it set out were the desirability of reducing the overall scale of government and publicly funded political activities; a dispersal of functions away from central authorities; an expansion of the power of elected office holders; and more direct involvement for the public in decisions.

The Plan engaged with many issues addressed in the present work. The authors, for instance, saw immense political potential in the Internet. They depicted this technological phenomenon as having had a democratising effect, and in leading to a significant expansion in personal choice. Such patterns, they observed, had already taken hold in areas including publishing and '[s]omething similar may be about to happen in the world of politics'.[143] Carswell and Hannan argued that in the US, '[t]he web has made it possible, as never before, for a politician to come from outside, appealing directly to voters over the heads of party bigwigs'.[144] It was becoming more difficult for elites such as donors, professional journalists and senior party figures to determine 'who is mainstream and who is eccentric'. Established parties, including in the UK, were not adapting effectively to these new tendencies, one manifestation of which was that 'parties can no longer deliver "their" voters. This is most clearly evinced in referendums on European integration'.[145] The authors described two occasions, in France in 2004 and Ireland in 2008, when a consensus among parties and press supporting a popular vote in favour of European integration had met with online resistance, and had been defeated, with 'no' results.[146] They concluded 'the political party as an organism … is dying. The modern political party will be protean: a series of *ad hoc*, issue-by-issue coalitions'.[147]

Another significant feature of the philosophy underpinning *The Plan* was its criticism of 'the fetichisation of the "expert"'. Carswell and Hannan disputed whether a genuinely neutral position founded solely in expertise was possible.[148] Moreover, to empower experts, they believed, was to undermine democracy, placing authority in the hands of the unaccountable.[149] The authors advocated measures to make Parliament more cost-effective and transparent, but stronger with respect to the executive.[150] They favoured abolition of the Human Rights Act 1998, withdrawal from the European Convention on Human Rights to which the 1998 Act gave domestic expression, special provisions to ensure that Parliament was not subordinate to international agreements; and

[143] ibid, 26.
[144] ibid, 27.
[145] ibid, 28.
[146] ibid, 28–29.
[147] ibid, 29.
[148] ibid, 29.
[149] ibid, 30.
[150] ibid, 45.

making senior judicial appointments subject to public hearings in Parliament.[151] *The Plan* supported an extensive dispersal of powers, including fiscal responsibility, to local authorities in England, to match devolution in other parts of the UK.[152]

Carswell and Hannan also complained of 'a shift in power from the legislature to the executive' of an 'insidious and colossal' nature, involving the use of statutory instruments, both to implement European law and for other purposes. Claiming that '[s]tatutory instruments were rare before the 1970s', they objected to them on the basis that they 'receive only occasional and cursory parliamentary oversight', and for the regulatory burden they imposed on the private sector. The authors proposed what they described as a 'Great Repeal Bill' to abolish the parent legislation creating inappropriate delegated powers.[153] In the field of foreign affairs, Carswell and Hannan advocated 'parliamentary control', making treaties subject to approval by the House of Commons. International agreements should also be time limited, meaning that regular Commons consent to their continued existence was required. The authors also proposed House of Commons hearings for individuals appointed to high level diplomatic posts.[154] They advocated direct democracy, which they argued was compatible with, and could potentially strengthen, the representative system of the UK. Carswell and Hannan held that members of the public should have the power to trigger referendums on particular issues (the 'initiative'); that they should be able to force a popular vote to approve or veto controversial parliamentary bills; and that major constitutional changes should be subject to referendums. In each case, the votes the authors envisaged taking place would be held on specific legislative measures. They also supported the extensive use of local level popular votes.[155]

While the authors included a quote from Hayek and the outset of their book and referred approvingly to his ideas in the main text,[156] they seemingly did not share the positive attitude towards 'interstate federalism' that, as we have seen, he once exhibited. Their book set out the simple proposal to '[r]eplace the existing terms of EU membership with a Swiss-style bilateral free-trade agreement'.[157] They held that 'the entire philosophy which underpins our ideas – that of devolution to the lowest possible level – is impossible to reconcile with European integration'.[158] *The Plan* argued that the 'choice' that faced the UK was not simply between 'integration and isolation – or, depending on your point of view, between subjugation and independence'. In fact, it held, there were

[151] ibid, 61.
[152] ibid, 89.
[153] ibid, 27.
[154] ibid, 125.
[155] ibid, 153.
[156] ibid, 116.
[157] ibid, 125.
[158] ibid, 146.

'many degrees of association with the EU that fall short of full membership'. It noted that Norway, Iceland and Liechtenstein were members of the European Economic Area (EEA) but not of the EU; and that they were part of the European Free Trade Association (EFTA) alongside Switzerland, which was itself not a participant in the EEA. The authors went on to observe that the Channel Islands were 'inside the single market' but not members of the EU, while Turkey participated in the customs union but not the remainder of the EU. Greenland, which had withdrawn when attaining partial independence from Denmark, nonetheless maintained certain connections. Within the EU there were various opt outs, for instance from the single currency and the Schengen area. Carswell and Hannan reasoned that it was appropriate to seek 'integration on an issue-by-issue basis: defence, fisheries, free movement of people and so on. It is plainly feasible to participate in some of these areas but not others'.[159]

They then set out a list of objectives that the UK should seek in its relationship with the EU. Among them were continued 'access to European markets'; the enjoyment of 'free-trade arrangements with non-EU states'; the minimising of 'budgetary contributions to Brussels'; 'control' over domestic resources such as fisheries and energy; freedom to determine agricultural policy; and '[t]o restore the supremacy of Parliament'. The authors acknowledged that it could not be predicted with certainty that all of these goals would be achieved, but asserted that '[t]he four EFTA countries … come close to meeting these objectives'. Furthermore, there was 'every reason to assume that Britain could secure an even more attractive settlement than the EFTA states', given the relative size of its economy and sustained trade deficit with the EU. The UK, *The Plan* concluded, should treat EFTA as 'the baseline: minimum terms, on which it would aim to improve'.[160]

The authors noted the argument that the EFTA states in practice had to apply rules that they did not have a formal role in passing, but claimed that 'it is a problem in theory rather than in practice. Remember that the legislation in question covers only a small and closely delineated part of the EFTA countries' public life'.[161] For them, the new arrangement they envisaged would leave the UK 'freer, more democratic and wealthier'. It would become possible to 'unbundle powers from Whitehall'. To attain this outcome securing 'parliamentary supremacy is a necessary first step. At present, an astonishing 84 per cent of national legislation in EU member states derives from Brussels. Before those powers can be devolved to local councils and private citizens, they must first be repatriated from the EU'.[162]

[159] ibid, 148.
[160] ibid, 149.
[161] ibid, 150.
[162] ibid, 152.

Carswell and Hannan were influential figures in the sustained movement for UK departure from the EU.[163] The programme set out in *The Plan* therefore merits close attention, both in its own right and in the context of the other texts considered in this chapter. First, for the authors, leaving the EU was part of a far larger programme. Key themes within it were a reduction in socio-economic interventionism and the decentralisation of political authority. The text placed a premium on mandates derived through elections or referendums. It could be seen as 'populist' in character,[164] in as far as such an outlook involves discerning and implementing the supposed will of the people, and preventing it from being frustrated by intermediary agencies representing elite interests. Challenges to the authority of a variety of established institutions and groups by proponents of leaving have been a recurring feature of the Brexit period. Disparagement of a public institution – namely the EU itself – was at the core of this campaign. Michael Gove, a Cabinet member and leave supporter, echoed Carswell and Hannan when, in June 2016, he famously asserted in a televised referendum debate that 'people in this country have had enough of experts'.[165] After the vote, a variety of high-level supposed saboteurs of exit were identified, including the Civil Service,[166] members of both Houses of Parliament[167] and the judiciary.[168]

A populist dimension might also be discerned in the assertion, by the UK government and others, of an obligation decisively to exit the EU following the referendum of 23 June 2016, overriding even the position of the UK Parliament as the principal organ of representative democracy. However, while *The Plan* was supportive of the use of referendums and of departure from the EU, it did not specifically promote the idea that the former would be the means of attaining the latter. Carswell and Hannan did, nonetheless, discuss referendums on EU-related matters elsewhere in the continent. Significantly, given more recent controversies, they did so in the context of considering the role that online campaigning could play in increasing the chances of anti-integrationist forces.

[163] Sebastian Payne, 'How Leave won: behind the scenes in the battle for Brexit', *Financial Times*, 11 November 2016: https://www.ft.com/content/18211880-a5e1-11e6-8b69-02899e8bd9d1.

[164] For a discussion of the populist concept in the light of the EU referendum, see: Michael Freeden. 'After the Brexit referendum: revisiting populism as an ideology' (2017) 22(1) *Journal of Political Ideologies* 1–11.

[165] Henry Mance, 'Britain has had enough of experts, says Gove', *Financial Times*, 3 June 2016: https://www.ft.com/content/3be49734-29cb-11e6-83e4-abc22d5d108c last accessed 6 September 2018.

[166] Charlotte Davis, 'Britain's civil servants are part of WORRYING plot to KEEP UK in EU, says Brexiteer MP' *Express*, 29 January 2018: https://www.express.co.uk/news/uk/911098/Brexit-news-UK-EU-European-Union-latest-deal-Labour-MP last accessed 6 September 2018.

[167] Laura Mowat, '"It's a threat to Brexit" Rees-Mogg hits out at MPs plot to STOP EU exit', *Express*, 14 January 2018: https://www.express.co.uk/news/politics/974221/brexit-news-jacob-rees-mogg-eu-vote-eu-withdrawal-bill-commons last accessed 6 September 2018.

[168] James Slack, 'Enemies of the people', *Mail*, 3 November 2016: http://www.dailymail.co.uk/news/article-3903436/Enemies-people-Fury-touch-judges-defied-17-4m-Brexit-voters-trigger-constitutional-crisis.html last accessed 6 September 2018.

Their general conclusions were that this technological development had helped bring about an ebbing of the power of established gatekeepers to manipulate the public; and that parties were struggling to adapt to the new environment.

The 'leave' result of 23 June 2016 can be seen as an historic achievement for the Carswell and Hannan agenda. However, the implementation of Brexit gave rise to tendencies that appeared to contradict other principles advocated in *The Plan*. There were complaints, as we have seen, that departing from the EU as planned by the UK government would bring about a concentration of power at UK level rather than a decentralisation; and that it would shift the balance between the executive and legislature problematically in favour of the former. At the centre of such controversies was the plan to expand significantly the delegated powers available to ministers: a tendency Carswell and Hannan had advocated reversing, not accelerating. They envisaged a 'Great Repeal Bill' for the abolition of enabling legislation. Ironically, the UK government initially intended to attach this title to what became the European Union (Withdrawal) Act 2018. Rather than restricting secondary law-making power, it extended it, on a substantial scale.

In this sense, the attainment of one aspect of *The Plan* appeared to compromise other elements within it. Furthermore, it would be difficult to judge whether the prospectus for a post-departure relationship with the EU was fully achieved, since it was expressed in such general terms. The authors, however, clearly hoped that the UK would be able to take a selective approach, maximising benefits while minimising obligations. Such an approach challenged the principles on which the EU was founded. Some critics on the UK side presented EU resistance to UK aspirations in this regard during the Brexit negotiations as unreasonable.[169] However, the idea that a single market must comprise a package of principles taken as a whole was not invented in Brussels in 2016. We can observe much earlier observations of this general principle, including those provided by Hayek and Jennings. In seeking partial exemption from this framework, the UK hoped to benefit at the expense of others who remained fully within it. Yet if the UK were successful in this approach, others within the EU might follow it. The consequence could then be that there was no more single market to which to gain access, on exceptional terms or otherwise.

Carswell and Hannan venerated Hayek. But in some ways Benn (writing with Hood in this particular work discussed above) was their more direct ancestor. His emphasis on popular democracy exercised at UK level had resemblance to their own; as did his aversion to a supposedly unaccountable, excessively controlling European bureaucracy, that he likened in its potential failings to the Soviet

[169] Henry Newman, 'Dear EU, please take Britain's Brexit plan seriously. It may be our best offer', *Guardian*, 12 July 2018: https://www.theguardian.com/commentisfree/2018/jul/12/eu-britain-brexit-plan-chequers-theresa-may last accessed 6 September 2018.

Union. As we will see, earlier in his career, Benn had expressed views regarding possible changes in political communications comparable to those found in *The Plan*. He, Carswell and Hannan all formed part of a UK political tradition, spread across parties, that found expression during the Brexit episode. There was a rival school. Promoting the development of multi-state organisations, it achieved substantial international influence during the twentieth century. But it drew its most powerful impetus from threats of a nature that were not keenly felt by sufficient numbers of voters in June 2016 to lead to a 'remain' result.

4

Advocating the Referendum

AMONG THE MOST distinctive features of the Brexit episode has been the way in which the decision to leave the EU was taken. It involved a referendum. The vote of 23 June 2016 was only the third of this type to have been held across the whole UK and the thirteenth to take place above local level. This event was even more unusual in that never before had a UK government held a referendum recommending a vote in favour of the more conservative option on the ballot paper, and been defeated, with a majority of those voting supporting radical change. (In 1975, the government formally advocated remaining within the EEC and won; while in 2011 there was no official recommendation when the UK voted on whether to adopt the Alternative Vote for elections to the Westminster Parliament, and rejected this idea.)[1] Yet, as we have seen, the 'leave' option was ambiguous. Legally, it placed no requirement on the government at all; and in formulating its Brexit policy, the executive inevitably applied its own interpretation to the result. In doing so it was driven primarily by the imperatives of the Conservative Party, just as it had been when bringing about the holding of the referendum itself.[2] Thus any assertion that the many and expansive consequences of Brexit as pursued under May were derived from the clearly expressed popular will, to which any resistance was an assault on democracy, was dubious.

Nonetheless, to a large extent such views were either firmly supported or deferred to. Among most parliamentarians, despite both Houses seemingly containing 'remain' majorities, there was a reluctant acceptance that the referendum they had provided for, despite its open-ended quality, had created an imperative to leave, though there was some quibbling about the precise execution by the government.[3] That a popular vote on a vague question with no firm legal force could acquire such practical importance calls for a closer examination of past views of how referendums should be implemented. There is a long history of advocacy in this area. By the time the first such vote was held above local level in 1973 (on the constitutional future of Northern Ireland), the idea of using such a mechanism had periodically been receiving serious attention since

[1] Lucy Atkinson, Andrew Blick and Matt Qvortrup, *The People's Veto: The history of the referendum in the United Kingdom* (Oxford, Oxford University Press, 2019 forthcoming), Introduction.

[2] See Conclusion.

[3] See ch 2.

the 1880s.[4] This chapter considers some of the more significant contributions from the early twentieth century.

I. 'THE ONLY WAY TO DEMOCRACY'

The socialist journalist (and playwright) Alex M Thompson wrote a pamphlet entitled *The Only Way to Democracy*, published by the *Clarion* journal (of which Thompson was a co-founder) in 1900.[5] He opened with a reference to William Gladstone, the former Liberal Prime Minister, stating that 'We are a self-governing people, i.e., a people governing ourselves by our majorities'. Thompson added a further quote from HG Reid, the state premier of New South Wales, Australia, when speaking to his Parliament, saying of voters 'that their yea and nay is to be the supreme power, the final word in the law-making of the nation'. Thompson went on to observe that all 'British' politicians presented themselves as recognising 'the people's fitness to exercise this power'. None would express doubt about the capacity of the public to take decisions on their own behalf, and all would hold that they 'could aspire to no higher distinction than the honour of *their* mandate to act as *their* agent to carry out *their* instructions in Parliament'.[6]

Parliamentary government fell short of this standard, Thompson believed, if it was possible to demonstrate 'that the laws are not the expression of the needs of the mass, but only the assertion of the privileges of the few'.[7] If this defect could be established, it would then be necessary to determine how to alter existing governmental arrangements properly to provide for 'an actual sovereignty of the people'.[8] In assessing the democratic fitness of the present system, Thompson found an imbalance between the two chambers of Parliament. If the elected Commons was the source of a blockage for a particular proposal, it could be 'dissolved, and the issue referred to … electors'; while the Lords could not. The purpose of the upper house, Thompson argued, was to preserve the special status of those who sat in it.[9] The existence of the Lords could not be reconciled with democracy. But, according to Thompson, the Commons was more insidious because, unlike the Lords, it purported 'to represent the nation, and to act only in obedience to the nation's instructions'.[10] By so doing it deluded genuine supporters of democracy into 'acceptance, more or less placid, of the existing system of government'. The Commons was, therefore, 'the greatest

[4] Lucy Atkinson, Andrew Blick and Matt Qvortrup, *The People's Veto: The history of the referendum in the United Kingdom* (Oxford, Oxford University Press, 2019 forthcoming), chs 1 and 2.

[5] Alex M Thompson, *The Only Way to Democracy* (London, Clarion Newspaper Co, 1900).

[6] ibid, 1.

[7] ibid, 2.

[8] ibid, 2.

[9] ibid, 2.

[10] ibid, 3.

obstacle to true democracy'. For Thompson, 'Parliamentary representation' was 'a mis-representation'.[11]

Voters were presented with a choice between two candidates, each of which was chosen by the respective 'partisans and wire-pullers' of the two main parties. In such circumstances, it was not clear how electors, in supporting 'this professional partisan or that professional place-hunter' could promote their 'views on … manifold and diverse issues'.[12] If they wished to pursue a particular end, they might be obliged to vote for a candidate with whom they disagreed on many other issues; or against one with whom they were generally in agreement, except over a crucial matter.[13] Thompson found it 'impossible that any delegate should completely represent the desires of ten or twenty thousand electors'.[14] Even if particular commitments could be obtained from individual candidates, once returned to Parliament they would vote in accordance with party policy. General elections, furthermore, could not be read as straight choices over any given issue, and contained within them many apparently contradictory tendencies.[15]

Thompson then turned to defects in the electoral system. Noting the limited nature of the franchise (comprising 6,600,000 of a total population of approximately 40,000,000) and the fact that not all who could vote exercised their right to do so, Thompson stressed the disproportionate way in which it operated. He observed its tendency to create parliamentary majorities on an unjustified scale, and to lead to wasted votes. Constituencies were far from equal in numbers of voters.[16] The Commons comprised members who were largely aligned with 'landed and sometimes … financial interests'. There were few 'workers' within the Commons and most MPs were 'parasites upon the people's backs'.[17]

Some political activists, Thompson noted, supported reform of the existing representative system, with measures such as 'automatic registration', full manhood suffrage; payment for MPs and their election expenses from public sources; preferential voting ('second ballot'); and the removal of the hereditary principle from Parliament.[18] Yet, Thompson reasoned, both France and the US had long adopted reforms of this type, and they had failed to deliver the advantages some might hope. Payment for MPs led to the recruitment of politicians who saw the role as a means of securing financial benefits for themselves, with no interest in furthering the interests of the public.[19] British Labour politicians were 'the most sturdy and honest in the world' precisely because 'their service has been disinterested'. While the bulk of them had 'worked at the bench, at the

[11] ibid, 3.
[12] ibid, 3.
[13] ibid, 4.
[14] ibid, 4.
[15] ibid, 5.
[16] ibid, 7.
[17] ibid, 8.
[18] ibid, 9.
[19] ibid, 9–10.

loom, or in the mine' by contrast prominent French, Italian and German socialists tended to be 'lawyers and writers'.[20] With this difference in mind, Thompson expounded: '[w]e stand in England at the parting of the ways. One leads to the Payment of Members and the creation of a class of professional political adventurers; the other leads to the Referendum and Initiative'.[21] Thompson favoured the latter option.[22] He proposed that the time it would take to secure parliamentary reform – 'twenty, perhaps fifty, years' – would be better expended on achieving his preferred option.

Thompson advocated two related mechanisms: the referendum and the initiative. The former was a popular protection against unwanted measures emanating from Parliament; the latter was a means by which the public could force laws with which it found favour onto the agenda. Avowedly drawing influence from practices employed in Switzerland, Thompson defined the referendum as a means by which a certain number of signatories could require a popular vote to be held to approve or nullify legislation that had already passed through Parliament, before it came into effect. The initiative, again involving the amassing of a defined level of support, enabled voters to present a measure of their own to Parliament. Elected representatives could choose to accept the proposals, or else it could be the subject of a referendum at the same time as the next General Election. Government could otherwise carry on in the normal way, and such measures would only be necessary 'when Parliament failed to provide legislation suited to the popular needs'.[23]

Thompson considered the main argument against the referendum and initiative as being that 'the people – not the man who makes the objection, but the *other* people – have not enough sense or understanding to vote on laws'. But he held that there was no reason to suppose that the popular judgement of candidates would be better than of policies. While some critics of his proposal could hold that the public might not feel motivated to take part, Thompson saw popular voting as a means of promoting better understanding and heightened engagement. It was a means of creating 'democratic character'.[24] He held '[t]he way to true Democracy will never be found through Delegacy. The only safe way is through direct legislation – through the Referendum and Initiative'. These reforms would 'educate the people in self-government, and ripen them for progress'.[25] Rather than leading to an increase in the volume of legislation, they would reduce it and make it more comprehensible in nature, lessening the influence of lawyers and their interest in greater complication. Debate would focus on values and specific proposals, and move away from the partisan contest,

[20] ibid, 11.
[21] ibid, 11.
[22] ibid, 11.
[23] ibid, 12.
[24] ibid, 14.
[25] ibid, 15.

replacing 'mud-slinging' with 'thinking'.[26] Change could take place at the pace that suited the public, whether fast or slow.[27] Thompson concluded: '[t]he only sure way to Democracy is through the Referendum and Initiative'.[28]

The previous chapter discussed how ideas from the political left regarding European integration, promoted by Tony Benn, subsequently found an echo in the Euroscepticism of the right. A similar pattern can be detected when considering the work of Thompson. His view of the referendum as a means by which the public could impose its will on a self-interested and unresponsive elite has a familiar tone in the Brexit era, more than a century later. However, there are important and instructive differences between the referendum as advocated by Thompson and the actual vote held on 23 June 2016. While Thompson envisaged a specific mechanism whereby given levels of support from below would trigger a referendum, the EU vote came about principally from above: driven by a Prime Minister seeking to manage difficulties within his own parliamentary party (though they were connected to a perceived threat from the outside in the form of UKIP).[29] The response to the result, moreover, was handled by his successor in the same context. Furthermore, while in the Thompson model voting would take place on specific measures – presumably bills – the 2016 referendum involved a choice between two propositions, one of which – that won – was far from precise. Nearly 40 years later, though still seeming to support the referendum in principle, Thompson wrote that he had come 'to agree with Sidney Webb that the principle cannot be usefully applied to complicated issues. And in the terribly difficult and ticklish problems of foreign affairs where the issues are not wholly within the control of our own Government, the effect may even be dangerous'.[30]

At the time Thompson wrote in 1900, democracy was visibly coming into being, but the process was far from complete and still subject to opposition. How, precisely, it would develop was unclear. Areas of uncertainty included what would be the future of the Lords; the voting system employed for parliamentary elections; and the pace at which change would take place. Thompson envisaged referendums forming a part of the system, complementing but not supplanting representative mechanisms. His model was not realised. Referendums on major issues have taken place since 1973. But as the example of the EU vote of 2016 demonstrates, they have not been incorporated into the political process in the systematic way he advocated. They take place at the behest

[26] ibid, 15.
[27] ibid, 15.
[28] ibid, 16.
[29] Nathaniel Copsey and Tim Haughton, 'Farewell Britannia? "Issue Capture" and the Politics of David Cameron's 2013 EU Referendum Pledge' (2014) 52 *JCMS: Journal of Common Market Studies* 74–89. For the idea that referendums as practised in the UK are elite-led exercises, see House of Lords Select Committee on the Constitution, *Referendums in the United Kingdom* (London, Stationery Office, 2010), 16–17. See ch 2 and Conclusion.
[30] Alex M Thompson, *Here I Lie* (London, George Routledge & Sons, 1937) 132.

of politicians, rather than being specifically triggered by the public; and they can be held on general propositions as well as more specific measures. Many reforms have taken place since 1900. But basic problems Thompson identified with the electoral system – the limited choice offered, and the wasting of votes, inequities and distortions produced – remain. There are possibly more direct means of correcting these problems than the use of the initiative and referendum, as will be discussed later.

II. JA HOBSON AND THE REFERENDUM

The Crisis of Liberalism: New Issues of Democracy, compiled from articles by the economic and political writer JA Hobson, appeared in 1909.[31] He was conscious that he wrote at a critical moment in the constitutional development of the UK. Hobson placed his work in the context of the struggle then ongoing between the reforming Liberal government, founded in a majority in the elected House of Commons, and the Conservative-dominated hereditary House of Lords. Following disputes between the two parliamentary chambers over various legislative measures, the contest would reach a peak after the Lords rejected the Liberal budget of 1909, using its legal powers that were then equal to those of the Commons. Eventually, after two general elections held during 1910 to try and resolve the matter, the Parliament Act 1911 decisively restricted the authority of the Lords with respect to legislation and finance. The Lords could from this point onwards only delay, rather than veto, most bills, and had no role in the passing of budgets. Hobson saw the Lords resistance to the Liberal programme as driven by a perception that David Lloyd George and Winston Churchill were 'reluctantly' directing their party towards 'the New Liberalism', entailing an intensifying 'attack upon the system of private property and private industrial enterprise'.[32] For Hobson the Lords was simply:

> the first line of trenches. Behind it lies a whole row of defences, represented by the laws and the judiciary, the bureaucracy, the Court, the electoral machinery (favouring at every turn the power of the purse), the secret unrepresentative character and working of Cabinet Government, the manipulation of electoral opinion through the public house, the Press, the pulpit, and those other instruments of popular instruction which depend for their financial support upon the charity of the propertied classes.[33]

Faced with this challenge, Liberalism, Hobson held, must 'accept and execute a positive progressive policy which involves a new conception of the functions of

[31] JA Hobson, *The Crisis of Liberalism: New Issues of Democracy* (London, FS King & Son, 1909).

[32] JA Hobson, *The Crisis of Liberalism: New Issues of Democracy* (London, FS King & Son, 1909) x.

[33] ibid, x–xi.

the State'.[34] He sought to explain 'the place which the fight around the Lords' veto occupies in the larger struggle for democratic government'.[35] Hobson speculated on the implications of the legislative veto currently possessed by the Lords being abolished. He argued that '[t]here can be no more foolish error than to represent the veto of the House of Lords as the only, or even the chief barrier to the free realisation of the will of the people in this country'.[36] While the Lords had been a threat to the Commons, so too was the Cabinet, that Hobson viewed as increasingly dominant in policy making, to the cost of parliamentary influence. As he put it, this 'process marks a diminution of representative government and a failure of democracy'.[37] Moreover, the rise of party caucuses and of groups seeking to commit MPs to particular causes had 'gone far towards changing a Member of Parliament from a representative into a delegate'.[38]

In such circumstances, the curtailing of the power of the Lords would lead not to Commons supremacy, but potentially to 'a Cabinet autocracy qualified in certain electoral conditions by the power of some enclave or "cave" in a party'. Hobson perceived that 'this state of affairs might easily lead to Caesarism, where a magnetic party leader either succeeded in capturing the imagination of the populace or in engineering a supremacy among competing politicians'.[39] Further changes, alongside the curbing of the Lords, were therefore required. For the Commons to be properly representative, a universal adult franchise, including women, was needed (in 1918 all men and some women would receive the vote in Westminster elections; and an equal franchise between women and men was attained in 1928). A proportional representation system was required for parliamentary elections, 'to provide a truer expression of the popular will'. The particular method Hobson favoured was the Single Transferable Vote (STV). Under STV, in which voters indicate their preferences for candidates in multi-member constituencies, the overall number of seats won by parties better reflects the proportion of the popular vote cast for them. Further changes Hobson advocated were the abolition of plural voting and the introduction of 'payment of members and electoral expenses out of public funds'. Taken together, these proposals would 'have secured the forms of sound representation'.[40]

Yet while proportional representation 'would mitigate the tyranny of majority rule, and would curb to some extent the autocracy of Governments', parliamentary manipulation would remain a possibility and the preeminence of Cabinet would be difficult to reverse. There would remain a need for '[a] real and firm check upon abuse of power on the part of a Cabinet and

[34] ibid, xi.
[35] ibid, xi.
[36] ibid, 7–8.
[37] ibid, 9–10.
[38] ibid, 13.
[39] ibid, 12.
[40] ibid, 13.

a House of Commons called upon to deal with new and urgent issues upon which the electorate had not been consulted'.[41] Another influence that might need checking was that of 'permanent officials who, in the intricate processes of modern government, must necessarily come to play a growing part in the construction and administration of laws'. Their contribution was generally positive. But the 'official mind, eminently serviceable, has its inevitable defects; authoritative, excessively conservative, mechanical, and usually contemptuous of the lay civic mind, it is apt to use every opportunity to impose itself upon new legislative proposals, and to substitute, as far as possible, the official will for the representative will'.[42] The sole possible corrective to these flaws in the system of 'representative government' was the 'Referendum'. It rested in the principle that 'no form of representation is perfect, and that certain particular defects in representative government can best be met by a special and direct appeal to the fount of government'.[43]

The basic thesis Hobson advanced was 'that a surgical operation upon the veto of the Lords must entail important after-treatment in the shape of constructive constitutional reforms'.[44] He wished to avoid vesting in the Commons 'an absolutism which is only checked by an intrusion of the popular will at intervals of five or six years'.[45] The model Hobson advanced was one of a second chamber composed of senior figures with some experience of administration, elected, either directly by proportional representation, or indirectly by local government representatives. This reformed body would not possess the power of legislative veto then attached to the Lords.[46] It would perform an 'advisory and deliberative' role.[47] However, Hobson envisaged it as being empowered to submit to referendum bills passed by the Commons that it judged not to have 'received the sanction of popular will'.[48] Certain measures, including money bills, legislation involving external relations, and emergency measures, would be exempt from this process.[49] The mechanism would mean that it was the public rather than the second chamber that was the ultimate wielder of a veto.[50] Hobson noted that, while it was difficult to establish whether any given legislative item had obtained a 'mandate' via a General Election, at which a variety of issues competed with one-another, a referendum was a means of detaching and testing popular approval for a specific measure.[51] Beyond applying a limit upon

[41] ibid, 13–14.
[42] ibid, 14.
[43] ibid, 15.
[44] ibid, 16.
[45] ibid, 25.
[46] ibid, 30.
[47] ibid, 31.
[48] ibid, 32.
[49] ibid, 39.
[50] ibid, 33.
[51] ibid, 35.

unchecked Commons dominance, the referendum could serve a more fundamental purpose still. As he put it:

> A people endowed even with a moderate measure of intelligence will recognise the advisability of deferring to the superior skill and knowledge of tried and trusted representatives upon the technique of legislation, but they will not give to these agents a perfectly free hand over a term of years to pass any laws that seem good to them. They will insist upon retaining the ordinary customer's right to refuse "misfits."[52]

The author recognised the possible objection that referendums would undermine the functioning of representative democracy, in which individual politicians were elected to apply their own judgement rather than follow specific instructions. However, he held that the party system served to bind members collectively, and that efforts to hold MPs to particular pledges similarly called into question the idea of their independence.[53] Furthermore, under present ways of operating, the Commons could come to be dominated by 'the pertinacious fanaticism of little organised groups representing a small minority of the electorate'.[54] Another potential objection was that a Conservative-dominated upper chamber would deploy its power to trigger a referendum only against the legislative programme of Liberal governments. To compensate for this possible imbalance, Hobson suggested an allowance for 200 Members of the House of Commons to submit a measure to a popular vote. A Liberal Opposition in the Commons might, therefore, be able to test public support for a Conservative-instigated bill it suspected was unpopular. Hobson did not anticipate the frequent use of referendums, partly because parliamentarians would be reluctant to bring them about and then lose.[55] Yet the mere prospect that they might be used would have an impact, causing those who drafted legislation to take into account the possibility of its being made subject to a direct popular verdict.[56]

Hobson saw the referendum as potentially educating and enhancing the responsibility of the electorate. The public 'may not understand the full details of the Bills presented for their judgment' and would not 'be competent to appraise the technical merits of the drafting.' However, 'they will find trusted advisers and exponents, skilled interpreters who will set forth effectively the substance of the Bills, and they will eke out their own understanding of the measure by the wisdom of accepted guides'. Such a process would lead to 'a genuine though doubtless limited expression of the general will, and an education in practical politics that is of inestimable value'. The public would gain greater 'respect for the law' once they were directly involved in making it.[57] The quality of legislation could also improve if those who framed it felt a pressing obligation to take

[52] ibid, 40.
[53] ibid, 35.
[54] ibid, 36.
[55] ibid, 37–38.
[56] ibid, 39.
[57] ibid, 41–42.

into account the popular perspective.[58] Hobson held that objections to the referendum were founded in a 'deep-seated distrust of democracy'.[59]

He did not believe that voters would always reach a desirable conclusion;[60] and accepted the idea that the referendum might tend towards conservative outcomes. But Hobson held that it was preferable to achieve reform that did not accelerate beyond the development of public opinion. He then dealt with the idea that 'an adverse vote would shake the authority of a Government and force frequent dissolutions'. Hobson noted that '[t]he Minister responsible for a defeated measure might be driven to resign, though even that course does not seem inevitable'.[61] He did however believe it 'possible that the popular rejection of a measure of the first importance might once or twice in a decade so damage the Government that they deemed a dissolution advisable'.[62] Moreover Hobson also accepted 'that the adoption of a Referendum, even for rare use, would probably produce some important changes in our unwritten Constitution, particularly as regards the collective responsibility of the Government'.[63]

In his analysis and in the model he advanced Hobson raised many points of contemporary significance. While Thompson took a socialist perspective, Hobson wrote as a radical liberal (who would come to assume an increasingly socialist outlook). For the latter, the referendum, rather than the alternative to other changes (as it was for Thompson), would be part of a package that included expansion of the franchise, electoral reform, and changes to the composition and powers of the House of Lords. Much of his programme was similar to that of constitutional reform campaigners more than a century later.[64] Hobson differed from Thompson in another sense. For Hobson, the referendum was a protective device more than a means of driving through change. Like a number of other reform advocates considered in this book, he identified a flaw in the UK constitutional system. The (gradual) coming of democracy entailed the aggrandizement of the Commons, as the directly elected chamber of Parliament, and the diminution of previously existing balancing mechanisms, in particular the Lords and the monarchy. The executive, through a more tightly organised party system, was able in turn to exercise powerful influence on the Commons, partially subject to small closely coordinated groups of MPs. The referendum, in the Hobson model, was a means of preventing the misuse or abuse of this power.

One fear for Hobson was what he described as 'Caesarism, where a magnetic party leader' seized 'the imagination of the populace' or successfully achieved

[58] ibid, 39.
[59] ibid, 45.
[60] ibid, 48.
[61] ibid, 47.
[62] ibid, 48.
[63] ibid, 48.
[64] See, for instance, the work of the pressure group, Unlock Democracy, (the elected governing council of which I am a member): http://www.unlockdemocracy.org last accessed 7 September 2018.

'supremacy among competing politicians'. The phenomenon he described shared features with that sometimes labelled 'populism'. For Hobson, the referendum was insurance against a charismatic ascendancy. However, some commentators today regard referendums – including the 2016 vote – as potentially providing a vehicle for, rather than check upon, populist tendencies.[65] Moreover, while Hobson saw referendums as a means by which voters could provide a clear view on a definite issue, critics of their use hold that voters may not make their decision solely on a basis of the specific question asked, if at all, using it, for example, to express dissatisfaction with the government.[66]

Hobson perceived popular votes as a means by which those taking part could become better informed about political issues. Public knowledge regarding the EU is surely greater now than it was before the referendum was called and in this sense the outcome Hobson hoped for has been achieved. However, in the Brexit context, the concept of information has itself become a subject of controversy. Hobson suggested that members of the public would 'find trusted advisers and exponents, skilled interpreters' to elucidate the subject matter for them. Yet we have seen how Carswell and Hannan promoted the very idea of 'experts' as suspect, characterising them as just another interest group invested in the existing system. Michael Gove appeared to echo this point during the campaign, which was representative of a wider attitude among public advocates of leaving.[67] On the 'remain' side, there have been complaints about the generation of misinformation and even psychological exploitation, both through traditional methods of campaigning and online initiatives.[68] The reference Hobson made to 'the manipulation of electoral opinion through the public house, the Press, the pulpit, and those other instruments of popular instruction which depend for their financial support upon the charity of the propertied classes' shows that suspicions regarding the exercise of covert influence long predate 2016. The account Hobson provided of such forces perhaps creates a flaw in his theory. Would they not also work to pollute referendums, undermining his hope that such popular votes might elicit an informed verdict on a specific issue from a public that became educated and engaged in the process? Harder to dispute from the perspective

[65] 'Brexit populism targets the democratic process', Opinion, *Financial Times*, 15 November 2017.

[66] House of Lords Select Committee on the Constitution, *Referendums in the United Kingdom* (London, Stationery Office, 2010) 19.

[67] See eg Dominic Cummings, 'On the referendum #20: the campaign, physics and data science – Vote Leave's "Voter Intention Collection System" (VICS) now available for all', *Dominic Cummings's Blog*, 29 October 2016: https://dominiccummings.com/2016/10/29/on-the-referendum-20-the-campaign-physics-and-data-science-vote-leaves-voter-intention-collection-system-vics-now-available-for-all/ last accessed 22 August 2018.

[68] eg John Lichfield, 'Boris Johnson's £350m claim is bogus. Here's why', *Guardian*, 18 September 2017: https://www.theguardian.com/commentisfree/2017/sep/18/boris-johnson-350-million-claim-bogus-foreign-secretary last accessed 7 September 2018. For controversy around online activities, see chs 2 and 10.

of 2016, however, is the potential Hobson foresaw for referendums to stimulate participation, with a turnout (of 72.2 per cent) higher than at any General Election since 1992 (77.7 per cent).

Some of the supposed tendencies against which Hobson aligned himself – such as the attempted manipulation of voters through established channels of influence and the aloofness of civil servants – were similar to those with which supporters of Brexit believed they were in conflict before and after the 2016 referendum. In asserting that to disagree with the use of the referendum was to doubt democracy itself, Hobson expressed a view like those who argued that to question the definitive nature of the EU vote of 2016 was to challenge the popular will.[69] However, as with Thompson, there were important differences between the referendum as advocated by Hobson and that which took place in June 2016. First, Hobson saw the referendum as a means by which the public could veto a course of action that the government of the day wished to pursue. The EU referendum involved the precisely the opposite: a vote that an administration should adopt a policy to which it was expressly opposed. Secondly, an assumption of the Hobson scheme was that the change being voted on was supported by a majority in the Commons. In 2016, it was not.[70] An important source of the immense disruption associated with Brexit was the fact many ministers within the UK government that sought to bring it about had opposed it as a policy, as had most MPs (alongside clear evidence of majority support for 'remain' in the Lords[71]).[72]

Thirdly, Hobson envisaged referendums being held on the passing into law or otherwise of specific legislative provisions. While they might be difficult to understand in all their technicality, they took a precise form that was defined in advance of the vote. As already discussed, the 2016 referendum was held on a vague proposition: remaining within or leaving the EU, rather than a definite measure. The winning option, 'leave', was especially open-ended. It could take many forms, the attainment of most of which was, anyway, dependent upon negotiations with the EU. This divergence from the Hobson model had consequences of a type he expressly sought to avoid. It led to the Cabinet – under the heavy influence of a minority group within the Conservatives – taking on the crucial role of interpreter of an ambiguous referendum result. Fourthly, the role of the Lords in relation to Brexit differed from that envisaged by Hobson.

[69] Brenan O'Neill, 'If Brexit doesn't happen, then Britain isn't a democracy', *Spectator*, 11 July 2017: https://blogs.spectator.co.uk/2017/07/if-brexit-doesnt-happen-then-britain-isnt-a-democracy/ last accessed 7 September 2018.

[70] 'EU vote: Where the Cabinet and other MPs stand', BBC, 22 June 2016: https://www.bbc.co.uk/news/uk-politics-eu-referendum-35616946 last accessed 7 September 2018. See also: Conclusion.

[71] Ashley Kirk L, Patrick Scott and Laura Hughes, 'How could the Lords vote on the Brexit Bill and how does it actually work? *Telegraph*, 1 March 2017: http://www.telegraph.co.uk/news/0/analysis-could-lords-vote-brexit-bill-does-actually-work/ last accessed 7 September 2018.

[72] 'EU vote: Where the Cabinet and other MPs stand', BBC, 22 June 2016: https://www.bbc.co.uk/news/uk-politics-eu-referendum-35616946 last accessed 7 September 2018. See also: Conclusion.

He argued that it should be able to trigger referendums. During the Brexit episode, however, the second chamber was not able unilaterally to force the holding of a second popular vote at a later stage in the process, had it wished to do so. Moreover, while the Lords was able to amend and delay legislation providing for the EU referendum and for the implementation of Brexit, it was subject to political constraints in deploying its powers heavily. It was vulnerable to being portrayed as an unelected body resisting both a popular vote and an elected chamber, and being subject to demands that it should be radically reformed or abolished.[73] Fifthly, Hobson anticipated that referendums would tend to be conservative in their impact, with voters often opposing change. On 23 June 2016 they did not.

In explaining the potential value of referendums Hobson described the danger that the Commons might become subordinate to 'the pertinacious fanaticism of little organised groups representing a small minority of the electorate'. How well did the EU referendum serve as a protection against such an outcome? It might be held that the vote held on 23 June 2016 enabled the preference of the majority to be discerned and followed, preventing the will of a minority from prevailing. However, another interpretation is possible. The sustained existence of a large body of Eurosceptic opinion among the UK public, including Conservative Party members, cannot and should not be disputed. However, the direct cause of the holding of the referendum itself came about because of the concerted and sustained efforts of a minority within a parliamentary Conservative Party which itself never had the support of a majority of those voting in a General Election, let alone of all who were registered to vote. Clear evidence that a majority of the public regarded an EU referendum as an overriding priority is lacking.[74] In any case, on 23 June, while 51.9 per cent of those voting supported 'leave', only slightly above 37 per cent of those who could have taken part favoured this outcome. Moreover, as already discussed, 'leave' was an uncertain proposition, and the interpretation of the result by the UK government – including that it necessitated departing from both the Single Market and the Customs Union – was driven by the same faction that had done most to force the holding of the referendum.[75] It is doubtful that all of those who opted for 'leave' specifically wanted such an outcome when they voted, or – if they were not aware of these details – would have wanted it were it explained to them at the time. It takes relatively little divergence from the

[73] For the tone of coverage, see eg: David Maddox '"You are playing with fire" Anger as unelected Lords vote to DERAIL Brexit', *Express*, 18 April 2018: https://www.express.co.uk/news/politics/948173/brexit-news-eu-uk-house-of-lords-brexit-bill-theresa-may-remain last accessed 7 September 2018.

[74] Nathaniel Copsey and Tim Haughton. 'Farewell Britannia? "Issue Capture" and the Politics of David Cameron's 2013 EU Referendum Pledge' (2014) 52 *JCMS: Journal of Common Market Studies* 74–89. See also Conclusion.

[75] See Conclusion.

variety of Brexit pursued for 51.9 per cent to become a minority. Rather than preventing it, then, the 2016 referendum arguably helped bring about precisely the minority subversion that Hobson feared.

A feature of the 2016 referendum that Hobson did anticipate involved its impact upon the operation of Cabinet. The reference Hobson made to the likelihood of referendums requiring an adjustment in the principle of collective responsibility was rather casual, given the historic importance and centrality of this rule. Like the 1975 European referendum,[76] the 2016 vote saw a suspension of normal rules, with ministers permitted publicly to disagree with the government support for 'remain'. In 2016, even after the campaign was concluded, the new Prime Minister, Theresa May, experienced pronounced difficulties in achieving public Cabinet unity over the appropriate approach.[77] Hobson also allowed for the possibility that referendum defeats could lead to resignations or dissolutions, though he suggested they were not inevitable. Arguably, both took place as a consequence of the 2016 referendum. David Cameron announced his planned departure the day after the vote; and the General Election of 2017 could be seen as a delayed response to the 'leave' result and the difficulties it had created.

III. JOHN ST. LOE STRACHEY: THE REFERENDUM

Hobson and Thompson were participants in a group called the 'Referendum League' that 'met a few times in a committee-room of the House of Commons to discuss preliminaries when the war broke out and men's thoughts were turned to more urgent matters'.[78] Another participant in the League was the political journalist John St. Loe Strachey. A sustained campaigner in this area, his interest dated back to the nineteenth century and his major work on the subject, *The Referendum*, appeared in 1924.[79] Strachey proceeded on the assumption that 'democracy has not only come to stay, but that with all its faults and drawbacks democracy is the fairest, the safest, the most just, and therefore the best way of government'. He defined democracy as 'government by the will of the majority legally and justly expressed'.[80] It was his support for 'the rule of the majority' that led him to advocate the referendum. The representative system, in particular when it involved political parties, meant that there was no guarantee 'that the will of the majority will prevail', unless the referendum

[76] Robert Saunders, *Yes to Europe! The 1975 Referendum and Seventies Britain* (Cambridge, Cambridge University Press, 2018) 96.

[77] See eg Rowena Mason, 'Theresa May defends decision not to sack Boris Johnson', *Guardian*, 3 October 2017: https://www.theguardian.com/politics/2017/oct/03/theresa-may-defends-decision-not-to-sack-boris-johnson last accessed 7 September 2018.

[78] Alex M Thompson, *Here I Lie* (London, George Routledge & Sons, 1937) 132.

[79] John St. Loe Strachey, *The Referendum: A Handbook to the Poll of the People, Referendum, or Democratic Right of Veto on Legislation* (London, T Fisher Unwin, 1924).

[80] ibid, 9.

were introduced.[81] Strachey argued that the use of the referendum would be within English historic traditions, since the idea of 'the Poll of the People' was developed during the Civil War period in the mid-seventeenth century.[82]

Strachey identified a particular fault in the party system, involving the operation of minority sub-groups within them pursuing specific objectives. In circumstances where 'the majority feel that the minority are quite fanatical enough to carry out their threats' to bring down a government if not acceded to 'they will yield to the minority and will use the appeal to Party loyalty to pass a Bill or an amendment which is contrary to the wishes of the majority of the Party, of the majority of the House as a whole, and of the majority of the people'. Faced with this problem Strachey held that 'a corrective is required. It is to be found in the Referendum'.[83] The reform he envisaged would attain a 'combination of representative institutions with pure democracy' that was 'not only necessary but sound'. While 'the people as a whole must say the final word on the really great things, the actual management of the affairs of the country must be conducted by the few'.[84] Strachey went as far as to state that he would 'accept the will of a tyrant' were it 'a majority tyrant'. He was more content to follow a majority that were in the wrong than a minority in the same position. There were, Strachey recognised, conceivable circumstances in which this principle would be problematic, for instance 'if a majority of the people were to decide to introduce slavery into this country'. At this point, 'resistance, even to a majority' would be acceptable. However, such scenarios were theoretical more than real.[85]

Strachey stressed that he favoured the referendum rather than the initiative. The latter, as we have seen, was a means by which members of the public could force an idea of their own onto the political agenda.[86] He regarded the case against the initiative as powerful. It was 'an encouragement to crude legislative schemes'.[87] Strachey then entered:

> a much needed caveat. The Referendum should never be used in answer to abstract questions, as "Are you in favour of a monarchy?" or an Emperor, or a War, or a Peace, or so forth. Those are questions that nobody can or ought to answer in the abstract. If a man of sense is asked, "Are you in favour of a monarchy" he naturally asks, "What kind of monarchy do you mean?" When you have got a definite statement of that kind you can say whether on the whole you are in favour of it or not, but you cannot give that answer to a purely abstract proposition.[88]

[81] ibid, 11.
[82] ibid, 17.
[83] ibid, 25.
[84] ibid, 26.
[85] ibid, 37.
[86] ibid, 24.
[87] ibid, 29.
[88] ibid, 37.

Consequently, a referendum 'ought never to be taken except in regard to a definite Bill in which the proposal to make a new law or to alter an existing law is set forth in the words of the proposed statute as it left the Legislature.' In response to the possible claim that regular voters would not be willing to study the Bill on which they were being asked to pronounce, he argued that most MPs were similarly unaware of the details of the legislation that passed through Parliament.[89] Moreover, while a referendum might be held on a 'complicated measure', an election might involve 'a complicated man like, say for example, Mr. Winston Churchill' or 'a complicated political programme'. Strachey insisted: 'if a man can vote at an election he can vote at a Poll of the People'.[90]

The specific mechanism Strachey advocated involved referendums being held when the House of Commons and House of Lords were in 'deadlock' over a bill. If approved in a referendum, it would pass in the form in which it left the Commons.[91] He argued that, generally, if it lost such a vote 'the Government would not resign, for the very good reason that they still commanded a majority in the House of Commons, which majority did not wish for a Dissolution'.[92] However, Strachey accepted that there might be exceptions to this rule in some circumstances.[93] He hoped that the introduction of the referendum would mean that in parliamentary elections votes were cast on a basis of the perceived strengths of particular candidates rather than their party affiliation.[94]

Strachey was driven by a faith in the majority, and suspicion of the inner machinations of parties, through which committed minorities could, he suspected, come to impose themselves. Once again, his version of the referendum differed substantially from its actual operation in 2016. The view Strachey took that referendums should be held on specific measures was similar to that of Thompson and Hobson, and was not adhered to in 2016. Strachey expressly opposed the use of 'abstract questions', holding that, were someone posed the question 'Are you in favour of a monarchy', it would be reasonable for them to inquire 'What kind of monarchy do you mean?' To extend this logic, if being asked whether the UK should remain within or leave the UK, a voter might wish to know the form which departure might take. The 2016 referendum question, therefore, appeared to be of the type that Strachey sought to preclude.

For Strachey, as for Hobson, the referendum was a means by which the electorate would be given (on the reference of the Lords) the right to approve or veto legislation desired by the government and its majority in the Commons. It was not, for Strachey, a means by which the public could impose laws upon

[89] ibid, 38.
[90] ibid, 38–39.
[91] ibid, 48.
[92] ibid, 48.
[93] ibid, 48–49.
[94] ibid, 49.

Parliament and the executive. In this context, he specifically opposed the initiative, of which Thompson was an advocate. The EU referendum was not the product of the initiative, in that it did not derive specifically from a mechanism for the public triggering of referendums (no such procedure exists in the UK). Yet nor was the 2016 vote in keeping with the Strachey model, since it was not held on a specific legislative measure, and did not involve a popular vote on whether to allow change which the government and Commons wished to bring about. In some ways, the Brexit episode represented success for just the type of group that Strachey hoped to neutralise: a minority (in this instance, within the Conservative Party), dedicated to its cause, to the point of being willing to damage its own party and government. In 2016 the referendum became a tool for such a faction rather than an obstacle to it. Through sustained pressure, it achieved the staging of a popular vote. The 'leave' result it subsequently obtained thereby provided the group with further leverage, working within the party and parliamentary system in pursuit of its goals.[95]

[95] See Conclusion.

5

Representative Democracy: Reform and Challenge

THE DECISION TO leave the European Union is attributable to more than the 2016 referendum. Mechanisms of representative democracy were involved. The development of the European issue in UK politics, for instance, owed much to inter and intra-party relations.[1] Parliamentary elections, their outcomes and the type of candidates that they returned were also significant, both to the holding of the referendum, the campaign that took place, and the response to the 'leave' outcome that it produced.[2] Later chapters will provide a perspective on certain institutions that were important to the Brexit process: the UK Parliament and the devolved legislatures and executives, and how they might change in future. The present focus is on various proposals made over time pertaining to the interface between the public and the organs that govern on its behalf. It is through this point of connection that democracy is able to attain and demonstrate that it has acquired the popular basis that is crucial to its legitimacy.

The chapter also takes into account that the Brexit episode figures in recent suggestions that the overall system of representative democracy might be under threat, in the UK and elsewhere.[3] Some depict Brexit as possibly produced by and contributing to a climate in which longer established principles, practices and institutions might struggle to retain their viability.[4] In such discussions perceived key sources of instability include the supposed rise of populism;[5] the impact of the Internet and social media;[6] and the potential impact of environmental problems such as climate change.[7] The following pages therefore consider past

[1] For an account of the long-term political history, see: Hugo Young, *This Blessed Plot: Britain and Europe from Churchill to Blair* (Basingstoke, Macmillan, 1998).

[2] See chs 1 and 2.

[3] See eg Andrew Hines, 'After Brexit, what does democracy mean?', *The Conversation*, 24 November 2016: http://theconversation.com/after-brexit-what-does-democracy-mean-69251 last accessed 7 September 2018.

[4] eg David Runciman, *How Democracy Ends* (London, Profile, 2018).

[5] eg Benjamin Moffitt, *The Global Rise of Populism: Performance, Political Style and Representation* (Palo Alto, Stanford University Press, 2017).

[6] eg Jamie Bartlett, *The People Vs Tech: How the internet is killing democracy (and how we save it)* (London, Ebury, 2018).

[7] For a critical discussion of this view, see: Daniel J Fiorino, *Can Democracy Handle Climate Change?* (Cambridge, Polity, 2018).

analysis of supposed malaise in the system of representative democracy, and proposed solutions to it, involving either specific alterations to the existing framework, or a more radical restructuring.[8]

I. PROPORTIONAL REPRESENTATION

John H Humphreys published *Proportional Representation: A Study in Methods of Election* in 1911.[9] Like JA Hobson, who had recently made his case for the referendum,[10] Humphreys was influenced by the prospect of a legal limitation on the power of the Lords. He wrote near the culmination of a protracted struggle between, on the one hand, the Liberal government and its base in the House of Commons and, on the other hand, the House of Lords and its inbuilt Conservative majority. Following two General Elections during 1910, the Liberals retained office (though without regaining the overall Commons majority they had won in 1906, becoming dependent on Irish Nationalists) and, at the time Humphreys produced his work, had introduced the Bill that would become the Parliament Act 1911. The Act would serve legally to circumscribe the powers of the Lords, removing it completely from authorisation (or otherwise) of the Budget, and meaning that, in nearly all other forms of legislation, the Commons could ultimately bypass the upper chamber. The passing of this statute would be a crucial stage in a far longer process whereby the Commons, propelled by successive expansions in the franchise from 1832 onwards that enhanced its legitimacy, became clearly the preeminent chamber in Parliament.[11] The rise of the Commons was in this sense a central feature of the coming of democracy to the UK (though the process was not complete by 1911, with the parliamentary franchise far from universal, excluding all women and many men). Humphreys noted that the 'conception of the House of Commons as the central and predominant factor in the constitution, exercising sovereign power because it represents the nation which it governs, has been notably strengthened during the last fifty years'.[12] Observing that the Lords had nonetheless obstructed the legislative programme of the radical Liberal government that first took office in 1905, winning a substantial election victory the following year, Humphreys remarked that:

> [t]hese assertions of authority on the part of the House of Lords called forth from the Commons a fresh demand for complete sovereignty – a demand based on the ground

[8] Online issues are addressed fully in ch 10.

[9] John H Humphreys, *Proportional Representation: A Study in Methods of Election* (Whitefish, Kessinger Publishing, 2004).

[10] See ch 4.

[11] For a classic study of this episode and its significance, see: Roy Jenkins, *Mr Balfour's Poodle* (London, Bloomsbury, 2012).

[12] John H Humphreys, *Proportional Representation: A Study in Methods of Election* (Whitefish, Kessinger Publishing, 2004) 8.

> that the House of Commons expresses the will of the people, and that the rejection by the hereditary House of measures desired by the nation's representatives is directly opposed to the true principles of representative government.[13]

The Parliament Bill, Humphreys held, represented an attempt to express this perception in hard legal form. In the new constitutional environment it would establish, 'the national will must remain the final authority in legislation, and the ultimate position of the House of Commons in the constitution and in public esteem will depend upon the confidence with which it can be regarded as giving expression to that will'. The Commons, Humphreys went on, was unable to 'claim to be the sole authority for legislation without provoking searching inquiries into the methods of election by which it is brought into being'.[14] When General Elections took place, voters were required to select 'representatives who shall have full power to speak in their name on all questions which may arise during the lifetime of a Parliament'. Yet while there were generally multiple matters that required attention, there were normally only two candidates on offer to electors.[15] Humphreys expressed the view that supporters of 'the final and complete triumph of representative institutions' and who hoped that 'the House of Commons shall not only maintain, but increase, the prestige that has hitherto been associated with it, must … endeavour to strengthen its position by making it in fact, as it is in theory, fully representative of the nation'.[16]

Alongside the recasting of the balance of power between the Commons and the Lords, Humphreys identified another tendency that called into question the existing electoral system. This additional development was what he referred to as 'the rise of a new organized party within the House of Commons itself'. Once again, the onset of democracy had raised questions about the functioning of the system. The expansion of the franchise had facilitated the appearance of the Labour Party as an electoral force, leading Humphrey to remark that 'a system which fails in many respects to meet the requirements of two political parties cannot possibly do justice to the claims of three parties to fair representation in the House of Commons'.[17] Humphreys felt further that there was a more general tendency towards reform intended to perfect the democratic system, and that wider social trends added to the case for change. He remarked '[a]ccuracy and precision are being demanded with ever-increasing force in all other departments of human activity; on what ground then can we in the most delicate of all – that of government – refuse to recognise their value?'[18]

[13] ibid, 9.
[14] ibid, 9.
[15] ibid, 10.
[16] ibid, 12.
[17] ibid, 14.
[18] ibid, 17.

Humphreys identified various flaws in the existing system. In analysing the eight general elections that had occurred since single-member constituencies had become standard under the *Redistribution of Seats Act 1885*, he found a tendency for inflated parliamentary majorities for the winning party;[19] and various problematic territorial distortions.[20] The delineation of boundaries, he found, was crucial to determining outcomes, prompting gerrymandering activities.[21] Other more general consequences of the electoral system included the generation of false impressions of public opinion, that in turn became the basis for legislative measures; the vulgarisation of political debate; and a tendency towards increasingly uniform discipline within parties.[22]

After considering two broad categories of proportional representation – the Single Transferable Vote (STV) and the party list system, Humphreys found both had advantages relative to the existing UK method. However, he concluded that, on balance, STV was more suitable for the UK.[23] As well as the Commons, Humphreys suggested that proportional representation in some form might be appropriate for the Lords as well.[24] He saw further potential uses for this general approach to voting. Were the UK to adopt a system of 'Federal Home Rule', any new sub-UK legislatures formed should use proportional representation.[25] Furthermore, Humphreys held that the formation of a Parliament for the whole empire, a project that had been promoted by campaigners and certain politicians for a number of decades, should if it took place also involve the use of a proportional voting mechanism.[26] He concluded that '[w]hether it is a question of improving existing institutions, or the creation of further representative bodies, the method of election is all important. All other departments of human activity show continuous improvement, and the substitution of scientific for rule-of-thumb methods of election is an improvement long-overdue'.[27]

Humphreys, like other authors discussed here, had identified a particular problem at the core the UK constitution. While not objecting to the coming (though not by this point full arrival) of democracy, he noted the tendency for it to remove a traditional balancing mechanism in the constitution. The predominance of the Commons would soon be legally confirmed, definitively removing key powers from the Lords. He might have added that the monarchy had already declined as a constitutional counterweight. The prospect of such a powerful, unchecked, force in the Commons was a source of apprehension for a number of observers. Their basic concern was that a single party could come to dominate

[19] ibid, 19–21.
[20] ibid, 21–27.
[21] ibid, 27–31.
[22] ibid, 39–51.
[23] ibid, 173.
[24] ibid, 224.
[25] ibid, 226.
[26] ibid, 9.
[27] ibid, 228.

the Commons (perhaps without justifying such a presence in terms of votes cast at an election) and, using tight parliamentary discipline, force through measures, possibly of a constitutionally objectionable nature, without being subject to effective restrictions.

Those vexed about such a scenario responded in a number of ways. One approach, as we have seen, was to propose the use of the referendum as a constraining mechanism under which the public could veto specific measures. For Humphreys, the solution was to ensure that the composition of the Commons genuinely reflected the preferences of voters, justifying its claim to be representative. His proposal has not yet been adopted. One of the consequences of retaining the so-called 'First-Past-the-Post' system has been that parties, especially in the period since World War II, have been able to secure outright Commons majorities having won only pluralities of votes cast (and possibly coming second in the popular vote). This tendency can in turn magnify the internal issues of a given party, subordinating the actions of government to these concerns. Both European referendums in the UK (1975 and 2016) were held by governments with small but unearned Commons majorities formed by single parties that were divided over the issue. It is reasonable to speculate that, under a proportional system, the imperative to hold such votes might not have manifested itself.

To focus on the specific case of 2016, it could be argued that, had seat totals reflected 7votes cast in the General Election of the previous year, then the Conservatives might well have formed a coalition with the United Kingdom Independence Party (the two parties respectively secured 36.8 per cent and 12.6 per cent of support from those who voted – perhaps they could have obtained help as well from the Democratic Unionist Party, with 0.6 per cent, and the Ulster Unionist Party had received 0.4 per cent). A referendum on EU membership, it might be concluded, would have come about anyway. However, under a different electoral system that removed the need for tactical voting, we could expect voters to behave differently, though it is difficult to predict what the precise outcome would be in such circumstances. A connected and more fundamental consequence of the use of proportional representation in some form would be that the party system as a whole would be likely to change. The First-Past-the-Post method creates an incentive for the maintenance of broad parties, combining within them often difficult to reconcile perspectives and factions. In recent decades, the strict parliamentary discipline within major parties to which Humphreys referred has eroded somewhat.[28] But this trend away from cohesion, including over the European issue, could partly be attributed to the imperative to sustain the existence of single parties, notwithstanding serious differences. The alternative course of action: to contest elections separately, would be, in electoral terms, unpalatable under First-Past-the-Post. This

[28] Philip Cowley, *The Rebels: How Blair Mislaid His Majority* (London, Politico's, 2005).

concern can reinforce the potential, noted by Strachey, for minorities within parties, if sufficiently determined and willing to inflict self-harm, to impose objectives on parties, that accept their agenda rather than succumb to electoral division. Splits would not be undertaken lightly under a proportional electoral system, but the possible negative consequences would be lessened. Moreover, if parties did not split, then others might form anyway, since the barriers to new entrants into the system would probably be lower. The outcome would be that voters were better served by a wider range of viable parties.

We might ask various questions, then, about how the UK party political system could be expected to function had a model similar to that recommended by Humphreys been introduced at some point. Would there be a single Conservative Party united around a referendum pledge, and another party, UKIP, also advocating such a vote? Or might there be a more moderate, Christian Democrat style, pro-EU party, and a Eurosceptic party? The same questions could be applied across the political spectrum. Would there, for instance, be multiple, viable, parties of the left? A more successful Green Party? Would the swing back towards two-party dominance at the General Election of 2017 have been possible if there were not a single Conservative Party and a single Labour Party as there is now? Would a government that wished or felt compelled to hold a European referendum ever have come about? To seek to provide answers is to speculate. But what would not be possible would be a party with a minority of votes winning a Commons majority, forming a government, and holding a referendum on a matter of major importance over which it was fundamentally divided but reluctant, for electoral reasons, to separate.

The powerful imperative for the maintenance of the two main parties – to which First-Past-the-Post is an important contributor – continued to manifest itself in the post-referendum environment. It is hard to imagine a more important issue over which to differ than the desirability or otherwise of leaving the EU with no agreement. Yet the Conservative Party sought to continue functioning while accommodating those who held opposing views on this subject.[29] In Labour, there was a division – involving the EU and other matters – between the leadership and the majority of the parliamentary party.[30] Fear of the electoral consequences of a split served to discourage a breakaway by MPs (partly based on observation of the experience of the Social Democratic Party in the 1980s, the formation of which indirectly helped the Conservative Party win the 1983 and 1987 general elections).[31] When considering what made the UK different

[29] 'Hardline Tories tell May: get ready for no deal Brexit', *Guardian*, 24 June 2018: https://www.theguardian.com/politics/2018/jun/24/hardline-tories-tell-theresa-may-get-ready-for-no-deal-brexit last accessed 7 September 2018.

[30] Steve Richards, 'Labour's Brexit chaos is now so exposed it threatens to tear the party apart', *Guardian*, 25 January 2017: https://www.theguardian.com/commentisfree/2017/jan/25/labour-brexit-chaos-tear-party-apart-splits-europe 7 September 2018.

[31] See: Polly Toynbee, 'Dear Labour, split the party and you'll regret it. Love from an SDP candidate', *Guardian*, 26 January 2016: https://www.theguardian.com/commentisfree/2016/jan/26/labour-party-split-sdp-candidate last accessed 7 September 2018.

to other EU member states, leading it to vote in 1975 and 2016 on whether it wished to continue participation in the process of continental integration, and adopting a policy of leaving in 2016, part of the explanation is that the parliamentary electoral system inadvertently produced a disposition in this direction. The UK parliamentary electoral system and the two-party predominance it encourages have been, according to their advocates, sources of stability and accountability.[32] Yet, they helped bring about a circumstance in which a flawed referendum was held on a subject of transcendent importance. Following the vote, many MPs were constrained in fully exercising their judgement as elected representatives – the system constrained them from functioning as proper representatives.

II. THE 'NEW BRITAIN'

In 1942, Richard Acland published *What it will be like in the new Britain*, the first of three texts considered in this work that were written during World War II.[33] He had previously been a Liberal MP; and would later sit for Labour in the Commons. In between, he was a co-founder of the Common Wealth Party, that successfully contested by-elections during the period of war-time truce between the Conservative and Labour parties. Ideas that infused Common Wealth can be found in *What it will be like*. He advocated the adoption of an economic model of 'Common Ownership'[34] that would 'be directed by a democratically elected Parliament'. Acland believed that, in the society he envisaged, the public would involve themselves politically 'with much greater vigour than they do today'. People would 'hold meetings and demonstrations. They will form organisations either to support or to oppose the Government, or to advance particular causes'. Faced with these various expressions of popular opinion, Parliament would 'decide to which all of the things that need doing we shall devote our resources, and in what proportions'. It would not, however, use 'some fixed Five-or Four-Year Plan', but would establish priorities for action.[35]

Subject to the views of Parliament and public, the Cabinet would set the overall policy, supported by an 'Economic General Staff'. The Staff would be 'a very substantial organisation' and would 'conduct a continuous review of our resources'. Acland described the division between the Cabinet and Parliament on the one hand and the Staff on the other hand in the following terms: '[w]hen Cabinet and Parliament have decided upon so many hospitals, so many schools,

[32] Dan Hodges, 'No, Britain does not want proportional representation', *Telegraph*, 1 June 2015: https://www.telegraph.co.uk/news/general-election-2015/politics-blog/11643323/The-electoral-reform-lobby-needs-to-sober-up.html last accessed 7 September 2018.

[33] Richard Acland, *What it will be like in the new Britain* (London, Victor Gollancz, 1942).

[34] ibid, 20.

[35] ibid, 24.

and so much re-housing in so many years, the General Staff, or one of its departments, will also exercise final responsibility over all questions of location of industry'. It would in turn issue instructions 'to the relevant industries'.[36]

Within this system, Acland saw a need for a reform of representative institutions. He recognised that parties would still be needed because '[d]emocracy, if it is to function, requires organized criticism directed by and centring upon a team of men who are prepared to back their criticism by taking over the task of government and doing it better'. Yet Acland hoped to 'diminish party-mindedness' on the part of members of the public.[37] He held that 'we should try to prevent the situation in which large numbers of citizens attach themselves to one of these teams and support them rather as the inhabitants of Chelsea support the Chelsea Football Club'.[38] For Acland, if his plans for a society based on common ownership were to be viable, it was necessary to achieve 'a change in the very nature of individuals', including 'a greater willingness to take a live interest in politics and to give support to the party which is right rather than to the party for which one's grandfather always voted'. Nonetheless, he saw merit in the existence of a group of opposition politicians 'united amongst themselves and divided from the Government on some fundamental issue or group of issues'. With this need in mind, Acland opposed the electoral 'truce' then in force between the main parties, which were participating in the wartime coalition government.[39] Under the common ownership system, Acland envisaged that, while party divisions would be necessary, they would take on a new form. Rather than disagreeing over whether or not this particular economic model was desirable, they would accept it as a given, with conflict taking place within this overall framework.[40]

Acland set out further changes to the representative system. The workload of MPs was rising, and they should be provided with 'secretaries, who have gone through a course of training in the principal acts and regulations which the member must master'. A more radical proposal was that MPs be permitted to nominate a 'deputy … whose views … correspond closely as possible with his own'. This individual would be able to participate in parliamentary proceedings in place of the Member. Possibly, the Commons could be divided into two bodies: 'the supreme Council of State' and 'the Council for Minor Matters', with the deputy attending the latter. Acland also held that MPs should receive 'a reasonable income for life even if they are defeated at a subsequent election'. This provision could address the problem of 'excessive party discipline' and an aversion to 'frank expression of opinion' on their part.[41] Within the Commons,

[36] ibid, 25.
[37] ibid, 167.
[38] ibid, 167–68.
[39] ibid, 168.
[40] ibid, 168–69.
[41] ibid, 170.

the Speaker might take on the additional role of a 'Judge', who, towards the end of major debates, would 'point out whether there were serious arguments advanced by one side which had not been referred to by the other'. Inside the executive, 'shadow Ministers of the Opposition' would be given the right to work within Whitehall departments, to give them access to information upon which government decisions were based.[42]

Acland then turned his attention to the press. He proposed a system that would secure a series of objectives: the end of control by the 'powerful individual owner or small group of owners'; no ability on the part of government to prevent 'criticism'; a 'reasonable probability that every kind of newspaper for which there is a substantial demand will in fact be published' and that 'any important set of opinions held by any substantial number of people' would have editorial backing from 'at least one newspapers'; and that minority opinions could be supported in some newspaper columns.[43] Printing presses would be subject to collective ownership; and decisions about what titles should be produced would fall to a Publications Commission.[44] To ensure independence, decisions about membership of the Commission would be subject to veto by the Leader of the Opposition.[45] Acland anticipated that 'under Common Ownership the community will desire to set aside quite substantial sums of public money for the support of journalistic enterprise'.[46]

The model of full common ownership Acland advanced may seem of its time – though the Labour Party seems to have become more disposed to such a position during the Corbyn era.[47] But aside from the relevance or otherwise of his core agenda, the subsidiary objectives Acland set out retain pertinence. He judged that meaningful opposition was necessary to a democratic constitution. It has been lacking from Labour over Brexit. For instance, despite its previous position to the contrary, the party supported the referendum bill in 2015; and the Labour leadership accepted the general principle that the 'leave' vote created an irresistible requirement to exit the EU, voting discretionary power to the executive in 2017.[48] The process that Acland regarded as essential – the public contestation of a government programme by a rival group with its own alternative values and policies – was compromised more fundamentally still over Brexit. Divisions over the issue in both the Conservative and Labour parties meant that

[42] ibid, 171.
[43] ibid, 173.
[44] ibid, 173.
[45] ibid, 174.
[46] ibid, 175.
[47] Benjamin Kentish, 'Corbyn supporters launch campaign to bring back Labour's historic Clause IV and "end capitalism"', *Independent*, 27 February 2018: https://www.independent.co.uk/news/uk/politics/jeremy-corbyn-labour-party-clause-iv-4-capitalism-labour4clause4-a8231351.html last accessed 7 September 2018.
[48] See ch 2.

at times it seemed that there was no coherent government position, and even if there had been the opposition lacked an internally agreed basis on which to challenge it.

The idea advanced by Acland that MPs lack the capacity properly to hold the government to account remains relevant. Brexit has been associated with a growth in the demands and importance of primary and secondary legislation. The suggestion of providing MPs with a guaranteed income for life would no doubt be controversial if proposed today. However, in the contemporary environment, the purpose of protecting the independence of MPs has an added significance. Acland had in mind pressure from above, with the party machine imposing itself on members. A further issue presently involves the threat of deselection from organised activists, both in the Conservatives and Labour, in pursuit of particular agendas, including in relation to Brexit.[49] The idea of high quality journalism as a public good, for which proper funding sources should be found, has resonance in the context of the debate about 'fake news' in the present era.[50]

Overall, Acland recognised – without enthusiasm – that, even given radical social reform, the basic features of the representative system, including the parties, ought to remain in place. His vision was more a reimagining of the landscape than a replacement. Acland saw one of his ambitions achieved in that a process known as 'partisan dealignment' took place in the UK from the 1960s, with automatic support for the two main parties generally declining (though the 2017 General Election saw a notable reversal of this process).[51] But in present circumstances, though the public might have become increasingly involved in politics, whether they have done so in an independent-minded fashion of which Acland would have approved is less clear. A strong case could be made that increases in participation, for instance in the 2016 referendum and 2017 General Election, seem to have operated in parallel with heightened polarisation of outlook, rather than an openness to diverse ideas and deliberation.[52] Frustrations about the functioning of the media in the Internet era are discussed in chapter ten. As we will see, though many aspects of the communications

[49] Patrick Macguire, 'Now it's Conservative, not Labour, MPs who fear deselection', *New Statesman*, 12 June 2018: https://www.newstatesman.com/politics/uk/2018/06/now-it-s-conservative-not-labour-mps-who-fear-deselection last accessed 7 September 2018.

[50] eg Mark Thompson, 'In a world of fake news, real journalism must be paid for', *Guardian*, 16 December 2016: https://www.theguardian.com/commentisfree/2016/dec/16/fake-news-journalism-digital last accessed 7 September 2018.

[51] Ivor Crewe, Bo Särlvik and James Alt, 'Partisan dealignment in Britain 1964–1974' (1977) 7(2) *British Journal of Political Science* 129–90; Ivor Crewe, 'The electorate: partisan dealignment ten years on' (1983) 6(4) *West European Politics* 183–91; Patrick Dunleavy, 'Facing up to multi-party politics: how partisan dealignment and PR voting have fundamentally changed Britain's party systems' (2005) 58(3) *Parliamentary affairs* 503–32.

[52] See eg Jonathan Wheatley, 'The polarisation of party supporters since 2015 and the problem of the "empty centre"', 6 June 2017: http://blogs.lse.ac.uk/politicsandpolicy/the-polarisation-of-party-supporters-since-2015/ last accessed 7 September 2018.

environment differ today, frustrations about it supposedly being imbalanced and dominated by privileged interests remain. The proposal Acland made for a Publications Commission demonstrates that schemes to achieve through public intervention a media more supportive of democratic processes can stray into difficult territory. The concept of an official committee deciding what can and cannot be published is not comforting.

III. PARLIAMENTARY REPRESENTATION

Parliamentary Representation by JFS Ross first appeared in 1943.[53] It opened by stating that '[i]n recent years dissatisfaction with the working of the parliamentary system has been widespread'. Democracy had collapsed in many parts of Europe, while in the UK and the US 'criticism of representative institutions has come from all sides and has given evidence that is based on deep-seated uneasiness and is not merely superficial or factitious'. While, in the circumstances of the conflict then taking place, such dissent was less prominent, a genuine 'recovery of confidence in the system' had not taken place. Ross insisted that it was not wise to:

> disregard the evidence that the system is not working well. With the adequacy of democratic institutions widely questioned and their efficiency unfavourably compared with that of the totalitarian dictatorships, it behoves upholders of representative government to see that it has a fair chance to function properly. Nay more; we must see that government is representative, that we are not fobbed off with a spurious article, that we do not allow oligarchy to masquerade as democracy.[54]

Ross identified a range of possible subjects of investigation, then explained that his particular focus would be on 'the *personnel* of parliament. What sort of people do we choose to represent us? How are they selected as candidates in the first case? Why are these kinds of people chosen and not others? Taking the whole House together, what are its outstanding personal characteristics?'[55] In a survey of the personal characteristics of members, he remarked on 'the *elderliness* of the House of Commons'; and on 'the dominating position of *public school* men' (Ross was not seemingly making a point about gender balance here, though he did do so elsewhere). He observed that 'the House is in no sense a microcosm of the community: the distribution of occupations is utterly dissimilar'. Ross found that 'a huge proportion of members belong to the *talking classes*, and in particular to the legal profession'. A further issue he

[53] JFS Ross, *Parliamentary Representation* (London, Eyre & Spottiswoode, 1948). This second edition reproduced the 1943 version in its original form and included additional material covering the 1945 General Election.

[54] ibid, 7.

[55] ibid, 8.

identified was 'the big proportion of members who hold, or are related to holders of, hereditary titles'. Lastly, Ross remarked upon 'the conspicuous failure of the House as a representation of the political opinion of the country, even as recorded in votes'. He noted that General Elections were frequently described as 'a *gamble*', a term he regarded as appropriate given that their 'results are not merely an exaggeration of prevalent public opinion – they are a capricious and unpredictable distortion of it'.[56] Ross summarised: 'In no single respect – age, education, occupation, sex, social standing, party – does the composition of the House of Commons reflect that of the community. The differences, moreover, are not the minor deviations inseparable from any system of representation: they are radical divergences.'[57] Members came from the 'privileged classes', he held. Within the Labour movement, trade union officials comprised the elite group, while beyond it, their political status was linked to their 'social position'. This echelon might be termed 'the upper classes' or 'wealthier classes' or 'political classes'.[58]

On the basis of his study, Ross reached conclusions about the need for a 'scheme of reform of parliamentary representation'.[59] He found that the existing 'single-member majority system' of election failed to provide voters with sufficient choice or means of expressing more sophisticated preferences.[60] Ross concluded that 'the present system of voting ... must give way to totally different system if the franchise is to be made a real instrument of democratic government'.[61] His second general proposal involved the quality of parliamentarians. While many of them were 'men and women of fine quality ... there are other members poorly qualified and lacking in the right spirit ... many members give little more than their spare time to their duties, and ... the general level of ability and character is not nearly as high as it could and should be'. Ross concluded '[t]he second-rate and third-rate are not good enough: we want first-rate members and we want their full service'. There was, he judged, a need to derive Members of Parliament from a far broader base.[62]

Ross proposed a programme to address the defects he identified. First, he advocated public subsidy for the election expenses of every candidate. To discourage what he termed '[s]ectional and "freak" candidates' it would be adjusted in accordance with votes actually received.[63] Secondly, Ross supported the payment of a 'full ... salary and expenses' to all MPs.[64] Thirdly, he proposed time-limited payments for MPs who had lost their seats. These three changes would, Ross

[56] ibid, 115.
[57] ibid, 116.
[58] ibid, 117.
[59] ibid, 198.
[60] ibid, 198.
[61] ibid, 199.
[62] ibid, 199.
[63] ibid, 205.
[64] ibid, 208.

hoped, make it more possible for those without privileged backgrounds to enter into politics.[65] To address distortions in party representation, Ross advocated abolishing the 'single-member majority system'.[66] Of other options available, he regarded 'the second ballot and the alternative vote' as intended 'to bolster up the old outworn method of election'. Ross preferred STV, which was 'a new method, essentially modern in its strength and flexibility and smoothness of working'.[67] Though these combined measures, he felt, would make a substantial contribution to an improvement in the composition of the Commons along the lines he desired, he recognised that 'we cannot by any direct means ensure that every member shall possess the high degree of integrity and intelligence and the particular kind of temperament and education that' was 'desirable'. Consequently he proposed a further measure, obliging 'every candidate to present verified credentials to the electorate he seeks to represent in Parliament'.[68] He described the process as follows:

> [The candidate] should be obliged to state his age, date of birth, and place of residence; to specify any university degrees, diplomas, professional qualifications, and so on, that he holds; to give the essential facts of his career, including his service on county councils, borough councils, education committees, etc. (if any), and his present occupation if he has one; and he should have to have all these facts verified by some such independent body as the Civil Service Commission, which would be quite impartial and trustworthy.[69]

While this first aspect of the procedure would be mandatory, there would also be an optional aspect. The candidate 'should ... be given the opportunity of undergoing voluntarily a series of psychological intelligence and aptitude tests ... These tests might be specially devised and prepared for the purpose by the National Institute [of Industrial Psychology]'.[70] They would be 'optional' and would not involve 'passing or failing'. However, if an individual had chosen to take them their results would be 'officially published' along with the compulsory information. Ross judged '[t]his would give the electors dependable information about each candidate – now sometimes sadly lacking – and some means of comparing the qualifications, experience, and personal characteristics of those who sought their votes'. While they were not compulsory, '[c]andidates who shirked the psychological tests would have to put up with the inferences that the electors might draw as to the reasons for their unwillingness to be tested'. Ross recognised that his proposals would be controversial among candidates, though he held that those that were suitable need not fear them; and those likely

[65] ibid, 209.
[66] ibid, 216.
[67] ibid, 217.
[68] ibid, 230.
[69] ibid, 230.
[70] ibid, 230–31.

to suffer included 'the rich non-entity who at present is able to "buy" a seat, and the shadier type of candidate with a plausible tongue and, like Chu Chin Chow, "a record strangely clean"'.[71]

In his analysis and proposals, Ross combined what seems today to be a flavour of both the contemporary and the anachronistic. Like many reform advocates before and since, and a number of current commentators, he judged the democratic or 'parliamentary system' across the world to face challenges. His complaint that parliamentarians were not properly representative either of the profile of voters or of their party preferences remains familiar to the twenty-first century reader.[72] His support for STV – repeating earlier recommendations from Humphreys and others – continues to be echoed today, as part of ongoing calls from electoral reformers for the introduction of proportional representation in parliamentary polls.[73] (In 2011, a referendum was held on the possibility of introducing the Alternative Vote, a system that Ross disliked. The proposal was defeated.)

Some of the Ross proposals could jar for a contemporary audience. His recommendation that public funding be used to support prospective, serving and former MPs, though to some extent now implemented, would be likely to generate controversy. Criticism of politicians as a group in recent years has often focused on the idea that they comprise a caste isolated from the rest of society for whom party politics is a life-long career, precluding other valuable experience.[74] For those who subscribe to such criticisms, the Ross proposals might appear to facilitate this undesirable tendency. But Ross makes his point well in this regard. To deny such subsidy for the political system seems likely to increase the likelihood that it will be dominated by the privileged. Another objection that the Ross scheme might have met in the current environment is that, although his avowed intention was to widen participation in parliamentary politics, his ideas were of elitist implication. For some today – perhaps including those of a similar persuasion to Carswell and Hannan, whose text we have already considered[75] – those that Ross dismissed as '[s]ectional and "freak" candidates' were precisely the types who should be encouraged, since they are sourced from outside the entrenched system. The idea of registering personal details with an independent body that would then verify their accuracy, and of taking 'psychological intelligence and aptitude tests', even if they were voluntary, would surely be

[71] ibid, 231.

[72] Though for evidence of a shift towards a more representative Commons, see: Cherry Wilson, 'Election Results 2017: The most diverse Parliament yet', BBC, 11 June 2017: https://www.bbc.co.uk/news/election-2017-40232272 last accessed 7 September 2018.

[73] See: the Electoral Reform Society website at: https://www.electoral-reform.org.uk/campaigns/electoral-reform/ last accessed 7 September 2018.

[74] See eg James Kirkup, 'Can we stop the rise of the career politician?', *Telegraph*, 25 November 2014: https://www.telegraph.co.uk/news/politics/11251185/Can-we-stop-the-rise-of-the-career-politician.html last accessed 7 September 2018.

[75] See ch 3.

controversial now. Who, we might ask, has the legitimacy to determine the criteria against which the appropriateness of a person to serve as a representative might be measured? Complaints about experts, 'establishment' manipulation and imposed uniformity would no doubt arise. However, a consideration of this aspect of the Ross model is a useful exercise. It suggests that, while some might take a view that the quality of politicians is unsatisfactory, measures intended to improve their calibre are likely to prove problematic.

IV. UNOFFICIAL CONSERVATIVE REFORM PROPOSALS

Some Proposals for Constitutional Reform was the work of a group of Conservatives, namely: The Right Hon Sir Cuthbert Headlam MP; Viscount Castlereagh; G Kitson Clark; Viscount Davidson MP; Major-General GP Dawnay; A Headlam-Morley (the sole female member); Douglas Jerrold; Lord Phillimore; KWM Pickthorne MP; Viscount Ridely; and Charles Taylor MP. They also took advice from the Marquess of Salisbury and Lord Hankey, though neither took responsibility for the product of the exercise. The text was completed in advance of the General Election of July 1945 (at which the Labour Party, to the surprise of many, decisively defeated the Conservatives). But owing to paper rationing it was not issued until after this event. It was not an official party statement, but clearly reflected prominent currents of Conservative thought.

The group proceeded 'on the assumption that there will be no revolutionary change in the Constitution, and that alterations in the machinery of government and in the procedure of Parliament will be carried out by traditional and orderly methods in order to meet new conditions and changing circumstances'.[76] It asserted that 'it would be idle to deny that the efficacy of our established institutions and traditional forms of government has in recent years been seriously called in question'.[77] This discontent arose from a view that interwar governments had not managed adequately to address both foreign and domestic challenges, such as the threat from the Axis powers and economic problems.[78] The gravest threat to existing structures, the paper held, came from Marxian socialists.[79] But it judged that a desire to supplant the parliamentary system of the UK was lacking among the public.[80]

The text considered a range of matters: making political careers more possible for those without financial means, the attainment of a more inclusive and outward-facing Civil Service, and the streamlining of Cabinet. It also gave

[76] *Some Proposals for Constitutional Reform: Being the Recommendations of a Group of Conservatives* (London, Eyre & Spotiswoode, 1946) 7.
[77] ibid.
[78] ibid, 9–10.
[79] ibid, 11.
[80] ibid, 19.

consideration to the House of Lords, which had seen its legislative and financial powers curbed in 1911 but was at this point almost wholly composed of hereditary members. The group held that an elected second chamber, under whatever system was used, would inevitably become more assertive in its dealings with the Commons, on the grounds that it had the necessary legitimacy to justify doing so. The text also warned against 'the duplication of elections', on the grounds that they could 'dissipate the force of democracy'. Moreover, there was a large reservoir of genuine ability in the Lords that would be lost were it to become elected.[81] The authors also rejected the idea of a mixed elected and hereditary Lords. Such schemes, it recorded, were motivated by a desire to enable the second chamber to regain powers to block legislation; but the continued presence of members of the Lords who had arrived by virtue of their parentage would undermine the claim for such a reversal. Nor did the group find favour with models – such as Beatrice and Sidney Webb and Winston Churchill had depicted, as we will see later in this book – for a second chamber 'elected by functional or vocational representation'. For the authors of the text, the second chamber had to engage with policy in its entirety, and not simply particular parts of it.[82] Society was an 'organic whole' and it should be represented as such.[83] Foreign efforts to implement such an idea did not suggest it was a desirable example to follow.[84]

The group set out a twin approach to be taken to Lords reform. Various qualifying restrictions would limit the number of hereditary participants in the Lords. The objective was to restrict membership primarily to Peers of the first creation, to those who had long or high-level experience of UK or local politics, and to those who had worked in the military or the Civil Service.[85] The group opposed the idea that peers should determine by vote who 'from among their own number' should sit in the Lords. It argued that this method would produce a Conservative bias because of the existing balance within the Lords. Alongside this hereditary cohort would be introduced a new category of 'Lords of Parliament for Life'.[86] They would not exceed the hereditary group in size. The Prime Minister would make recommendations in consultation with other party leaders. The system would partly be a means of redressing the party imbalance that favoured the Conservatives within the Lords; but non-party political appointment could be made of individuals eminent in different areas of public life.[87] The judicial members of the Lords, and the Anglican Bishops, would remain. The group considered whether specific arrangements

[81] ibid, 53.
[82] ibid, 54.
[83] ibid, 55.
[84] ibid, 55–56.
[85] ibid, 57.
[86] ibid, 59.
[87] ibid, 60.

should be put in place for incorporating senior figures from 'other churches and religious communities'. It decided that the best means of attaining such representation would be through the creation of appropriate individuals as Lords of Parliament.[88] Under the new model envisaged, women would have equal status to men.[89]

The proposals by the Group of Conservatives for the House of Lords are significant both for their analysis and their content. In many ways, the model they set out is similar to the one arrived at today (allowing for the fact that the creation of new hereditary peerages has fallen into disuse). The Life Peerages Act 1958 and House of Lords Act 1999 transformed the second chamber into a mainly appointed, mixed gender, body. Members of the type the Group of Conservatives envisaged: politicians with UK or local level experience, former civil and military servants and prominent individuals from other walks of life now reach the Lords via Life Peerages. The Bishops remain, and there are Peers from senior judicial backgrounds, though the Law Lords themselves have gone (following the creation of a separate Supreme Court under the Constitutional Reform Act 2005, operating from 2009). The Conservatives no longer constitute a majority in the Lords – and nor does any other party. But, contrary to the demands of successive reform campaigners (though not the Group of Conservatives), the second chamber remains unelected.

It was a second chamber in this condition that engaged with Brexit; an episode that has served to emphasise both its strengths and weaknesses. Advantages it displayed included an ability, drawing on the range of expertise and experience contained within it, to address complex issues and work in a cross-party fashion to uphold fundamental matters of constitutional principle. It has performed all of these functions in ways that the House of Commons could not. Yet its shortcomings arose from a lack of democratic legitimacy relative to the House of Commons – a deficiency the Group of Conservatives, alongside others, held should be maintained. Alongside the legal limitations on its powers contained in the Parliament Act 1911 (added to by the Parliament Act 1949) the Lords is politically constrained by its not being elected while the Commons is. The Lords has become more assertive than it was before 1999 and the transition away from the hereditary principle, often working with the Commons to secure legislative amendments.[90] However, it is principally a reactive institution, and when it does engage is wary of overplaying its hand. The House of Lords Select Committee on the Constitution, for instance, as we have seen, carried out excellent work scrutinising the European Union (Amendment) Bill. But its consideration of the legislation providing for the 2016 referendum was conducted in the narrowest

[88] ibid, 60–61.

[89] ibid, 61.

[90] Meg Russell and Maria Sciara, *The House of Lords in 2006: Negotiating a Stronger Second Chamber* (London, Constitution Unit, 2007).

possible terms. In the post-referendum phase, the Lords was largely dealing with the consequences of a major decision already taken in a questionable way. It helped to bring about alterations to some of the details (important nonetheless) of the Brexit policy. But the House of Lords was less effective in challenging the basic premise that leaving the EU was the only proper outcome of the vote held on 23 June 2016; that this obligation to leave had to take a particular form, as discerned by the UK executive; and that the UK constitution had to change in whatever way was necessary to accommodate Brexit, with other principles ultimately subordinate to this overriding imperative.

A role traditionally ascribed to the Lords is to act as a constitutional guardian.[91] Within the political and legal limitations imposed upon it, the UK second chamber performs this task well. But it is problematic that when the stakes are at their highest – involving matters fundamental to the operation of the political system – that the upholding of key principles is vested in a body that is, as many in the Commons and elsewhere have wanted it to be, both of limited formal authority, and reluctant heavily to deploy those powers that it does possess. Humphreys and a variety of other analysts discussed in this work have expressed concern that the decline and neutering of the House of Lords removed a crucial systemic safeguard. The Brexit experience suggests that their concerns were well founded; and that no wholly satisfactory substitute has yet been found.

If we return to the question considered previously in this chapter (in relation to the voting system) – what was different about the UK, making it unlike (so far) any other full EU Member State in seeking to leave[92] – this lack of firmer intra-parliamentary constitutional protections can help to provide another part of the explanation. Were the systemic changes that Brexit necessitated – such as those pertaining to devolution – more difficult to implement, for instance requiring legislative supermajorities, or being subject to an absolute, legally enforceable veto by a more legitimate second chamber or the devolved legislatures, then events would presumably have played out differently. Perhaps the domestic constitutional implications of Brexit would have been considered more thoroughly, in public, in advance. Prior discussion and negotiation might have taken place involving the different actors who would have a role in approving (or vetoing) the measures necessary to facilitate leaving. Some, including supporters of Brexit, might complain that requirements of this kind would have had the effect of making UK departure from the EU impossible, and would therefore be undemocratic in nature. It would be more accurate to conclude that Brexit,

[91] Dawn Oliver, *Constitutional Guardians: The House of Lords* (The Constitution Society, London, 2015): https://consoc.org.uk/wp-content/uploads/2015/12/COSJ3942_Constitutional_guardians_WEB.pdf last accessed 7 September 2018; Lucy Atkinson, *Talking to the Guardians: The Constitutional Role of the House of Lords* (The Constitution Society, London, 2016): https://consoc.org.uk/wp-content/uploads/2016/10/House-of-Lords-PDF.pdf last accessed 7 September 2018.

[92] Algeria and Greenland, who have both exited predecessor organisaions of the EU, do not properly fit the category of full member states.

were it to happen within such a framework, would have to take place differently, involving more prior consideration, a better-informed public decision-making process, and a higher level of consensus. All of these qualities would be desirable for a course of action of this magnitude.

V. EDWARD GOLDSMITH: ENVIRONMENT AND DEMOCRACY

In 1971, the editor of the *Ecologist* journal, Edward Goldsmith, both edited and contributed to a book entitled *Can Britain Survive?* One of the chapters he wrote himself, 'What of the Future?', dealt with the political implications of a perceived looming environmental crisis.[93] Goldsmith held it was 'certain that, well before the end of the century, there will be a very severe food crisis' impacting upon the UK.[94] It would produce 'chaos' and a need to 'reduce our population in one way or another'.[95] Further difficulties would arise from shortages of essential resources and pollution.[96] Health problems and epidemics would multiply; and 'social disintegration' was in prospect.[97] Racial tensions would arise from inward migration.[98] Unemployment, inflation and international protectionism would intensify.[99]

Goldsmith asked '[t]o what extent can all this be avoided? Industrial society can clearly not survive for long. Nevertheless it should be possible to ensure a gradual transition to a different type of society', that eschewed '[t]he totally absurd notion that bigger things are better'.[100] He therefore proposed that:

> it should be a precept of government, as it is of the organization of nature, that everywhere there should be the maximum decentralization. Nothing should be done at village level which could be done by the family, nothing at county level which could be done by the village, and so on all the way up.[101]

Goldsmith asserted that '[a] nation consisting of 56 million people can constitute a society only if it is highly organized into families, small communities, provinces, *etc*'. Those within these groups 'must be responsible for running their own affairs. They must be self-regulating for only in this way can they be stable'. Welfare policy, economic activity and agriculture would all be 'radically decentralized'.[102]

[93] Edward Goldsmith, 'What of the Future?' in Edward Goldsmith (ed), *Can Britain Survive?* (London, Tom Stacey, 1971).
[94] ibid, 244.
[95] ibid, 246.
[96] ibid, 246–47.
[97] ibid, 248.
[98] ibid, 249.
[99] ibid, 249–50.
[100] ibid, 251.
[101] ibid, 252.
[102] ibid, 252.

Yet 'the transition to such a society would not be easy'. It might involve introducing '[a] sort of national service for conservation'. The act of achieving this 'stable society' would need to be executed 'as a single programme'. It would require 'a government having a mandate to plan and implement such a programme as painlessly as possible, *i.e.* over the maximum period consistent with avoiding the catastrophes with which our society is at present menaced'. However, Goldsmith doubted that 'the British government will undertake a programme of this sort'.[103] He judged that it lacked the capacity to carry out the necessary 'long-term planning'; and that subordinating the short-term interests of the whole of society to long-term objectives would be problematic. Goldsmith wrote:

> [a] politician must win votes if he is to remain in office and to do this he must satisfy the countless short-term requirements of a predominantly ignorant and egoistic electorate, even when they are in direct conflict with the long-term interests of the society he has been called upon to direct.[104]

Goldsmith therefore concluded that bringing 'growth' to an end would be brought about not through deliberate action, but the pressure of events that failure to act induced.[105]

The following year, Goldsmith, along with the other editors of the *Ecologist* journal: Robert Allen, Michael Allaby, John Davoll and Sam Lawrence, issued *A Blueprint for Survival*, first as a special edition of their publication, and then as a Penguin Special.[106] It included an endorsement from an impressive list of eminent scientists and other prominent public figures, supporting the general principles contained within it if not every detail.[107] The text opened with the statement that '[t]he principal defect of the industrial way of life with its ethos of expansion is that it is not sustainable'. In the judgement of the authors it would cease 'within the lifetime of someone born today'. The circumstances of this 'termination' would be 'either against our will, in a succession of famines, epidemics, social crises and wars; or because we want it to – because we wish to create a society which will not impose hardship and cruelty upon our children – in a succession of thoughtful, humane and measured changes'. The source of the threat the authors identified was a combination of global population growth and increased consumption per head, with the effect of 'disrupting ecosystems and depleting resources'. It was 'undermining the very foundations of survival'.[108]

[103] ibid, 253.
[104] ibid, 254.
[105] ibid, 255.
[106] The editors of the Ecologist, *A Blueprint for Survival* (London, Penguin, 1972). I am grateful to my research student, Mitya Pearson, for bringing this book to my attention.
[107] ibid, 10–13.
[108] ibid, 15.

The authors regretted that the government had not recognised 'the impending crisis'. One reason for this failure was the lack of a 'machinery for looking at energy, as a whole, as part of a general, global, pattern'. The Central Policy Review Staff, that the Conservative Prime Minister Edward Heath had formed under Lord Rothschild in 1971, was the sole entity within Whitehall that could have feasibly have been expected to make good this omission, yet it seemed 'not to think it worthwhile'. Furthermore, the two main parties appeared 'to be mesmerized by two dominating notions: that economic expansion is essential for survival and is the best possible index of progress and well-being; and that unless solutions can be devised that do not threaten this notion, then the problems should not be regarded as existing'.[109] The book proposed a programme for change, part of which was a 'decentralization of polity and economy at all levels, and the formation of communities small enough to be reasonably self-regulating and self-supporting'.[110] The authors advocated various anti-pollution measures,[111] a move towards a managed economy,[112] and population control, including free contraception, abortion and sterilisation.[113]

Of all the transformations the authors proposed, the 'most radical', they felt, was that of 'decentralization'. It was needed for a number of reasons (though not because of 'nostalgia for a mythical little England of fêtes, olde worlde pubs, and perpetual conversations over garden fences'). First was:

> that the long transitional stage that we and our children must go through will impose a heavy burden on our moral courage and will require great restraint. Legislation and the operations of police forces and the courts will be necessary to reinforce this restraint, but we believe that such external controls can never be so subtle or so effective as internal controls.[114]

The authors held that it would be appropriate 'to promote the social conditions in which public opinion and full public participation in decision-making becomes as far as possible the means whereby communities are ordered'. In units of greater size, this quality would be more difficult to achieve, since the attainment of the necessary social stability 'would appear as so much outside coercion'. However, 'in communities small enough for the general will to be worked out and expressed by individuals confident of themselves and their fellows as individuals, "us and them" situations are less likely to occur'. Once aware of the social constraints to which they were necessarily subject, the public would determine for themselves how to operate within these parameters, rather than feeling that they were under the control of a 'remote and unsympathetic government'.[115]

[109] ibid, 27.
[110] ibid, 30–31.
[111] ibid, 32–37.
[112] ibid, 37–45.
[113] ibid, 45–50.
[114] ibid, 50.
[115] ibid, 50.

The second motive for decentralisation was that it would fit with the envisaged shift towards smaller scale agricultural and industrial production.[116] Third was that the 'small community' was an 'essential source of pleasure and stimulation for the individual', who was in contemporary 'large agglomerations … merely an isolate'.[117] The authors observed a centralisation of political authority in recent times that had 'been accompanied by the rise of self-conscious individualism, an individualism that feels threatened unless it is harped upon', and found fulfilment in consumerism. They noted that in small communities that were the subject of anthropological study, such individualism did not prevail, 'yet no man controls another and each has very great freedom of action'. Alongside this benefit, participants in such societies 'enjoy the rewards of … knowing and being known, of an intensity of relationships with a few, rather than urban man's variety of innumerable, superficial relationships'. These advantages would 'provide ample compensation for the decreasing emphasis on consumption'.[118] The fourth and final motive of the promotion of small communities was that population dispersal minimised human environmental disruption.[119]

A Blueprint for Survival stressed that these small communities would be outward looking and interconnected rather than insular. The political structure the authors envisaged was of a neighbourhood unit of perhaps 500, with communities of 5,000. These communities would be 'as self-sufficient and self-regulating as possible'. But there would be mechanisms whereby decisions of wider implications could be considered in regions of 500,000, as well as national and global representation. The book stressed: 'our goal should be to create *community feeling* and *global awareness*, rather than that dangerous and sterile compromise which is nationalism'.[120] The book closed with a call for a 'Movement for Survival', an organisation which existed in embryonic form that would seek 'to influence governments, and in particular that of Britain, into taking those measures most likely to lead to the stabilization and hence the survival of our society'.[121]

Brexit, as we have seen, figures in a wider contemporary discussion about possible threats to democracy. The Goldsmith contributions provide an historical insight into another aspect of that general theme, that has connections with the prospect of UK departure from the EU: the environment. He suspected that the political existing system was innately disposed towards short-termism and therefore not capable of delivering an appropriate response to the problems he identified. The firmer intervention required would therefore be driven by events. In the second, co-authored, text we encounter a more detailed account of the

[116] ibid, 50–51.
[117] ibid, 51.
[118] ibid, 52.
[119] ibid, 52.
[120] ibid, 53.
[121] ibid, 134.

practices and structures that would supposedly be necessary to preserve human existence. They contain a central contradiction. On the one hand, they emphasise dispersed organisation, self-governance and local responsibility. But, on the other hand, it is clear that all activity will take place within rigid limitations, that will have to be imposed somehow, from somewhere. During the 'long transitional stage' requiring 'great restraint', one source of regulation might be '[l]egislation and the operations of police forces and the courts'. Another will be 'internal controls', judged by the authors to be far more 'subtle' and 'effective'. A telling recommendation is for the establishment of 'social conditions in which public opinion and full public participation in decision-making becomes as far as possible the means whereby communities are ordered'. The model seems to be one of self-imposed authoritarianism. The tone is fatalistic, conveying the sense that society is inevitably headed in this direction, either preemptively now or in response to crisis later. Moreover, the text suggests that the polity envisaged is not only necessary as a response to ecological challenges, but is desirable in itself.

A Blueprint for Survival made a significant public impact at the time it appeared and was an influence on the formation of what is now the Green Party.[122] While the agenda of the environmental movement has changed, with a key focus now on climate change,[123] the ideas for social organisation Goldsmith and his colleagues advanced remain significant. We should not dismiss him *merely* as the eccentric he undoubtedly was. Similar miscalculations were made in the past about those who sought to achieve UK withdrawal from the EU. They included Goldsmith's younger brother, James, who formed the Referendum Party, contesting over 500 parliamentary seats at the 1997 General Election on the specific platform of holding a popular vote on exit from the EU.[124] In April 1999, the *Economist* described how:

> D[uring] the last election, the public got used to the sight of Jimmy Goldsmith, leading his troops in the Referendum Party on a crusade against the European Union. The Referendum Party flopped, and shortly afterwards its tycoon leader died. But the death of Jimmy has not removed the Goldsmith influence from British politics. Jimmy's older brother, Teddy, who celebrated his 70th birthday earlier this year, is on a crusade of his own – and may ultimately prove more influential than his late brother in changing mainstream politics.[125]

The article clearly failed to foresee the extent to which the agenda that James Goldsmith had supported would be attained, albeit posthumously. But what

[122] 'Teddy Goldsmith', *Telegraph*, 25 August 2009.

[123] For a political perspective on this issue, see: Anthony Giddens, *The Politics of Climate Change* (Cambridge, Polity, 2011).

[124] Neil Carter et al, 'Europe, Goldsmith and the Referendum party.' (1998) 51(3) *Parliamentary Affairs* 470–86.

[125] 'The Other Goldsmith', *Economist*, 15 April 1999.

of the ideas of Edward Goldsmith? Political scientists are beginning to discuss what might be the consequences for political institutions of the perceived onset of an epoch called the Anthropocene, in which humanity is the primary force in the shaping of the global environment.[126] As Goldsmith did in an earlier era, some more recent observers have expressed doubt regarding the capacity of democratic systems to provide the necessary response, and have advocated the introduction of some form of enlightened despotism to devise and impose appropriate policies.[127] Such ideas are likely to gain currency as the climate instability associated with the Anthropocene intensifies. Some will regretfully conclude that authoritarianism is unavoidable, while others will welcome it and see an environmental crisis as the means of achieving their goal.

The environmental threat certainly implies a need for more coordinated activity, presumably involving greater governmental intervention and coercion, both to mitigate and respond to difficulties. Ironically, the attainment of one objective associated with the Goldsmith family, departure from the EU, makes the Edward Goldsmith prediction of the early 1970s more likely to prove accurate. Outside the EU, it will be harder to achieve more concerted action on the environment through the democratic system of the UK. As the Environmental Audit Committee (of which Zac Goldsmith MP, nephew of Edward and son of James, and a supporter of leaving the EU[128] was and is a member) put it shortly before the 2016 referendum:

> The UK's membership of the EU has been a crucial factor in the shaping of its environmental policy since it joined the Union in the 1970s. The overwhelming view of our witnesses was that EU membership has been positive for the UK environment. None of the witnesses to our inquiry, even those who made criticisms, made an environmental case for leaving the European Union ... The process of EU environmental policy development has been a two-way street. On the one hand, the EU has led the UK to improve environmental standards in areas such as air and water pollution and biodiversity. It has also given the UK a platform to pursue its environmental objectives internationally and has provided access to a useful pool of knowledge. On the other hand, the UK has been a major player in the EU, influencing the strategic and long term direction of EU environmental policy and the design of specific laws and policies. The UK's membership of the EU has ensured environmental action was taken on a faster timetable and more thoroughly than would otherwise have been the case. There has been frustration that EU policy can be difficult to change once introduced, but this also has benefits, allowing longer-term planning and greater certainty for businesses looking to make green investment decisions.[129]

[126] John S Dryzek, 'Institutions for the anthropocene: governance in a changing earth system' (2016) 46(4) *British Journal of Political Science* 937–56; Robun Eckersley, 'Geopolitan democracy in the Anthropocene' (2017) 65(4) *Political Studies* 983–99.

[127] Dan Coby Shahar, 'Rejecting eco-authoritarianism, again' (2015) 24(3) *Environmental Values* 345–66; David JC Shearman and Joseph Wayne Smith, *The climate change challenge and the failure of democracy* (Santa Barbara, Greenwood Publishing group, 2007).

[128] See Zac Goldsmith, 'How my Dad saved Britain', *Spectator*, 28 February 2015.

[129] House of Commons Environmental Audit Committee, *EU and UK Environmental Policy* (London, House of Commons, 2016) 3.

It may shortly be necessary to address growing environmental concerns and disruption from without the formal EU framework. Those who dislike ready-made authoritarian responses that continue in the same tradition as Goldsmith need to find convincing answers to them, developing constitutional mechanisms able to reconcile popular control with effective climate governance.

VI. BEYOND PARTIES AND VOTING

The remainder of this chapter considers proposals, produced from the late 1970s onwards, to extend beyond – or possibly break altogether with – one or both of two key features of the representative democratic system: voting and parties. The first text, by the political writer Brian Crozier, entitled *The Minimum State: Beyond Party Politics*, appeared in 1979.[130] His stated purpose was to 'devote an entire book to the theme of bad government and the possibility of improvement'.[131] Crozier opened with the announcement that '[t]he era of party democracy is nearing its close'. He saw 'men and women of goodwill' as being engaged in 'the preservation of a threatened way of life against external and internal enemies', by which he meant the Soviet Union and its proxies.[132] He saw governments across the democratic world, including in the UK, as failing to deliver on the basic tasks required of them: internal security, external defence, and sound money.[133] Crozier perceived a decline in the public credibility of politicians, exacerbated by the decision in 1978 to broadcast parliamentary proceedings, coupled with a deterioration in the quality of those attracted to such a career path. He suspected that 'for years the best young brains have been decreasingly attracted to the prospects of a career in politics, but have opted instead for business, industry, the professions or finance'.[134] To correct these problems and avoid a shift into Communist absolutism, Crozier made a series of recommendations of a constitutional nature, intended 'to strengthen the authority of government … prevent the imposition of the views of an extremist minority upon Parliament and therefore the country as a whole' and reestablish 'good government' while discouraging 'frivolous or unnecessary legislation'.[135]

At the core of the Crozier programme was the idea of removing party from the business of government. Parties, Crozier judged, imposed inappropriate governors on the public through their control over the selection of candidates, leading to the wider problems he identified in his work.[136] He proposed

[130] Brian Crozier, *The Minimum State: Beyond Party Politics* (London, Hamish Hamilton, 1979).
[131] ibid, vii.
[132] ibid, 3 and footnote.
[133] ibid, 5–7.
[134] ibid, 11.
[135] ibid, 171.
[136] ibid, 173.

replacing the party-centred system through the creation of a 'profession of politics'. In making his case, he remarked:

> [i]f I need a heart-valve operation, I go to a heart specialist, not to the local butcher. If I seek legal advice, I go to someone with the appropriate degree and legal background. If my teeth are giving trouble I go to a dentist, not to a veterinary surgeon. Is it not astonishing that in a matter of such universal concern as the laws of the land, we entrust our destinies to the unqualified?[137]

Crozier accepted that many MPs were of a high quality, but he insisted that there was scope for improvement. Under his model, a professional body, 'the College of Politicians', would play a central role. At election time, the College would put forward two candidates in each constituency. They would run as individuals, and not on party platforms. After the vote, the individuals who won their contests would comprise the government, while those who lost would become the opposition. When the next election came, all candidates would have to run in different constituencies, and could not compete against the same rival as previously.[138] Those who held office would apply their individual judgement to their work, rather than that of a collective party perspective.[139]

Candidates for a political career would train at a School of Political Service. Their entrance into the College of Politicians would be subject to a written examination and interview. The main purpose of this filtering process would be to determine the ability of those being tested to apply knowledge in practice. The oral stage would assess qualities including 'fluency of speech and suitability of personality and temperament'. It would also seek to ascertain that the candidate was in 'opposition to all forms of collectivism' and establish their 'awareness of the Marxist problem and of Leninist techniques, general reliability and probity of character'.[140] Subject to these requirements, entry would be open to all members of society, regardless of 'race, religion, class or social origin'.[141] Once they had passed through the recruitment process, they could look forward to secure careers as politicians.[142]

Crozier also proposed a written constitution within which his system would operate. Among its provisions would be a 'specific upper limit on State participation in the economy'. The text would include a Charter of Rights. While it would guarantee 'free inquiry and advocacy' for the press, Crozier stressed that 'the freedom to inquire does not necessarily imply the freedom of access to State secrets … And the right to advocate does not mean the right to distort, smear and subvert'.

[137] ibid, 174.
[138] ibid, 175.
[139] ibid, 179.
[140] ibid, 176.
[141] ibid, 177.
[142] ibid, 179.

He hoped for voluntary restraint in this area.[143] Under the constitution, parties would be permitted to exist as 'pressure groups' but would 'be deprived of the right to compete for political power'.[144] Some local-level decisions would be taken by referendums.[145]

The apocalyptic tone Crozier conveyed regarding the future of party-based democracy was pervasive at time the he wrote. The economic and industrial problems of the 1970s were often linked to fears about coups from the left or right, depending on the perspective of the individual concerned, or a more general sense of serious constitutional malaise.[146] Crozier himself promoted his ideas energetically, including in circles surrounding Margaret Thatcher.[147] The remedies he proposed to the problem he claimed to have identified had a sinister character. For instance, his qualification of the principle of 'freedom of inquiry and advocacy' risked rendering it meaningless. Moreover, rather than there being no parties, in his model the College of Politicians seemed likely to become the only party in a one-party state, carefully filtering candidates for admission, with other groups denied the right to contest elections. Even for those in government, policy options would be seriously constrained by the constitutional limitations on economic intervention. Whatever flaws there might be in the party system, the Crozier proposal demonstrates the difficulties inherent in conceiving of a contemporary democracy without them, with their absence negating the value of voting in elections.

We can reject the conclusions Crozier reached as worse than whatever problem they were addressing, and also unnecessary on his own terms – democracy survived in the UK and elsewhere without their being implemented. Indeed, at the time he wrote, a sustained period of worldwide growth in this system of government – now known as the 'third wave of democratisation' – was commencing.[148] Nonetheless, his programme has aspects to it which merit consideration for present purposes. In focusing on the idea of obtaining the correct type of public office holder – perhaps through an emphasis on expertise and the creation of new career structures – Crozier shared ground with the authors of other texts discussed in this work.

[143] ibid, 182.

[144] ibid, 187.

[145] ibid, 178.

[146] See eg Andrew Blick, *People Who Live in the Dark: the history of the special adviser in British politics* (London, Methuen, 2004) 155; Stephen Haseler, *The Death of British Democracy* (London, HarperCollins, 1976); William Waldegrave, *The Binding of Leviathan: Conservatism & the Future* (London, Hamish Hamilton, 1978) 74.

[147] Richard Norton-Taylor, 'Brian Crozier obituary', *Guardian*, 9 August 2012: https://www.theguardian.com/politics/2012/aug/09/brian-crozier last accessed 28 August 2018; John Hoskyns, *Just in Time: Inside the Thatcher Revolution* (London, Aurum Press, 2000) 129, footnote.

[148] Samuel P Huntington, *Third Wave: Democratization in the late twentieth century* (Norman, University of Oklahoma Press, 1993).

Some of his ideas also have a perverse contemporary salience. Where Crozier feared Soviet attempts to undermine democracy from within, the possibility of Russian interference in elections or referendums in the UK and elsewhere is a concern today.[149] Moreover, his reference to the need to 'prevent the imposition of the views of an extremist minority upon Parliament and therefore the country as a whole' is poignant. In some ways, Brexit has involved just such a scenario. As already discussed, the holding of the 2016 referendum was attributable in large part to the demands of a minority of Conservative MPs,[150] a party that itself formed a government on a basis of a minority of votes cast.[151] Following the vote of 23 June, it was that same minority within a minority that continued to exert pressure to interpret the vote as inescapably binding, and to impose a particular interpretation of leaving the EU.[152] The power seizure Crozier feared, in this instance, took place on the right rather than the left. Rather than placing one of their own at the head of the party, the 'extremist minority' exerted themselves when they deemed it necessary to impose decisions upon a leader who had supported 'remain'.[153]

There have, however, also been developments relevant from the point of view of the Crozier scenario on the left. The ascendancy of Jeremy Corbyn has involved a small minority within the Parliamentary Labour Party securing control. It achieved this success by channelling mass support from outside Parliament, in the form of participants in the leadership election contested under new rules used for the first time in 2015.[154] In this sense, the party system in the UK has proved to be vulnerable to extremist (though not overtly anti-democratic) capture. Both the Conservatives and Labour have been driven towards radical positions with which many MPs are uncomfortable. Activists and members associated with both parties may tend towards a more favourable view of this development; and the 2017 General Election, with a reversion in the direction of two-party dominance, suggests that the public were at least not repelled by the Conservative and Labour stances.[155] Regardless of how

[149] For an example of this outlook see Sarah Jones, 'Russian Interference 2.0', *New Republic*, 27 July 2018: https://newrepublic.com/article/150244/russian-interference-20 last accessed 8 September 2018.

[150] Andrew Grice, 'Tory rebels form new Eurosceptic group', *Independent*, 2 November 2011: https://www.independent.co.uk/news/uk/politics/exclusive-tory-rebels-form-new-eurosceptic-group-6255896.html last accessed 8 September 2018.

[151] See ch 2.

[152] Heather Stewart, '"We're the opposition": Rees-Mogg and his European Research Group', *Guardian*, 20 July 2018: https://www.theguardian.com/politics/2018/jul/20/opposition-jacob-rees-mogg-european-research-group-profile last accessed 8 September 2018.

[153] See Conclusion.

[154] 'Jeremy Corbyn elected Labour leader: How did he win?', BBC, 12 September 2015: https://www.bbc.co.uk/news/uk-politics-34126758 last accessed 8 September 2018.

[155] Andreas Whittam Smith, 'After three decades of splintering, two-party politics is back – sort of', *Independent*, 9 June 2017: https://www.independent.co.uk/voices/election-results-hung-parliament-two-party-politics-back-return-labour-conservative-tory-jeremy-a7781256.html last accessed 8 September 2018.

voting patterns may develop in future, one important observation can be made. The UK system seems not to be as immune to extremism as has often been claimed.[156]

The political writers Anthony Barnett and Peter Carty first published *The Athenian Option: radical reform for the House of Lords* in 1998.[157] At that point, following the election of a Labour government under Tony Blair the previous year, changes to the upper chamber of the UK Parliament were in prospect. The House of Lords Act 1999, noted above, would remove most of the hereditaries, supposedly as a preliminary to more transformation still, perhaps even a House with elected members in it.[158] In their pamphlet, written for the think tank Demos, regarded as influential on the government of the time, Barnett and Carty supported the application of methods of deliberative, participatory democracy then being developed.[159] The authors argued that, while these techniques were largely being considered for use in relation to local and regional affairs, they could be adapted to UK level. They presented their proposal in a wider context, holding that 'it is now clear that over the next few years Britain will move towards a new constitutional settlement'. Barnett and Carty saw their recommendation as '[o]ne that closes the gap between rulers and ruled; one that increases, in a practical and efficient manner, the capacity of citizens to participate in the process of democratic government'.[160] Their proposal was 'that a reformed upper chamber should consist largely, but not entirely, of representative groups of citizens chosen by lot from among the electorate along the lines of a jury'.[161]

Their idea avowedly derived inspiration from the ancient 'Athenian principles of selection and deliberation'.[162] Barnett and Carty recognised that in many senses, for instance through its exclusion of women and slaves from the political system, Athens did not conform to contemporary democratic norms. However, they found it intriguing that one of its organs of governance was a council or a 'boule', composed of 500 citizens. Members were chosen by sortition, but with provision to ensure that every sub-Athenian locality received a specified level of

[156] For some historical examples of this perception, critically assessed, see: Andrew Blick, *Beyond Magna Carta: A constitution for the United Kingdom* (Oxford, Hart Publishing, 2015) 4–18. For a recent expression of this outlook, see: Dan Hodges, 'No, Britain does not want proportional representation', *Telegraph*, 1 June 2015: https://www.telegraph.co.uk/news/general-election-2015/politics-blog/11643323/The-electoral-reform-lobby-needs-to-sober-up.html last accessed 7 September 2018.

[157] Anthony Barnett and Peter Carty, *The Athenian Option: radical reform for the House of Lords* (Exeter, Imprint Academic, 2008).

[158] Michael Cockerell, 'The politics of second chamber reform: a case study of the House of Lords and the passage of the House of Lords Act 1999' (2001) 7(1) *Journal of Legislative Studies* 119–134.

[159] Anthony Barnett and Peter Carty, *The Athenian Option: radical reform for the House of Lords* (Exeter, Imprint Academic, 2008) 20–21.

[160] ibid, 21.

[161] ibid, 22.

[162] ibid, 25.

representation.[163] The application of this approach to the UK second chamber, would, the authors argued, imbue the House of Lords with 'genuinely representative character', affording it greater legitimacy and therefore making it stronger, yet not so powerful as to create stalemate between it and the Commons. The authors held that their proposed innovation would generate enhanced 'interest among the public in policy making'. They saw their model as working in tandem with, rather than in opposition to, 'party politics'.[164] Barnett and Carty held that 'representative democracy is central and essential'. However, in the case of Lords reform, they felt the establishment of an elected second chamber was 'likely to create a potentially destructive alternative to the House of Commons'. Their 'Athenian solution' was, therefore valuable both for its democratic virtue and because other options were less desirable.[165]

While the new members – that the authors labelled PPs ('Peers in Parliament') – would be chosen at random, certain quotas could be applied to their selection, for instance having an even gender balance and ensuring that different territories of the UK were represented in accordance with their populations.[166] The reconstituted second chamber of which PPs were members would retain the existing powers of the House of Lords, but add to them in three areas: being able to block legislation that compromised 'principles of constitutional democracy'; to 'return' bills (provided they were of a non-financial nature) on the grounds that they 'will not achieve the objectives that the government claims'; and to require 'that legislation be drafted in a way that citizens can understand'.[167] But while PPs would scrutinise legislative measures, the initiation of bills would fall to the Commons, from which the government would also be drawn.[168] Peers of Parliament might sit for terms of perhaps four years, with rolling annual recruitment, or they could be taken on specifically for the purposes of scrutinising particular measures.[169] The hope of the authors was that '[t]he last state to cling to the hereditary principle might become the first to apply modern, direct democratic processes within its parliament'.[170]

The Party's Over: Blueprint for a Very English Revolution, by the political writer and publisher Keith Sutherland, appeared in 2004.[171] His overall thesis was that '[t]he political party is an anachronism. It serves no useful purpose and we are better off without it. Furthermore, it is a danger to democracy and an affront to the constitutional dignity of this country'.[172] Employing historical

[163] ibid, 38–39.
[164] ibid, 25.
[165] ibid, 39.
[166] ibid, 39–40.
[167] ibid, 37.
[168] ibid, 43.
[169] ibid, 45.
[170] ibid, 22.
[171] Keith Sutherland, *The Party's Over: Blueprint for a Very English Revolution* (Exeter, Imprint Academic, 2004).
[172] ibid, 21.

analysis, he argued that the division between parties had once been meaningful, entailing the struggle between different material interests in the period from their instigation in the seventeenth century through to the 1980s. But the promotion of popular capitalism under Margaret Thatcher had undermined traditional class divisions, while the failure of centralised socialism reduced the ideological distance between the Conservatives and Labour. Sutherland viewed parties as subsequently becoming 'uneasy marriages of convenience'. Political outlooks, he believed, had fragmented to the point that as a minimum there should be six different parties to accommodate them. But the UK electoral system promoted a 'binary model of politics'. This mismatch engendered public 'apathy, confusion and a dramatic decline in voting'.[173] Parties were devoid of any 'underlying political philosophy'.[174] Sutherland asked:

> How can we describe a party that was responsible for the destruction of much of the professional and institutional infrastructure of the country as "conservative" in any sense that Burke or Oakeshott might have understood? And can the career opportunists, carpetbaggers and asset-strippers who picked up the capital of the Labour Party for a song at the liquidation sale make any plausible claim to represent the tradition of Keir Hardy and Nye Bevan?[175]

Political activities were now 'technocratic-managerial' in nature. Consequently, Sutherland concluded, parties were obsolete. He held that there were 'other ways of appointing managers and holding them to account'.[176] He rejected direct democracy as a solution since, while it might appear to promise to incorporate the public into government, it was vulnerable to capture by strident minorities.[177] Sutherland argued that that measures intended to increase electoral turnout and other forms of participation did not address the underlying issues.[178] Furthermore, he judged that an attempt to adapt US constitutional models, such as a directly elected head of state, would not succeed, since they rested on an overly positive view of the actual US experience.[179]

In proposing his scheme for reform, Sutherland asserted that the current parliamentary system, in which MPs were elected by a minority of registered voters many of whom could not name them, was not properly representative.[180] Like Barnett and Carty, he suggested a model derived from the jury system used for trials, a process that he held still commanded public confidence. He contrasted the position in a court, where a verdict was reached after close consideration of the evidence, with the political environment in which 'party leaders can get away

[173] ibid, 24.
[174] ibid, 25.
[175] ibid, 25–26.
[176] ibid, 27.
[177] ibid, 27.
[178] ibid, 29–30.
[179] ibid, 32.
[180] ibid, 38–39.

with misrepresenting themselves and their policies outrageously'.[181] In a sense, Sutherland noted, something similar to juries already played a part in politics, since the parties made extensive use of focus groups. The difference between a focus group and a jury in an actual legal proceeding was that the latter reached its opinion once the evidence had been presented to it, rather than – as in the case of the former – instantly.[182] He therefore concluded that MPs should be chosen at random, rather than being elected on party platforms. As a cross-section of regular members of the public, they would not speak in debates, but they would scrutinise measures proposed by ministers, who would be challenged by individuals drawn from the Lords, an institution Sutherland judged to be effective in its current form.[183] Commons and Lords would therefore need to meet as a single entity, in a different location more suited to the purpose.[184]

Ministers under this system would no longer be drawn from Parliament. Sutherland discussed a range of means by which they might be appointed. He held that 'the Crown could, if it chose, select its own ministers with the aid of advisors'.[185] Indeed, Sutherland thought, it would be entirely proper were the monarch to become openly politically assertive. The 'future King Charles III', the Prince of Wales, had 'often shown himself to be more in tune with public opinion than the government, which tends to reflect the view of the metropolitan elite'. Charles might, for instance 'attempt the appointment of an anti-vivisectionist as minister of agriculture'. Such action would be reminiscent of mediaeval times in which 'monarchs frequently shared an interest with the commons against the feudal aristocracy'.[186]

But a monarch might prefer to leave governing to others. If so, the task of recruiting ministers might be handled by recruitment consultants, selecting individuals on a basis of their suitability for the particular task.[187] However they were chosen, ministers would remain individually responsible to Parliament for their actions (and those of their civil servants), which could potentially remove them from office. However, ministers would not share joint responsibility for their government, and the fall of one minister would not have implications for others.[188] Under such a system, there would not strictly be a need for a Prime Minister at all, though in practice one minister might become the focus for the administration – unless the monarch sought to fulfill that role.[189] In summarising his essay, Sutherland concluded that 'Britain isn't, never was, and never should be a *democracy*. We are a constitutional monarchy which has generated into an

[181] ibid, 39.
[182] ibid, 39–40.
[183] ibid, 41–44.
[184] ibid, 117.
[185] ibid, 102.
[186] ibid, 103.
[187] ibid, 104–06.
[188] ibid, 106–12.
[189] ibid, 112–14.

electoral dictatorship. The way to resolve the problem is not more democracy, it is to re-create the essential balance that Aristotle argued constituted the ideal polity.'[190]

It is useful to consider the Barnett and Carty programme, on the one hand, and that of Sutherland, on the other hand, in parallel. Both were concerned with the way in which members of the legislature were chosen, though the former were focused on the Lords, while the latter concentrated on the Commons. The most important similarity between them is the method they proposed: sortition. It has clear attractions: long lineage, dating back to what are commonly regarded as the earliest of experiments in popular government; and proven effectiveness in the UK today in the form of the jury system. It is democratic in the sense that selection is blind, and every member of society has an equal chance of being chosen, subject to the use of quotas.

A key difference between the two schemes is that, while Barnett and Carty envisaged integrating the method into the existing system, improving its operation in the process, Sutherland sought to supplant it. Of particular interest from the point of view of earlier discussions in this chapter, it is notable that Barnett and Carty hoped that the Lords, reformed in the manner they advocated, could take on a role in approving or blocking measures of a constitutional nature. In this respect the new recruits to the second chamber would play a stabilising more than revolutionary role. Sutherland, by contrast, sought radically to alter the composition of the Commons, the primary chamber, upon which governments – under current arrangements – depend for their existence. Some aspects of the analysis Sutherland provided were perceptive; in particular the difficulties inherent in condensing multiple disparate outlooks into each of the two main parties. But it might be preferable to consider reform to the electoral system, as discussed above, as a means of addressing this problem, than the solution Sutherland offered. Like Crozier, his model suggests that, while the party system has its flaws, attempts to propose a different approach to political organisation – perhaps entailing reversion to monarchical activism or the selection of ministers by management consultants – tend to produce alternatives that are less appealing still. Viable political parties are a valuable component of contemporary democracy. Indeed, such are their merits that it would be desirable to see them multiply.

[190] ibid, 170–71.

6

Programmes for Parliament

Parliament was both central and peripheral to Brexit. In some senses it instigated events, and in others it reacted to them. The referendum was held in large measure as a consequence of sustained pressure from Conservative backbench MPs, who continued to exert influence after it took place. Parliament provided the legislative basis for the vote that took place on 23 June 2016; and for various consequences of departure from the EU. It exercised detailed scrutiny of Brexit once adopted as a policy by the UK government – or at least attempted to do so. Parliament was the site for various political battles about the way in which the UK should leave the EU and asserted a right to some kind of vote on the outcome of negotiations. However, many parliamentarians who voted for the referendum bill did so not because it was their preferred course of action, but because they felt it was politically inescapable, and they saw it as a means of managing political controversy connected to the EU. Indeed, for a large number within Parliament, such a vote was primarily a means of inflicting a defeat upon Euroscepticism. Partly because of the influence of this premise, Parliament mandated an open-ended referendum question and did not prescribe what a 'leave' result might mean, or what would follow were it to be the outcome of the vote. In practice, Parliament had relinquished primary control over interpretation of the vote, with the executive asserting responsibility for this task. Despite both Houses seemingly containing majorities who were in favour of 'remain' at the time of the referendum, Parliament proved reluctant seriously to challenge the premise – adopted by the UK government – that the result created an irresistible imperative to leave the EU, and to depart from both the Single Market and the Customs Union in the process. After the courts insisted that the activation of Article 50 of the Treaty on European Union by the executive required specific statutory authorisation, Parliament provided it in unconditional form.[1]

At the time of writing, whether circumstances will arise in which Parliament (and within it the Commons) asserts its latent ability to impose a course of action on the government (or replace it with a more amenable administration) remains to be seen. But the Brexit experience to date has in many ways undermined parliamentary credibility. Collectively, the legislature has appeared

[1] See ch 2.

subordinate both to an exercise in direct democracy, and to the executive as custodian of its result (though the government in turn has been heavily pressurised by a coordinated minority of Conservative MPs). In as far as the Brexit episode has proved unsatisfactory from a constitutional perspective, Parliament has emerged as a culprit in this failure, for its less than optimal performance. These tendencies alone are sufficient reason for reflection, informed by past reform proposals, on the constitutional role of Parliament. Further grounds for such an assessment arise from the systemic reconfiguration that exit from the EU appears likely to bring about. Advocates of leaving the EU present it as a means of restoring or protecting the authority of the UK Parliament. Responsibilities may return from the EU after departure. The precise role that the UK Parliament will play in their exercise is unclear, but is a central democratic concern.

I. THE WEBBS, CHURCHILL AND SUB-PARLIAMENTS

Published in 1920, Beatrice and Sidney Webb produced *A Constitution for the Socialist Commonwealth of Great Britain* in response to a 'request' from the International Socialist Bureau.[2] The Webbs wrote, in their view, in a context in which events were propelling all the industrialised countries towards socialism: '[g]reat changes are everywhere at hand'.[3] Socialist governments had come to power in many parts of Europe; and the ideas underpinning their ideological approach had become 'avowedly accepted as the basis' for the reconstruction of society.[4] It was therefore valuable to give consideration to 'the changes in the British Constitution and in the social and economic structure of the nation' that a 'Socialist Ministry', backed by a parliamentary and public majority, would need to pursue.[5]

The Webbs held that the 'Capitalist System', as they described it, had 'demonstrably broken down'.[6] Throughout the 'civilised world', this mode of organisation had 'at least among the young generation … lost its moral authority'. They identified a wave of change, with some countries completely discarding capitalism, while in others large movements against it were developing.[7] In a section headed 'The Dictatorship of the Capitalist', they set out their objection to the economic inequality they saw as arising from capitalism, whereby

[2] Sidney and Beatrice Webb, *A Constitution for the Socialist Commonwealth of Great Britain* (Cambridge and London, London School of Economics and Political Science/Cambridge University Press, 1975), xxxv.

[3] ibid, xxxv.

[4] ibid, xxxv.

[5] ibid, xxxvi.

[6] ibid, xxxvii.

[7] ibid, xxxvii.

'[n]ine-tenths of all the accumulated wealth belongs to one-tenth of the population'.[8] However, the Webbs' principal ground for opposition to this system was 'the power which the mere ownership of the instruments of production gives to a relatively small section of the community over the actions of their fellow-citizens and over the mental and physical environment of successive generations'.[9] The purpose of socialists, as they saw it, was to replace the 'Dictatorship of the Capitalist' with 'government of the people by the people and for the people, in all the industries and services by which the people live'.[10]

Central to the Webbs' proposal was their discernment of a development in the definition of the concept of democracy. In their analysis, socialists had once shared the 'Victorian' belief in 'the equality of voting power' and the view that 'human beings in society needed only to be represented as human beings'.[11] Yet in the present century a different conception had emerged. It entailed 'the acceptance of the representation not of man as man, but of man in the leading aspects of his life in society'. These dimensions were 'man as producer, man as consumer, man as a citizen concerned with the continued existence and independence of his race or community, or with the character of the civilisation that he desires; possibly also man as a seeker after knowledge, or man as a religious believer'.[12] This mode of classification for political representation presented a rival to that derived from 'mere inhabitancy of a particular geographical area'.[13] With this conception of democracy in mind, the Webbs set out to explain how the existing constitutional structures and arrangements might suitably be adapted.[14]

The main purposes of the reorganisation the Webbs proposed were to 'arrest the growing dissatisfaction with' constitutional arrangements, especially 'Parliamentary Government', and to achieve a 'progressive democratisation of industry'.[15] They recognised that some, disliking the idea of change, would oppose their plans. But they stressed that since the social environment was constantly developing, it was inevitable that governmental arrangements had to alter to reflect this process. Change in the developed world had become 'amazingly rapid'.[16] Tendencies they identified as requiring a systemic overhaul included 'growth and mobility of population'; 'successive transformation of the methods of production and distribution'; the pace at 'which ideas are now disseminated over the whole globe'; and 'the common accessibility of knowledge' previously 'monopolised' by a small group.[17] For the Webbs, the future of

[8] ibid, xxxviii.
[9] ibid, xxxviii.
[10] ibid, xxxix.
[11] ibid, xl.
[12] ibid, xl–xli.
[13] ibid, xli.
[14] ibid, xliv.
[15] ibid, 97.
[16] ibid, 97.
[17] ibid, 97.

'European civilisation' was dependent upon its ability to adapt institutionally.[18] The Webbs held that democracy was clearly preferable to other systems.[19] Rather than 'Utopian' in character, they saw their scheme as building upon existing tendencies.[20]

The Webbs began with the monarchy. Their far from enthusiastic endorsement of this institution was that '[i]t does not seem necessary to propose any change in the system, to which the nation is accustomed'.[21] The House of Lords received less generous treatment. The single paragraph dealing with the second chamber opened by explaining that there was 'of course, in the Socialist Commonwealth no place for the House of Lords, which will simply cease to exist as part of the Legislature'.[22] They allowed that the Law Lords might – or might not – continue to exist as a remnant of the Lords.[23] The Webbs then moved on to the remaining chamber of Parliament. In perhaps the most striking proposal contained in *A Constitution for the Socialist Commonwealth of Great Britain*, they called for a 'splitting of the House of Commons, as regards powers and functions, into two coordinate national assemblies'. Each would have a 'sphere' of its own, though it would connect to the other; neither would be superior nor inferior to its counterpart. Of these bodies, one would be concerned with 'Political Democracy', that is 'with criminal law and political dominion', while the other would address 'Social Democracy', that is 'economic and social administration'. For the Webbs this division of the Commons was a means of managing the excessive workload presently faced by Parliament; and of creating a system that supported pursuit of the common interest, in place of the seeking after particular benefits associated with capitalism.[24]

The first task of the Political Parliament would be 'Foreign Affairs'.[25] It might be, the Webbs noted, that at some point in the future a 'Supernational Authority of a League of Peoples' would take on responsibility for governing and law making, rendering such functions irrelevant. But as yet, no such body was in sight. The Political Parliament would also be responsible for internal protection against criminality and in resolving disputes between individuals, so law and order and justice would be in its remit. The 'chief executive officers' of this Parliament would be a 'Premier', a 'Minister for Foreign Affairs' a Minister for the Dominions, a Minister for India, a Minister for the Crown Colonies, a Minister for the Dependencies, at least one Minister for National Defence, and a Minister responsible for Justice.[26] They would comprise a Cabinet that was

[18] ibid, 99.
[19] ibid, 99–101.
[20] ibid, 101–02.
[21] ibid, 108.
[22] ibid, 110.
[23] ibid, 110.
[24] ibid, 111.
[25] ibid, 111.
[26] ibid, 112.

smaller in size than its predecessor, because of the transfer of functions to the Social Parliament. It would continue to assume collective responsibility for its actions, and would hold or lose office as a group on a basis of the confidence of the Commons.[27]

The Webbs then moved to consideration of their envisaged 'Social Parliament'. It would have two broad spheres of interest: the nature of the present social environment, and of the future; both of which were interconnected. They held that the second of the two areas was 'usually too lightly regarded'.[28] The Social Parliament and the Social Executive would be charged with 'exercising whatever national control may from time to time be required over the nation's economic and social activities'.[29] This role would entail control of existing 'public services' and spheres in which the crown had responsibility; and the ability to decide when it was appropriate to extend the remit of governmental supervision further.[30] While the Political Executive would continue to resemble the old Cabinet, retaining the principle of collective responsibility, the Social Executive would not. Presenting the London County Council and other municipal authorities as the appropriate model, the Webbs argued that the Social Parliament should operate a standing committee in every sphere of work, which would elect a chair.[31]

Members of each Parliament would be full-time and have 'an adequate livelihood provided for them'.[32] The two Parliaments would operate differently from one another, in accordance with their particular functions. They need not, the Webbs held, be elected simultaneously, or using the same constituency boundaries, or for the same term length, or under the same electoral system. The authors rejected the idea of 'devolution' to 'new regional or provincial Parliaments'.[33] Their grounds for this view were that dividing the provision of public services within Great Britain would come at a cost in efficiency, though they accepted that 'national feeling' might make legislative and administrative devolution unavoidable.[34] The two parliaments and executives would be 'equal and co-ordinate', with each superior in its particular field. If there were a clash between them, the courts would resolve the dispute by interpreting whether a particular measure was genuinely founded in the powers allotted to the particular Parliament.[35] The Webbs acknowledged some possible criticisms of their plan for a twin Parliament: that it would involve 'constant deadlocks' or that the Parliament with ultimate responsibility for finance would dominate.[36]

[27] ibid, 116–17.
[28] ibid, 117.
[29] ibid, 118.
[30] ibid, 118–19.
[31] ibid, 119–20.
[32] ibid, 121.
[33] ibid, 122.
[34] ibid, 122 fn 1.
[35] ibid, 122–23.
[36] ibid, 126.

But it was, as they saw it, the proper response to 'the failure of Parliament to cope with the collective business of the community, and the dangerous disillusionment with parliamentary institutions, and even with Democracy itself, which this failure has caused'.[37]

A comparable scheme was advanced by Winston Churchill in his Romanes Lecture, delivered at the Sheldonian Theatre, Oxford, on 19 June 1930.[38] He began by observing that '[i]t has been accepted generally until quite recent times that the best way of governing is by talking. An assemblage of persons who represent, or who claim to represent, the nation meet together face to face and argue out our affairs'. The general population tended to abide by the conclusions reached, even if they were not wholly content with them, given that they had chosen those who governed for them. The UK exemplified this approach to government. Yet, Churchill went on, it 'seems to lose much of its authority when based upon universal suffrage'.[39] The political complexities and pressures that arose made it difficult to sustain. As he put it, '[m]any of the parliaments so hopefully erected in Europe in the nineteenth century have already in the first quarter of the twentieth century been pulled down'.[40] Churchill praised domestic 'parliamentary institutions' as being 'precious to us almost beyond compare', and for their ability to adapt to circumstances.[41] Yet there had been a change in the nature of the debates that took place within them, from 'political and social' to 'economic'. The House of Commons was effective at dealing with 'political issues'.[42] However, the Commons was currently:

> engaged in digesting and assimilating a large new party founded, in theory at any rate, upon the basis of manual labour. It is a very heavy meal and the process of deglutition must take time. The constitutional boa-constrictor which has already devoured and absorbed the donkeys of so many generations only requires reasonable time to convert to its own nourishment and advantage almost any number of rabbits. And similarly the House of Commons tames, calms, instructs, reconciles, and rallies to the fundamental institutions of the State all sorts and conditions of men; and even women![43]

Yet digesting economic problems was a different challenge.[44] While it was possible to conclude political disputes by an 'expression … of the national will … [y]ou cannot cure cancer by a majority. What is wanted is a remedy.'[45] The public desired greater 'prosperity' and the task to be performed was finding a

[37] ibid, 131.
[38] Winston L Spencer-Churchill, *Parliamentary Government and the Economic Problem* (Oxford, Clarendon Press, 1930).
[39] ibid, 6.
[40] ibid, 6.
[41] ibid, 6.
[42] ibid, 7.
[43] ibid, 8.
[44] ibid, 8.
[45] ibid, 15.

means of providing it for them. Churchill observed '[a]ll kinds of popular cries can be presented for an election, and each may contain some measure of the truth. None in itself will provide us with the key'.[46] Consequently the idea of dealing with economic issues on a 'national and non-party' basis had gained currency. However, any effort at a cross-party combination of senior politicians would lead them largely 'to restate in civil terms the well-known differences and antagonisms which they represent'. Churchill called, therefore, for 'a non-political body, free altogether from party exigencies, and composed of persons possessing special qualifications in economic matters'. This 'Economic sub-Parliament', 'subordinate' to the full Parliament, would discuss the crucial and controversial issues 'of Finance and Trade', and arrive at 'conclusions by voting'.[47]

While being 'an innovation', it would be possible for the adaptable 'constitutional system' to absorb. It could be approximately one-fifth the size of the 'political Parliament', selected 'in proportion to its party groupings'. Churchill referred to the support for such an institution in Germany.[48] The views the Economic sub-Parliament reached would not be legally binding. But they could gain in force by virtue of their foundation in a 'consensus of opinion', creating the possibility of their being adopted whole at political level. Churchill stressed the 'urgent, vital, and dominant' problems that called for this measure. The existing 'constitutional machinery' could not cope with the policy challenges that arose. There was a danger that 'our Parliamentary institutions ... may well fall under a far-reaching condemnation'.[49] Emphasising the historic nature of the challenge, Churchill claimed that it was 'not less serious for us than the years of the Great War'.[50]

Beatrice Webb returned to the theme of parliamentary reform in a 1931 *Political Quarterly* article entitled 'A Reform Bill for 1932'.[51] She opened by referring to the existence of a strengthening perception that the present 'machinery of government' was not adequate to perform the functions required of it. A number of observers even believed that, were there a failure to 'rationalise the constitution and activities of British Parliamentary institutions', enabling them able properly to effect 'continuous social readjustment and progress', the outcome would be 'a slow decay of our standards of civilisation'. According to such prognoses, this decline would entail an authoritarian regime of the fascist or communist variety. Hence, Webb judged, it was essential to identify the cause of the problem and how it might be corrected.[52]

[46] ibid, 15.
[47] ibid, 16.
[48] ibid, 16.
[49] ibid, 17.
[50] ibid, 18.
[51] ibid, 1–22.
[52] Mrs Sidney Webb, 'A Reform Bill for 1932' in *The Political Quarterly*, Vol II, Nos 1–4 (London, Macmillan, 1931) 1–22, p 1.

She identified the overload of the Cabinet as a core difficulty, with growing demands for social intervention and economic management.[53] Moreover, there was a clogging of work to be transacted in the House of Commons.[54] As regards the latter difficulty, Webb held that 'British Parliamentary Government ... is to-day like the stomach of a man who habitually over-eats. The only remedy is to reduce the amount of food he has to digest.' For this reason the idea of 'devolution' had attained currency.[55] Webb insisted she intended no sweeping changes: Parliament would continue to be the ultimate source of constitutional authority, with the Commons and the Cabinet in practice dominating. She listed a number of changes that could be of value. One was to 'mend or end' the Lords. For the Commons, she noted the possible desirability of changing the way in which it was elected, altering the 'procedure' by which it operated and lowering the membership to around 300.[56]

Yet all these changes were entirely separate from the proposal Webb advanced for the 'devolution of business from the Cabinet and the House of Commons to another authority'. The new body she envisaged, to be established through 'a Parliamentary statute' was a 'National Assembly', with a 'national executive'. Possibly, Webb conceded, there would be a need for separate Scottish and English entities, and perhaps even distinct Welsh institutions. However, Webb clearly favoured a full assembly for Great Britain.[57] Advancing a logic counterposed to that more usually underpinning schemes for devolution, home rule or federalism, Webb held that the greater the size of the territory involved, the more fully the purposes of the proposal could be fulfilled. She identified a series of fields of operation the division of which between Wales, Scotland and England would be inappropriate. They included industrial and economic regulation and benefits. Webb judged, furthermore, that innovations such as motorised transport, the telephone and large scale manufacture and 'distribution' of products meant that the smaller territory 'as a unit of administration' was 'tending to become obsolete'.[58] Webb accepted, nonetheless, that forces other than the desire for administrative efficiency were also involved. The 'consciousness of consent'[59] might assume a 'form of racial self-consciousness', calling for separate institutions for the three nations, serving 'what are deemed to be distinct species of human beings'. Furthermore, Scotland had certain distinguishing constitutional features already: with separate arrangements at Whitehall level, different arrangements for local government, and its own legal system.[60]

[53] ibid, 1–22, pp 2–3.
[54] ibid, 4–5.
[55] ibid, 1-22, p 8.
[56] ibid, 1-22, p 9.
[57] ibid, 1-22, p 6.
[58] ibid, 1-22, p 10.
[59] ibid, 1-22, p 10.
[60] ibid, 1–22, p 11.

To reconcile her instincts and objectives with these centrifugal influences, she suggested two potential 'compromises'. One option would be to create three distinct units, but providing for 'the services necessarily common to the United Kingdom' to be 'administered by a series of Joint Committees' – following the example of the Joint Committees for Health Insurance – 'the decisions of these indirectly elected bodies being ratified by each assembly'. The second possibility was that there would be a single National Assembly for Great Britain, but for the handling of 'purely sectional business', members from Wales, Scotland and England might convene respectively in Cardiff, Edinburgh and London; with full meetings in London providing approval of the conclusions they reached and for dealing with matters of common interest.[61]

Webb found the second proposal the more agreeable, and proceeded on the premise that it were the one chosen.[62] She proposed a National Assembly of around 350 members (300 for England and Wales, 50 for Scotland), elected on three-year fixed terms. The choice of electoral system employed could be left to the Commons at the time it implemented the new system. She noted that in federal systems, whole classes of activity were apportioned to states or retained at the centre; sometimes in a loosely defined fashion. Webb favoured a more precise and circumscribed approach, with 'specific statutes or groups of statutes' bestowed upon the National Assembly.[63] The assembly would thereby be in possession of delegated power. Webb acknowledged the ongoing controversy surrounding 'administrative law' – that is the conferral upon a minister by Act of Parliament of the power to make regulations, perhaps even enabling the amendment of the parent legislation, and potentially protected from judicial intervention. She felt, however, that there would be less resistance to the proposition of vesting such delegated authority in an elected body 'having exactly the same moral authority, from the standpoint of political democracy, as the House of Commons itself'.[64]

The functions responsibility for which Webb anticipated being transferred in this way included the work of six 'or more' current ministries and boards: Agriculture and Fisheries, Health, Education, Labour, Mines, Transport, Works; as well as portions of the activities of the Board of Trade and the Home Office. Not only the existing Parliament but the Cabinet would cease to operate in these areas, since along with the Assembly a new executive would come into being. The Assembly would also become responsible for the oversight of local government and of 'specialised Commissions' such as the British Broadcasting Corporation, the Electricity Commission and the London Traffic Board.[65] Private bills would

[61] ibid, 1–22, p 11.
[62] ibid, 1–22, p 11.
[63] ibid, 1–22, p 12.
[64] ibid, 1–22, p 13.
[65] ibid, 1–22, p 14.

come within the remit of the National Assembly; and more functions might be devolved in future 'of public services yet undreamt of'.[66]

Discussing the way in which the National Assembly might operate, Webb identified two broad options. The first was to follow the model provided by the UK Parliament, within which individual members were 'practically powerless'. The second was to emulate the methods used by municipal and county councils. An adaption of this model would entail the Assembly electing a series of committees, in which all members would participate. Their purpose would be 'to direct the work of the Whitehall Departments'. As well as a 'General Purposes Committee' and a 'Finance Committee',[67] other committees would each deal with specialised policy subject areas. The members would elect a chair, who would, alongside a committee role 'become the head of the executive department concerned'.[68] Webb saw this approach as a far better means of securing 'control … by the elected representatives than' the present House of Commons.[69]

Webb concluded by presenting her scheme as entailing 'the advance of the British Constitution to a new kind of federalism'. In other countries – Australia, Canada, the US and parts of Europe – there were 'federations based on unions of geographical areas'. But for Great Britain, which was 'relatively small and densely populated', such a model was inappropriate. What was required, if the problem of excessive demand on executive and legislature was to be addressed, rather than 'federation by areas', was 'federation by subjects'.[70] A particular value of this system would be that it would allow for voters to express their dispositions in a more sophisticated form. For instance, 'an internationalist and a pacifist' might be a supporter of free market economics; while an imperial enthusiast might also favour social reform.[71] Creating two different elected bodies would provide a democratic outlet for this dualism.[72]

The proposals produced by the Webbs and by Churchill are relevant in the contemporary environment for a variety of reasons. All three texts depicted democracy as under threat, demonstrating the recurring nature of such claims. The sources of pressure upon the system that the Webbs discerned were similar to those often singled out today: rapid social transformation; increased movements of people; changes in the functioning of the economy; enhancements in the speed and ease with which information could be disseminated, reaching a far wider proportion of the public. For Beatrice Webb, developments in transport and communications technology, and in methods of distribution of products,

[66] ibid, 1–22, p 15.
[67] ibid, 1–22, pp 17–18.
[68] ibid, 1–22, p 18.
[69] ibid, 1–22, p 18.
[70] ibid, 1–22, p 21.
[71] ibid, 1–22, p 21.
[72] ibid, 1–22, p 22.

were rendering distance less important (though perversely, from her perspective, there was a simultaneous if unfortunate pressure for national differentiation within the UK).

The Webb schemes have a special salience in relation to Brexit. A significant source of controversy surrounding the policy of UK departure from the EU has involved the nature of the mandates and obligations created by democratic votes. What is the nature and force of a referendum result? What is its strength relative to that of an election to the UK Parliament? How does it operate from a territorial perspective? Beatrice and Sidney Webb considered questions of this nature, presenting a sophisticated conclusion: that the idea of one, single, 'Common Will' was not viable and needed to be replaced, as a minimum, with two different streams: political and social. They felt that a single institution, Parliament, suitably adjusted and segmented, could channel the different two forces. In her later article, Webb grudgingly conceded that a third territorial aspect might also be necessary. A crucial aspect to their scheme was that it could invest public authority with a democratic validity that current arrangements providing only for one form of parliamentary expression lacked. In this respect, an important dimension to the Beatrice Webb 1931 article, from the point of view of Brexit, was her proposition that a sub-parliamentary body could vest legitimacy in the exercise of delegated powers that might be lacking were they attached to ministers.

A challenge to the system that figured in the analysis of both the Webbs and Churchill involved the burden of work falling upon governmental institutions. These responsibilities, they felt, were growing in volume, and taking on new forms. To ensure that Parliament properly handled the expanding and shifting challenge it faced, their programmes were designed to secure enhancements in the capacity of this institution, enabling it to focus on specific tasks more effectively. Brexit, albeit depending on whether and how, precisely, it is enacted, brings with it the prospect of responsibilities previously within the remit of the EU being transferred (or restored) to the UK. The exact level at which they will each come to be based domestically – be it devolved or central – has been a matter of contention. But, whatever arrangements are arrived at, Parliament will have a significant role of some kind, for both producing legislation in new areas, and holding the UK executive to account for the way in which it operates within them. The proposals put forward by the Webbs and Churchill are probably the most prominent examples of the idea that some kind of sub-division should be introduced into Parliament.[73] It was never implemented. A different model, discussed below, for enhancing parliamentary accountability, involving permanently sitting, specialist select committees shadowing Whitehall departments, was ultimately favoured. Any effort to secure a major enhancement in

[73] For a post-war proposal along these lines, first published in 1947, see LS Amery, *Thoughts on the Constitution* (Oxford, Oxford University Press, 1964), 65–69.

parliamentary capability to match future challenges would be advised to take into account proposals not previously adopted, rather than simply modifying existing mechanisms. The schemes proposed by the Webbs repay particularly close consideration, though not because they should be implemented in all their details (as the Webbs themselves recognised). Their interest today derives from the way in which they sought to combine more specialist handling of specific policy areas with augmentations and reconfigurations in democratic authorisation for the performance of such tasks. Here lies a clue as to how objections to the rule of expertise might be overcome, aligning the two objectives of more effective and more accountable popular government.

II. PARLIAMENTARY REFORM AND THE ROLE OF COMMITTEES

At the time he published *Parliamentary Reform* in 1934, Ivor Jennings (whose work on a Western European federation we have already encountered)[74] was a Barrister-at-Law at Gray's Inn and a Reader in English Law at the University of London. He opened by noting that '[i]n a parliamentary democracy the legislature is the most important branch of the Governmental machine'. However, 'during the past fifty years', Jennings went on, 'the British Parliament has become progressively less efficient'.[75] Jennings held that the consequence of the weaknesses of the Commons was a constraint on the law-making capacity of Parliament.[76] The outcome was that '[m]any parts of the law are in a shocking state of obscurity and confusion. Others are archaic and unjust'.[77] Jennings took the view that all parties could broadly agree on the existence of weaknesses in the way Parliament functioned.[78] Nonetheless, his work was aimed primarily at Labour policy-makers;[79] and he recognised that his ideas were most likely to become a reality under a Labour administration. In this context he noted that his recommendations came in two different categories. First were those changes that would facilitate 'easier' law-making while not bringing about a 'dangerous' accretion of authority to the executive. Secondly were reforms that would enable 'effective' consideration by Parliament 'of the activities of a Government.'[80]

In Jennings's analysis, a Labour government would initially be more engaged with the first of his categories, focusing for the opening two-year period on introducing 'a number of measures of major importance'. Plans included in his

[74] See ch 3.

[75] W Ivor Jennings, *Parliamentary Reform* (London, Victor Gollancz for the New Fabian Research Bureau, 1934) 7.

[76] ibid, 7.

[77] ibid, 9.

[78] ibid, 9–10.

[79] ibid, 10–12.

[80] ibid, 12.

first group would enable Labour to carry out this programme 'without assuming any powers which could justly be represented as a temporary dictatorship'. His concern was that '[i]n the modern world, "emergencies" tend to become rather frequent'. While Jennings did not see Labour as a threat, he feared that 'in the name of patriotism, or its opposite, injustices to the individual will be committed and justified'.[81] He wrote at a time when authoritarian regimes of various hues were violating democratic values and personal freedom, including in Germany the Nazi government under Adolf Hitler, which founded its unpicking of the constitutional protections of the Weimar Republic in the supposed requirements of public safety. For Jennings it was 'fundamental that the law of Parliament should provide for justice and order, for it is the basis of all law. If Parliament permits the laws to be warped, there is no remedy but revolution'.[82] Working on the assumption that 'no democratic party desires to create precedents that anti-democratic parties might follow, I have felt it necessary to consider to what extent elasticity can be permitted'.[83] Having implemented its initial programme while affording 'ample protection to what will then have become minorities', a Labour government after two years might shift its focus to ensuring that Parliament was 'a more effective democratic machine.'[84]

Jennings opened the first full chapter of his book by proclaiming that '"Government by the people"' has in all countries proved to be a myth'. However, he held, realisation that literal popular rule had not been attained had not 'in Britain at least, destroyed belief in the Parliamentary system'.[85] Jennings then went on advocate the merits of the system of representative democracy, though he did not use the precise term. While the House of Commons was not fully representative of the public, 'at least it is a kind of representation'.[86] As Jennings put it: 'Elected representatives must have their ears to the ground; and, even if sometimes they do hear strange noises they do, in the mass, give expression to something which is not completely a travesty of public opinion.'[87] The operation of parties enabled differing outlooks to be advanced and for a debate of some sort to take place, which in turn enabled public opinions to manifest themselves, in turn feeding back into Westminster.[88] An ongoing dialogue between Parliament and people was thereby possible; and, despite many divergences it was possible to establish and discern 'common opinion' over certain issues, especially over 'social and economic conditions'.[89]

[81] ibid, 13.
[82] ibid, 13.
[83] ibid, 13–14.
[84] ibid, 14–15.
[85] ibid, 17.
[86] ibid, 17.
[87] ibid, 17.
[88] ibid, 17–18.
[89] ibid, 18.

Having discussed what he saw as the necessarily subtle relationship between electors and elected in the Commons, Jennings then discussed another key representative institution that was not itself directly accountable to voters and was therefore a stage removed from them. Parliament did 'not govern'. Rather, the 'General Election puts a small body of persons in charge of the governmental machine'. They were dependent upon the executive machinery, that is, the Civil Service. To some extent it influenced them, while they also shaped its actions. These ministers possessed only 'control', though it was 'in itself a vast power'. Though they were perhaps extraordinary people they were nonetheless fallible, liable to various forms of enticement and persuasion. Parliament had an important role: maintaining two-way contact between ministers and 'public opinion'.[90] While it was 'necessary to govern by public opinion',[91] Jennings observed, 'public opinion must be educated'.[92]

In discussing the relationship between the executive and Parliament, Jennings argued that 'the Government has control over the House of Commons'.[93] The loyalty of backbenchers could be relied on because 'fear of a dissolution or of the entry into office of the Opposition enables the Government to override even a majority opinion on its own side'.[94] Even in circumstances of minority government, a party that holds the 'balance of power' had to be cautious about moving its support from one side to another.[95] The Commons, then, had two core functions: to facilitate the discussion of 'the actions and proposals of the government'; and of possible policies that might 'be adopted … by the present Government or by some future Government'.[96] In performing them, the channeling of public opinion was crucial. For this reason, 'Parliamentary procedure must be adapted' so to ensure that 'debates' were 'about general principles'.[97] Consideration of more detailed points was needed but was more appropriate for committees.[98] It was a means of ensuring 'supervision' of the activities of civil servants by Parliament, since ministers could not exercise complete oversight of those who were technically responsible to them.[99]

Jennings identified five chief flaws in the existing operation of Parliament. First, there was not enough space in the schedule for the executive to pass more than a small portion of the measures it wanted.[100] Secondly, the increasingly 'technical' nature of law made proper scrutiny difficult.[101] Thirdly, there was a

[90] ibid, 19.
[91] ibid, 19.
[92] ibid, 20.
[93] ibid, 20.
[94] ibid, 21.
[95] ibid, 21.
[96] ibid, 22.
[97] ibid, 23.
[98] ibid, 23.
[99] ibid, 25.
[100] ibid, 31–33.
[101] ibid, 33–34.

tendency – albeit sometimes overstated by the judiciary – towards inadequate drafting.[102] Fourthly, there was a lack of allowance for the production of legislation not emanating from the government.[103] Fifthly, a means of ensuring that close contact was established between the executive and the Commons – and by extension, the public – was absent.[104] In discussing means of correcting these faults, one model Jennings considered, and discarded, was the use of the referendum. His reason was 'that there is no "general will"'.[105] Jennings went on '[t]here is, of course, a majority for or against any specific proposal at any given time. But it does not follow that a referendum taken on Saturday will have the same result as it would if it were taken on the following Monday'.[106] Moreover, even where a specific vote satisfactorily discerned the wishes of the people, it did not follow that they would be content with the consequences of its implementation: for instance, if a reduction in taxes led to the removal of public services. Jennings concluded: '[g]overnment is a single problem that demands unified control'.[107] External policy and economic policy, for instance, could not be separated in the way the Webbs (whose proposal he discussed) envisaged. If every voter was able fully to grasp all the considerations of government, then 'direct democracy' might be viable. But such a position did not prevail.[108]

Having also dismissed devolution in various forms, Jennings went on to consider what he saw as the remaining credible solution to the difficulties of parliamentary overload: reform of the House of Commons. He expressly left aside discussion of the House of Lords.[109] Jennings made a wide variety of proposals in his work, including, for instance, for enhancements to the House of Commons library staff, enabling it to produce briefing papers for members.[110] He considered the legislative process in full and made various recommendations, such as requiring the government to provide in advance of the second reading stage 'an explanation of what a Bill proposes to do, and *why*'.[111] The most substantial proposal Jennings made in this area involved changes to the system of legislative standing committees, where he believed all bills should be sent, with no use made of Committees of the Whole House.[112] This measure would make overall time-savings for the Commons and improve the quality of legislative scrutiny.[113]

[102] ibid, 34–35.
[103] ibid, 35.
[104] ibid, 35–36.
[105] ibid, 52.
[106] ibid, 52.
[107] ibid, 52–53.
[108] ibid, 55.
[109] ibid, 56.
[110] ibid, 161–63.
[111] ibid, 69.
[112] ibid, 82.
[113] ibid, 92.

Crucially, he insisted, these bodies should not be microcosms of the Commons, but should aspire towards 'unity'. Discussions and votes on a partisan basis were without value. Standing committees also needed access to advice on par with that provided to the relevant minister, either from the minister, or better still from the actual officials who had furnished it. For civil servants to deal directly with a parliamentary committee, though the preferable option, would require an adjustment of existing constitutional understandings. Jennings hoped that standing committees could obtain 'other expert opinion', to assist them in their deliberations.[114] This approach would enable outside groups to input directly into the law-making process. Jennings regarded this possibility favourably, though recognised 'dangers'. As he put it '[t]he practice of lobbying has already gone further than the comparatively unbiased person desires'.[115] Yet it was better for this kind of activity to take place in the open than through existing covert means.[116] Jennings called for these standing committees to 'be as specialist in character as a committee of members of Parliament can ever be'.[117] A committee would therefore be formed to handle bills issued by each department, or in some instances connected groups of departments. The members would have an interest in the subject matter.[118] A government minister, possibly the relevant Parliamentary Secretary, would attend but not – in the interests of the autonomy of the committee – be the chair, who would be appointed by the Committee of Selection.[119]

The plans Jennings advanced for committees in the Commons extended further, taking in not only legislation but also policy. He held that existing parliamentary working methods reflected the concerns of a time before the extension of governmental activity into the social and economic spheres. The election of a future Labour government would entail more such expansion. Oversight of government policy in plenary was no longer sufficient. One problematic aspect of this tendency was the loss of effective parliamentary control over civil servants, who were often in practice those who made the decisions. Jennings therefore advocated the formation of cross-party committees, reflecting the make-up of the Commons, attached to particular departments or sometimes groups thereof.[120] Each such committee:

> would obtain information, discuss the need for legislation, and debate policy generally. It would report to the House anything which it regarded as important. It would publish anything necessary to create or inform public opinion. It would be, in short, a permanent Departmental Committee or Royal Commission.[121]

[114] ibid, 83.
[115] ibid, 90.
[116] ibid, 91.
[117] ibid, 84.
[118] ibid, 85–86.
[119] ibid, 99–100.
[120] ibid, 140–44.
[121] ibid, 144.

Jennings proposed that the specialist legislative and policy committees he described be merged into one, creating bodies that could investigate policy, identify a need for legislation, scrutinise any bills that were consequently brought forward, and consider their impact after they came into force.[122] Jennings was insistent that the committees he advocated would not supplant the functions of the executive, but that they would help the Commons in its proper functions, which were to 'discuss and assent to the Government's proposals', proposing alterations to them, discussing 'political issues' and scrutinising the 'detail'.[123] Jennings saw it as important that policy as well as legislation should be overseen, since it was 'largely a historical accident whether a Government proposal does or does not need legislation'.[124] If, as he accepted was likely to be the case, the powers delegated to ministers were to increase, it was important that they could properly be held accountable.[125]

Jennings discussed the future of delegated legislation. He was concerned primarily with the means by which it could lessen the burden upon the Commons timetable without violating key constitutional values.[126] Jennings proposed six general categories of activity that could be dealt with by 'Ministerial Regulations',[127] involving organisational and procedural matters. He then went on to consider the less regular 'emergency' use of delegated legislation, 'such as might be necessary when a Labour Government assumed office'.[128] Jennings held that a Labour administration would need to create both 'the powers necessary to transfer existing capitalist enterprises to public control and the powers necessary to prevent sabotage by a minority'.[129] The 'sabotage' scenario he had in mind seemed to involve, while socialisation measures were passing through Parliament, 'the City of London' creating 'such financial difficulties that all progress would be stopped and the energies of the Government directed solely to maintaining the existing state of affairs'. In other words, he feared disruption from financial traders seeking to frustrate the government in the implementation of its policy programme. Jennings felt that a Labour administration 'would be justified in taking powers' to preclude this outcome.[130] These authorities, Jennings concluded, should be 'penal' and could be achieved through modification of the Emergency Powers Act 1920. The capacity for 'transferring industry' could be acquired through adapting the model provided by the Economy Act 1931.[131]

[122] ibid, 144–46.
[123] ibid, 148.
[124] ibid, 149.
[125] ibid, 150.
[126] ibid, 110.
[127] ibid, 110.
[128] ibid, 111.
[129] ibid, 113.
[130] ibid, 112.
[131] ibid, 113.

Jennings, then, anticipated the extensive use of delegated legislation both for immediate policy objectives and for the use, if necessary, of the legal system to prevent speculation against their attainment. The safeguards he advocated were that a bill providing for these powers would set out the details of the precise sectors of the economy that were to be taken into public ownership and the control to which they would be subject. A tribunal for determining compensation would be established. The powers created by the legislation – which would be no more than 12 sections in total – would be exercised through Orders in Council, which would have force for a limited period, extendable only by a Commons resolution. The Commons would be able to override judicial decisions that an Order exceeded the powers provided for under the legislation.[132]

The Jennings programme represents a firm assertion of the value of representative democracy, focused on Parliament. It expressly counters, among other approaches, the idea that referendums offer a purer means of popular government. In doing so it engages with a perennial concern of democratic analysis encountered frequently in this work: the mandate, something necessary in principle, but complicated in practice. Another familiar theme is the idea of the system of government in general and Parliament in particular encountering difficulties. The most significant of the solutions he offered involved a shift in the emphasis of Parliament, away from the partisan battleground of the plenary and towards a more cooperative and focused committee environment. Some of the Jennings proposals have been realised in the Commons select committee system first introduced in 1979. These committees address the work of specific departments, obtaining access to ministers (though not as committee members) and officials, making use of other experts as evidence givers and performing a role as conduit between Parliament and the outside world.[133] Yet the insight Jennings offered: that legislation and policy should be considered as an integrated whole, has been overlooked. Though select committees may play some part in considering legislation, the main work in this area is not carried out by these specialist, permanently operating bodies.[134] Jennings feared it was policy, rather than legislation, that would be inappropriately excluded from the system he advocated. But the arguments he advanced apply generally: any separation of the two is artificial from the point of view of parliamentary oversight, and to the detriment of meaningful accountability. Jennings's views on delegated powers are a reminder that forms of law-making other than primary legislation have long been available. Governments of differing political orientations can

[132] ibid, 114–15.

[133] See the 'Core Tasks' for House of Commons select committees, issued by the House of Commons Liaison Committee, 31 January 2013: https://www.parliament.uk/business/committees/committees-a-z/commons-select/liaison-committee/core-tasks/ last accessed 8 September 2018.

[134] See: Meg Russell, Bob Morris and Phil Larkin, *Fitting the Bill: Bringing Commons legislation committees into line with best practice* (London, Constitution Unit, 2013).

be attracted to the use of regulations as a means of overcoming administrative blockages.[135] Their prospective use in the past has raised potentially contentious questions about the role of Parliament, just as it has lately in relation to Brexit.

Bernard Crick, a political scientist, published his Fabian pamphlet *Reform of the Commons* in 1959.[136] He started from the principle 'that Parliament is ceasing to be an efficient critic of the Executive'. Referring specifically to Jennings, Crick noted that '[r]oot and branch schemes for reform, such as were canvassed in the 1930s, are no longer the fashion and … no longer relevant'. He noted that Jennings had presumed that the advent of a radical Labour government would have necessitated a full overhaul of parliamentary procedure. Yet the Clement Attlee administration of 1945–51 had managed to implement its programme – albeit having to overcome significant resistance in the process – without modifying the basics of the existing system. Yet he cautioned that 'the danger of ceasing to think big is ceasing to think at all'. The reality of Parliament did not merit its standing in the outside world; and the public was beginning to sense defects. Crick held that in 'comparison with the popular assembly of almost any other free country, Parliament has fallen hideously behind the times, both in its procedures and in the facilities it extends to its members, and there is good ground for thinking that it would benefit from some fairly drastic internal alterations and repairs which would go far beyond mere patching'.[137] Crick saw reform to the Commons as needed to match a parallel tendency, that he did not object to in itself, but that he perceived as requiring offsetting: the expansion of executive power.[138]

He made a series of recommendations. First, he advocated that MPs receive enhanced secretarial assistance, facilities, expenses and salaries. Crick held, secondly, that MPs should have access to research support provided by the Commons, benefiting them with sources of knowledge separate from those of the executive. Thirdly, he argued, being an MP should be the main occupation of those who filled the role, enabling them to dedicate maximum time to the performance of it. Fourthly, a system of 'standing specialised committees should be established' – not necessarily all at once – enabling the Commons to be 'an informed and effective critic of Government policy and administration which, at the moment, in so many respects, it is not'.[139] Crick made broad proposals as to how these bodies, each with a policy area allocated to it,[140] might operate. Convening in the mornings, their proceedings would be 'reported both by

[135] For a classic criticism of the use of secondary legislation, see Lord Hewart of Bury, *The New Despotism* (London, Ernest Benn, 1929).

[136] Bernard Crick, *Reform of the Commons* (London, Fabian Society, 1959).

[137] ibid, 1.

[138] ibid, 2.

[139] ibid, 38.

[140] ibid, 35–36.

press and by *Hansard*'. They would 'draw staff for purposes of research and investigation either from an expanded office of the Clerks to the House or from an expanded Library'. While the committees would not have a 'power to send for persons and papers' automatically vested in them, they would be able to request the House to vote in favour of their receiving such access for 'specific purposes'. Provision would be made in the parliamentary schedule for the discussion of their reports. Members could serve on committees according to their own personal inclination (though not being allowed to join more than two such bodies at once), though there might be a need for a Selection and Allocation Committee, partly to ensure that there was 'a normal working majority for the Government'.[141]

Crick held that the committee stage of all bills could be taken before these committees; and perhaps eventually the report stage as well. Each of them might take on a role in scrutinising financial estimates, performed at that point by the Committee of Estimates. This distribution of responsibility could 'ensure a far closer scrutiny of estimates than is at present possible'. Crick concluded that '[t]he work of the present Scrutiny Committee on delegated legislation might well be better performed by sub-committees of the proposed specialised committees – with the power, for this purpose, of sending for persons and papers'.[142] Committees regularly considering legislation would be chaired by MPs from the governing party; but in other cases, following the model of the Committee of Public Accounts, there would be Opposition chairs.[143]

Crick was avowedly not as radical as Jennings, particularly as regards the supposed need to instigate enabling powers for a Labour government. Crick was also far less ambitious than the Webbs with their plans to create multiple mandates and their objective – shared with Churchill – of establishing sub-parliaments, rather than simply systems of committees. However, like Jennings, he perceived value in the creation of a set of specialist committees to assist in the oversight of the executive. His ideas in this area would attain substantial influence, as part of a current of thought that grew from the 1960s, prompting certain experiments and leading to the previously mentioned reforms of 1979.[144] But his ideas were not fully attained. Again like Jennings, he envisaged a firm legislative role for specialist committees, one that has not yet been attached to them. In as far as Brexit is likely to create new policy responsibilities for Parliament to oversee, it is appropriate to revisit this idea – including the specific suggestion Crick made regarding the handling of delegated legislation. But it may also be wise to consider more far reaching reforms than he chose to countenance.

[141] ibid, 37.
[142] ibid, 37.
[143] ibid, 38.
[144] Gavin Drewry (ed), *The New Select Committees* (Oxford, Clarendon, 1989).

7

The Territorial Constitution

Discussion conducted in advance of the EU referendum, and the question on the ballot paper itself, failed to convey the full constitutional connotations involved.[1] Leaving the EU, it transpired, had immense implications for the internal governance of the UK, just as being a member of it had.[2] Among the many – and to a large extent unforeseen – domestic constitutional issues Brexit has engaged, the distribution of legal and political responsibility at particular levels of governance has been one of the most charged. A first strand to this controversy involved that, while there was a relatively bare majority across the UK in favour of 'leave' among those who voted on 23 June 2016, there were substantial 'remain' victories in Northern Ireland and Scotland (and London). No formal provision was made for recognising possible divergence of this kind in advance of the vote, nor was it accepted as directly relevant by the UK government afterwards, when it manifested itself as a reality. Secondly, a strand in its own right, was the particular delicacy created by the implications of Brexit for Northern Ireland. In this territory there had been an overall 'remain' vote, but the position became more complicated, with a 'leave' majority among the Protestant, unionist community (as opposed to the Catholic, nationalist group).[3] There were, furthermore, difficulties in reconciling the special position of Northern Ireland in its relationship with the Republic of Ireland, underpinned by the 1998 Belfast or 'Good Friday' Agreement.[4]

A third strand of territorial complexity to Brexit involved how powers that might be repatriated from the EU after the UK left would be divided between UK and devolved level. While the UK had been a member of the EU, numerous policy remits allocated to the devolved legislatures had come within the overall remit of the EU. A dispute therefore arose as to which of these powers might appropriately be wielded according to the discretion of the devolved institutions, and which needed to be exercised at UK level to ensure that the integrity of the UK as a single state with an integrated market was maintained. An associated

[1] See ch 2.
[2] See ch 1.
[3] See ch 1.
[4] See Introduction.

consideration involved how decisions about the use of those powers that were to be used in a uniform fashion for the whole UK should be made, and the degree and nature of territorial input. Fourthly, there was disagreement about process, in particular where the power to make decisions about the shaping of new arrangements should lie: ultimately at UK level, or by consensus, and what were the appropriate mechanisms for consultation. Naturally, within these discussions, the devolved executives (or those that were operational) sought to promote their autonomy and role, while the UK government had a more expansive view of its position.[5]

It should also be noted that these third and fourth strands had two sub-aspects to them: how to ensure that the necessary degree of continuity at the point of Brexit; and what arrangements would then prevail in the post-departure environment. The following chapter seeks, therefore, through assessment of sources, to provide perspectives on two subjects. The first is the importance of the internal territorial governance of the UK to its relationship with the EU, and why exit from the latter should create such tension with regard to the latter. The second is that of possible constitutional arrangements for the UK in the future.

I. A FEDERAL UK: THE CHURCHILL PROPOSAL

On 13 September 1912, *The Times* reported a speech delivered the day before by Winston Churchill, then First Lord of the Admiralty, during 'his annual visit to his constituents in Dundee'.[6] It took place 'at a meeting of women' arranged by the Dundee and District Women's Liberal Federation, and was subject to continuous interruptions by campaigners for women's suffrage. Churchill explained that he wanted to discuss the implications of the Home Rule legislation then passing through Parliament for 'the general question of a federal system for the United Kingdom'. Churchill stressed that he was speaking on his own account, and not that of the government, because he saw an urgent need to stimulate debate in this area. The government, he explained, intended that the introduction of this form of autonomy for Ireland would be a precursor 'to a genuine system of self-government in all the four countries', while remaining as they were at present forever 'united under the Crown and the Imperial Parliament'. Churchill envisaged the establishment of between 10 and 12 legislatures exercising authorities vested in them by the UK Parliament. No particular obstacles would arise in introducing 'a Parliament or National Council' to Wales and Scotland. But while 'applying the

[5] See ch 1.
[6] 'Local Parliaments For England', *The Times*, Friday 13 September, p 4, Issue 40003.

federal system' to Wales and Scotland alongside Ireland would be straightforward, the case of England was more complex. Churchill explained that:

> England was so great and populous that an English Parliament, whatever its functions or limitations might be, could not fail in the nature of things to be almost as powerful as the Imperial Parliament, side by side with which it would have to live; and if there were, as there very easily might be, a divergence of feeling and policy between the English Parliament and the Imperial Parliament, the quarrel between these two tremendously powerful bodies might tear the State in half and bring great evils upon all.

If the establishment of 'a workable federal system' for the UK was sought, Churchill held, then it would be necessary 'to face the task of dividing England into several great self-governing areas'. Identifying some of these territorial units was straightforward. Lancashire, Yorkshire and the Midlands were all distinct and cohesive entities. The London County Council, 'to which it would be quite easy to add additional power' could form the basis for a further component of a federation. There were, therefore, Churchill judged, 'four great areas in England which might well have a conscious political identity, and might have an effective political machinery bestowed upon them'. Dealing with other areas in England in this way was more difficult. Yet Churchill felt that the obstacles could be overcome, given popular support and if 'public men of the country should give the best of their minds to solving the problem'.

He found the prospect of a federal UK entirely plausible, arguing that a country of 45 million people required 'a far closer attention and a far more intimate knowledge than they can possibly receive from one Imperial Parliament'. Churchill saw the task in part as an upscaling of local government, asserting that 'larger units ... are required for the welfare and active development of our country'. He noted the examples of the US, Germany, Canada, South Africa and Australia as viable examples of 'federal systems ... in which you can reconcile the general interest of an organised State with the special and particular development of each part and portion of it'. Though establishing 'a federal system would be an immense task' it would deliver substantial benefits for each component of the UK, and the whole. It would provide openings into politics for 'men' of ability who might otherwise be excluded. They might then work their way up to the UK Parliament, improving the quality of personnel within this institution, providing it with people who were 'not ... mere politicians and orators, but who had made their mark as administrators in their own country or province'. Churchill held that 'our public life would become richer; and our administration more sympathetic and more searching'. The transfer of work to these new legislators would lighten the load upon Parliament, enabling it to focus more on external policy. Finally, the formation of a UK federation could help 'open the way to that close union with the great Dominions beyond the seas which must be achieved if the greatness of Great Britain is to endure'. However, before any of these goals could be attained, Churchill stressed, the Irish issue must be resolved.

A century on, both the potential and challenges Churchill identified appear prescient. He perceived, correctly, that a model first driven by the contingencies of Ireland might have wider applicability to the whole UK. Yet Churchill also recognised, as is clear in the circumstances of Brexit, that the status of Ireland – or Northern Ireland – could be a huge complicating factor, potentially restricting more comprehensive constitutional settlements. If self-government were to be extended to the point of blanket coverage, then England, in his judgement, would have to be included as regions, not a single unit. The debate over the 'English question' continues today. Some support an English Parliament as a counterpart to legislatures in Northern Ireland, Scotland and Wales. Others – to whom Churchill was a precursor – oppose this view.[7] As a politician he recognised that the parallel existence of English and UK bodies would create an unstable power balance. He also identified that a full set of English regions was not immediately apparent, but that they could be discerned were there sufficient will to do so. For him, federation was beneficial both as a means of serving the particular needs of given areas, but also for the cohesion of the whole. It also created the potential for strengthened links with the outside world, in this instance the Empire. But how far the Churchill model fully merited the federal label is doubtful. Rather than a true sharing of sovereignty between 'federal' and 'state' levels, it seemed to involve power vested by the UK or 'Imperial' Parliament, that would retain ultimate authority.

II. RAMSAY MUIR AND DEVOLUTION

In 1930 Ramsay Muir, the political writer and Liberal activist, published *How Britain is Governed*.[8] In this work he sought 'to take an independent, critical, and realistic view of the actual working of the British system of government'. In tandem with this analytical task he intended, where he had identified 'defects and distortions' in 'our system', to propose how they 'might be amended without any revolutionary change'.[9] Central to his thesis was the dismissal of a prevailing perception he discerned:

> It is often said that the nineteenth century was a period of constitutional and political change, but that this work is now complete, and the twentieth century will be a period of social and economic change. This statement, which is repeated as if it were an axiom, is mere nonsense.[10]

[7] See eg Andrew Blick, *Federalism: the UK"s future?* (London, Federal Trust for Education and Research, 2016); Robert Hazell, 'The English Question' (2006) 36(1) *Publius: The Journal of Federalism* 37–56. A post-EU referendum discussion of these issues can be found in: Meg Russell and Jack Sheldon, *Options for an English Parliament* (London, Constitution Unit, 2018).

[8] Ramsay Muir, *How Britain is Governed: A critical analysis of modern developments in the British system of government* (New York, Richard R Smith, 1930).

[9] ibid, Preface.

[10] ibid, 319.

The nineteenth century, Muir argued, saw only three laws that 'directly affected our system of government' – that is, the electoral reform Acts of 1832, 1867 and 1884. But the twentieth century had already seen two such enlargements of the franchise, in 1918 and 1928, the introduction of restrictions on the House of Lords contained in the Parliament Act 1911, the provision for self-government in Ireland by legislation of 1920, and the recognition of the Irish Free State in 1924. This latter group of reforms was far more extensive than the former, Muir judged. Moreover 'the twentieth century will have to make yet greater constitutional changes if our system of government is not to break down'.[11] Efforts to achieve 'economic and social reconstruction'[12] had expanded the role of government, thereby placing 'so serious a strain upon its machinery, that very substantial changes are necessary if our system is to be adequate to the demands upon it'.[13]

Muir regarded practical developments – to 'conditions and conventions' – as more significant than alterations in 'formal law'. He observed that over 'the last half-century, and more particularly during the last thirty years, a series of changes have come about, almost unnoticed, in the working of our institutions which have completely transformed their character'.[14] The tendencies he noted included, first, an expansion in the scale and strength of the 'bureaucracy, which is now the most potent influence in our system' and which was subject to unsatisfactory control. Second was the rise of 'Cabinet dictatorship', taking authority upon itself of which it was unable effectively to dispose. This second tendency was supported by a third: the 'increased rigidity of party organisation', a trend that had 'almost reduced the House of Commons to a mere registering machine'. Fourth was the 'distortion of our electoral system', with results not properly expressing 'the mind of the nation'.[15] Fifth, the Commons was struggling effectively to carry out its tasks, because of the burden of work, procedural defects, Cabinet dominance, and the confusing way in which the government presented financial information. The sixth tendency was the compromising of the ability of the House of Lords to fulfill the role of a second chamber. It had come about partially because of the limitations imposed on the Lords by the Parliament Act. But the primary cause was 'the enormous increase of its size owing to wholesale creations of undistinguished peers for the purpose of financing party organisations'. Seventh and last, the combined ineffectiveness of the two Houses of Parliament in holding government to account, and an observation of this defect, entailed 'organised interests not recognised by the constitution … beginning to exercise direct pressure upon, or even control over, the Government, which often pays a greater deference to

[11] ibid, 319.
[12] ibid, 319.
[13] ibid, 320.
[14] ibid, 320.
[15] ibid, 320.

them than to Parliament'. The cumulative impact of these developments was 'a complete transformation of our system of government, which is now so different from the system described by Mill and Bagehot that their generalisations are no longer valid'.[16]

Muir discussed reforms in a variety of areas to address the problems he had identified. They included the introduction of proportional representation for parliamentary elections; a reduction in the size and responsibilities of Cabinet; and changes to the House of Commons and House of Lords. An important focus of his work was on devolution. He argued that even if significant improvements in its performance were achieved, Parliament could not fully cope with the expansions in the role of government that were ongoing. Furthermore, this pattern of growth entailed 'an excessive centralisation which is sapping the vitality of the nation'.[17] In this context Muir discussed devolution of two varieties: 'regional' and 'functional'.[18]

He defined the regional brand of devolution as 'the creation of subordinate legislative bodies for defined areas of the country, upon which various responsibilities now inadequately performed by Parliament would be "devolved"'.[19] In making the basic case for such a change, he noted that the only country internationally in which a population on the scale of the UK was subject to a single legislature and executive was Japan (France and Italy, though 'unitary' in nature, had smaller populations and less extensive external roles to manage). By contrast, the US had 48 states; Germany 18; Canada nine provinces; and Australia six states. While the UK had a population of approximately 45,000,000, Canada and Australia had, respectively, 10,000,000 and 6,000,000. However, while there might be general support for the idea of devolution in the UK, detailed plans with firm backing from a political party were absent.[20]

Muir noted that an extensive form of 'devolution' had been introduced to Northern Ireland; and asserted that had it been offered to Ireland sooner, then the formation of the Irish Free State could have been avoided.[21] He judged the Northern Ireland experiment to be 'working well', reducing the pressure of business on the UK Parliament.[22] Muir described how there were also long-standing calls from Wales and Scotland for a similar constitutional measure. As in the case of Ireland, the motive was nationalist in nature. Muir judged that independence was not on the agenda in the case of Wales and Scotland, but that 'both of them value their distinctive national characteristics, and want to cultivate them'. Both nations feared the imposition of homogeneity from

[16] ibid, 321.
[17] ibid, 323.
[18] ibid, 324.
[19] ibid, 277.
[20] ibid, 278.
[21] ibid, 278–79.
[22] ibid, 280.

London, Muir argued. In his assessment, '[t]he more active and powerful the highly organised bureaucracy of Whitehall becomes, the more these fears grow'.[23]

Muir observed that some interpreted devolution as entailing solely 'the establishment of subordinate legislatures in Scotland and Wales'. While this approach might 'satisfy the nationalist sentiment of these countries', if presented in these terms it would meet with resistance in England, as well as in Wales and Scotland. Furthermore, it would not achieve a substantial reduction in the workload of the UK Parliament. Muir therefore judged that devolution would need to be introduced to England. He seemed to take as a given that it would not involve the establishment of a legislature for the whole of England. Rather, his model entailed 'setting up perhaps half a dozen provincial legislatures, and assigning to them full responsibility for substantial departments of government, which would be withdrawn from the purview of the central Parliament'. Muir recalled that Winston Churchill had once set out, in vague terms, such a scheme, but that no other senior politician had done so.[24]

As well as addressing sub-UK nationalism and the overloading of Parliament, Muir saw devolution as a response to a debilitating social trend in the UK. Not only was local government becoming subordinate to the centre, London had come to dominate in a range of other fields: trade, finance, industry, the press and the arts.[25] Considering this powerful 'centralising tendency', Muir remarked:

> There is no country in the world, except France, where it is so strong as in Britain; there is no capital in the world, except Paris, which threatens so seriously as London does to suck into itself the vitality of the whole nation. Germany, for example, has many centres of vitality that rival Berlin; America has many that rival New York. The explanation of this contrast is that in this country government is completely centralised in London; while in Germany and in America it is largely decentralised.[26]

Muir considered the geographical units to which devolution would take place, putting forward a tentative proposal to facilitate discussion.[27] The identification of the first two components of this system was straightforward: the 'Kingdom of Scotland', the population of which was about 4,000,000; and the 'Principality of Wales (and Monmouthshire)', the population of which was approximately 2,000,000.[28] The division of England into 'Provinces' was a more complicated task. One candidate would be London, with 'the whole residential area dependent upon it'. Numbering about 9,000,000, its inhabitancy would

[23] ibid, 280.
[24] ibid, 281.
[25] ibid, 282–86.
[26] ibid, 282.
[27] ibid, 289.
[28] ibid, 286.

exceed that of nineteen states in Europe.[29] A further 'natural region' would be the 'North-west – Lancashire, Cheshire, Cumberland and Westmoreland, the lands between the Pennines and the Irish Sea', with a 6,000,000 population.[30] Next was '[t]he ancient realm of Northumbria – Yorkshire, Durham and Northumberland' (6,000,000). Then came East Anglia, along with various countries and territories that covered roughly the same area as 'Cromwell's Eastern Association' (2,500,000). Peterborough could be the capital for this region. Ten Midlands counties, centred on Birmingham, would comprise a population of about 5,000,000. A 'south-western' territory 'from Hampshire and Gloucestershire to Cornwall' would account for approximately 4,500,000 people, focused on either Bristol or Plymouth. The final Province would be composed of the 'south-eastern counties' of Surrey, Sussex and Kent, with about 2,000,000.[31]

Muir judged his draft proposal to have demonstrated that it was feasible 'to devise a scheme which would give us Provinces of substantial size, and of more or less distinctive character, each capable of being administered from a convenient centre'. Each would have its own legislature and departments, taking over those responsibilities transferred from the Westminster and Whitehall centre. It would be required to 'raise its own revenue' for expenditure purposes, through means defined in the statute that created it.[32] In determining the powers that would be 'transferred' to the devolved institutions, Muir began by setting out those responsibilities that had to be reserved to the centre: 'foreign relations, imperial relations, defence, currency, tariffs, the administration of the National Debt, the Post Office'.[33] What functions, precisely, should be devolved? In the case of Northern Ireland, there were departments for Agriculture, Commerce, Education, Home Affairs and Labour. While Northern Ireland was a useful model to some extent, Muir concluded that some of the functions exercised at devolved level in this instance were not applicable to the remainder of the UK. They included 'justice'. Scotland had its own legal system, but the emergence of multiple legal systems in other areas was undesirable – though responsibility for the police and prisons, he held, could be transferred. Divergence in 'the regulation of trade and industry' and in commercial and industrial law was also to be avoided.[34] Similarly, social insurance should be retained at the centre.[35] The powers remaining that were suitable for devolution were: '[a]griculture and fisheries, public health, housing, education, the relief of poverty, the regulation and organisation of local government, the maintenance of order'.[36]

[29] ibid, 287.
[30] ibid, 286–87.
[31] ibid, 288.
[32] ibid, 289.
[33] ibid, 289.
[34] ibid, 290.
[35] ibid, 291.
[36] ibid, 291.

While within these areas, the devolved institutions could appropriately 'wield large powers', they would do so, Muir held 'subject to the ultimate sovereignty of the Imperial Parliament'.[37] Some kind of central limiting mechanism was necessary, he argued, to prevent excessive variations of approach. It was not desirable for the 'Imperial Government' to exercise '[d]irect control', since to do so would undermine the devolved authorities. However:

> some means of co-ordination and consultation would clearly be necessary. The Secretary of State for Home Affairs might perhaps be charged with the duty of keeping in touch with the work of the subordinate administrations, holding, possibly periodical conferences with their chiefs, and advising the Cabinet as to the use of that reserve power of over-riding legislation of which the Imperial Parliament could not divest itself, though it would use it as little as possible.[38]

In considering the role of the 'Imperial Parliament' in relation to devolved legislation, Muir first discussed whether bills ought to be tabled at Westminster, possibly for scrutiny by a Committee of Both Houses. He rejected this idea as 'time-devouring' and likely to generate tension between devolved and central tiers. Muir then proposed another procedure that might reconcile provincial autonomy with the need to retain the overall integrity of the UK. It rested on his express assumption that the provincial legislatures would be unicameral, and that they could refer bills to the 'Second Chamber of the Imperial Parliament'.[39] Such a procedure would be more legitimate, Muir argued, if it was coupled with a reform of the composition of the House of Lords.[40] This particular model was influenced by observation of federal constitutions such as those of Australia, Germany and the US, 'in which the Second Chamber specifically represents the component members of the federation'.[41] The possible scheme he set out for the UK, in the context of the introduction of devolution, involved 'the subordinate legislatures each electing a number of members proportionate to their population. A body elected in this way, by the methods of proportional representation, might be an excellent Second Chamber; it might even be strong enough to oppose an effective barrier to ill-considered revolutionary changes'.[42]

Having put forward his broad outline for a system of devolution, Muir concluded 'that a large scheme of devolution is quite practical', provided it took account of the issues he had identified.[43] He suspected that as a subject it was likely to achieve added salience in future, particularly 'under the impetus of national sentiment in Scotland and Wales'.[44] For Muir, devolution was

[37] ibid, 291.
[38] ibid, 292.
[39] ibid, 292.
[40] ibid, 293.
[41] ibid, 267.
[42] ibid, 268.
[43] ibid, 295.
[44] ibid, 294.

part of a broader package of constitutional change, that would promote transformation in the nature of UK society, including challenging the cultural and economic hegemony of London. To introduce it in some parts of the country but not others, he believed, would be to court difficulties. Like Churchill, Muir envisaged an England of the regions rather than a single English unit, with both men recognising that discerning precise divisions for the whole of England required effort. Unlike Churchill, Muir did not use the term 'federal', though used analogies with federal systems in presenting his case. In that he envisaged the UK Parliament retaining ultimate authority, including to override the devolved institutions in their spheres of operation, he was correct to avoid the 'federal' label. The idea that there would exist such a right of intervention, but that it would be deployed 'as little as possible', demonstrated foresight. In the late 1990s the UK Parliament legislated for three devolved systems while expressly retaining a right of intervention. This power came to be subject to the Sewel Convention, the status and workings of which became a focus of controversy in relation to Brexit.[45]

At the core of this Brexit-related dispute was an argument over powers that needed to be located at UK level after departure from the EU. Muir had in fact provided an insightful account of those authorities that could and could not be devolved. He identified powers that would become part of the devolved systems from the late 1990s, in particular agriculture and education. Muir supported fiscal devolution, something that the UK would move towards only cautiously. In identifying what should be reserved, alongside such remits as foreign affairs, tariffs, defence and monetary policy, Muir also discerned the need for unified control over 'the regulation of trade and industry', industry and commerce. These types of powers were a potential source of non-tariff barriers. Their unification was necessary to the maintenance of a single UK market. The Muir programme, then, is a useful illustration of how devolution might have been designed were it developed at a time when the UK was not a participant in the EU.

Another aspect of the Muir programme that arguably prefigured actual developments was his suggestion for a mechanism to facilitate liaison between the UK and devolved administrations. The Joint Ministerial Committee has performed such a role, though its effectiveness is open to debate.[46] However, Muir made further related proposals that have not yet been realised: namely, for incorporation of the devolved territories into the second chamber of the UK Parliament. In this sense, through a structure that had a federal quality to it, the continued supremacy of the Westminster legislature could be reconciled with a guaranteed role for the sub-UK components, which would possess a share in

[45] See ch 1.

[46] Institute for Government, 'Devolution and the Joint Ministerial Committee', 23 February 2018: https://www.instituteforgovernment.org.uk/explainers/brexit-devolution-joint-ministerial-committee last accessed 9 September 2018.

that 'sovereignty'. The ideas of Muir offer a particularly useful guide for the present in this respect. Devolution as it has developed in the UK has emphasised the dispersal of power. There has been a tendency to neglect means of ensuring that territorial points of authority, once established, might be integrated into the whole, ensuring cohesion at the centre, both through providing them with protections against arbitrary interference and a role in decisions taken on behalf of the whole. Muir also recognised the wider impact that governmental arrangements could have. The location of the most important political institutions in London was more than an organisational detail – it had physical and material consequences for the territorial distribution of economic and cultural power within the UK. This observation demonstrates the fundamental social importance of a constitution, and why it is so important for it to be handled and configured in accordance with democratic principles.

III. MACKINTOSH, BANKS AND THE REVIVAL OF DEVOLUTION

In 1968 the Labour politician and academic John P Mackintosh published a Penguin Special entitled *The Devolution of Power: Local democracy, regionalism and nationalism*.[47] He began by arguing that local government in the UK was defective. Elections were unsatisfactory, with many seats uncontested and desirable candidates not forthcoming. The geographical boundaries of authorities were outmoded and not matched to the requirements of the areas they were supposed to serve. Local government was subject to growing interference from the centre and lacked control over its own finances.[48] In response Mackintosh called for 'a new form of regional government' that would involve 'sweeping changes of structure and attitude on the part of the existing central government and on the part of the new local authorities and their officials'.[49]

The need for change was compounded by the rise of nationalism in Wales and Scotland, most dramatically expressed in the form of parliamentary by-election victories for Plaid Cymru in Carmarthen 1966 and the Scottish National Party at Hamilton in 1967.[50] Mackintosh expected that 'an all-Wales elected authority' would be a controversial proposition, attracting criticism from 'the older Labour MPs as dangerous, and by Plaid Cymru as inadequate'. However, after functioning for a sufficient period it could 'begin to engage people's loyalties and diminish nationalist support till the demand for total separation was lost in a healthy competition over Welsh affairs and for control of the Welsh Parliament or Assembly'.[51] In the case of Scotland, '[o]nly an

[47] JP Mackintosh, *The Devolution of Power: Local democracy, regionalism and nationalism* (Harmondsworth, Penguin, 1968).

[48] ibid, 38.

[49] ibid, 141.

[50] ibid, 142.

[51] ibid, 150.

elected assembly or Parliament which had powers to debate and decide Scottish matters would meet this desire for greater involvement and local control'.[52]

In discussing the form his proposed new system would take, Mackintosh rejected the idea of 'a federal solution', with the sub-UK units possessing tax-raising powers as well as the central authority. He did so on the grounds that a 'clean' separation of fiscal authority that this model required was not possible.[53] He favoured instead bodies without primary legislative or substantial money-raising responsibility, but with regional planning functions, and certain powers transferred to them from central government. The units he proposed were Wales and Scotland, along with nine English regions. Six of the territories in England would be based on existing 'economic planning regions': Northern; North Western; Yorkshire and Humberside; West Midlands; East Midlands; and East Anglia. Problems arose with defining the South West; the area surrounding London; and 'the residual territory in the Bristol-Oxford-Southampton-Bournemouth quadrilateral'.[54]

For the South West, the difficulty was 'that the sentiments and interests of Devon and Cornwall plus parts of Somerset and Dorset are distinct and could in time have a certain unity, while Plymouth could be accepted as the administrative centre of such a region'. However, Bristol, which was 'the present location of the South-West Planning council', was 'far away and has a quite different area of interests around Sevenside'.[55] Another subdivision including Bristol, Bath and north east Somerset might be necessary; leaving eastern Dorset with Bournemouth and Southampton. There was some disagreement among experts regarding how far the South East region should extend beyond the boundaries of the Greater London Authority. Mackintosh argued for a maximalist approach, stretching 'to the borders of East Anglia … in the north, including Bedfordshire, Hertfordshire, Buckinghamshire, the south – east of Oxfordshire and Berkshire around Reading and the north-east corner of Hampshire'. Such a zone would cover almost the entirety of the area that 'in any way looks to London and whose communications network cannot avoid London'.[56]

He described the Welsh and Scottish institutions as 'assemblies' and the English bodies as 'regional councils'.[57] They would each be responsible for agriculture; countryside amenities; drainage; education; fire services; fishing; forestry; highways; hospitals; housing; police; refuse disposal; regional planning; regional transport; river pollution; support for the arts; and water supplies. They would also possess a 'general competence', allowing them to

[52] ibid, 170.
[53] ibid.
[54] ibid, 188.
[55] ibid, 188.
[56] ibid, 188–90.
[57] ibid, 198.

engage in any activity that was not expressly forbidden to them.[58] The English regions would have broadly the same powers as Wales and Scotland, an arrangement Mackintosh recognised might be regarded as an affront by some in the latter two nations. He seems to have envisaged that Northern Ireland (which still had a functioning devolved system of its own at this point) would also have a similar range of powers.[59] The UK Parliament would create the overall statutory framework within which the devolved authorities would then operate, possibly passing subordinate legislation as appropriate.[60] Mackintosh argued that this approach would:

> be an improvement on the formal federalism attempted in the various Home Rule Bills. It is unsuitable in modern times to try and allocate functions in their entirety, because there is a real popular pressure for uniformity of standards in some fields and the extent of this demand may alter rapidly. For instance in education the most appropriate model would be for the U.K. Parliament to pass an Act declaring that all state education must be free, compulsory to a certain age, and that certain minimum standards of pay and qualification for teachers must be maintained. Thereafter, the regional councils would be empowered to organize and run all aspects of education, making, where necessary, subordinate legislation for their own region.[61]

Direct elections to the new bodies (with approximately 100 to 150 members) would take place on a three-yearly basis.[62] Mackintosh anticipated that it would be possible to attract higher quality candidates than were presently willing to stand for local authorities.[63] He discussed whether the executive might be elected separately, 'a Governor of the kind elected for each state in the U.S.A'. Mackintosh judged that '[s]uch a person would have a very strong position and be able both to speak for the region and to represent its view to the central government'. But this approach would require 'a total rearrangement of the relations between the executive and the assemblies on lines unfamiliar to British politicians'.[64] Mackintosh concluded that direct elections for the executive were not desirable. However, the local government committee system 'should be swept aside. Governments as large and complex as those to be created in the regions cannot be run by groups of elected members deciding both policy and administrative detail'. The executive would be composed of a Prime Minister and a Cabinet including within it ministers with defined portfolios across a range of policy areas.[65]

[58] ibid, 193–94.
[59] ibid, 196.
[60] ibid, 196–98.
[61] ibid, 197.
[62] ibid, 199.
[63] ibid, 199.
[64] ibid, 200.
[65] ibid, 200.

Mackintosh was an important constitutional thinker within Labour.[66] Partly under his influence, the party would twice attempt to implement devolution programmes, though the idea was internally divisive for it. It did so first in the 1970s, but was unsuccessful; then finally implemented the system for Wales and Scotland, and reintroduced it to Northern Ireland, from the late 1990s.[67] As the analysis Mackintosh advanced suggested, an important driver for this project was the upsurge in nationalism in Wales and Scotland.[68] Muir – like Beatrice Webb – had recognised the significance of sub-UK national sentiment. But the point of intensity it had appeared to reach by the time Mackintosh wrote was of a different order. The model Mackintosh proposed, therefore, while intended to cover the entire UK, was to a significant extent a response to tensions in particular parts of it. He anticipated that in Wales devolution would be controversial at first, both within Labour and among nationalists, for different reasons. But he expected it would then gain support. In this prediction Mackintosh was broadly correct.[69] It is more difficult to argue that, so far, hopes of undercutting independence movements have proved to be realistic, particularly in the case of Scotland.[70]

Mackintosh was wise to deny the applicability of the term 'federal' to his system. Not providing for legislative or fiscal power at sub-UK level, it was more modest than that of Muir (who himself eschewed the 'federal' label). The Mackintosh model was in many ways an augmented form of local government with a national element to it. The actual devolution systems have acquired powers – in the law-making and fiscal fields – more extensive than Mackintosh envisaged for them. But his vision of a more comprehensive system has not yet come about. England has been left behind. Though there have been limited devolution initiatives since the Scottish independence referendum of 2014, they do not have the scope of those in Wales, Scotland or Northern Ireland. Moreover, they have tended to involve the imposition from the centre of a directly elected mayor – a structure that Mackintosh discussed and specifically ruled out.[71]

[66] For an acknowledgement of his influence by a critic, see: Tony Wright, 'The referendum: the case against John Mackintosh' (1975) 46(2) *The Political Quarterly* 153–60.

[67] For a classic study in this area, see: Vernon Bogdanor, *Devolution in the United Kingdom* (Oxford, Oxford University Press, 2001).

[68] See eg HM Drucker and Gordon Brown, *The Politics of Nationalism and Devolution* (London, Longman, 1980); John Tomaney, 'End of the empire state? New Labour and devolution in the United Kingdom.' (2000) 24(3) *International Journal of Urban and Regional Research* 675–88.

[69] For instance, in the referendum held in 2011, there was a substantial majority in favour of enhanced devolution, though on a relatively low turnout. For an account of the referendum, see: Richard Wyn Jones, *Wales says yes: Devolution and the 2011 Welsh referendum* (Cardiff, University of Wales Press, 2012).

[70] For the view that devolution has the opposite of the intended effect in Scotland, see: Tam Dalyell, *The Question of Scotland: Devolution and After* (Edinburgh, Birlinn, 2016).

[71] Inquiry into better devolution for the whole UK, *Devolution and the Union: a higher ambition* (London, All-Party Parliamentary Group on Reform, Decentralisation and Devolution in the United Kingdom, 2017): https://www.local.gov.uk/sites/default/files/documents/devolution-and-union-high-637.pdf last accessed 9 September 2018.

Federal Britain? by JC Banks appeared in 1971.[72] He noted that he wrote in the context of an upsurge of interest in sub UK self-government, both in Wales and Scotland and in the English regions.[73] As he put it:

> Western man demands from government a high degree of security and certainty conjoined with personal liberty and some measure of self-government. The unitary British constitution until yesterday had seemed to serve succeeding generations well in each of these respects, and Britons shied away from changing its basic rules for fear of losing what they had...In the sixties deflation and devaluation, unfavourable economic performance in relation to European rivals, excessive immigration into England, and excessive immigration from Scotland have between them played havoc with the traditional feeling of domestic security and certainty. Liberty has seemed threatened...As for self-government, this has been increasingly regarded mirage, and the demand for its reassertion in one form or another has grown as the sense of security and freedom has diminished.[74]

Applying an historical analysis, Banks argued that political thought in the UK had been characterised by a 'unionist myth', minimising the multinational and regional divergence of the state.[75] Challenges to this perception had developed in the past decade, derived – he argued – from territorial disparities in economic performance.[76] As he put it: 'The sudden widening of the regional gap between the haves and have-nots brought about by the deflationary policies of central government in the 1960s no doubt explains the simultaneous reassertion of English regionalism and the dramatic revival of nationalism in Scotland and Wales'. (Banks accepted, however, that the two phenomena of 'regionalism and nationalism' were distinct.)[77] A further aspect to his analysis of territorial governance was his view that there was an 'over-concentration of power' at the centre, associated with excessive demands upon Cabinet and 'the over-burdening of the legislature. Much needed legislation is postponed session after session, debate on what does reach the Order Paper is restricted to the point that whole sections go unexamined, members' lives must be regimented to meet the exigencies of a relentless timetable, provincial needs come last in any queue'. Furthermore, the system required 'secrecy', since challenges to policy were inconvenient.[78]

In proposing a solution, Banks argued that devolution was in a sense an established principle of the UK system. It had been implemented for Northern Ireland, and calls for it to be introduced in Wales and Scotland were long-standing. Furthermore, it was not as challenging as another possible

[72] JC Banks, *Federal Britain?* (London, George G Harap & Co, 1971).
[73] ibid, 11.
[74] ibid, 236.
[75] ibid, 23–42.
[76] ibid, 43–47.
[77] ibid, 79.
[78] ibid, 188.

model, federalism, since it 'does not destroy the essence of the unitary state'. Any meaningful 'constitutional change' would need to 'aim at a positive diffusion of power', involving the establishment of directly elected bodies.[79] Banks rejected the idea of city-regional devolution, since it would not be applicable to the whole of Great Britain. He proposed, therefore, the formation, alongside Wales and Scotland, of 12 English provinces.[80]

They would be: Northumbria; Yorkshire; Trent; East Anglia; South-east; Wessex; Bristol; Kernow (Cornwall); Central Anglia; Severn; Mersey; and Cambria. Banks envisaged a process taking place in stages over a number of years. At first the devolved authorities would have administrative powers transferred to them, with responsibility for law-making potentially following subsequently. He anticipated that Wales, Scotland and perhaps Northern Ireland would develop more autonomy than other parts of the UK. The possible extent of this process would be difficult to predict in advance, but he noted that, while the UK remained a single state, functions such as defence and foreign affairs would need to be reserved to the centre. Another area that might become more decentralised was taxation. Banks argued, however, that grant support from the centre would be necessary, distributed in accordance with a formula taking into account the varied needs of different territories.[81]

In discussing the implications for the UK Parliament, Banks suggested a reconfiguration of the second chamber. While retaining the basic limitations that applied to the powers of the Lords relative to the Commons, the composition could alter to provide for 'regional representation'. One model might be to provide each nation and province with two members per million of population. It would produce 118 representatives in total (including Northern Ireland with 3), the largest being the South-east with 32, the smallest, Cornwall, with one. Alternatively, if each territory were provided with ten members, the overall figure would be 150.[82]

Banks closed with a consideration of the European dimension to devolution, suggesting a model he labelled the 'European Federation of Nations'.[83] He argued that the means by which 'European unity' might become 'an acceptable reality' was not through integrating the participating states, nor through a legislature elected on universal suffrage, but through 'a federal or confederal system based on small nations and regions of large nations as its political units. These units would be represented in a European parliament indirectly elected through their own legislatures, not by direct election'. One benefit of such an approach would be to remove 'any threat to unity posed by the existence of the larger national constituents of a European Union'.[84] Secondly, it would bring

[79] ibid, 237.
[80] ibid, 238–39.
[81] ibid, 236–57.
[82] ibid, 244.
[83] ibid, 297.
[84] ibid, 295.

government closer to those on whose behalf it was carried out, and provide protection for the position of the sub-member state components.[85]

Banks saw devolution as in keeping with UK constitutional traditions, and favoured its introduction for the whole UK. He regarded it as a means of meeting demands for heightened sub-UK autonomy, and of lessening the burdens on an excessively interventionist, central system. Like other plans considered here from Churchill onwards, he favoured an England of the regions – but like each of his predecessors, proposed territorial divisions that differed from the others. While Banks wanted self-government to encompass the whole country, he held that it was likely to be introduced to varying extents in different areas. Banks was correct in anticipating this outcome. Each of the three systems established in Wales, Scotland and Northern Ireland (and London) differed from one-another; and limited variants introduced across England are all distinct.[86] Banks was reluctant fully to embrace the federal label alluded to in the title of his book. But he employed some aspects of the concept in the model he set out. Like Muir, he envisaged the second chamber of the UK Parliament providing for territorial representation, thereby coupling dispersal of power with the establishment of a focal point at the centre. He also presented ideas that, as he recognised, had a European federalist dimension to them. Like Churchill, Banks recognised that multi-level governance could extend both to smaller units below the level of a given state, and larger entities above it. For Churchill, the Empire was the larger body in question while for Banks it was Europe. Equally, like Pinder and Pryce,[87] he saw European federalism (or confederalism) as a means of guaranteeing territorial autonomy. Building on historic continental links, the devolved institutions of Wales, Northern Ireland and Scotland all worked to deepen the attachments of the areas they represented to the EU.[88] Severing these links in the context of Brexit would prove controversial.

[85] ibid, 295–96.

[86] See eg Charlies Jeffery and Daniel Wincott. 'Devolution in the United Kingdom: statehood and citizenship in transition.' (2006) 36(1) *Publius: the journal of federalism* 3–18.

[87] See ch 3.

[88] Carolyn Moore, 'The Impact of Devolution on EU-Level Representation: British Regional Offices in Brussels' (2007) 17(3) *Regional and Federal Studies* 275–91.

8

The Executive: Organisation, Power and Constraint

BREXIT WAS PRESENTED as an exercise in popular decision-making.[1] But the UK executive was an important player throughout – and its role was a subject of controversy. The referendum took place to a large extent because of the internal imperatives of the party that formed the government at the time it took place.[2] After the referendum, the new Prime Minister, Theresa May, asserted a preeminent role for the executive as interpreter and implementer of the referendum result. This claim became subject to various challenges of a legal and political nature, through the *Miller* case, and pressure within Parliament and from a devolved level. The 'May doctrine' was thereby eroded somewhat as the Brexit period progressed. However, the executive remained the core actor in the Brexit process, devising policy (or at least endeavouring to) and conducting negotiations with the EU – albeit subject to various political pressures, and associated internal divisions. Executive power became an important and divisive concept in a further sense. A key source of the disputes surrounding the European Union (Withdrawal) Bill was the extent to which it would provide the executive with discretionary power necessary to attain the necessary continuity at the point of departure.[3] By extension, the role that UK ministers might play in determining the legal framework for repatriated authorities in the post-Brexit environment was also an implied point of contention. Executive power – its proper place in the constitution, how it should operate, and how it might be constrained – have long been issues of concern in the UK. Various reform proposals have provided insight into the subject, and possible models for the future.

I. EXPERT CONSTRAINT

In 1912 the constitutional historian and political commentator William Sharp McKechnie published *The New Democracy and the Constitution*.[4] Like other

[1] See chs 1 and 2.
[2] See Conclusion.
[3] See ch 1.
[4] William Sharp McKechnie, *The New Democracy and the Constitution* (London, John Murray, 1912) 1.

commentators discussed in this book, he saw the historic development of popular government from the nineteenth century onwards as having upset the traditional constitutional balance. Members of the lower classes, in his account, who had been incorporated into the electorate were growing more assertive of their own perceived interests and less inclined to deference. Candidates returned to Parliament were increasingly subject to the set programmes of the parties with which they were associated. The effect was to strengthen not Parliament but the executive. McKechnie felt that previous restraints on abuse of this power had been lost, and sought a substitute. He opened with the statement that '[i]f professions of politicians mean anything, the triumph of Democracy in Great Britain is now assured ... A fervent and almost servile eagerness to interpret and to execute "the people's will" is as persistently proclaimed by Conservatives and Liberals as by Socialists and Labour leaders.'[5] The author saw the realisation of this principle, if not subject to effective limitations, as in practice creating threats to the rights of minority groups (by which he meant those in a position of relative socio-economic privilege), from the majority group within a dominant House of Commons. Constitutional changes – the most significant and recent of which was the Parliament Act 1911, curtailing the powers of the Lords – had removed some of the most important constraints.[6] McKechnie was uneasy about the preeminence of democracy. As he put it:

> [i]gnorant multitudes know the bitterness of their own needs, but know nothing of their causes; and but little of the difficulties and dangers that surround all suggested methods for relieving them. They can by no means be trusted to select the alternative that is least likely to inflict injustice on individuals, or to bequest injury to posterity. If left to their own guidance, they will take the straightest and most wasteful course to the immediate satisfaction of their wants.[7]

He concluded that '[s]omething is needed to take the place of the ancient checks and balances that have been destroyed. Some new device is urgently required to restore government by free discussion to its ancient throne'.[8] In other countries a 'written Constitution' could perform this role.[9] For the UK, McKechnie proposed the formation of:

> [a]n advisory council...with the legal right to be consulted by the Treasury Board and to give advice upon all financial schemes, but without any powers of enforcing its opinions ... appointed under statutory authority. The number and qualifications of members of this body, with the rules ensuring the communication of information in sufficient time to make realities of their rights of criticism, remonstrance, and protest, would be defined in the statute creating the council. The Chancellor of

[5] ibid, 1.
[6] ibid, 164; 185–86.
[7] ibid, 128–29.
[8] ibid, 174–75.
[9] ibid, 177.

> Exchequer would be bound to make public, not only his own arguments and opinions, but also those of the committee. The members would be men who were not engaged in politics on either side. … Their qualifications would be carefully defined. Membership would be confined to financial and scientific experts with long practical experience, men of acknowledged theoretical eminence, or holders of high official positions.[10]

McKechnie believed that '[a] small non-partisan body of' the type he proposed, if made up of 'men of scientific standing and acknowledged impartiality' could play a part both 'in moderating the extreme views of successive Treasury Boards', as well as shaping 'public opinion'. Even '[t]he most optimistic Chancellors would hardly persevere in unsound finance in face of their united protest'. By this means it would be possible to provide some degree of 'protection' to 'even the most unpopular or the most helpless of minorities'. Equally, a Chancellor of the Exchequer with the approval of the entity McKechnie advocated for a course of action would be strengthened in its pursuit, though still responsible for it.[11]

Those – including the present author – who seek to query the executive response to the EU referendum, or those who raise concerns about supposedly 'populist' political tendencies in the UK and elsewhere should reflect upon the tone of analysis that McKechnie provided. He made some valid points about the dangers inherent in a democratic system, and in particular one in which a single mandate, vested in the executive, was afforded overweening systemic primacy. However, his work today reads as that of a supporter of elite interests in opposition to the possibility of meaningful social reform. The idea that a group of experts might possess the credibility necessary to check the executive might seem to stretch plausibility in the current climate. Opposition to such influences, as we have seen, has formed part of the programme advanced by leading opponents of EU membership.[12] It may be that any future efforts to limit the executive that rest on expertise will risk suffering from a lack of democratic legitimacy.

Yet the ideas McKechnie advanced should not entirely be dismissed as either anachronistic or unworkable. His focus on the protection of minorities may seem unattractive, since he defined these groups as those in possession of privilege. However, there are other less well-placed categories for whom protection is needed within a democracy. Moreover, in some senses the model he advocated for limitation on the executive has been implemented, most notably in the form of the Office for Budget Responsibility. The Budget Responsibility and National Audit Act 2011[13] requires that appointments to the Office are made by the Chancellor of the Exchequer subject to approval of or nomination by the

[10] ibid, 199.
[11] ibid, 199–200.
[12] See ch 3.
[13] Schedule 1.

House of Commons Treasury Select Committee. The Act contains requirements to ensure that members of the Office are appropriately qualified. It sets out the functions of the Office as being 'to examine and report on the sustainability of the public finances'. The Office is required to 'on at least two occasions for each financial year, prepare … fiscal and economic forecasts, and … an assessment of the extent to which the fiscal mandate has been, or is likely to be, achieved'. The Act also obliges the Office, at a minimum of once per financial year, to issue 'an assessment of the accuracy of fiscal and economic forecasts previously prepared by it, and … an analysis of the sustainability of the public finances'.[14] The parallels between the Office for Budget Responsibility and the body that McKechnie proposed are clear; and the Office provides evidence that experts can, within a democracy, make a contribution to good governance.[15]

II. ARTHUR PONSONBY AND DEMOCRATIC CONTROL OF FOREIGN POLICY

In 1914, the Liberal MP, Arthur Ponsonby, published a pamphlet entitled *Parliament and Foreign Policy*.[16] Written for the pressure group the Union of Democratic Control in in the early stages of World War I, he opened with the words 'Diplomacy has failed'. His thesis was that while the public mood internationally was more disposed towards peace than it had once been, politicians had somehow achieved an outcome that confounded this inclination.[17] Ponsonby therefore set out to answer the questions '*how* can the people exercise control over foreign affairs, in what way can their influence be felt and their opinions asked, and how can a Foreign Secretary be relieved of some of the unlimited power he at present possesses?'[18] The main flaw he found in the current system was that the functions of the Foreign Secretary were 'for the most part conducted in private, and no part of his executive action is subjected to the same scrutiny as that of the head of any other department'.[19]

Ponsonby made a series of proposals for reform. He advocated more socially inclusive recruitment practices for Foreign Office staff and a broadening of the skills contained within it. More importantly, Ponsonby held, there was a need for 'democratic control … over the present unfettered power of the Foreign Secretary. This can only be done through the House of Commons'.[20] To achieve this end,

[14] Section 4.

[15] For a critical review of the Office that takes issue with certain arrangements connected to it, but recognises the value of the organisation, see: House of Commons Treasury Committee, *Reviewing the Office for Budget Responsibility* (London, House of Commons, 2016): https://publications.parliament.uk/pa/cm201516/cmselect/cmtreasy/514/514.pdf last accessed 9 September 2018.

[16] Arthur Ponsonby, *Parliament and Foreign Policy* (London, Union of Democratic Control, 1914).

[17] ibid.

[18] ibid, 3.

[19] ibid, 3–4.

[20] ibid, 7.

he called, first, for a two-day debate of the Foreign Office Vote in the Commons every year. Secondly, Ponsonby argued that '[n]o treaty should be drawn up with any foreign country without Parliamentary sanction being given to its clauses in detail as well as to its formal ratification'. Thirdly, he held that '[n]o treaty, alliance, or commitment should be entered upon without the express consent of Parliament'. Finally, '[w]ar should not be declared without the consent of Parliament'. Ponsonby depicted his changes as part of an historic progression. In an earlier era, the monarch had 'delegated' treaty and war making functions, which were (and remain in our present) Royal Prerogative powers, to ministers. It was, consequently, 'only one further step that they should pass into the control of Parliament'.[21]

Ponsonby noted two possible objections to his proposals: that they would compromise the discretion that was necessary to international diplomacy; and that the Commons was too large an entity to carry out meaningful discussions of external policy. He insisted that there was no threat to secrecy, as all that was required was a general overview of diplomatic activity, not confidential details.[22] While Ponsonby accepted that the Commons might not be the perfect place for a debate about foreign affairs, the problem, he observed, was partly that it had been starved of information about the issues, a deficiency his plans were intended to correct. Moreover, a debate in the Commons was necessary from a democratic standpoint. Potentially, he held, the formation of a Commons Foreign Affairs Committee could provide for more effective oversight, though, he stressed, it would not seek to supplant 'the executive responsibility of the Minister'.[23] Ponsonby suspected that the arguments being deployed against the democratisation of foreign policy were the same that had previously been leveled against the application of similar reforms in the oversight of home affairs. He judged that, were his proposals put into effect, it would be more difficult for a Foreign Secretary to act in a surreptitious fashion (as he felt had regrettably been the case in the lead up to World War I, contributing to the occurrence of the conflict[24]), though success would partly depend on the minister concerned being willing to abide by the principles involved.[25]

Ponsonby was mainly focused on war and how to prevent it, or at least how to exert control over policy that might lead towards it. But his ideas had a wider application. Moreover, they remain significant today, in relation to armed conflict and other forms of activity. External policy remains an area of significant executive discretion, over which parliamentary oversight is a problematic proposition. To some extent, the proposals Ponsonby advanced have been implemented. For instance, under the 1979 reforms, there is a permanently sitting

[21] ibid, 8.
[22] ibid, 9.
[23] ibid, 10.
[24] ibid, 7.
[25] ibid, 11.

Foreign Affairs Committee in the Commons. Moreover, during the first two decades of the twenty-first century, a convention has begun to form that the UK government should, if appropriate, hold a vote on a substantive motion in the House of Commons before entry into armed combat (declarations of war, to which Ponsonby referred, are no longer in use).[26] However, there is no legal force attached to this requirement. Furthermore, the exact conditions in which it should or need not be invoked are unclear. This problem is likely to become more pronounced.[27] Democratic mechanisms that were developed with more conventional forms of conflict in mind will probably become increasingly difficult to apply as methods such as the use of Unmanned Aerial Vehicles (UAVs, or 'drones') and cyber-attacks become more prominent.[28]

The Constitutional Reform and Governance Act 2010 implemented a version of the so-called 'Ponsonby Rule', derived from an undertaking Ponsonby gave when serving as Parliamentary Under-Secretary of State for Foreign Affairs in the first Labour government of 1924.[29] Under this Act, the Commons now possesses – in theory – the legal right to veto ratification of a treaty.[30] Brexit, it can reasonably be anticipated, is likely to lead to numerous international agreements that might be subject to rejection. However, the means by which the Commons might go about exercising this power are not entirely clear. Moreover, the political restraints on such action could be immense. To reject a treaty could be perceived as detrimental to the wider interests of the UK; and would inflict damage – possibly fatal – on a government that, by definition, had enjoyed the confidence of a majority in the Commons. Similar considerations apply to the vote that has been promised to Parliament on any deal that the UK manages to reach with the EU in advance of exit. Ponsonby noted the importance of ministers being willing to cooperate with any system of enhanced democratic control. But it is equally important that those charged with operating the system from the parliamentary end are willing sufficiently to assert themselves with respect to the executive, if necessary acting collectively across party lines. Under a constitutional model in which governments are drawn from Parliament, there is a powerful structural urge not to do so. In such circumstances, a minority group that is willing to break ranks can force its will on the majority.

[26] Andrew Blick, 'Emergency powers and the withering of the Royal Prerogative' (2014) 18(2) *The International Journal of Human Rights* 195–210; Veronika Fikfak and Hayley Hooper, *Parliament's Secret War* (Oxford, Hart Publishing, 2018).

[27] James Strong, 'The war powers of the British parliament: What has been established and what remains unclear?' (2018) 20(1) *The British Journal of Politics and International Relations* 19–34.

[28] For the complications in relation to UAVs, see House of Lords/House of Commons Joint Committee on Human Rights, *The government's policy on the use of drones for targeted killing* (London, House of Lords/House of Commons, 2016) 32–35.

[29] Arabella Lang, *Parliament's role in ratifying treaties* (London, House of Commons Library, 2017) 10.

[30] *Constitutional Reform and Governance Act*, ch 2, Pt 2.

III. DELEGATED POWER: STRENGTHENING THE EXECUTIVE

John Strachey MP (whose father, John St Loe Strachey, we have already encountered as a leading exponent of the referendum[31]) and CEM Joad published the article 'Parliamentary Reform: the New Party's Proposals' in *The Political Quarterly* in 1931. It was described as 'an official statement of the proposals of Sir Oswald Mosley's New Party, relating to the Reform of Parliament'.[32] A former Labour minister, Mosley had resigned office in 1930 in frustration at the failure of the Labour government to respond effectively to the global economic downturn and the mass unemployment it created. He subsequently formed the New Party to pursue his interventionist ideas.[33] The article by Strachey and Joad is the only formal statement of party policy considered in this book, included because it does not resemble a regular document of this type, owing to its discursive nature; and because of the significance of the subject matter it addresses. The authors opened with the statement that 'Parliament is dying, and dying discreditably. Nobody except the professional Parliamentarians, can sit through its languid and half-hearted proceedings and doubt it'.[34] They observed that, since the end of World War I 'unemployment has sapped the strength of Great Britain', creating insecurity for the labour force, causing suffering for families, and absorbing public money that might otherwise have been invested in a renewal project. This problem of joblessness had also undermined the global credibility of the UK. While Parliament had frequently discussed the issue, the nature of such proceedings served to confirm the poor prospects the country faced. 'Year after year, session after session, under Government after Government, these debates have gone on. The endless, futile speeches have all been made – and re-made. To those who care for the future of Great Britain nothing is more horrible than to sit through these debates. In the ornate and hideous Chamber the nation's breath seems to grow fainter, speech by speech.'[35] Because Parliament was passing away, the country lacked the 'wide and good government' it needed.[36]

The authors identified two 'functions' of Parliament.[37] The first was that of placing a government in office in accordance with the party affiliation of those who were elected members. Strachey and Joad judged that Parliament was effective at this task. However, the second role was that 'it attempts itself

[31] See ch 4.

[32] John Strachey and CEM Joad, 'Parliamentary Reform: the New Party's Proposals' *The Political Quarterly*, Vol II, Nos 1–4 (London, Macmillan, 1931) 319–36, p 319.

[33] Matthew Worley, 'What Was the New Party? Sir Oswald Mosley and Associated Responses to the "Crisis", 1931–1932' (2007) 92(305) *History* 39–63.

[34] John Strachey and CEM Joad, 'Parliamentary Reform: the New Party's Proposals' *The Political Quarterly*, Vol II, Nos 1–4 (London, Macmillan, 1931) 319–36, p 319.

[35] ibid, 319–36, p 319.

[36] ibid, 319–36, p 319.

[37] ibid, 319–36, p 319.

to govern.'[38] Performance of the latter was not compatible with fulfillment of the first. Parliament was a legislature, scrutinising and altering every proposed law, even to the point of engaging in 'administrative details of the measures by which the law are put into effect'.[39] Strachey and Joad offered as an example of the latter activity a recent prolonged debate about the choice of trees to be grown in Kensington Gardens.[40] The consequence of this second parliamentary function was the existence of 'a body of 615 men and women selected partly by chance, partly by caprice' endeavouring 'to do the work of governing this vast Empire'.[41]

The outcome was pronounced confusion.[42] Important matters were neglected, while extended space was afforded to trivia. Debate was often retrospective, and informed neither by expertise or knowledge.[43] Government itself was prevented from performing its task because it was 'checked, harassed and interminably delayed by Parliament', while Parliament was excessively large, ungainly and too ignorant properly to carry out the role it sought to take upon itself.[44] The authors drew an initial conclusion. 'Democracy, in theory so perfected and completed in the Great Britain of 1931, has never in practice been more mocked and impotent.'[45] While the public could choose and replace governments, administrations once installed made little impact on economic malaise, and the approaches they took did not differ. A central source of 'this impotence of the people' was 'the decadence of Parliament'.[46]

To resolve this problem, the authors held that Parliament had to concentrate on its first role, that of providing a government, and cease its second, that of carrying out the work of government. This approach was the only means by which '[d]emocracy' could 'become a reality instead of a sham'.[47] The authors proposed four core changes. First, '[t]he initiation of legislation must be formally transferred to the executive'.[48] Secondly, legislation would come into force through 'Orders in Council'. In a revival of wartime practices, the monarch, following ministerial advice, would issue these instruments.[49] They would be tabled before the House of Commons for a period of a week. If, before this deadline was reached, 200 members or more requested it, a debate would take place on the measure. Were it voted down in these circumstances, it would

[38] ibid, 319–36, p 320.
[39] ibid, 319–36, p 320.
[40] ibid, 319–36, p 320.
[41] ibid, 319–36, p 320.
[42] ibid, 319–36, p 320.
[43] ibid, 319–36, pp 320–1.
[44] ibid, 319–36, p 321.
[45] ibid, 319–36, p 321.
[46] ibid, 319–36, p 321.
[47] ibid, 319–36, p 322.
[48] ibid, 319–36, p 322.
[49] ibid, 319–36, p 330.

be void. Otherwise, the order would come into force.[50] The authors envisaged that the outcome of this change would be a transformation in the character of parliamentary oversight of law-making: from positive to negative. Parliament, they held, ought to keep its ability to identify and veto individual measures, but should not devise and shape laws as a whole.[51]

Thirdly, Parliament would continue to be responsible for voting supply to the government in the same way as it already did, though with some tighter time limitations.[52] Fourthly, Private Bills (as distinct from Private Members' Bills, also being abolished), the devices used by public bodies to obtain legislative change, would cease to exist.[53] One important feature of the system advocated here was that Parliament would no longer have the ability to amend, but simply to reject, proposals.[54] Law making, Strachey and Joad held, had become too detailed and specialised for '600 amateurs' to alter in a worthwhile fashion.[55] Whitehall officials, while not perfect, possessed far more of the relevant expertise. Bodies meeting inside government departments, including outsiders who might or might not be MPs, could provide a superior substitute for legislative committees in Westminster.[56] Parliament, the article explained, would be able to remove a government from office and force a General Election ahead of the five-year limit of a Parliament; or to take the less drastic step of passing 'admonitory resolutions' on subjects about which concern existed.[57] The authors envisaged a more focused version of ministerial questions, and daily half-hour sessions with the Prime Minister (or nominated delegate).[58]

Having described how Parliament would 'abandon its present pretence of governing and legislating', Strachey and Joad then set out to define 'in whom or what is the power of legislation to be vested'.[59] The Cabinet would continue to be the central body. But the entity that advised the monarch on the issuing of Orders in Council, rather than the full Cabinet, would be a 'Prime Minister's Committee', comprising five individuals. Supplanting much of the role of the existing Cabinet, these Ministers without Portfolio would be responsible for 'the planning of a comprehensive policy envisaged as a whole in the light of a comprehensive survey of the nation's needs as a whole'.[60] The article then sought to deal with the anticipated charge that the scheme it set out would represent 'the establishment of a virtual dictatorship'.[61] First, they insisted

[50] ibid, 319–36, pp 322–3.
[51] ibid, 319–36, p 323.
[52] ibid, 319–36, pp 323–4.
[53] ibid, 319–36, p 324.
[54] ibid, 319–36, p 330.
[55] ibid, 319–36, p 324.
[56] ibid, 319–36, p 325.
[57] ibid, 319–36, p 325.
[58] ibid, 319–36, p 327.
[59] ibid, 319–36, p 329.
[60] ibid, 319–36, p 330.
[61] ibid, 319–36, p 335.

that the Committee would have no more power than the present Cabinet.[62] Secondly, they noted that Parliament would be able to remove the Committee at any point that it wished to, though it could only do so through a 'direct vote of censure'.[63] The article closed by noting that it might be possible to put its proposals into force through 'a "General Powers' Bill", transferring to the Executive the functions outlined above'. The authors also referred to the absence of the House of Lords from its proposals. 'The omission is deliberate. We are prepared, that is to say, to let sleeping peers lie, but only if they are content to lie. If they wake up, we are prepared to dismiss them, bed and baggage.'[64]

Stafford Cripps, a future Labour Chancellor of the Exchequer, wrote a *Political Quarterly* article in 1933 entitled 'Democracy and Dictatorship: The Issue for the Labour Party', tackling similar themes. He concerned himself with the charge he attributed to 'antagonists of Socialism' that, were they elected to office, 'the wicked Socialists will establish a dictatorship!' The objective of such claims, Cripps held, was to present 'our existing "democratic" institutions' as '[t]he only alternative to dictatorship'. Yet it was only through reform of the existing system that it would be possible to achieve socialism.[65] Cripps held that the Labour Party should formulate and publicise a clear policy in this area,[66] to ensure that it had a mandate when it took office.[67] He argued that the existing 'method of government' was consciously configured in such a way as to preclude a 'rapid or fundamental change of system'.[68] Two of the three components of Parliament – the Lords and the monarchy – were 'wholly undemocratic'.[69] It was not easy to predict what would be their response to an effort to implement socialism.[70] A government committed to such a programme might be stalled for two years by the House of Lords; during which time financial and commercial interests could work to undermine it.[71] Yet were a social democratic reform prevented, the outcome might be 'a revolution by force, followed by a dictatorship of the Proletariat'.[72]

Cripps supported, therefore, the abolition of the Lords.[73] A Labour government could recommend to the monarch the creation of sufficient numbers of peers to force through this policy. If necessary a General Election could be held on this single issue, to demonstrate public support.[74] Following the removal

[62] ibid, 319–36, p 335.
[63] ibid, 319–36, p 336.
[64] ibid, 319–36, p 336.
[65] Sir Stafford Cripps, 'Democracy and Dictatorship: The Issue for the Labour Party' (1933) IV(4) *The Political Quarterly* October–December, 467–81, p 467.
[66] ibid, 468.
[67] ibid, 475.
[68] ibid, 468.
[69] ibid, 468.
[70] ibid, 468–69.
[71] ibid, 469.
[72] ibid, 470.
[73] ibid, 471.
[74] ibid, 472–73.

of 'the dead hand of the second chamber, the problem would then arise of transforming the House of Commons into an efficient machine for socialist democracy'.[75] An abrupt change of approach would be needed, requiring in turn 'rapidity of action'[76] to overcome those who would, if there were delay, be able to 'bring about the fall of the Government by extra-Parliamentary means'.[77] It would be necessary to 'adapt the House of Commons procedure so that it may become more rapid and effective than it is at present'. Otherwise there was a danger that the government might succumb to an urge to 'act dictatorially'.[78]

The condition prevailing at the time of the formation of a socialist administration would be, Cripps contended, akin to a 'state of emergency'.[79] It was likely to take place in the context of 'a financial and probably an industrial crisis or emergency'. In such tumultuous circumstances, it was well established that 'the House of Commons gives the Government special powers to deal with the emergency'.[80] As a first stage, there would be a need for an 'Emergency Powers Act', drafted broadly enough to make it possible 'to protect the community from any economic attack by the Capitalists', including the possible authority to restrict the transactions of the City of London.[81] In considering the idea of such a measure, Cripps noted that there had been an expansion in recent decades in the 'legislative power delegated by Parliament to ministers and local authorities'. Cripps saw this trend as arising from the need to offset some of the harsher injustices of capitalism. At present it fell to the courts to decide whether the use of such powers fitted with the expectations of Parliament when it created them.[82] However, Cripps thought that, under the model he envisaged, the Commons should adjudicate, since it was best placed to determine what it had intended.[83]

Within this framework of extended delegated power, the role of the Commons would be to oversee 'the main lines of the National programme of legislation and to control the National finances in their broad outline'.[84] A 'small' Cabinet would issue a 'Finance and Planning Bill' once or twice a year, containing in it proposed legislation and associated financial consequences. The Budget would no longer be drawn up secretly by the Chancellor of the Exchequer, in isolation from planning for bills. Discussing and agreeing upon the Finance and Planning Bill would be the main function of the Commons in plenary. However, it might usefully divide into committees that would be formed 'upon a functional basis', providing a valuable outlet for the energies

[75] ibid, 473.
[76] ibid, 473.
[77] ibid, 474.
[78] ibid, 474.
[79] ibid, 475.
[80] ibid. 476.
[81] ibid, 476–67.
[82] ibid, 477.
[83] ibid, 478.
[84] ibid, 478.

of backbench MPs. These bodies would be able to 'control' the deployment of delegated powers by ministers.[85] They might consider 'supply'; and scrutinise bills in their committee stages. The opposition would be given clear opportunities to criticise the government, to prevent an excessive growth of executive authority.[86] Cripps wanted the grounds on which a government might resign following a Commons defeat to be narrowed, though retaining the possibility for its removal by elected representatives. This change would make debate in the Commons more meaningful, with alterations to bills possible without carrying the risk of destroying the government.[87]

The following year, *The Political Quarterly* published an article by another future Labour Chancellor of the Exchequer, Hugh Dalton, entitled 'The Labour Party's Proposals for the Reform of Parliamentary Procedure'.[88] Dalton believed that changes to the way in which the Commons operated were vital if Labour was fully to implement its plans for legislation with sufficient speed. A Labour government 'must have tools to fit the job'.[89] He dealt only with reforms to the Commons, writing: '[t]he House of Lords must go. We may speculate on the time and manner of its going, but not in this article'. He noted that Labour policy was 'to treat the House of Lords as an antiquated traffic obstruction on the democratic highway, and to remove it'.[90]

The changes Dalton sought for the Commons did not necessitate statutory enactment, in his view, and could be put into force simply by alteration to the Commons Standing Orders, an approach that did not require the involvement of the Lords.[91] He identified two areas in which improvements were needed: the 'allocation of Parliamentary time' and the 'form of legislation'.[92] Concerning the first category, Dalton wrote '[t]he present waste of time in Parliament must be experienced at close quarters to be clearly realised'.[93] It was important to make it possible for more bills to be passed, while continuing to allow for meaningful discussion, and preventing duplication of discussion of certain matters and the needless loss of time. To ensure these objectives were achieved, Dalton advocated the formation of a 'Committee on the Allocation of Parliamentary Time' or simply a 'Committee on Time'.[94] He felt that this approach could bring about 'a practical revolution in parliamentary procedure'.[95] For Dalton,

[85] ibid, 479.
[86] ibid, 480.
[87] ibid, 480–81.
[88] Hugh Dalton, 'The Labour Party's Proposals for the Reform of Parliamentary Procedure' (1934) V(4) *The Political Quarterly* October–December, 469–79, p 469.
[89] ibid, 470.
[90] ibid, 470.
[91] ibid, 470–71.
[92] ibid, 472.
[93] ibid, 472.
[94] ibid, 474.
[95] ibid, 476.

it was preferable to other proposals, such as the formation of 'an "Industrial Parliament," or of a system of Departmental Parliamentary Committees based on foreign models, or on false analogies from the procedure of British local authorities'. Committees of the sort others had advocated would in fact act as a brake upon parliamentary work.[96]

The second aspect of the programme Dalton outlined involved legislation. He held it should take a 'form … more general and less detailed than has been the case hitherto. Bills with a hundred clauses and a dozen schedules are a legislative monstrosity, and should be discontinued'. Dalton preferred that '[d]etail should … be embodied in Ministerial Orders, authorised to be made within limits laid down by a comparatively short and simple Statute'.[97] Dalton regarded this model as an extension of the approach already taken by the National government, citing the example of its application of import duties.[98] It could fall to parliamentary committees in some instances to decide whether a particular use of delegated responsibility came under the intended purpose of the parent Act.[99]

What do these three contributions from the early 1930s reveal? Clearly, they show that a perceived need to expand the delegated power vested in the executive is far from new. This desire can be in some senses well-motivated. Parliament will never be entirely optimal in its performance, and always has the potential to seem an encumbrance when urgent action is required. Yet the obstacles it creates are surmountable. Both Cripps and Dalton participated in a Labour government that delivered on its radical manifesto without a curtailment of Parliament of the type they envisaged. Moreover, there are dangers in such an approach. All three proposals described above sought to eliminate the Lords and even the courts from the equation of delegated law-making; and the power of the Commons was to be requisitioned, with its scope to limit the executive reduced. Even removing a government might become more difficult. Unchecked power can contribute to mistakes, and is vulnerable to abuse. It is an irony that Mosley himself, along with thousands of others, was detained without trial during World War II through a regulation issued under the Emergency Powers (Defence) Act 1939.[100]

Advocates of the expansion of delegated executive power can hold a variety of different political perspectives and motivations. In the 1930s it was Labour and the centrist (and in some senses proto-Fascist) New Party that were

[96] ibid, 477.
[97] ibid, 477.
[98] ibid, 478.
[99] ibid, 478.
[100] AW Brian Simpson, *In the Highest Degree Odious: Detention Without Trial in Wartime Britain* (Oxford, Oxford University Press, 1994); Aaron L Goldman, 'Defence Regulation 18B: Emergency Internment of Aliens and Political Dissenters in Great Britain during World War II' (1973) 12(2) *Journal of British Studies* 120–36.

interested in enhancing the capacity for governmental action. Their objective was economic intervention at a time of depression. In more recent times, controversial efforts to create wide-ranging delegated powers have arisen in connection to legislation aimed at achieving less regulation: the opposite purpose.[101] In the Brexit context, the main purpose of delegated powers so far has been ensuring that exit from the EU does not create a chaos-inducing legal vacuum.[102]

Assuming this projected departure takes place, it seems likely that there will be a permanent need on the part of the UK executive for new delegated powers, to help fill the law-making void left by the EU. This development will create an accountability gap. At present, European law is subject to scrutiny processes at EU level including by the directly elected European Parliament. Powers transferred to the UK will no longer be subject to these EU-level controls. Unless new ways are found of overseeing activity in these patriated areas, one of the outcomes will be a relative diminution in the extent to which executive authority in the UK is subject to democratic limitations. The remit of the executive will have expanded; but the ability of Parliament or other entities to keep it in check will not. Moreover, if the UK has entered a period in which parties of government are more extreme in their objectives, they may wish to utilise such powers more vigorously. For those who are uncomfortable with the idea of extensive executive discretion – varieties of which are set out in the models described above – it will be important to ensure that the expansion in UK executive capacity is matched by equivalent enhancements in the ability of Parliament (and perhaps other institutions) to hold it to account.

IV. REFORMING THE CIVIL SERVICE

In 1942, the socialist political scientist, Harold Laski, wrote an introduction to a book entitled *'Passed to you please': Britain's red-tape machine at war* by the journalist JPW Mallalieu.[103] Both Laski and Mallalieu were concerned with the internal workings of the executive, and in particular the body of staff responsible for supporting ministers: the Civil Service. Writing in the midst of the conflict with the Axis powers, Laski held that:

> we entered the war with the conviction that the Civil Service was broadly adequate to any task to which it might be called; and Mr. Mallalieu has provided at least an index to the reasons why this is one of the articles our faith least likely to survive

[101] See Legislative and Regulatory Reform Act 2006.

[102] Simon Patrick, *Scrutiny of Delegated Legislation in Relation to the UK's Withdrawal from the European Union* (London, The Constitution Society, 2017): https://consoc.org.uk/wp-content/uploads/2017/10/delegated-legislation-and-brexit-2.pdf last accessed 9 September 2018; Hansard Society, *Taking Back Control for Brexit and Beyond* (London, Hansard Society, 2017): https://assets.ctfassets.net/rdwvqctnt75b/4mZb6S8t3yukaqAqKYkskC/b1366a34a9086f7fb81edb1c4ab10f87/Taking_Back_Control_FINAL.pdf last accessed 9 September 2018.

[103] Harold J Laski, 'Introduction' to *'Passed to you, please': Britain's red-tape machine at war* (London, Victor Gollancz, 1942).

> the war. The administrative class, above all, has shown an absence of imagination and audacity, an unwillingness to press for experiments proportionate to the urgency, which make a new Bentham one of the supreme requirements of the post-war age.[104]

Laski believed that 'the adjustments the post-war Civil Service will require are likely to be profound'. He made a series of recommendations to this end. While 'competitive examination' would probably remain the main method of recruitment, there would be a need to appoint 'persons above the normal age of entry to the Administrative Class on the grounds of special qualifications'.[105] Laski referred to Churchill's installment of Beveridge as 'Director of Labour Exchanges' in 1908 as an example to emulate.[106] Responsibility within the Civil Service for personnel matters, he proposed, should be transferred away from the Treasury, so that decisions in this area were not subordinate to 'financial considerations'. Laski advocated the formation of a 'Staff College' for training senior officials; and the creation of educational opportunities for 'the younger members of the lower grades to qualify for promotion to the upper grades'. He advocated the instigation of 'the comparative study of public administration' as 'an academic subject of university status'.[107]

Officials, Laski believed, should be given the opportunity to spend time gaining experience of foreign practices. Free movement between service for local authorities and in Whitehall should be encouraged. Laksi argued that staff should be allowed to retire after five years of employment, to avoid inducing 'men to stay in the Service who have neither interest in nor aptitude for administration'.[108] There should be greater possibilities for staff engaged in technical or scientific activities to be moved into administrative roles, where they could potentially make a worthwhile contribution.[109] Laski believed that '[w]here the administrator and the scientific specialist disagree over a policy in which the expertise of the specialist is important, it should be customary for the Minister to hear the specialist's view directly if that is desired by the specialist'. He firmly opposed the ban on married women working in the Civil Service and supported 'equal pay for equal work'. Laski identified the need for a 'Central Bureau of Statistics and Information', serving the whole of government, attached to the Cabinet Secretariat.[110] Government should, in his view, establish firmer links with academia, habitually obtaining the benefit of its expertise. (This relationship would, Laski noted, require specific safeguards for the freedom of the universities, which should control their own work, the results of which would be published.)[111]

[104] ibid, 6–7.
[105] ibid, 10.
[106] ibid, 10–11.
[107] ibid, 11.
[108] ibid, 11.
[109] ibid, 11–12.
[110] ibid, 12.
[111] ibid, 12–13.

Laski advocated that officials be brought 'in closer relation' with MPs. One means of achieving this objective would be through the formation of 'an advisory committee' in the Commons for each Whitehall department. These bodies would 'discuss policy with the Minister and his officials, initiate enquiries into administration, and be consulted on the issue of orders and regulations arising out of delegated powers'. Civil servants should be allowed to publish research in their fields of interest.[112] They should also, Laski argued, dedicate more effort to meaningful communications with the outside world, presenting information in a more intelligible fashion, and seeking input into their work from individuals and groups with particular interests in it.[113] He advocated the holding of more 'independent enquiries' into administrative matters.[114]

In 1964 a 'Fabian Group' published a report entitled *The Administrators*. It was concerned with 'the Administrative Class ... the governing class in the Civil Service', accounting for about 3,000 of a total of more than a million employees.[115] It opened with the statement that '[f]or many years it has been customary to say that Britain has the best civil service in the world. The depth of this conviction has perhaps deflected people from considering what they mean'.[116] The general thesis of the report was that the Civil Service was no longer properly equipped for the task required of it. During its formative era in the nineteenth century, government intervention in society was minimal. But – especially since World War II – it had become far more active. The range of functions taken on called for skills and capacity that the Civil Service did not fully possess.[117] The group identified three central faults among civil servants: '[a]mateurism', with an emphasis on generalist all-rounders, rather than experts; a 'tendency ... to be too negative in their approach', focusing on 'procedure' rather than underlying issues, and to be disposed to find 'compromises'; and a propensity 'to be too closed and secretive in the formulation of policy'.[118]

To address these faults, like Laski, the group proposed that responsibility for personnel be transferred from the Treasury, to the Civil Service Commission. The Commission would be charged with considering ways of recruiting staff from a broader range of backgrounds, in particular outside Oxford and Cambridge, qualified in areas other than 'the liberal arts'. Mobility of personnel both into and out of the Civil Service should be facilitated, the group recommended, with outside placements elsewhere in the public and – 'subject to safeguards' – private sectors.[119] Again echoing Laski, the report advocated

[112] ibid, 13.
[113] ibid, 13–14.
[114] ibid, 14.
[115] Fabian Group, *The Administrators* (London, Fabian Society, 1964) 1.
[116] ibid, 2.
[117] ibid, 2–5.
[118] ibid, 14.
[119] ibid, 41.

a 'School of Administrative Studies' for the training of officials. Career paths, the group argued, should be better planned, avoiding transfers between unconnected roles, with improved 'mid-career training'. Replicating Laski once more, the group supported a breaking down of the barriers between 'specialists and administrators' at high level, forming a new 'Senior Civil Service'. A greater number of 'specialists' should be employed, with more extensive utilisation of 'outside research'. The Fabian Group believed that 'outside study and discussion of long range policy issues' should be 'encouraged, not discouraged by excessive secrecy'. Finally the report called for the introduction of 'two types of political appointment'. The first would comprise 'experts who are called in to help implement the particular policies of the government of the day'. In the second category would be 'personal aides', whose task would be 'to provide general help to ministers in their private office'.[120]

In the years and decades that followed the publication of *The Administrators*, a succession of reform initiatives sought to implement ideas similar to those the Fabian Group and before it Laski advocated. Responsibility for personnel management, for instance, was removed from the Treasury in 1968, first to a specially created Civil Service Department, and by 1983 to the Cabinet Office.[121] Both more experts and a small group of politically appointed ministerial aides – known as special advisers – have been recruited into government.[122] Measures including the *Freedom of Information Act* have facilitated more open government. Yet criticism of the Civil Service for its lack of ability to perform the tasks that fall to it, and for the preeminence of generalism, persist.[123] Brexit has created enormous challenges for the organisational capacity of Whitehall; and a post-EU environment, if it involves the patriation of significant new powers, will create further strains.[124] But it seems likely that any administrative machine, however it was organised and composed, would struggle to withstand the pressures created by Brexit, that lie in the nature of the policy of departure itself, and the unprepared way in which it was adopted, more than the quality of Civil Service support.

Both Laski and the Fabian Group placed a premium on expertise. They differed from Mckechnie in that he envisaged a group of outside, public assessors, while they saw specialists as being integrated into the government machine, though operating more publicly and interacting with the outside. A number of other commentators in the period covered by this book shared the

[120] ibid, 42.

[121] For the definitive history of the Civil Service up to the late 1980s, that covers this episode thoroughly, see Peter Hennessy, *Whitehall* (London, Fontana, 1990).

[122] Andrew Blick, *People Who Live in the Dark: the history of the special adviser in British politics* (London, Politico's/Methuen, 2004).

[123] House of Commons Public Administration and Constitutional Affairs Committee, *The Minister and the Official: The Fulcrum of Whitehall Effectiveness* (London, House of Commons, 2018).

[124] For discussion of Brexit and Whitehall, see eg Joe Owen, Lewis Lloyd and Jill Rutter, *Preparing Brexit: How ready is Whitehall?* (London, Institute for Government, 2018).

outlook of Laski and the Fabian group. From the 1920s onwards, for instance, William Beveridge supported the formation of an 'Economic General Staff', a 'permanent, expert, responsible body examining the economic problems of the country as a whole, giving to the Government the materials for a consistent general policy'.[125] In the contemporary climate, the value of experts is a subject of controversy that arose partly in connection to the Brexit issue.[126] A reading of Laski and the Fabian group suggests how this contention can come about. For them, the need to enhance specialist knowledge within government arose from a particular conception of the role of government: that it was and ought to be responsible for social intervention. Experts can become associated with a particular outlook, and can be targeted as proxies for it, becoming contaminated in political discourse. But to strive – through the close study of empirical evidence – for the attainment of shared truths is an essential function in a stable society. Small groups of trained individuals engaged in doing so are an indispensable necessity. How they might better be integrated into public decision making in future is a subject to which I will return in the concluding chapter of this book. Part of the answer may lie in the parliamentary committees of which Laski was a prescient advocate.

V. CONSTRAINT AND SEPARATION

While the New Party, Cripps and Dalton saw UK parliamentary government as entailing excessive constraints upon the executive, others have taken a different view. In a work that appeared in 1978, *The Binding of Leviathan: Conservatism and the Future*, the Conservative politician William Waldegrave observed an ability on the part of the executive to dominate the House of Commons, through which it could wield an inordinate degree of authority. He presented this thesis in the context of a discussion of possible shared philosophical ground between conservatism and liberalism.[127] He held that '[t]he aspect of Liberalism most interesting to a Conservative is its constitutional theory designed to preserve the capacity to dissent.' Conservatives, Waldegrave held, should along with Liberals:

> greatly fear the present tyranny of the House of Commons. Unchecked…by the House of Lords or the Monarch; dominating the courts and the traditions of common law with an ever-increasing volume of statute-law and an ever-increasing number of special administrative tribunals from which appeal lies to a Minister and not to a

[125] William Beveridge, 'An Economic General Staff', 5 March 1935, in Sir William Beveridge, *Planning under Socialism and other addresses* (London, Longmans, 1936) 57.

[126] See ch 3.

[127] William Waldegrave, *The Binding of Leviathan: Conservatism & the Future* (London, Hamish Hamilton, 1978) 73.

> court; brandishing the theory of the detailed mandate in the face of reasoned argument, the legal power of a majority in the British House of Commons has increased, is increasing and ought to be diminished.[128]

Waldegrave recognised the practical political constraints that applied. He also noted that the Treaty of Rome, providing for participation in European integration, represented another limiting force. However, he doubted the effectiveness of external pressure if tested.[129] He therefore believed that 'our constitution is dangerously vulnerable to capture by the minority who can get hold of a political party which then, for one reason or another, gains a majority in the House'. It was therefore 'all too plausible that the ... nightmare of ... capture of the executive by a totalitarian clique which would subsequently impose its intellectually disreputable certainties at the barrel of a gun – could become a reality'. Short of this extreme outcome, other problems arising from the position of the Commons included the tendency for whichever group controlled it to produce an excess of legislation, to disruptive effect. Furthermore, it meant that 'paradoxically, that executive power drains away from backbench members of the House of Commons since the majority, once obtained, can be whipped into line on virtually any measure'.[130] Given this position of institutional weakness, there were difficulties in attracting high quality MPs, which in turn led to a further decline in the autonomy of the Commons. Power had transferred into 'the Whitehall village – a closed, quiet community with its own values and its own objectives'.[131]

Having identified these problems, Waldegrave then made a series of recommendations to address them. An effective second chamber was desirable. It could only legitimately offer more resistance to potential abuses from the Commons if it was elected, and in a different way to the Commons. Using 'a pure proportional system' would prevent any one party from winning a majority. It would be 'something akin to a national jury to set against the initiating Lower House – indeed the inventors of democracy, the Athenians, might well have used the lot to select a random membership for it, and thus divorce it from electoral politics entirely'. Waldegrave regretted that he felt such an approach was not viable in the contemporary UK (though as we have seen, others would later advocate this method).[132] While regarding confidentiality within government to be necessary in some areas, he supported an overall reduction in the level of official secrecy. In particular, Waldegrave argued that 'analysis' should be made more open. He wrote '[t]he facts, or supposed facts, on which policy is based should always be published, in advance, for scrutiny. The options and

[128] ibid, 73.
[129] ibid, 73–74.
[130] ibid, 74.
[131] ibid, 75.
[132] ibid, 77–78.

counter-options should always be open to outside scrutiny. Not only would this improve the quality of the information on which government finally acts, but it might help to generate a new breed of political commentators and policy experts in Britain'.[133]

To expand ministerial influence within the Civil Service, Waldegrave advocated the development of the system of special advisers: temporary, partisan appointments made on ministerial patronage. He proposed the imitation of the 'European "Cabinet"', composed in equal numbers of career officials and outside appointments, supporting the minister.[134] However, Waldegrave stressed that strengthening the autonomy of Parliament, through Lords reform, was of higher order importance than internal reform in Whitehall, though desirable. Finally, Waldegrave saw the establishment of a UK Bill of Rights as attractive in principle as a means of 'restoring some protection to the individual and the community against the overweening state'.[135] But he doubted, short of a major crisis of some kind, that it would politically be possible to secure agreement to a viable instrument of this type. However, Waldegrave observed that:

> [t]he nearest we may get to it is a watershed we have already, relatively, passed: entry into the European Community. And…the full implications of our adherence to the European Convention of Human Rights may not yet have been understood. In so far as this adherence can be used to revivify traditional rights, Conservatives and Liberals alike should welcome it, and seek to use it. More may not be possible.[136]

A consideration of the Waldegrave proposals from the perspective of Brexit prompts a number of observations. Among the changes that he contemplated, the introduction of elected members of the House of Lords has not yet taken place. Though the second chamber has become more assertive during the twenty-first century, it remains reluctant to deploy its full power, including in relation to Brexit. There is far greater openness surrounding official information than prevailed in the 1970s.[137] Yet to base major decisions on the interpretation of referendum results is in a sense to reject the concept of evidence-based policy, rendering access to such materials less relevant.

Like Brian Crozier, among others around the same time, Waldegrave appeared to fear a minority group from the political left using the constitutional supremacy of the House of Commons to enforce its extreme ideas. Brexit, conversely, has seen Eurosceptics from the right – within (and beyond) the Conservative parliamentary party – seek to impose an agenda involving major and difficult-to-reverse systemic changes and alterations to individual rights (though there was also a – smaller – 'leave' contingent within Labour). They have done so

[133] ibid, 83.
[134] ibid, 84.
[135] ibid, 84.
[136] ibid, 84–85.
[137] See Freedom of Information Act 2000.

through exerting pressure on the executive, first to secure the holding of a referendum, and then to insist on a particular interpretation of the result. Deploying dubious claims about obligations to fulfil the popular will, they have pursued constitutional transformation over which a broad consensus is manifestly lacking. Waldegrave saw participation in the predecessor to the EU as a bulwark against the kind of manoeuvre he feared. Yet, rather than preventing the pursuit of Brexit, participation in continental integration has been the target of this operation.

The potential for EU membership to play a part in the upholding of rights has expanded further in the period since Waldegrave wrote. As noted in chapter one, the attempted copying across of European law into the UK system at the point of departure provided for under the European Union (Withdrawal) Act 2018 deliberately did not extend to the EU Charter of Fundamental Rights (see appendix). Vernon Bogdanor has stressed the importance of this development. The Charter, that applies to the application of European law, was first agreed by the EU in 2000, gained domestic force in the UK though the 2007 Treaty of Lisbon (that, among its other provisions, provided for the Article 50 mechanism). The Charter rights are listed in the Appendix to this chapter. Its implementation in the UK meant that courts could disapply Acts of Parliament in as far as they were incompatible with European law: an equivalent to the constitutional review of many other states. While many of the rights contained in the Charter might be provided for in other ways after the projected exit from the EU, they will not have this degree of hard enforcement.[138]

Removing the other protective barrier that Waldegrave identified, the European Convention on Human Rights, (and the Human Rights Act 1998 that incorporates it into UK law) has been another objective of prominent supporters of Brexit,[139] that could well become their priority in future.

Protections such as the European Convention on Human Rights have been one means of reducing the perceived problems connected to a government-dominated House of Commons. Another approach, more radical, might be to break the existing link between the executive and the legislature. Setting out such a view, the first edition of *The Last Prime Minister: Being Honest About the UK Presidency* by the Labour MP Graham Allen appeared in 2001.[140] He argued that the traditional model for understanding the UK constitution, that it involved a Prime Minister who was the chair of a Cabinet of equals, was no longer appropriate.[141] The premier, Allen held, had in practice become a president.[142]

[138] Vernon Bogdanor, *Brexit and our unprotected constitution* (London, The Constitution Society, 2018) 13–22.

[139] See ch 3.

[140] Graham Allen, *The Last Prime Minister: Being Honest About the UK Presidency* (London, Graham Allen, 2001).

[141] ibid, 3.

[142] ibid, 4.

In contrast to the equivalent office in the US, the UK version was not subject to constitutional limitations, such as those provided by a separately elected congress, and the Supreme Court, which interpreted a written constitution.[143] Members of the House of Commons were simple 'rubber stamps' for this informal presidency.[144] The House of Lords, given that it was unelected, lacked the authority to challenge the executive.[145] Again in contrast to the US President, the UK head of government was able to deploy patronage extensively within the legislature, compromising its autonomy.[146] Allen saw the office of Prime Minister as being driven increasingly in a presidential direction by a number of factors: the concentration of power at the centre of the UK political system; the focus of the media on the person of the premier; the decline of Cabinet as the supreme body within government; the development of cohesive mass parties; support from the Civil Service; and a transition towards personality driven, non-ideological politics.[147]

Allen recognised that he was not the first to have detected a drift towards presidentialism in the UK system. However, he was unusual in that he expressly depicted this outcome as desirable, and as meeting the demands of the contemporary domestic and international environment.[148] He therefore argued that: '[t]he choice now for the UK is not between a Presidency or a Prime Ministership, but between an unregulated Presidency and a regulated one'.[149] Preferring the latter option, Allen concluded that the UK premiership lacked the democratic mandate it needed to justify the way in which it had come to operate. Therefore, a separation of powers should be implemented, with Parliament and the UK 'president' elected separately from each other. While the 'president' would continue to be powerful, the holder of the office would operate in the context of a stronger Parliament. Allen hoped this new arrangement would be brought about as part of the adoption of a written constitution for the UK.[150]

Allen identified features of the system that contributed to Brexit playing out in the way it did, in particular the fusion between executive and legislature in the UK and the lack of a written constitution. But often during the Brexit episode the holder of the office of Prime Minister did not appear dominant. Cameron had to resign after a referendum he was forced to initiate had destroyed his authority. May at times struggled to hold together her Cabinet and party. Both appeared subordinate to various forces, within the Conservative Party, Parliament, their own Cabinets, the European Union, the Democratic Unionist Party,

[143] ibid, 5.
[144] ibid, 12.
[145] ibid, 13–14.
[146] ibid, 13.
[147] ibid, 16.
[148] ibid, 40–41.
[149] ibid, 55.
[150] ibid, 63–68.

and the UK electorate. Yet they were presidential in as far as the head of state in a system such as that of the United States can at times appear weak, subject to alignments in Congress and the constitution as interpreted by the courts.

I worked in the office of the UK Prime Minister in 1999. The premier then in office, Tony Blair, for much of his tenure an exceptionally powerful Prime Minister, was at the time at the peak of his political authority. Yet the impression I gained from the inside was not one of unchallenged ascendancy. Substantial effort was directed towards preempting or managing problems. Three years later I was working for Allen, author of *The Last Prime Minister*, in the Commons. From this standpoint I witnessed how much difficulty a skillful backbencher, working with others, could create for a Prime Minister. In particular, through forming a cross-party alliance, Allen was a key organiser of the two largest Commons rebellions in parliamentary history, in February and March 2003, over proposed participation in the invasion of Iraq. I do not seek, however, to dispute the range of authorities available to the prime ministers, or their capacity, potentially at least, to achieve desire outcomes. But political power is a subtle and complex material.

A number of observers have disputed the idea of an increasingly dominant Prime Minister.[151] Michael Barber was Chief Adviser on Delivery to Blair and Head of the Prime Minister's Delivery Unit from 2001–05. Barber's book, *Instruction to Deliver: Tony Blair, Public Services and the Challenge of Achieving Targets*, first appeared in 2007.[152] In his discussion of the developing role of the Prime Minister, he argued that '[t]he ever-increasing demands of the job suggest the task is becoming more difficult to do'. In his view, 'unless further institutional change is made', then on present trends there would be 'a weakening rather than a strengthening of prime ministerial power'.[153] Barber therefore advocated the formation of 'a Department of the Prime Minister and the Cabinet, incorporating No.10 and the Cabinet Office' to provide the necessary additional support.[154] Such an entity has yet to be created. But whether, if it had been formed, it would have helped prime ministers substantially with the challenges they faced in connection to Brexit, is doubtful. The difficulties faced by Cameron and then May did not arise primarily from a lack of administrative support, but from the impact of external tendencies upon the executive, and their response to them.

[151] For an account of this debate, see George Jones, *The Power of the Prime Minister: 50 Years On* (London, The Constitution Society, 2016); Andrew Blick and George Jones, *Premiership: the development, nature and power of the office of the British Prime Minister* (Exeter, Imprint Academic, 2010).

[152] Michael Barber, *Instruction to Deliver: Tony Blair, Public Services and the Challenge of Achieving Targets* (London, Politico's/Methuen, 2007).

[153] Michael Barber, *Instruction to Deliver: Tony Blair, Public Services and the Challenge of Achieving Targets* (London, Politico's/Methuen, 2007) 298.

[154] ibid, 315.

APPENDIX

Excerpts from the Charter of Fundamental Rights of the European Union (first proclaimed 2000)

The European Parliament, the Council and the Commission solemnly proclaim the following text as the Charter of Fundamental Rights of the European Union.

CHARTER OF FUNDAMENTAL RIGHTS OF THE EUROPEAN UNION

The peoples of Europe, in creating an ever closer union among them, are resolved to share a peaceful future based on common values.

Conscious of its spiritual and moral heritage, the Union is founded on the indivisible, universal values of human dignity, freedom, equality and solidarity; it is based on the principles of democracy and the rule of law. It places the individual at the heart of its activities, by establishing the citizenship of the Union and by creating an area of freedom, security and justice.

The Union contributes to the preservation and to the development of these common values while respecting the diversity of the cultures and traditions of the peoples of Europe as well as the national identities of the Member States and the organisation of their public authorities at national, regional and local levels; it seeks to promote balanced and sustainable development and ensures free movement of persons, services, goods and capital, and the freedom of establishment.

To this end, it is necessary to strengthen the protection of fundamental rights in the light of changes in society, social progress and scientific and technological developments by making those rights more visible in a Charter.

This Charter reaffirms, with due regard for the powers and tasks of the Union and for the principle of subsidiarity, the rights as they result, in particular, from the constitutional traditions and international obligations common to the Member States, the European Convention for the Protection of Human Rights and Fundamental Freedoms, the Social Charters adopted by the Union and by the Council of Europe and the case-law of the Court of Justice of the European Union and of the European Court of Human Rights. In this context the Charter will be interpreted by the courts of the Union and the Member States with due regard to the explanations prepared under the authority of the Praesidium of the Convention which drafted the Charter and updated under the responsibility of the Praesidium of the European Convention.

Enjoyment of these rights entails responsibilities and duties with regard to other persons, to the human community and to future generations.

The Union therefore recognises the rights, freedoms and principles set out hereafter.

TITLE I

DIGNITY

Article 1

Human dignity

...

Article 2

Right to life

...

Article 3

Right to the integrity of the person

...

Article 4

Prohibition of torture and inhuman or degrading treatment or punishment

Article 5

Prohibition of slavery and forced labour

...

TITLE II

FREEDOMS

Article 6

Right to liberty and security

...

Article 7

Respect for private and family life

...

Article 8

Protection of personal data

...

Article 9

Right to marry and right to found a family

...

Article 10

Freedom of thought, conscience and religion

...

Article 11

Freedom of expression and information

...

Article 12

Freedom of assembly and of association

...

Article 13

Freedom of the arts and sciences

...

Article 14

Right to education

...

Article 15

Freedom to choose an occupation and right to engage in work

...

Article 16

Freedom to conduct a business

...

Article 17

Right to property

...

Article 18

Right to asylum

...

Article 19

Protection in the event of removal, expulsion or extradition

...

TITLE III

EQUALITY

Article 20

Equality before the law

...

Article 21

Non-discrimination

...

Article 22

Cultural, religious and linguistic diversity

...

Article 23

Equality between women and men

...

Article 24

The rights of the child

...

Article 25

The rights of the elderly

...

Article 26

Integration of persons with disabilities

...

TITLE IV

SOLIDARITY

Article 27

Workers' right to information and consultation within the undertaking

...

Article 28

Right of collective bargaining and action

...

Article 29

Right of access to placement services

...

Article 30

Protection in the event of unjustified dismissal

...

Article 31

Fair and just working conditions

...

Article 32

Prohibition of child labour and protection of young people at work

...

Article 33

Family and professional life

...

Article 34

Social security and social assistance

...

Article 35

Health care

....

Article 36

Access to services of general economic interest

...

Article 37

Environmental protection

...

Article 38

Consumer protection

...

TITLE V

CITIZENS' RIGHTS

Article 39

Right to vote and to stand as a candidate at elections to the European Parliament

...

Article 40

Right to vote and to stand as a candidate at municipal elections

...

Article 41

Right to good administration

...

Article 42

Right of access to documents

...

Article 43

European Ombudsman

...

Article 44

Right to petition

...

Article 45

Freedom of movement and of residence

...

Article 46

Diplomatic and consular protection

...

TITLE VI

JUSTICE

Article 47

Right to an effective remedy and to a fair trial

...

Article 48

Presumption of innocence and right of defence

...

Article 49

Principles of legality and proportionality of criminal offences and penalties

...

Article 50

Right not to be tried or punished twice in criminal proceedings for the same criminal offence

...

9

The Digital Constitution

THE BREXIT EPISODE has a technological dimension. We have seen how subsequent examinations of the conduct of the referendum campaign raised concerns connected to the use of the Internet and social media, in particular by the winning 'leave' side.[1] Debate and investigation (both by journalists[2] and official bodies)[3] focused on a range of suspected problems and misdeeds.[4] Some involved actual and possible violation of the law,[5] others areas not clearly covered by legislation, but that perhaps should be; others still patterns of behaviour considered worrisome, but that should not or could not be formally prohibited.[6] They were: the violation of spending rules; the misuse of personal data; the dissemination of misleading information; the creation of an environment detrimental to the conduct of constructive public political discourse; and covert interference from outside the UK.[7]

This aspect of Brexit controversy connected to a developing international debate about the relationship between digital technologies and democracy,

[1] See ch 1.

[2] Such as Carole Cadwalldr. See eg '"I made Steve Bannon's psychological warfare tool": meet the data war whistle blower', *Guardian*, 18 March 2018: https://www.theguardian.com/news/2018/mar/17/data-war-whistleblower-christopher-wylie-faceook-nix-bannon-trump last accessed 18 September 2018.

[3] Such as the House of Commons Digital, Culture, Media and Sport Committee, the Electoral Commission and the Information Commissioner's Office.

[4] For a discussion of the issues, see: Independent Commission on Referendums, *Report of the Independent Commission on Referendums* (London, Constitution Unit, 2018) 178–90.

[5] Electoral Commission, *Report of an investigation in respect of – Vote Leave Limited – Mr Darren Grimes – BeLeave – Veterans for Britain* (London, Electoral Commission, 2018): http://www.electoralcommission.org.uk/__data/assets/pdf_file/0019/244900/Report-of-an-investigation-in-respect-of-Vote-Leave-Limited-Mr-Darren-Grimes-BeLeave-and-Veterans-for-Britain.pdf last accessed 13 September 2018.

[6] For a series of recommendations for changes in the law and non-legal modifications in practice, see Electoral Commission, *Digital campaigning: increasing transparency for voters* (London, Electoral Commission, 2018) 24–26.

[7] For an overview see: Stephanie Hankey, Julianne Kerr and Ravi Naik, *Data and Democracy in the Digital Age* (London, The Constitution Society, 2018) 8–11: https://consoc.org.uk/wp-content/uploads/2018/07/Stephanie-Hankey-Julianne-Kerr-Morrison-Ravi-Naik-Data-and-Democracy-in-the-Digital-Age.pdf last accessed 11 September 2018; Julia Carrie Wong, '"It might work too well": the dark art of political advertising online', *Guardian*, 19 March 2018: https://www.theguardian.com/technology/2018/mar/19/facebook-political-ads-social-media-history-online-democracy last accessed 18 September 2018.

and whether it was healthy.[8] Concern already existed about the extent and nature of electronic surveillance by intelligence agencies for security purposes in democracies.[9] The discussion has now expanded to cover a series of new categories, sometimes grouping them together as a whole.[10] One was the Internet and its implications for political behaviour. A link is frequently drawn, for instance, between social media and 'populism', however defined.[11] Another area of interest is the gathering, processing and use of 'big data' – that is, information digitally accumulated on a scale previously inconceivable.[12] This developing practice, conducted both by public and private agencies, is particularly sensitive in that it partially relates to details of individual behaviour.[13] 'Big data' is utilised through the application of algorithms – that is sets of instructions regarding how to identify and respond to patterns within it – for making, or informing, decisions. A process known as 'machine learning' enables computer systems to devise new algorithms of their own in the light of experience.[14] Machine learning and algorithms connect to a third aspect of digital technology and democracy: Artificial Intelligence (AI). This term generally refers to the mimicking by machines of human functions such as the classification of objects and reasoning. There is a degree of overlap between this concept and that of algorithms and machine learning.[15] At present a high level of expectation exists

[8] For various perspectives on this issue, see: Jamie Bartlett, *The People Vs Tech: How the internet is killing democracy (and how we save it)* (London, Ebury, 2018); David Runciman, *How Democracy Ends* (London, Profile, 2018); Philip N Howard, *Pax Technica: How the Internet of Things May Set Us Free Or Lock Us Up* (New Haven, Yale University Press, 2015); Stephen Coleman, *Can the Internet Strengthen Democracy?* (Cambridge, Polity, 2017); Helen Margetts, Peter John, Scott Hale and Taha Yasseri, *Political Turbulence: How Social Media Shape Collective Action* (Princeton, Princeton University Press, 2015).

[9] Intelligence and Security Committee of Parliament, *Privacy and Security: A modern and transparent legal framework* (London, House of Commons, 2015): http://isc.independent.gov.uk/committee-reports/special-reports.

[10] Jamie Bartlett, *The People Vs Tech: How the internet is killing democracy (and how we save it)* (London, Ebury, 2018).

[11] Sven Engesser, Nicole Ernst, Frank Esser, and Florin Büchel, 'Populism and social media: How politicians spread a fragmented ideology' (2017) 20(8) *Information, Communication & Society* 1109–26; Paolo Gerbaudo, 'Populism 2.0: Social media activism, the generic Internet user and interactive direct democracy' in Daniel Trottier and Christian Fuchs (eds), *Social media, politics and the state: Protests, revolutions, riots, crime and policing in the age of facebook, twitter and youtube* (London, Routledge, 2014) 79–99.

[12] Dawn E Holmes, *Big Data: A Very Short Introduction* (Oxford, Oxford University Press, 2017).

[13] See eg House of Lords Select Committee on Artificial Intelligence, *AI in the UK: ready, willing and able?* (London, House of Lords, 2018) 95–105.

[14] Government Office for Science, *Artificial Intelligence: opportunities and implications for the future of decision-making* (London, Government Office for Science, 2015) 6–7.

[15] For a discussion of big data, machine learning and Artificial Intelligence, and the distinctions between them, see House of Commons Science and Technology Committee, *Algorithms in decision-making* (London, House of Commons, 2018) 7.

among participants in and observers of government in the UK and elsewhere that machine learning and AI will become increasingly pervasive in the public (as well as the private) sector, and will prove effective.[16] Beyond being associated with automated decisions in specific areas, AI can also imply the development of a more general intelligence, that might in some accounts come to rival and then surpass that of the human creator. Whether and when this transition might come about are matters of contention and uncertainty.[17] Even more controversially, some speculate that machines could one day become conscious beings, however defined.[18]

The consideration of all of these issues in the particular context of democracy is a task as immense in its scope as its importance. Much is being written; much more remains to be. Attention has tended to focus so far on the implications for popular government in general.[19] A more specific focus on the rules, structures and institutions of a given polity that facilitate democracy – that is, its constitution – has been neglected. This chapter therefore considers, through the analysis of historic proposals, the implications of and possible response to digital technology from this particular perspective.

I. HG WELLS: THE WORLD BRAIN

The novelist and political writer, HG Wells, published in 1938 a collection of lectures and essays from 1936 and 1937, under the collective title *World Brain*.[20] He saw technological progress as bringing with it a threat of civilian destruction on a previously unimaginable scale, through aerial bombing. This danger created a need for 'Common Control of the Air', that in turn necessitated the establishment of 'something with at least the authority of a World Federal government'.[21] Such an entity would encompass 'a common federal protection of everyone in the world from private, sectarian, or national violence, a common federal protection of the natural resources of the planet from national, class or individual appropriation, and a world system of money or credit'.[22] For Wells, the attainment 'of a world-wide network being woven between all men about the earth' was both desirable and inevitable. But there was a

[16] See eg House of Lords Select Committee on Artificial Intelligence, *AI in the UK: ready, willing and able?* (London, House of Lords, 2018) 8–11.

[17] See Nick Bostrom, *Superintelligence: Paths, Dangers, Strategies* (Oxford, Oxford University Press, 2016) 22–25.

[18] For a discussion of this issues see Max Tegmark, *Life 3.0: Being human in the age of Artificial Intelligence* (London, Penguin, 2018) esp ch 8.

[19] eg Jane AGM van Dijk and Kenneth L Hacker, *The Internet and Democracy in the Network Society* (London, Routledge, 2018).

[20] HG Wells, *World Brain* (New Delhi, Isha Books, 2013).

[21] HG Wells, 'The Brain Organization of the Modern World', Lecture delivered in America, October and November 1937; ibid, 38–39.

[22] ibid, 39.

'prior necessity, of linking together its mental organizations into a much closer accord' than presently prevailed. Humanity needed 'a unified mind'.[23]

In explaining how this initial requirement might be met, Wells referred to 'thinkers of the forward-looking type' who were 'beginning to realize that the most helpful line for the development of our racial intelligence lies in the direction of creating a new world organ for the collection, indexing, summarizing and release of knowledge'. They anticipated 'a unified ... world organ to "pull the mind of the world together"'.[24] Central to this initiative 'would be a world synthesis of bibliography and documentation with the indexed archives of the world.' Wells envisaged a large team of 'workers ... engaged perpetually in perfecting this index of human knowledge and keeping it up to date'. They would utilise an emergent technology of the time by drawing on 'the resources of microphotography'. This 'Permanent World Encyclopaedia [sic]' would comprise 'a complete planetary memory for all mankind'. Furthermore, it was more than 'simply an index; the direct reproduction of the thing itself can be summoned to any properly prepared spot. A microfilm, coloured where necessary, occupying an inch or so of space and weighing little more than a letter, can be duplicated from the records and sent anywhere, and thrown enlarged upon the screen so that the student may study it in every detail'.[25] The encyclopaedia would supply 'the mental background of every intelligent man in the world. It would be alive and growing and changing continually under revision, extension and replacement from the original thinkers in the world everywhere'. Suppliers of its content would include academic and research groups throughout the world; and it would become 'the standard source of material for the instructional side of school and college work, for the verification of facts and the testing of statements ... Even journalists would deign to use it; even newspaper proprietors might be made to respect it'.[26]

Wells anticipated this innovation would prove successful because of his belief that:

> human brains are very much of a pattern, that under the same conditions they react in the same way, and that were it not for tradition, upbringing, accidents of circumstance and particularly of accidental individual obsessions, we should find ourselves – since we all face the same universe – much more in agreement than is superficially apparent.[27]

The enterprise Wells proposed, then, was intended to 'bring together into close juxtaposition and under critical scrutiny many apparently conflicting systems

[23] ibid, 40.

[24] HG Wells, 'The Idea of a Permanent World Encyclopedia [sic]', Contribution to the new 'Encyclopedia Francaise', August 1937; HG Wells, *World Brain* (New Delhi, Isha Books, 2013) 59.

[25] ibid, 60.

[26] HG Wells, 'World Encyclopaedia', Royal Institution of Great Britain Weekly Evening Meeting, 20 November 1936; HG Wells, *World Brain* (New Delhi, Isha Books, 2013) 14.

[27] ibid, 15.

of statement'. More than simply 'an assembly of fact and statement' it would serve 'as an organ of adjustment and adjudication, a clearing house of misunderstandings'. The encyclopaedia would 'act as a flux and a filter for a very great quantity of human misapprehension. It would compel men to come to terms with one another'.[28] To bring this project about, Wells called for the formation of an 'Encyclopaedia Society' to promote its establishment.[29] One danger it would be necessary to avoid was that of 'private mercenary exploitation of this world-wide need'.[30] Over time it would 'spread like a nervous network, a system of mental control about the globe'; and come to 'exert a very great influence upon everyone who controls administrations, makes wars, directs mass behaviour, feeds, moves, starves and kills populations'.[31] It was, Wells insisted 'a way to world peace'.[32]

Recent decades have seen the 'world brain' concept Wells promoted reassessed in the light of the invention and rise of the Internet.[33] The urge to draw comparisons (and contrasts) between the global communications system he imagined and the actual digital network that has developed since the 1960s[34] is understandable. But for present purposes the scheme Wells proposed is more useful as an example of how the political possibilities of technology can be perceived and presented. Wells had a specific constitutional preference: the establishment of a world federation. He argued it was inevitable and that the innovation he depicted would help bring it about. Wells, therefore, described an invention that was embedded within a particular agenda and was inherently disposed towards realising it. Anyone objecting to his agenda – which could be interpreted as authoritarian in its implications[35] – was, it seemed, already on the losing side of an historical contest before it had begun.

The development of actual communications technology has exceeded even the imagination of Wells. Multiple media can be accessed by anyone with an appropriate connection without a need for the physical transfer of microfilms. Moreover, the Internet has certainly attained the level of ubiquity he envisaged for the 'world brain' and is for a significant proportion of the

[28] ibid, 15–16.

[29] ibid, 19.

[30] ibid, 21.

[31] ibid, 23.

[32] 'The Idea of a Permanent World Encyclopedia', Contribution to the new 'Encyclopedia Francaise', August 1937; HG Wells, *World Brain* (New Delhi, Isha Books, 2013) 62.

[33] W Boyd Rayward, 'HG Wells's idea of a world brain: a critical reassessment' (1999) 50(7) *Journal of the American Society for information science* 557–73, p 571; Dave Muddiman, 'The universal library as modern utopia: The information society of HG Wells' (1998) 14(2) *Library History* 85–101.

[34] The forerunner to the Internet, the ARPANET, became operational on 29 October 1969. For a history of the Internet, see Jane Abbate, *Inventing the Internet* (Cambridge, MIT Press, 1999).

[35] W Boyd Rayward, 'HG Wells's idea of a world brain: a critical reassessment' (1999) 50(7) *Journal of the American Society for information science* 557–73.

population of the globe a primary source of information.[36] Yet current perceptions of the Internet, partly prompted by the Brexit experience, suggest that many of the expectations of Wells have not been realised. Obviously, global federation and world peace have not yet come about. Whether the Internet has or will have made these outcomes more or less likely (aside from whether they are plausible at all) are difficult questions to answer. But what of the intermediate changes Wells projected?

Technological innovation seems not to have facilitated a unified discourse around an agreed body of factual information of the sort for which he hoped.[37] Nor has it seemingly led to a reconciliation of groups with conflicting perceptions.[38] Indeed, in both of these areas the Internet is often perceived as having the opposite of the effect Wells hoped for. The Internet is in part a repository for advanced research and knowledge and a medium for discourse surrounding such information.[39] But it also contains trivia, inaccuracies and intentionally misleading content.[40] The 'private mercenary exploitation' that Wells hoped could be avoided has become a defining feature of the Internet.[41] Digital communications technology is in part a means of exerting pressure upon elite groups; but the authorities can also use it for their own purposes, for surveillance of and propagandising to their own populations.[42] Wells stressed the universal aspect of his conception, as do exponents of the Internet.[43] But the degree of access that an individual can obtain to online content, and the use that can be made of it, varies considerably according to the degree of official control and censorship exercised in different regions.[44] Wells was

[36] For data for the UK, see 'All data related to home internet and social media usage', Office for National Statistics: https://www.ons.gov.uk/peoplepopulationandcommunity/householdcharacteristics/homeinternetandsocialmediausage/datalist last accessed 11 September 2018.

[37] See eg Nathaniel Persily, 'The 2016 US Election: Can democracy survive the internet?' (2017) 28(2) *Journal of democracy* 63–76.

[38] For a nuanced assessment of this point, see: Seth Flaxman, Sharad Goel, and Justin M Rao, 'Filter bubbles, echo chambers, and online news consumption' (2016) 80.S1 *Public opinion quarterly* 298–320.

[39] Christine L Borgman, *Scholarship in the digital age: Information, infrastructure, and the Internet* (Cambridge, MIT Press, 2010).

[40] For data on public usage of and attitudes to the Internet in the UK, see: Ofcom, *Internet use and attitudes* (London, Ofcom, 2017) 9–15: https://www.ofcom.org.uk/__data/assets/pdf_file/0018/105507/internet-use-attitudes-bulletin-2017.pdf last accessed 11 September 2018.

[41] Andrew Keen, *The Internet is Not the Answer* (London, Atlantic, 2015).

[42] For instance, in authoritarian regimes see Espen Geelmuyden Rød, and Nils B Weidmann, 'Empowering activists or autocrats? The Internet in authoritarian regimes' (2015) 52(3) *Journal of Peace Research* 338–51.

[43] For this perception and the challenges it faces, see Tim Berners-Lee, 'I invented the web. Here are three things that need to change to save it', *Guardian*, 12 March 2017: https://www.theguardian.com/technology/2017/mar/11/tim-berners-lee-web-inventor-save-internet last accessed 19 September 2018.

[44] eg Philip N Howard, Sheetal D Agarwal, and Muzammil M Hussain, 'When do states disconnect their digital networks? Regime responses to the political uses of social media' (2011) 14(3) *The Communication Review* 216–32; Barney Warf, 'Geographies of global Internet censorship' (2011) 76(1) *GeoJournal* 1–23.

interested in 'human brains' and how they would react to a communications technology. He saw them as 'very much of a pattern, that under the same conditions they react in the same way'. Some practitioners of online campaigning are also interested in mental functions. Yet, arguably, rather than appealing to common characteristics to achieve better-informed mutual understanding, reconciliation and cooperation, their aim is to exploit differential cultural and personal traits for the purposes of psychological manipulation, often of a deliberately divisive character.[45] Complaints about such practices lie at the core of the current mood of digital despondency.[46]

Wells imagined a system that would serve the specific political and constitutional goals he favoured. Advocates of the Internet have similarly seen it as being innately supportive of their ends. They have differed from Wells in their emphasis on the supposed democratic[47] or even libertarian[48] potential of the network. Such perceptions promoted by Internet enthusiasts are now being called seriously into doubt. But perhaps the conclusion that should be drawn is not that these technologies are inherently bad, any more than they are necessarily good, but that they operate within a wider framework that helps determine how they are used and the effect that they have.[49] This context can itself be shaped, including through the use of constitutional mechanisms.

II. 1968, TECHNOLOGY AND POLITICS

Tony Benn, Minister for Technology in the Labour government of Harold Wilson, addressed the Welsh Council of Labour Annual Conference at Llandudno on 24 May 1968. It was a time of international political dislocation and unrest; and Benn spoke in the immediate wake of riots breaking out in Paris.[50] A key theme for Benn was analysis of 'the present wave of anxiety, disenchantment and discontent' that he saw as manifesting itself in

[45] Stephanie Hankey, Julianne Kerr and Ravi Naik, *Data and Democracy in the Digital Age* (London, The Constitution Society, 2018) 8–11: https://consoc.org.uk/wp-content/uploads/2018/07/Stephanie-Hankey-Julianne-Kerr-Morrison-Ravi-Naik-Data-and-Democracy-in-the-Digital-Age.pdf last accessed 11 September 2018.

[46] eg Jamie Bartlett, *The People Vs Tech: How the internet is killing democracy (and how we save it)* (London, Ebury, 2018).

[47] Patrice Flichy, *The Internet Imaginaire* (Cambridge, The MIT Press, 2007) 156–60.

[48] See eg John Perry Barlow, 'Declaration of the Independence of Cyberspace', *Electronic Frontier Foundation*, 8 February 1996: www.eff.org/cyberspace-independence last accessed 11 September 2018. For a statement of 'crypto anarchism' dating to 1988, see: Timothy C May, *The Crypto Anarchist Manifesto*: https://www.activism.net/cypherpunk/crypto-anarchy.html last accessed 19 September 2018.

[49] See eg Zizi Papacharissi, 'The virtual sphere: The internet as a public sphere' (2002) 4(1) *New media & society* 9–27.

[50] Tony Benn, 'Developing a Participating Democracy', speech to the Annual Conference of the Welsh Council of Labour given at the Winter Garden Pavillion, Llandudno in Joan Bedington (ed), *Speeches by Tony Benn* (Nottingham, Spokesman Books, 1974).

the UK as well.[51] He described how 'technology ... is outdating our political institutions'. According to Benn, the 'education system, our system of local government, the civil service and the legal system are all now under critical examination because technology has made them obsolescent'. Asking himself whether Parliament, too, could continue to function as it had in the past, Benn answered 'I very much doubt it'.[52] He judged that social unrest of the time was a reaction to a parliamentary system that '[m]any people do not think ... is responding quickly enough to the mounting pressure of events or the individual or collective aspirations of the community'. It was 'foolish to assume that people will be satisfied, for much longer, with a system which confines their national political role to the marking of a ballot paper with a single cross once every five years'.[53]

Benn regarded this general discontent as responsible for a range of contemporary tendencies, including 'student protests against the authoritarian hierarchies in some of our universities ... industrial unrest ... nationalism in Wales and Scotland ... the Black Power movement'. He discerned a general pattern of development 'away from authoritarianism and towards personal responsibility' and judged that 'the redistribution of political power will have to be faced as a major political issue'. There would be extensive consequences 'for our system of Parliamentary democracy, and for the Labour Party which works within it'. The outcome would not in every case involve dispersal of power and might in some areas entail the concentration of functions – for instance, in 'military, industrial and technical areas'. Furthermore, decentralisation was not simply a 'geographical' matter and an important aspect of it was the shift of 'power right back to the individual'.[54]

Presenting an historical analysis, Benn depicted a series of shifts in the 'Parliamentary system' whereby, over time, various groups had secured representation for themselves: the landowners, the industrialists, the middle classes and finally, through the establishment of the Labour Party, the workers. He judged that in future 'we must expect equally radical changes to be made in our system of government to meet the requirements of a new generation'. On this occasion, Benn noted, he was not referring to collective ownership of property, but to 'the demand for more political responsibility and power for the individual than the present system of Parliamentary democracy provides'. The model he envisaged was 'a participating democracy under which more and more people will have an opportunity to make their influence felt on decisions that affect them'.[55]

[51] ibid, 202.
[52] ibid, 201.
[53] ibid, 202.
[54] ibid, 202.
[55] ibid, 203.

The attainment of this 'participating democracy' required the fulfilment of a number of conditions. First, the public should be provided with 'the right to know more about government and what it is doing'. He saw the recent establishment of a Parliamentary Ombudsman and developments in the select committee system as valuable contributions in this area, and felt that televising the Commons would be a further welcome step. Benn held that the publication of internal Whitehall papers was also a possible outcome. In his view, '[t]he more light we throw on the workings of government the less we shall have of the obsession with personalities'.[56]

The second 'requirement for a participating democracy' was 'that government should be allowed to know a great deal more than it does know about the community it was elected to serve'.[57] This change was 'essential if we want to see decisions made on the basis of accurate fact. You cannot manage an advanced society, which is a vast complex inter-connecting system, unless the facts are available'. Benn described steps being taken within government to facilitate better predictions of the impact of economic policy, and for ongoing assessment of the outcomes 'to provide for rapid feedback'. He then claimed that in the 1970s 'computers will be widely used for managing the economy by means of a sophisticated process-control system not dissimilar from that now used in large automated plants'. He insisted that '[t]he value judgements will all be human and political but we shall have a reasonable chance of doing what we want to do and achieving what we set out to achieve'. However, attaining this outcome rested upon 'having information available to programme the system'. Considering the field of 'social policy', Benn anticipated that, were these data obtained, 'the present arguments about selectivity would fade away'. It would be possible 'not long hence' to achieve a 'complete integration' of benefits and taxation. The requirements and means of each individual could then be assessed individually, 'entirely free from anomalies'. Every person would then be able make financial contributions or receive payment 'according to his circumstances'. Benn recognised that there were 'serious dangers' associated with such an approach. The use of '[p]rocessed information about individuals could be the basis for a police state'. It would be necessary to establish 'a mass of new safeguards'. However, the benefit was that 'this information could and should compel government to take account of every single individual in the development of its policy. Just to exist will be to participate. We are a long way from that now'.[58]

Thirdly, 'a participating democracy will certainly involve the direct sharing of decision-making with the electorate as a whole'. Given his belief that voting twice a decade was no longer sufficient, it would be necessary to reexamine

[56] ibid, 203.
[57] ibid, 203.
[58] ibid, 204.

previous objections to the idea of using referendums. While opinion research was utilised extensively in politics, given that it rested on small groups of selected individuals, and that those taking part 'share no responsibility for the answers they give' it was 'no substitute' for full popular voting. He proposed as a first initiative that referendums be held on social issues of the type that were at the time resolved through parliamentary Private Members' Bills. For Benn, while decisions taken in this way might produce outcomes he did not agree with, they would involve 'real responsibility' and would stimulate a wide 'interest in public policy'.[59] He envisaged that 'technology may ultimately help us', asserting that '[e]lectronic referenda will be feasible within a generation and with it could come a considerable up-rating of the responsibility and understanding of ordinary people'.[60]

Fourthly, Benn advocated 'a radical re-examination of the way in which our mass communications are handled'. He regretted, given the importance of the contemporary 'mass media', the lack of attention afforded to their relationship with democracy. Prime ministers could, if required, broadcast to the entire country and newspaper proprietors could place their own views in front of millions of readers. Yet:

> for ordinary people, or even for extraordinary people with minority views, the only way of answering back is to walk about with a placard and hope the press or television cameras will take a picture. Compared with the technology available to the mass media, the public is still stuck with a communications system that has hardly changed since the Stone Age.[61]

He suspected that this disparity was an incentive for a drift towards violence among those with dissenting views since they had 'precious little access to the community through the mass media'. They might achieve exposure through 'books and through relatively small-circulation papers and magazines'. However, 'access to the microphone or T.V. camera is very strictly limited – both by the B.B.C. and the commercial T.V. companies'. Benn concluded that '[w]hat broadcasting now lacks is any equivalent to the publishing function. At the moment it is controlled by editors with slots to fill and a few selected minority views get in some of the slots'. But this arrangement was 'no substitute for the right to speak'. He speculated that in the future 'independent groups of publishers would be allocated so many hours of broadcasting a month and told to help those who have something to say, to say it clearly and well, to national audiences'. Failure to implement such a practice would entail 'denying ourselves access to a whole range of ideas – good, bad and indifferent – which we ought, as responsible citizens, to be allowed to know about through the mass media'.[62]

[59] ibid, 204.
[60] ibid, 205.
[61] ibid, 205.
[62] ibid, 205.

Fifthly, Benn argued that 'representative organisations of all kinds' such as trade unions and pressure groups should receive public funding to facilitate their contribution to democracy and the process of government. Sixthly, he called for 'the devolution of much more responsibility to regions and localities'. He held that through allocating responsibilities to the tier of government at which they could most appropriately be exercised, the effectiveness of Whitehall could be enhanced, since it could focus more clearly on those tasks it retained. In conclusion, Benn asserted that the momentum for reform he had identified was 'as inevitable as was the incoming tide that ultimately engulfed King Canute'. It would dominate the 1970s, he felt, and would apply to the Labour Party as well as the parliamentary system. Those unwilling to act upon it risked 'discontent, expressing itself in despairing apathy or violent protest' that might 'engulf us all in bloodshed. It is no good saying that it could never happen here. It could'.[63] In his assessment 'the question of whether ordinary people can govern themselves is still on trial – as it always has been and always will be. Beyond parliamentary democracy as we know it we shall have to find a new popular democracy to replace it'.[64]

Not all of the technologies and techniques that are the subject of this chapter existed in May 1968. Even an embryonic version of the Internet, the ARPANET, only became operational the following year.[65] But Benn addressed some important themes related to the possible political and constitutional role of computerised data processing and electronic communications. He saw technological development in part as a source of instability. It was, for Benn, a source of social turmoil that challenged the practices and institutions of representative democracy, including Parliament. To fail to recognise and address this trend was in his view to invite descent into violent unrest. Yet technology could help provide solutions to the problems of which it was a cause. He saw it as playing a part in a radical restructuring of the political governmental system. Power would in some instances be centralised; but often it would be transferred downwards, to territorial tiers, and to the individual. The public could take part directly and on an ongoing basis in the making of specific decisions, rather than simply electing representatives periodically. Moreover, Benn envisaged a future in which, without any express actions on their part '[j]ust to exist will be to participate'. This form of passive democratic incorporation would be achieved through the gathering and processing of data, which would in turn deliver more effective and responsive public services. Another aspect of the model Benn set out involved the role played by electronic media (for him, television and radio). Their range of content would be widened to achieve more inclusive political debate.

[63] ibid, 207.
[64] ibid, 207.
[65] See n 32 above.

The thesis Benn advanced in 1968 prompts numerous observations from the perspective of the twenty-first century, Brexit era. In a sense the Internet has provided the 'equivalent to the publishing function' he regretted was lacking from 'broadcasting'. This digital network has made it possible for any individual to communicate ideas, whatever they may be, to a potentially vast audience, in the UK and elsewhere. However, whether the Internet has enriched political debate – especially since the advent of social media – is open to question. Some analysts complain that, rather than broadening the range of outlooks to which users are exposed, it has narrowed them.[66] Algorithms present them with content that, based on their previous consumption habits, is tailored to fit within, rather than challenge, their existing outlook – part of a tendency labelled 'homophily'.[67] The Internet, it is now often held, has inspired anger and irrationality more than informed discussion and careful judgement.[68] In such an environment, rather than being empowered, as Benn advocated, individuals, have become susceptible to manipulation.[69] Such conditions – assuming they do prevail – are perhaps not conducive to satisfactory exercises in direct democracy. Complaints about the 2016 campaign often focus on its online dimension.[70] More frequent popular votes, as suggested by Benn, might be more problematic still. (It could of course be held that any difficulties the Internet creates for the integrity of referendums also apply to elections.)

An important component of complaints about the democratic impact of the Internet involves the role of private sector entities, determining the basis on which information is disseminated (for instance Google, Facebook and Twitter), or actively assisting with campaigns (most controversially, Cambridge Analytica).[71] Non-governmental actors, however, were largely absent from the assessments Benn presented. In his discussion of the future of data analysis, for instance, Benn saw the public sector as the accumulator and user of the personal details of the population. While governments in the UK and elsewhere are major players in this field,[72] they are far from a position of monopoly. Facebook, to

[66] See eg Cass R Sunstein, *# Republic: Divided democracy in the age of social media* (Princeton, Princeton University Press, 2018).

[67] See eg Yosh Halberstam and Brian Knight, 'Homophily, group size, and the diffusion of political information in social networks: Evidence from Twitter' (2016) 143 *Journal of Public Economics* 73–88.

[68] See eg Fabiana Zollo, Petra Kralj Novak, Michela Del Vicario, Alessandro Bessi, Igor Mozetič, Antonio Scala, Guido Caldarelli and Walter Quattrociocchi. 'Emotional dynamics in the age of misinformation' (2015) 10(9) *PloS one*.

[69] Andrew Prat and Patrick Kennedy, *LSE US Centre*, 5 May 2018, 'Information inequality makes voters vulnerable to manipulation': http://blogs.lse.ac.uk/usappblog/2018/05/05/information-inequality-makes-voters-vulnerable-to-manipulation/ last accessed 19 September 2018.

[70] See chs 1 and 2. For a measured assessment of some of the democratic issues, see: Philip N Howard and Bence Kollanyi, *Bots,#StrongerIn, and# Brexit: computational propaganda during the UK-EU referendum* (2016): https://arxiv.org/pdf/1606.06356.pdf last accessed 19 September 2018.

[71] Jamie Bartlett, *The People Vs Tech: How the internet is killing democracy (and how we save it)* (London, Ebury, 2018) 45–50; 69–101.

[72] John Manzoni, Chief Executive of the Civil Service, 'Big data in government: the challenges and opportunities', speech given 21 February 2017: https://www.gov.uk/government/speeches/big-data-in-government-the-challenges-and-opportunities last accessed 19 September 2018.

choose one prominent example, has gathered an immense volume of personal data from its members, and its possible deployment for the influence of voting has been a recent subject of international controversy.[73] The activities of multinational corporations such as facebook create ethical difficulties of an order that – though he recognised there were concerns to be addressed – Benn did not fully foresee in 1968. Benn hoped that a 'publishing function' in broadcasting could combine with the mass acquisition and processing of personal data to enhance democracy and further the public interest. Arguably the reverse scenario has come about, with self-serving commercial entities compromising political processes.

In his discussion of the role of data in policy making Benn insisted that '[t]he value judgements will all be human and political', with the processes simply intended to ensure that the goals set were achieved. This was an important observation. Some of the contemporary excitement about the potential of data analytics to achieve enhancements in the effectiveness of public policy should be tempered by the observation that systems cannot be neutral. Initial objectives are set by those who create them, reflecting their perspectives and priorities.[74] Any policy, regardless of whether it contains an automated component, is liable to criticism, for instance from those who feel that it is detrimental to them. Moreover – and a point that Benn seems to have neglected – even within the frame of a given objective, a system can deliver perverse, arbitrary or discriminatory results, and might perhaps contradict its purported aims. In a democracy, it is important that those in positions of political authority are accountable, and cannot hide behind processes, whether analogue or digital.

In the UK context, the relevant principle is that of individual ministerial responsibility, under which secretaries of state (or equivalent) answer to Parliament (with certain exceptions) for the policies and activities within their particular remit. In the words of the *Ministerial Code*, 'Ministers have a duty to Parliament to account, and be held to account, for the policies, decisions and actions of their departments and agencies'.[75] Assuming the prominence of machine learning in government continues to increase as presently projected, its impact on accountability will need close attention. The formulation and implementation of policy must remain the responsibility of ministers. If algorithms have played a part in it, ministers must nonetheless be able to explain the underlying rationale. Parliament needs the capacity meaningfully to scrutinise the policy itself and whether the system is properly delivering what it is supposed to. One problem here may be the distance that develops between the minister, setting the overall direction, and the actual detail of implementation. The primary purpose of data analytics is to identify patterns and

[73] 'Facebook scandal "hit 87 million users"', *BBC*, 4 April 2018: https://www.bbc.co.uk/news/technology-43649018 last accessed 19 September 2018.

[74] For possible bias in algorithms, see: House of Commons Science and Technology Committee, *Algorithms in decision-making* (London, House of Commons, 2018) 18–23.

[75] *Ministerial Code* (London, Cabinet Office, 2018), para 1.3(a), p 1.

make predictions on a basis of them – but not to explain why a given combination of characteristics creates a particular propensity. As Chris Anderson, the editor-in-chief of *Wired* magazine, put it a decade ago:

> This is a world where massive amounts of data and applied mathematics replace every other tool that might be brought to bear. Out with every theory of human behaviour ... With enough data, the numbers speak for themselves ... The new availability of huge amounts of data, along with the statistical tools to crunch these numbers, offers a whole new way of understanding the world. Correlation supersedes causation.[76]

It is not necessary fully to accept this thesis to realise that it might be difficult for a minister to explain why a particular decision reached via machine learning serves an overall purpose; or to discern whether it does at all. Such confusion is detrimental to democratic accountability. Close consideration must be given to the formulation of rules and practices that might minimise it.

Another significant assertion from Benn was that the incorporation of data analysis into public policy might ensure that '[j]ust to exist will be to participate'. This claim is contestable. A different view of such practices – in governmental and private sectors – is possible. They could be seen as involving the making of decisions on behalf of individuals without their express input. Their needs might be assessed on a basis of their personal characteristics. But the criteria used will be defined by others, and conclusions reached will be based on aggregations of collective behaviour rather than their own. Decisions will rest in predictions that apply to someone who matches this artificial profile, not themselves. The basis for such calculations may be secret, or incomprehensible, and might not involve any explanation of causality.

The need to reconcile social modelling with government by consent is a fundamental challenge for democracy. Previous chapters have shown how various reforms in earlier eras sought to combine a perceived growth in the role of government with genuine and meaningful public input. This issue, therefore, does not arise specifically from a particular application of digital technology – but its salience has certainly been heightened. Some may take the view that greater precision is needed. For them, the use of big data will help resolve this tension, moving ever closer to perfection in personalised interventions. The alternative view is that the conflict arises from the project itself, the refinement of which will perhaps worsen the dilemma it addresses. Taken to their extreme, data analytics can imply that individuals lack the ability to help determine, or even to understand, their future and that of their society. This bleak scenario represents the opposite of participation. It could undermine the very concept of free will, raising difficult questions about the nature of humanity.

[76] Chris Anderson, 'The End of Theory: the data deluge makes the scientific method obsolete', 27 June 2008, *Wired*: https://www.wired.com/2008/06/pb-theory/ last accessed 29 September 2018.

One contemporary of Benn was aware of the difficulties associated with the idea of what might today be termed predictive analytics. An economist and former protégé of John Maynard Keynes, Ernest Friedrich Schumacher, born in Germany, was resident in the UK from 1937. His work *Small Is Beautiful: Economics as if People Mattered*, first published in 1973, is best known for its influence on the environmental movement.[77] But it contains an important discussion of issues relevant today in the context of machine learning, data analytics and big data. The chapter 'A Machine to Foretell the Future?', was drawn from a lecture the author gave at the First British Conference on the Social and Economic Effects of Automation, at Harrogate in June 1961. He opened by remarking that '[t]here have never been so many futurologists, planners, forecasters, and model-builders as there are today, and the most intriguing product of technological progress, the computer, seems to offer untold new possibilities. People talk freely about "machines to foretell the future".'[78] Proposing historical context for this outlook, Schumacher noted that 'the Greeks – and I suppose most other nations – went to living oracles'. However, 'the Chinese … went to a book setting out the universal and necessary pattern of changes'. Like the ancient Chinese, '[m]odern man goes to the computer'. While conceding the limitations of the analogy, he insisted that 'a machine to foretell the future is based on metaphysical assumptions of a very definite kind. It is based on the implicit assumption that "the future is already here", that it exists already in a determinate form, so that it requires merely good instruments and good techniques to get it into focus and make it visible'. This assumption was expansive in its implications. Moreover, it 'seems to go against all direct personal experience. It implies that human freedom does not exist or, in any case, that it cannot alter the predetermined course of events'.[79]

Schumacher urged cognisance of the 'decisive practical consequences' of this perception.[80] However, he explained that he adhered to 'a rather negative opinion about the usefulness of "automation" in matters of economic forecasting and the like'. While accepting 'the value of electronic computers and similar apparatus for other tasks, like solving mathematical problems or programming production runs',[81] Schumacher reached 'the cheerful conclusion that life … is still worth living because it is sufficiently unpredictable to be interesting … we are still masters of our individual and collective destiny'. The task of experts was 'to clarify the limits within which our destiny is confined. The future cannot be forecast, but it can be explored'.[82]

[77] EF Schumacher, *Small Is Beautiful: Economics as if People Mattered* (New York Harper Perennial 2010 reprint, first published 1973).

[78] ibid, 237.

[79] ibid, 238.

[80] ibid, 239.

[81] ibid, 254.

[82] ibid, 255.

This expression of doubt about projected developments is a reminder that perceptions of the impact of technology – in political as in other areas – rest on assumptions about the future. Perhaps some today would argue that Schumacher was misguided in his scepticism regarding the potential applications of computerised data analysis. Benn, on the other hand, seems to have overestimated what would be the pace of innovation in areas such as the establishment of a universal taxation and benefits system, with which the present government appears still to be struggling.[83] A lesson from history is that some kind of working assumption about the future is essential to decision making, but it might well be incorrect. At a given time, radically different views of what is to come might be on offer; and prevailing wisdoms can change over time. A consideration of attitudes towards the feasibility of AI illustrates this point well. There have been both regular disagreements at particular points; and periods of more and less aggregate optimism. It is important to explore this point in more historical depth since, of all the tendencies considered in this book in their constitutional implications, that connected to digital technologies is possibly the most dynamic and difficult to assess in its implications and extent.

Alan Turing opened his 1950 article 'Computing Machinery and Intelligence' with the statement 'I propose to consider the question, "Can machines think?"'[84] He recognised that he was entering a philosophical field of longstanding controversy. Turing recalled Charles Babbage, credited with his 'Analytical Engine' as having originated the concept of the computer in the early nineteenth century, though he never managed to construct a finished product. Ada Lovelace, a close colleague of Babbage, Turing noted, had once insisted that '"The Analytical Engine has no pretensions to *originate* anything. It can do *whatever we know how to order it* to perform" (her italics).'[85] Turing, however, disputed whether Lovelace was completely ruling out the possibility of a thinking machine; and he boldly advanced his belief 'that at the end of the century the use of words and general educated opinion will have altered so much that one will be able to speak of machines thinking without expecting to be contradicted'.[86] It is reasonable to conclude that, by the deadline Turing set, though the idea of 'machines thinking' had attained a degree of acceptance, it remained contested. It continues to divide opinion, as indeed does the very meaning of the concept of 'thinking'.[87] Whether and when the technological

[83] Jessica Morgan, 'Universal credit forces people into debt because application process is so complicated, says charity' *Independent*, 23 July 2018: https://www.independent.co.uk/news/uk/home-news/universal-credit-debt-benefits-dwp-application-poor-money-a8459786.html last accessed 19 Spetmber 2018.

[84] AM Turing, 'Computing Machinery and Intelligence' (1950) 433–60 *Mind 49* 1.

[85] ibid.

[86] ibid, 8.

[87] See eg Rob Sparrow, 'Can Machines Be People? Reflections on the Turing Triage Test' in Patrick Lin, Keith Abney and George A Bekey, *Robot Ethics: the ethical and social implications of robotics* (Cambridge, MIT Press, 2012) 301–16.

development he envisaged as prompting it would ever be attained also remain points of disagreement.[88]

Irving John Good was a former colleague of Turing. In an essay based on talks he gave in 1962 and 1963 entitled, 'Speculations Concerning the First Ultraintelligent Machine' he defined his subject 'as a machine that can far surpass the intellectual activities of any man'. The 'intellectual activities' concerned included 'the design of machines'. Consequently 'an ultraintelligent machine could design even better machines'. What Good referred to as 'an intelligence explosion' would inevitably follow, with 'the intelligence of man … left far behind'. Consequently, 'the first ultraintelligent machine is the last invention that man need ever make, provided that the machine is docile enough to tell us how to keep it under control'.[89] Good did not offer a definite timetable, though he made reference to developments in 'very close man-machine interaction' – an intermediary step towards the end goal – as prompting major financial investments in the technology 'by say 1980'.[90]

Despite the continued existence of doubters about what precisely it can and will achieve, confidence in AI and associated technologies, in governmental and other spheres, is high at present, hence the intensity of recent parliamentary interest in the subject shown in the reports cited above. The present author does not presume to comment directly on science and technology. However, it is worth noting that, in the past, following periods of optimism, disputes have arisen over the prospects for AI, and there have been both increases and declines in political and financial support for research. An example of downturn came in the UK in the early 1970s. In July 1972 James Lighthill, a mathematician but not an AI specialist, completed a review of work ongoing in the field at the request of the Science Research Council, which was considering applications amounting to a substantial volume of funding in the area.[91] Lighthill found that, though there had been some progress in the field to date:

> '[m]ost workers in AI research and in related fields confess to a pronounced feeling of disappointment in what has been achieved in the past twenty-five years. Workers entered the field around 1950, and even around 1960, with high hopes that are very far from having been realised in 1972. In no part of the field have the discoveries made so far produced the major impact that was then promised …
>
> When able and respected scientists write in letters to the present author that AI, the major goal of computing science, represents another step in the general process of evolution; that possibilities in the nineteen-eighties include an all-purpose intelligence

[88] See n 15 above.

[89] Irving John Good, 'Speculations concerning the first ultraintelligent machine' (1965) 6(99) *Advances in computers* 31–83, p 33.

[90] ibid, 35.

[91] Professor Sir James Lighthill FRS, 'Artificial Intelligence: A General Survey', July 1972. Available at: http://www.chilton-computing.org.uk/inf/literature/reports/lighthill_report/contents.htm last accessed 21 August 2018.

> on a human-scale knowledge base; that awe-inspiring possibilities suggest themselves based on machine intelligence exceeding human intelligence by the year 2000; when such predictions are made in 1972 one may be wise to compare the predictions of the past against performance as well as considering prospects for the realisation of today's predictions in the future.

The pessimistic view Lighthill advanced was challenged by other experts, as was his methodology.[92] Nonetheless, it prompted retrenchment in the area by the Social Research Council.[93] The 1970s saw the first occurrence of a so-called 'AI winter', in which international support for the industry dropped significantly. The following decade experienced a revival and a further 'winter'; with another resurgence occurring in the 1990s.[94] The lesson to derive from this history is that there is no single conclusion to be drawn. Predictions are unlikely to be wholly correct and they may be entirely wrong. But they can contain elements of accuracy that are difficult to discern at the time they are made. Perceptions of the present necessarily involve extrapolations into the future. They in turn rest on interpretations of the past. To deploy history as a means of restricting expectations – for instance, to conclude that because some past predictions made by those involved in AI research have proved incorrect, their efforts must continue to be futile – is to misuse it. That practitioners have overclaimed in the past does not in itself prove they will not succeed. (Though it would be reasonable to conclude that ambitious assertions of this type made today should be approached with scepticism.) Technology is certain to develop in some ways not predicted. The Internet, for instance, is relatively new and has already passed through radically different and unforeseen phases of development. It could continue to do so. Furthermore, other inventions we cannot yet – by definition – fully conceive of may appear to supplant, or more likely interact with those that already exist.[95] It is better to consider the widest range of potential outcomes.

One extreme would be the emergence of general AI that rivals or surpasses that of humans, as Good speculated. Such a scenario might add political salience to an existing philosophical debate about whether such AI systems should be regarded as conscious beings.[96] If the answer was yes, then should

[92] Professor NS Sutherland, 'Some Comments on the Lighthill report and on Artificial Intelligence', August 1972. Available at: http://www.chilton-computing.org.uk/inf/literature/reports/lighthill_report/contents.htm last accessed 21 August 2018.

[93] Brian Oakley and Kenneth Owen, *Alvey: Britain's Strategic Computing Initiative* (Cambridge, The MIT Press, 1989) 15.

[94] Nick Bostrom, *Superintelligence: Paths, Dangers, Strategies* (Oxford, Oxford University Press, 2016) 6–9.

[95] For a more sophisticated perspective on technology in history, see: David Edgerton, *The Shock of the Old: Technology and Global History since 1900* (London, Profile, 2008). See also Evgeney Morozov, *To Save Everything, Click Here: The folly of technological solutionism* (London, Penguin, 2014) ch 9, 318–52.

[96] See eg Murray Shanahan, *The Technological Singularity* (Cambridge, MIT Press, 2015) 117–50.

they possess rights?[97] If they were of equal or greater intelligence to humans, then should they enjoy a socially recognised status at least on a par with that of their creators? In the constitutional sphere, how would these rights be defined and enforced? Would they extend to participation in political processes? If so, would they take part in the same processes as us, or be self-governing? More fanciful still, some might hold, but taken seriously by some seemingly credible commentators, would be a circumstance in which AI subordinated or destroyed humanity, in which case human constitutional agendas would become irrelevant.[98] (What could be termed an optimistic variant on this kind of model involves the advent of a 'singularity' in which humans transcend their present physical existence altogether.[99] Dilemmas such as the West Lothian Question seem trivial in this context.)

Perhaps other possibilities merit consideration. Could another AI 'winter' come about, involving a loss of confidence, followed by a decline in financial and other support, and the scaling down of research and innovation in the field, precluding projected achievements, even if they were attainable? This scenario might seem implausible to many at present. Alternatively, could breakthroughs occur but not be implemented, for economic, legal, cultural, moral or political reasons? Important constitutional conclusions follow from these points. Technological possibilities alone do not determine outcomes. Our governmental institutions need not only respond to AI and the other innovations discussed in this chapter. Those who act on behalf of the political community can and should shape developments in ways that reflect prevailing democratic values.

III. 1995, 2001, 2008: ONLINE GOVERNMENT, DEMOCRACY AND THE INTERNET

In 1995 the Conservative-associated Bow Group published a pamphlet entitled *On-line Government*.[100] The author, Julian Roche, opened by asking: '[a]fter the disappearance of the socialist mirage, is there now a new threat to our society: a rapidly evolving divergence between government and people?' Among the problems he identified as comprising this malaise – which were, he observed, common to 'Western' countries – were declining 'confidence in institutions'; the disappearance of 'a sense of political community'; less participation in elections; and increased criminality. Roche described the purpose of his pamphlet as being to describe 'new technology in the dissemination of information and

[97] Patrick Lin, Keith Abney and George A Bekey, *Robot Ethics: the ethical and social implications of robotics* (Cambridge, MIT Press, 2012) Pt VII, 'Rights and Ethics', 299–364.

[98] See, eg Stuart Armstrong, *Smarter Than Us: The rise of machine intelligence* (Berkeley, Machine Intelligence Research Institute, 2014) 1–2.

[99] See eg Raymond Kurzweil, *The Singularity is Near* (London, Gerald Duckworth & Co, 2006).

[100] Julian Roche, *On-line Government* (London, Bow Group, 1995).

how it might be used to create a national system of interactive terminals which could become the way that a large part of politics operates'. He held that '[m]any more people would be encouraged into politics if they could participate from their homes'. Roche urged the government to give proper consideration to the potentials of 'on-line government' as a means of preventing increasing popular disengagement with the system.[101]

Noting the existence at the time of various constitutional reform proposals, including for strengthened local government, proportional representation and the increased use of referendums, Roche presented his ideas as a new addition to this list. He viewed his concepts as applicable to democracies worldwide as a means by which they could 'rejuvenate' themselves. More 'effective ... communication' between governors and governed could enhance the 'trust' in that relationship.[102] Roche observed that it was no longer necessary to speculate about possible future technology being used for mass political participation, since it 'now exists ... and it is relatively inexpensive and becoming cheaper'. He identified the French 'Minitel' system as one possible foundation for 'on-line government'.[103] Roche discerned an important development he held to be imminent: the wide availability of a device he called the 'Smart Box', combining in one device 'computer, modem and television technologies'. It would mean that people could transmit and receive large quantities of 'visual, audial and numerical' data, either from their homes or other suitably equipped locations.[104]

Roche set out proposals for what he termed '[o]n line government', utilising the Smart Box. He took the view that '[p]aper and democracy ... do not mix'. The former reduced the speed at which government could operate and circumscribed 'access to information'. 'Electronic information', conversely, was 'much closer to the spoken word'. Government should, therefore, shift to the latter format. The Stationery Office, already beginning an electronic publishing programme, should intensify this effort. But it should do more than simply make green papers, white papers and bills available online. Electronic copies of these texts – which might, for reasons of economy, begin to replace hard copies altogether – should become the basis for consultation and engagement.[105] Eventually '[e]very citizen ... would be able ... to intervene with suggestions, comments and proposals on legislative schemes'.[106] Roche went on: '[t]he monopoly of drafting power that currently resides with the Civil Service would be replaced with a marketplace of ideas in which the role of the (perhaps privatised) drafting services would be to draw together the numerous democratic strands of comment into fresh versions of the proposed legislation'.[107]

[101] ibid, 1.
[102] ibid, 3.
[103] ibid, 4.
[104] ibid, 5.
[105] ibid, 9.
[106] ibid, 10.
[107] ibid, 10.

Roche saw such an approach as compatible with the Conservative outlook, being inclined towards the dispersal of political power. He envisaged the extension of this practice into the parliamentary process. A bill would be introduced into the Commons, at which point 'MPs would then communicate electronically amongst themselves with proposed amendments and establish eventual concord amongst themselves and their party as to how the amendments should be phrased. The amendments would be received electronically by the Government and acted upon either by accepting them … or by putting them to the vote'.[108] In the Roche model, the Lords would also adopt this practice.[109] It would not be necessary for parliamentary debates to take place in either Chamber, since members could participate and vote using Smart Boxes. Hansard could be made available instantly throughout the country, as could ministerial 'press releases, and speeches'. Roche speculated that 'our descendants will regard it as characteristic of an advanced democracy that citizens receive such real-time information and even to use the quantity and quality of such networks as analytical criteria of democratic status'.[110]

Similar principles could be applied to other parts of the constitution, with 'On-Line Councils' and 'On-Line Political Parties', able to consult with their members on policy issues.[111] Roche proposed that '[s]etpiece Party Political Broadcasts would be replaced – or at least augmented – by constant interactive dialogue between the citizens of our democracy and the political parties to which they owed their allegiance'. Recognising difficulties that might emerge, Roche noted that there would be a need for procedures intended to 'prevent either espionage, nuisance or obscenity'.[112] In describing an 'On-Line Civil Service', Roche proposed 'the principle that all Civil Service documents should be accessible to the general public unless there are commercial or security reasons for them not to be so'.[113] Smart Boxes could help attain meaningful accessibility to official information for members of the public. A 'Civil Service interactive system' would operate by 'opening up government, through its electronic systems … to the outside world'.[114]

Roche identified certain possible areas of contention in his scheme. One involved how this access would be funded, whether publicly or by individual users, a discussion which had clear political connotations.[115] He anticipated certain problems in the introductory phase, including cultural resistance from various quarters. Yet Roche stressed 'the evidence from a younger generation is mounting that unless an event occurs on a computer screen, it is not to be

[108] ibid, 11.
[109] ibid, 11.
[110] ibid, 12.
[111] ibid, 13–14.
[112] ibid, 16.
[113] ibid, 16.
[114] ibid, 17.
[115] ibid, 21.

taken very seriously … politics must go on the offensive, if it is to recapture its vitality, and that offensive must be straight onto the very screens that are the key connection between the individuals of the generations to come'.[116]

Roche identified three key possible objections. First, that ministers would be bombarded with so many communications that they were in effect able to evade any kind of accountability. Roche suspected that a way of offsetting this problem would be 'the creation of "intermediate" points between the active citizenry and the government, at which comments and ideas would be combined and submitted.' A second objection was that private or public sector organisations might 'access private files and interrogate people' using their Smart Boxes. Roche called for strict rules on the handling of information. Thirdly there was the prospect of what he described as 'on-line demagogues'. Roche judged:

> [i]t seems highly questionable as to whether such people would gain much from on-line government. The British people have been trusted by their governments, in the round at least since 1688 and more specifically since 1832 … the British electorate has seen off the blandishments and enticements of a series of demagogues, from the Chartists to the Blackshirts. On-line government serves to widen the political net, and therefore make it less likely that individual zealots will gain authority for their ideas.[117]

Roche concluded by noting the central case in favour of the programme he advanced: that it would save expenditure; that it would improve 'accessibility' inside government and between it and the outside world; that it would make business and government work more effectively together; that it would accelerate the legislative process; and that it would help promote Conservative ideas. Identifying and seeking to rebut an important potential criticism of his plans, Roche stated: '[s]ome will argue that far from improving Parliamentary democracy, these measures will diminish it'. For him the best response to such views was that 'the technological advances referred to in this paper are inescapable … Conservatives have always recognised the need to adapt and react to changes such as these'. He described a possible 'Conservative view of democracy for the 21st Century' comprising 'three elements: the executive, the people and the experts', alongside 'three pillars: judiciary, executive and legislature. Each will balance the others and all will participate through the network. On line government may be the means to extract the best from all three' and offset 'fears that Western democratic institutions are under threat … from cynicism and apathy'.[118]

Though it will be assessed critically below, the Roche work was powerful, important, and gains in significance as time passes. He might be seen as

[116] ibid, 23.
[117] ibid, 24.
[118] ibid, 26.

advancing a UK, Conservative variant on Internet enthusiasm, that favoured the use and re-enforcement of existing institutions and methods, in contrast to more revolutionary libertarian ideas promoted on the other side of the Atlantic Ocean. Like many of the contributors considered in this book, he detected social difficulties, including deteriorating public support for and participation in the political system, that he believed were characteristic of the particular period in which he wrote. Like those other authors, he presented changes that he hoped could address the problem. Though he did not use the term 'Internet', it seems to be this network that he had in mind for most of the functions he envisaged. The Roche pamphlet is therefore another important reminder that democracy is often held to be in peril; and that – before it was fully incorporated into the system as it is now – the Internet was seen by some as a solution to the perceived problem, not the culprit. While Roche in 1995 made the provocative statement that '[p]aper and democracy … do not mix' doubts are now commonly voiced about the compatibility of the Internet and democracy.

Two key strands in the digitally-led programme Roche advocated were the provision of more information to the public, and the development of means by which they could become more actively involved in the business of government and politics. Rather than supplanting the existing system or creating new institutions, Roche presented a model in which the established organs of representative government – Parliament, the executive and Civil Service, local government and parties – would alter their ways of working as a means of reviving their status through reconnecting with the public. He did, however, vaguely allude to the possible need for 'intermediate' agencies, to make interactions between 'citizenry' and 'government' workable, avoiding the overload of the latter by the former. Roche assumed greater rapidity – in debate and in the production of legislation – would be beneficial. Yet it could be argued that proceeding with caution in deliberation and law making, even if enforced by limitations derived from earlier technology that no longer need apply, has merits, and should not be abandoned simply because the possibility for greater speed has emerged. Roche, however, took an excessively fatalistic approach to technology, perceiving it as presenting unavoidable consequences. While he was probably correct to regard its use in some form as a coming fact, he underplayed the possibilities for determining the precise usage adopted.

Some of the more radical aspects of the Roche vision – such as the opening up of legislative drafting to outside inputs – have not come about as he envisaged. But government and politics in the UK as worldwide have come to embrace the Internet, affording it a high priority as a means of communication and as a policy area in itself. Online petitioning, though it does not provide direct access to the working of government, has created a new means of exerting pressure.[119]

[119] Scott Wright, 'Populism and Downing street e-petitions: connective action, hybridity, and the changing nature of organizing' (2015) 32(3) *Political Communication* 414–33.

Contemporary Whitehall initiatives such as 'Open Policy Making' have traces of the Roche agenda in them.[120] A wider range of information is now readily available to the public, thanks to a combination of the Internet, and freedom of information law and policy. Yet like Benn before him – who hoped that more open government would reduce the importance of personality in political coverage – Roche was overly optimistic about the likely beneficial impact of this change. He seems to have assumed a popular appetite for knowledge of and participation in official processes that was never likely to materialise. The same might be said of his hopes for 'constant interactive dialogue between the citizens of our democracy and the political parties to which they owed their allegiance'. On the one hand, it may be the case that because of the Internet, participation levels are higher than they would otherwise be. Furthermore, had the Roche agenda of opening up processes been pursued more fully, there might be more incentive still to take part. But, on the other hand, even if it is made more convenient and more relevant, there are surely limits to the quantity and quality of involvement that can be expected from the public.

Alongside overestimating the benefits, Roche also perhaps underplayed some of the potential difficulties, for instance with his brief consideration of the need to prevent 'espionage, nuisance or obscenity'. However, he certainly anticipated some future problems and controversies (though perhaps not their scale): the inundation of representatives with electronic communications; the gathering of personal information for commercial or political purposes; and what he described as 'on-line demagogues'. All of these issues are significant from the Brexit perspective. In the first category – the deluge of demands upon MPs – the prolonged pressure upon Parliament and government that helped move the referendum idea to the forefront of the political agenda had an important electronic dimension, for instance the use of online petitioning.[121] But the possible criticism Roche identified – that MPs might be able to evade accountability through hiding behind a myriad of digital campaigns – did not apply in this instance. Petitioners saw this particular objective achieved, though other cases might well be different. In the second category, involving personal information, the provenance of such data used during the 2016 campaign has been a subject of controversy.[122]

But what does recent experience reveal about the 'on-line demagogues' that Roche thought would not be a serious threat in the UK? The phrase 'online

[120] For details of the 'Open Policy Making Toolkit', see the *Policy Lab*: https://openpolicy.blog.gov.uk/2018/03/28/opm-toolkit/ last accessed 19 September 2018.

[121] See eg James Kirkup, 'EU referendum: why the vote is a big deal for David Cameron' *Telegraph*, 24 October 2011: https://www.telegraph.co.uk/news/newstopics/eureferendum/8845930/EU-referendum-why-the-vote-is-a-big-deal-for-David-Cameron.html last accessed 22 August 2018.

[122] See eg Aliya Ram, 'Leave.EU accused of data misuse during Brexit campaign', *Financial Times*, 17 April 2018: https://www.ft.com/content/fdf8f2ba-4243-11e8-803a-295c97e6fd0b last accessed 22 August 2018.

demagogues' conjures the image of a tweeting US President. But what is its applicability to the UK? The Internet has provided an outlet for forces that to some might seem fringe or extreme, or aimed at stimulating and channeling urges of a populist (however defined) nature. A decade after Roche wrote, the British National Party (BNP) was making effective use of the medium.[123] Perhaps it is useful to avoid the use of pejorative terminology such as 'demagogues', or indeed 'populists'. What to some might be a victory for demagoguery is for others a triumph of the will of the people in favour of change, in the face of elite resistance. To approach the subject in a more neutral sense, it is perhaps appropriate to focus instead on the idea of the promotion of an individual, a movement, or a specific goal to which there was much opposition within the institutions of representative democracy, but which attained mass support among the wider public.

The 'leave' result of 23 June 2016 can be seen in these terms; but the exact difference that online activities made is difficult to discern. Commentators on,[124] opponents of,[125] and participants in[126] the winning campaign have depicted online activities and related technologies as significant to the outcome. It is necessary to be cautious about accepting wholly the views of those who perhaps have an interest in relating an exciting story about the impact of technology, or explaining away the result as the consequence of some kind of underhand – or perhaps illegal – digital ploy, or to maximise the importance of their bold decision taking. Moreover, because a particular approach is relatively new it should not be focused on at the expense of more established methods. A bus – or rather a coach – with the slogan '[w]e send the EU £350 million a week, let's fund our NHS instead' written on the side was perhaps the most memorable feature of the entire campaign.[127] Moreover, while the traditional press was perhaps once overrated in its influence upon elections, we are now in danger of committing the opposite error and overlooking it.[128] When seeking out

[123] See eg Chris Atton, 'Far-right media on the internet: culture, discourse and power' (2006) 8(4) *New media & society* 573–87.

[124] eg Vyacheslav Polonaki, 'Impact of social media on the outcome of the referendum' (2016): https://www.referendumanalysis.eu/eu-referendum-analysis-2016/section-7-social-media/impact-of-social-media-on-the-outcome-of-the-eu-referendum/ last accessed 19 September 2018.

[125] See eg Rob Merrick, 'Brexit result has been thrown into question by the Cambridge Analytica data scandal, says Tory MP', *Independent*, 30 April 2018: https://www.independent.co.uk/news/uk/politics/brexit-vote-result-second-referendum-cambridge-analytica-antoinette-sandbach-mp-a8325636.html last accessed 24 August 2018.

[126] Dominic Cummings, 'On the referendum #20: the campaign, physics and data science – Vote Leave's "Voter Intention Collection System' (VICS) now available for all", *Dominic Cummings's Blog*, 29 October 2016: https://dominiccummings.com/2016/10/29/on-the-referendum-20-the-campaign-physics-and-data-science-vote-leaves-voter-intention-collection-system-vics-now-available-for-all/ last accessed 22 August 2018.

[127] Matt Chorley, 'That sodding Brexit bus', *Times*, 24 May 2018.

[128] For discussion of press influence on voters in the UK, see: Kenneth Newton and Malcolm Brynin, 'The national press and party voting in the UK' (2001) 49(2) *Political Studies* 265–85.

differences between the experiences of the 1975 and 2016 referendums, the existence of social media is significant, but so too is the fact that, in contrast to 1975, in 2016, overall, press coverage was more negative than positive regarding European integration.[129] It is necessary also to consider how different media, older and newer, work together, rather than operating in isolation. For instance, the online edition of a newspaper can contain an image of a coach with a slogan written on its side; which can be shared on the Internet by others.

Nonetheless, it is worth taking into account some testimony regarding the specific role of online communications in 2016 when considering the significance of the Roche agenda today. Dominic Cummings – who ran the nominated lead 'leave' campaign, 'Vote Leave' – suggested in a subsequent blog that its distinctive and innovative digital, data-led approach was 'one of the reasons we won'. He wrote:

> One of our central ideas was that the campaign had to do things in the field of data that have never been done before. This included a) integrating data from social media, online advertising, websites, apps, canvassing, direct mail, polls, online fundraising, activist feedback, and some new things we tried such as a new way to do polling … and b) having experts in physics and machine learning do proper data science in the way only they can – i.e. far beyond the normal skills applied in political campaigns. We were the first campaign in the UK to put almost all our money into digital communication then have it partly controlled by people whose normal work was subjects like quantum information (combined with political input from Paul Stephenson and Henry de Zoete, and digital specialists AIQ [Aggregate IQ]).[130]

Cummings went on, in the same blog, to distinguish the experts who he valued from those who, in keeping with a theme that came to be associated with supporters of departure from the EU, he derided:

> If you want to make big improvements in communication, my advice is – hire physicists, not communications people from normal companies and never believe what advertising companies tell you about 'data' unless you can independently verify it. Physics, mathematics, and computer science are domains in which there are real experts, unlike macro-economic forecasting … Physicists and mathematicians regularly invade other fields but other fields do not invade theirs … It is no surprise that they can successfully invade politics and devise things that rout those who wrongly think they know what they are doing.[131]

The Cummings testimony demonstrates that the Internet and connected techniques had come to be applied in a way Roche did not emphasise. While he saw

[129] 'UK newspapers' position on Brexit', *University of Oxford*, 23 May 2016: http://www.ox.ac.uk/news/2016-05-23-uk-newspapers-positions-brexit last accessed 30 September 2018.

[130] Dominic Cummings, 'On the referendum #20: the campaign, physics and data science – Vote Leave's "Voter Intention Collection System" (VICS) now available for all', *Dominic Cummings's Blog*, 29 October 2016: https://dominiccummings.com/2016/10/29/on-the-referendum-20-the-campaign-physics-and-data-science-vote-leaves-voter-intention-collection-system-vics-now-available-for-all/ last accessed 22 August 2018.

[131] Ibid.

them as a means of enabling the public to wield an enhanced role within the system, by the time of the Brexit episode another aspect had become prominent: the use of digital networks to influence people. Roche hoped that party political broadcasts might be replaced with two-way online dialogues. This straightforward progression to more interaction did not take place. The Internet could be and was used for purposes other than promotional messaging, but it also became a medium for ever more sophisticated exercises in this craft, arranged by parties and other groups, some of obscure nature. In this context, as far as input from the public was sought, it was as a provider of big data, to enable it the better to be manipulated.

In 2001, two academics specialising in communications, Jay G Bulmler and Stephen Coleman, published a pamphlet entitled *Realising Democracy Online: A Civic Commons in Cyberspace*.[132] It built on an earlier paper presented at an event held by the centre-left Institute of Public Policy Research at the London School of Economics and Political Science in May 2000.[133] The 2001 pamphlet called for an 'electronic commons', that 'would be neither a talking shop in splendid isolation, nor a replacement of representative by direct democracy'. The project they envisaged would be a broad channel enabling the public to participate more fully in decisions made on their behalf. It would become 'part of the democratic furniture: an integral component of the representative system' as well as a public debating forum.[134] As the two authors saw it, '[t]he public does not speak with one voice, so representatives will still have the important job of distinguishing between the messages they receive, as well as between relevant information and mere noise offstage'. They found it implausible, for practical reasons, that voters would be able fully to engage with all public business.[135]

Blumler and Coleman identified weaknesses in the existing environment for political communications that they hoped to correct. The chief problems derived from a decline in social deference and in lasting attachments to particular parties and collections of viewpoints; and 'the increased intractability of the central problems of politics'. In this setting, 'the political communication scene has become more turbulent and less manageably containable than before'.[136] The Internet, the authors believed, could potentially be deployed to improve the position for a number of reasons. Unlike broadcast media, Internet users were without doubt 'active' rather than 'passive'. The medium was also more suited to the hosting of meaningful discussion. It could make considerable quantities of data available to those who used it. It allowed more fully for

[132] Jay G Blumler and Stephen Coleman, *Realising Democracy Online: A Civic Commons in Cyberspace* (London, ippr/Citizens Online, 2001).
[133] ibid, 3.
[134] ibid, 5.
[135] ibid, 8.
[136] ibid, 11.

two-way communication than other channels. Lastly, it was effective as a means by which people could find specific content and information for themselves, at a low cost.[137]

To capitalise on the potential advantages of the Internet, the two authors called for the instigation of 'a civic commons in cyberspace' through the creation of 'an entirely new kind of public agency, designed to forge fresh links between communications and politics and to connect the voice of the people more meaningfully to the daily activities of democratic institutions'.[138] While this entity would be financed from public sources it would be independent of the government. It would be charged with 'eliciting, gathering, and coordinating citizens' deliberations upon and reactions to problems faced and proposals issued by public bodies', including local authorities, assemblies and parliaments, and Whitehall departments. It would prompt those involved in governing, both officials and politicians, to attach greater significance to 'the stimulation of increased participation', regarding such initiatives as more than simply 'citizens' playgrounds'.[139] Rather than replacing existing projects for the attainment of popular engagement it would place them 'under a more capacious electronic roof', supporting them with its 'resources and expertise' and augmenting their prominence and impact. The agency would respond to suggestions from others, and instigate its own projects, seeking to involve members of previously excluded sectors of society. It would rest on principles of 'transparency' as well as 'accountability'.[140] Operating flexibly, the initiative would seek to encapsulate the dynamism of the amateur alongside the methodical approach of the professional. It would perceive and present itself as engaged in 'a cumulative civic learning exercise'.[141]

The agency would be responsible for 'promoting, publicising, regulating, moderating, summarizing, and evaluating the broadest and most inclusive range of online deliberation via various new media platforms, including the web, e-mail, newsgroups, and digital TV'.[142] It would spread its message as widely and inclusively as possible, ensuring that access to online participation was made available 'in such places as libraries, schools, doctors' surgeries, community centres and municipal offices'.[143] A particular challenge for the body would be in reconciling the need for free speech with the moderation of the debates it sponsored, to ensure that they did not become offensive or mutual attempts at drowning out opponents.[144] The agency would distil the discussions it had facilitated and communicate them on to the relevant public body. The authors

[137] ibid, 13.
[138] ibid, 16.
[139] ibid, 16.
[140] ibid, 16.
[141] ibid, 17.
[142] ibid, 17.
[143] ibid, 17.
[144] ibid, 17–18.

suggested that, while creating a 'civic commons' for the UK was the most practical initial step, ultimately a transnational entity might be more appropriate, in the context of 'an increasingly interdependent world'.[145]

The pamphlet recognised a possible criticism: that there was no obvious necessity for this 'civic commons' in addition to already proliferating online democratic activity. In defending their proposal and its ambitious nature, Blumler and Coleman stressed a need to avoid a repetition of the disappointment that had followed expectations for engagement raised by cable television and before that local radio. It was important therefore that the initiative was imbued with 'legitimate authority'.[146] Furthermore, the civic commons would ensure that access to online deliberation was universal, a vital requirement from a democratic standpoint. The institution Blumler and Coleman envisaged would also be an antidote to purported exercises in engagement that were in fact merely disguised efforts to promote pre-determined agendas or serve particular interests. For the civic commons, in contrast, democracy itself would be the end. The initiative could also be useful to organs of representative democracy. Local authorities had 'weakened in terms of both powers and legitimacy in recent years' while the Westminster Parliament had 'been undergoing a crisis of legitimacy and confidence about its role'. Both could reconnect with the public through the civic commons.[147] For this benefit to be attained, however, it would be necessary for politicians genuinely to take part, rather than simply create the impression that they were.[148]

Blumler and Coleman then listed some possible intiatives that could take place: the Chancellor of the Exchequer consulting in advance on the Budget; engagement by Whitehall with the target users of public services; '[p]ublic kiosks' for local government consultations; online evidence sessions for parliamentary select committees; EU consultations; and '[d]eliberative polls'. They closed with an assertion that their model rested on a particular view of democracy, making it possible for 'the active citizen, enabled by effective, accessible technologies as well as effective, accessible representative institutions, to feel democratically empowered beyond their few seconds in the polling booth'.[149]

Blumler and Coleman found problems in the political system similar to those identified by Roche, centring on shifting popular attitudes and policy difficulties, that they hoped the Internet could help correct. While Roche focused mainly on changes within the established framework, the central Blumler and Coleman proposal was for a new institution to act as intermediary with governmental institutions and facilitator on behalf of the public. But some

[145] ibid, 18.
[146] ibid, 19.
[147] ibid, 19.
[148] ibid, 20.
[149] ibid, 20.

of the activities they envisaged, such as participation in policy processes and dialogue with representatives, were comparable to those included in the Roche programme. They also shared with Roche (and Benn) the hope that the availability of more official information would improve the quality and quantity of engagement.

The *Realising Democracy Online* programme was not implemented. In the interim, the online environment has changed substantially. In particular, social media including facebook have come to provide online platforms for interactions of various types, including political communication. But they are not publicly accountable and consequently not transparent in their operations or objectives. Whether, within this context, members of the public are, as Blumler and Coleman anticipated, 'active', or whether they are 'passive', is debatable. From the perspective of the individual, it may seem the former; but from the point of view of a political data analytics team, they might seem more to resemble one of a mass of recipients of stimuli intended to trigger the response desired by whoever is facilitating a given campaign.

A project devised to integrate the public more fully and in a more constructive sense into political processes, as advocated in *Realising Democracy Online*, appears attractive today. Particular challenges it would need to address would include the apparent difficulty involved, in a divisive political landscape, in establishing the neutrality of any agency, and securing trust for its integrity across different competing, conflicting or alienated groups. While support from senior politicians would be essential to success, it could also be perceived as a form of contamination. A further daunting task would be in utilising the Internet as a forum for considered, respectful yet rigorous debate. In 2001 Blumler and Coleman complained that 'the political communication scene has become more turbulent and less manageably containable than before'. They hoped that the Internet might assist with this problem, but the model they proposed was not adopted. With the rise of social media and non-conventional sources of information, the tendency they identified as a difficulty seems to have intensified. The technology they hoped would solve certain problems may have worsened them.

Politics, Policy and the Internet, a pamphlet by the journalist Robert Colville, was published by the Conservative-orientated think tank, the Centre for Policy Studies, in 2008.[150] He argued that the Internet was having a transformative effect upon the political environment similar to that attained by the advent of radio and television in the previous century. However, politicians in the UK, Colville observed, had been slow to respond relative to their counterparts elsewhere, including in the US. The political parties were especially sluggish, and needed to change 'their mindset from "send" to "receive"'. Potentially, MPs could use the Internet to provide them with greater autonomy from their parties,

[150] Robert Colville, *Politics, Policy and the Internet* (London, Centre for Policy Studies, 2008).

responding directly to the needs of their citizens.[151] Colville attached significance to the possible importance of political bloggers.[152] He also argued that the Internet led to an 'empowerment of individuals', allowing them to organise in ways they had not previously, and exert immense pressure over single issues. 'Politics', Colville held, 'is slowly but surely escaping from the hands of the politicians'.[153] One facet of the tendency he detected was that it made it more difficult for 'ministers' to 'tailor their speeches to different audiences – putting one gloss on things for *The Mirror*, another for *The Times*, and yet another when appearing on News at Ten'. Because of the existence of a 'vast archive of material available in fractions of a second via the major search engines' it was now 'far harder to go back on your word – pronouncements made in different places and different times can be compared and contrasted. In other words, your past is always there, and cannot be disowned'.[154] Moreover, 'the politician speak that has evolved over recent decades is almost uniquely ill-suited to the internet, which privileges verbal flair and/or straight talking'.[155]

When discussing the implications of these trends, the first proposal Colville made was that 'people will have to think before they open their mouths – or, if they are changing a policy position, will need to explain more clearly just why and how the alteration has come about'. He hoped that '[i]f this does not lead to a more ideologically coherent set of policies, it ought certainly to lead to policies which are more intellectual [sic] coherent, or at least more comprehensible to voters'. Colville also anticipated that the decentralising effect upon political activity he attributed to the Internet might be applied to the conduct of government.[156] One means of achieving this outcome would be an 'open source' approach, allowing members of the public to comment on line on government proposals, and to put forward their own initiatives.[157] Potentially, the Internet could facilitate more extensive use of referendums.[158] The government could also shift to a 'presumption' that 'every of piece of data' be made 'public automatically, unless there are pressing objections in terms of security or privacy'.[159] Colville cautioned that the government was seeking to amass data about members of the public to deploy for its own purposes.[160] Nonetheless, he concluded that '[t]he individual, and not the state, will be the master in the digital age'.[161]

[151] ibid, i.
[152] ibid, 6–10.
[153] ibid, 36.
[154] ibid, 38.
[155] ibid, 38.
[156] ibid, 39.
[157] ibid, 41.
[158] ibid, 43.
[159] ibid, 45.
[160] ibid, 40.
[161] ibid, ii.

To suppose today that the Internet has entailed a straightforward shift for politicians from sending to receiving messages, and the 'empowerment of individuals' would be to fail fully to comprehend actual developments. Some receiving certainly takes place, but it is used in part to ensure that more effective persuasion can then be generated. For some, the rise of the outsider blogger as described by Colville might be perceived as a further deterioration in the political system and drift towards 'demagoguery', facilitated rather than prevented by the Internet. While focusing on the impact of tenacious individuals, he did not anticipate that online influence might come from sources that were not human at all: automated systems or 'bots'.[162] Nonetheless, the idea that the public might seek out information online from less conventional sources than they once did has certainly proved prescient in the decade since Colville wrote his pamphlet. Whether this trend has proved to be democratically beneficial is another question.

While Colville correctly drew attention to the governmental harvesting of personal information, he did not anticipate a tendency that is possibly of equal concern: the amassing of big data from Internet users by online multinational corporations such as google and facebook.[163] Perhaps the most important way in which actual developments have followed a path different to that projected by Colville involves the idea of consistency of messages. It is true that the Internet creates an environment in which it is more difficult for politicians to hide from statements or actions that they may later regret. David Davis, while on the Conservative backbenches, tweeted in advance of the 2016 referendum that 'The first calling point of the UK's negotiator immediately after #Brexit will not be Brussels, it will be Berlin, to strike a deal'.[164] (He made a number of similar tweets on the same day, 26 May 2016, drawing on a speech he was delivering.) The idea that the UK would deal primarily with Germany rather than the EU as a whole on such matters was incorrect in law and in practice. As Secretary of State for Exiting the European Union, a post to which he was appointed when Theresa May became Prime Minister, his public prediction was publicly revealed to be wrong.[165]

Yet it is not clear that such exposure necessarily has negative consequences for the person involved. It was possible to draw attention to the Davis tweet – and indeed it remains available online – but whether doing so amounted to

[162] For bots in the EU referendum, see: Philip N. Howard and Bence Kollanyi, *Bots,# StrongerIn, and# Brexit: computational propaganda during the UK-EU referendum* (2016): https://arxiv.org/pdf/1606.06356.pdf last accessed 19 September 2018.

[163] Greg Elmer, Ganaele Langlois and Joanna Redden (eds), *Compromised data: From social media to big data* (London, Bloomsbury, 2015).

[164] Available at: David Davis @DavidDavisMP 26 May 2016: https://twitter.com/daviddavismp/status/735770073822961664?lang=en last accessed 19 September 2018. For a further tweet of this ilk from Davis, see: https://twitter.com/daviddavismp/status/735770127564607489?lang=en.

[165] See eg 'These David Davis tweets really haven't aged well', *Indy 100*: https://www.indy100.com/article/brexit-secretary-david-davis-twitter-resign-theresa-may-conservative-party-8438651 last accessed 20 September 2018.

any more than point-scoring is uncertain. Indeed, to speculate, it could be that the enormous expansion in public political statements associated with the Internet and social media have served to make more rather than less difficult the task of holding politicians to account for their utterances. Perhaps one consequence of such scrutiny is simply to reveal human fallibility; and in the process bring about not an increase in standards but a lowering of public expectations. In such circumstances, with discourse on a basis of coherent positions appearing to deteriorate, people on all sides of a debate may be increasingly inclined to reject rational analysis and cling more strongly to their emotionally founded beliefs.

Moreover, there is another aspect to the online dissemination of information that could have the effect of lessening consistency and by extension accountability. This form of communication is not public in the sense of being universally available. It is possible to target voters with messages specifically tailored to their profile, who are not aware of different and possibly even contradictory messages sent from the same source to others. The Internet environment does not, then, seem to create pressure in the direction of a single, intelligible programme against which a party can be judged by the whole electorate. Instead it can facilitate and even encourage fragmentation into a myriad of discrete and not necessarily logically integrated components, of which a public overview is impossible, to the detriment of democratic accountability.[166]

Consideration of these publications from 1995, 2001 and 2008 re-enforces the point made previously in this chapter regarding the difficulties involved in predicting events and tendencies yet to come. The environment in which these texts was issued changed in the intervening periods between them, and it has continued to do so since 2008. Many of the hopes they expressed were not realised, or were even inverted. But the pessimism that now surrounds the subject of digital democracy might itself prove to be excessive. The ways in which technologies and their political applications and receptions can transform suggests that there are no predetermined outcomes. It might be possible, therefore, to shape the future, and the design of governmental mechanisms should take such opportunities into account. The technological optimism expressed by the authors analysed in this chapter should not be completely dismissed. Supporters of democracy should continue to explore the potential of a communications network that can reduce the barriers to participation for those who have previously been excluded, but they should do so with a newly-acquired caution, and set out to correct emergent problems. Taking this more nuanced perspective, I will discuss potential institutional reforms in the conclusion of this book. But before proposing any changes of this nature, if they are to prove effective, it is essential to discern the fundamental principles in which they must

[166] Jamie Bartlett, *The People Vs Tech: How the internet is killing democracy (and how we save it)* (London, Ebury, 2018) 84–85.

rest. In the relatively new and developing field that is the subject of this chapter, from where should these values be derived?

There is in fact an historic tradition to which to turn. As long ago as 1968, the year Benn gave his speech on participation in democracy discussed in this chapter, the Council of Europe Parliamentary Assembly anticipated some of the challenges faced today. Its Recommendation 509 of 31 January 1968, cited in appendix a to this chapter, referred to 'the serious dangers for the rights of the individual inherent in certain aspects of modern scientific and technological development'. These words have a contemporary resonance, as does the description in the recommendation of this threat as involving 'phone-tapping, eavesdropping, surreptitious observation, the illegitimate use of official statistical and similar surveys to obtain private information, and subliminal advertising and propaganda'. The precise technology has changed, but the feared abuses have come to pass.

The 1968 Council of Europe recommendation was an initial entry in a series of efforts by multi-state organisations at European and international level to manage democratic risks associated with information technology.[167] Building on this tradition, a significant contemporary text in this field (passed in 2016) is the EU General Data Protection Regulation (GDPR), an excerpt from which is provided in appendix b. It sets out a body of '[p]rinciples relating to processing of personal data' with full legal force. The UK will presumably not be directly subject to GDPR upon exit from the EU. However, it will retain a domestic equivalent to this regime; and has also begun to develop various codes of practice intended to help address issues connected to the Internet, big data and its deployment (see appendices c and d). They represent a recognition of many of the problems and opportunities identified in this chapter, though they are aspirational statements rather direct hard law. If the technologies that have lately become so prominent in political discourse continue to gain in importance it may be that future generations look to the 1968 Council of Europe text (and perhaps some of those that followed it) in the way that we view such documents as Magna Carta, the Bill of Rights 1689 and the European Convention on Human Rights. Each of these instruments sought to address the concerns of the particular periods in which they were drafted. They were subsequently adapted and applied to circumstances their authors could not have envisaged, taking on an immutable quality.[168] Key principles in the field of digital democracy have been established: the challenge of implementing, promoting and adapting them as necessary remains.

[167] Stephanie Hankey, Julianne Kerr and Ravi Naik, *Data and Democracy in the Digital Age* (The Constitution Society, London, 2018), pp.32-35 <https://consoc.org.uk/wp-content/uploads/2018/07/Stephanie-Hankey-Julianne-Kerr-Morrison-Ravi-Naik-Data-and-Democracy-in-the-Digital-Age.pdf> last accessed 11 September 2018.

[168] Andrew Blick, *Beyond Magna Carta: a constitution for the United Kingdom* (Hart/Bloomsbury, Oxford, 2015).

APPENDICES: DEMOCRATIC NORMS AND DIGITAL TECHNOLOGY

Appendix A

Human rights and modern scientific and technological developments
Recommendation 509 adopted by Council of Europe Parliamentary Assembly, 31 January 1968

The Assembly,

1. Considering that member States under the Statute of the Council of Europe accept the principle of the enjoyment by all persons within their jurisdiction of human rights and fundamental freedoms;
2. Having regard to the serious dangers for the rights of the individual inherent in certain aspects of modern scientific and technological development;
3. Believing that newly developed techniques such as phone-tapping, eavesdropping, surreptitious observation, the illegitimate use of official statistical and similar surveys to obtain private information, and subliminal advertising and propaganda are a threat to the rights and freedoms of individuals and, in particular, to the right to privacy which is protected by Article 8 of the European Convention on Human Rights;
4. Considering that the law in the majority of the member States does not provide adequate protection against such threats to the right of privacy, and that there is in consequence danger of violation of Article 8 of the Convention on Human Rights;
5. Noting that some member States of the Council of Europe are planning to revise their legislation on this subject and that it would be desirable for any such reform to tend towards a greater harmonisation of the law;
6. Considering that it would be useful to make a detailed study of the legal problems arising in connection with the right to privacy and its violation by modern technical devices, with special reference to the European Convention on Human Rights;
7. Reserving the right to continue its own studies and to make further proposals on the questions concerned,
8. Recommends that the Committee of Ministers instruct the Committee of Experts on Human Rights:

    8.1. to study and report on the question whether, having regard to Article 8 of the Convention on Human Rights, the national legislation in the member States adequately protects the right to privacy against violations which may be committed by the use of modern scientific and technical methods;

    8.2. if the answer to this question is in the negative, to make recommendations for the better protection of the right of privacy.

Appendix B

Excerpts from European Union *General Data Protection Regulation*, (EU) 2016/679, 14 April 2016, entry into force 25 May 2018

Article 5

Principles relating to processing of personal data

1. Personal data shall be:
    1. processed lawfully, fairly and in a transparent manner in relation to the data subject ('lawfulness, fairness and transparency');
    2. collected for specified, explicit and legitimate purposes and not further processed in a manner that is incompatible with those purposes...
    3. adequate, relevant and limited to what is necessary in relation to the purposes for which they are processed ('data minimisation');
    4. accurate and, where necessary, kept up to date; every reasonable step must be taken to ensure that personal data that are inaccurate, having regard to the purposes for which they are processed, are erased or rectified without delay ('accuracy');
    5. kept in a form which permits identification of data subjects for no longer than is necessary for the purposes for which the personal data are processed...
    6. processed in a manner that ensures appropriate security of the personal data, including protection against unauthorised or unlawful processing and against accidental loss, destruction or damage, using appropriate technical or organisational measures ('integrity and confidentiality').
2. The controller shall be responsible for, and be able to demonstrate compliance with, paragraph 1 ('accountability').

Appendix C

Excerpts from Department for Digital, Culture, Media and Sport, *Digital Charter*, published 25 January 2018

... The internet is a powerful force for good. It serves humanity, spreads ideas and enhances freedom and opportunity across the world. Combined with new technologies such as artificial intelligence, it is set to change society perhaps more than any previous technological revolution – growing the economy, making us more productive, and raising living standards.

Alongside these new opportunities come new challenges and risks. The internet can be used to spread terrorist material; it can be a tool for abuse and bullying; and it can be used to undermine civil discourse, objective news and intellectual property. Citizens rightly want to know that they will be safe and secure online. Tackling these challenges in an effective and responsible way is critical for digital technology to thrive.

The Digital Charter is our response: a rolling programme of work to agree norms and rules for the online world and put them into practice. In some cases this will be through shifting expectations of behaviour; in some we will need to agree new standards; and in others we may need to update our laws and regulations. Our starting point will be that we will have the same rights and expect the same behaviour online as we do offline.

The Charter's core purpose is to make the internet work for everyone – for citizens, businesses and society as a whole. It is based on liberal values that cherish freedom, but not the freedom to harm others. These are challenges with which every nation is grappling. The internet is a global network and we will work with other countries that share both our values and our determination to get this right.

We will be guided by these principles:

- the internet should be free, open and accessible
- people should understand the rules that apply to them when they are online
- personal data should be respected and used appropriately
- protections should be in place to help keep people safe online, especially children
- the same rights that people have offline must be protected online
- the social and economic benefits brought by new technologies should be fairly shared

Work programme

The Charter brings together a broad, ongoing programme, which will evolve as technology changes. Our current priorities include:

- Digital economy – building a thriving ecosystem where technology companies can start and grow.
- Online harms – protecting people from harmful content and behaviour, including building understanding and resilience, and working with industry to encourage the development of technological solutions.
- Liability – looking at the legal liability that online platforms have for the content shared on their sites, including considering how we could get more effective action through better use of the existing legal frameworks and definitions.
- Data and artificial intelligence (AI) ethics and innovation – ensuring data is used in safe and ethical way, and when decisions are made based on data, these are fair and appropriately transparent.

- Digital markets – ensuring digital markets are working well, including through supporting data portability and the better use, control and sharing of data.
- Disinformation – limiting the spread and impact of disinformation intended to mislead for political, personal and/or financial gain.
- Cyber security – supporting businesses and other organisations to take the steps necessary to keep themselves and individuals safe from malicious cyber activity, including by reducing the burden of responsibility on end-users.

Appendix D

Excerpts from Department for Digital, Culture, Media and Sport, *Data Ethics Framework*, updated 30 August 2018

The Data Ethics Framework guides the design of appropriate data use in government and the wider public sector. This guidance is aimed at anyone working directly or indirectly with data in the public sector, including data practitioners (statisticians, analysts and data scientists), policymakers, operational staff and those helping produce data-informed insight…

The Data Ethics Framework principles

Your project, service or procured software should be assessed against the 7 data ethics principles.

1. Start with clear user need and public benefit
Using data in more innovative ways has the potential to transform how public services are delivered. We must always be clear about what we are trying to achieve for users – both citizens and public servants.

2. Be aware of relevant legislation and codes of practice
You must have an understanding of the relevant laws and codes of practice that relate to the use of data. When in doubt, you must consult relevant experts.

3. Use data that is proportionate to the user need
The use of data must be proportionate to the user need. You must use the minimum data necessary to achieve the desired outcome.

4. Understand the limitations of the data
Data used to inform policy and service design in government must be well understood. It is essential to consider the limitations of data when assessing if it is appropriate to use it for a user need.

5. Ensure robust practices and work within your skillset
Insights from new technology are only as good as the data and practices used to create them. You must work within your skillset recognising where you do

not have the skills or experience to use a particular approach or tool to a high standard.

6. Make your work transparent and be accountable
You should be transparent about the tools, data and algorithms you used to conduct your work, working in the open where possible. This allows other researchers to scrutinise your findings and citizens to understand the new types of work we are doing.

7. Embed data use responsibly
It is essential that there is a plan to make sure insights from data are used responsibly. This means that both development and implementation teams understand how findings and data models should be used and monitored with a robust evaluation plan.

Conclusions

THIS BOOK HAS considered a momentous episode in UK history. The implications of the subject matter are substantial, not only domestically, but on an international scale. Through applying methodology adapted from history, the work has considered various themes that are relevant across the democratic world. They include the role of the EU (and by extension other multi-state organisations) and the issues raised by an attempt to withdraw from it. I have investigated how long-term constitutional controversies, such as those pertaining to voting systems, the territorial power balance, and the configuration of the legislature, can manifest themselves in new circumstances. The book has also addressed perceived emerging challenges to democracy associated with the Internet, social media and other connected technologies, focusing in particular on their constitutional connotations.

I have considered a particularly fraught subject: the supposed rise of populism in mature democracies. Previous chapters have shown that clear traces of this doctrine, if defined in descriptive (as opposed to pejorative) terms, can be found in the campaign to leave the EU, in the means by which this goal was pursued (that is, though a referendum), and in the way in which the popular vote itself was presented. Populism, in the case of the UK and Brexit, was not confined to less mainstream parties such as UKIP, but found its way, for instance, into the governing Conservatives. Even the UK Prime Minister, Theresa May, in asserting what is labelled in this work the 'May Doctrine', incorporated populist aspects into her programme. However, that is not to say that either May or her party became wholly populist in nature. Moreover, the effort to attain departure from the EU unavoidably relied heavily upon the use of more established representative institutions.

An important lesson can be derived regarding the intertwining of populist and elite movements. An episode such as Brexit must be understood as more than simply an expression of populism, however useful this concept is as an analytical tool. The proposition I advanced in the introduction, that of a recent and ongoing 'reassertion of the political', may be a more comprehensive means of assessing contemporary turbulence in the UK and elsewhere. It involves, as I suggested, an interaction between governors and governed, leading to a widening of the options on offer; an increase in the chances that previously more marginal proposals will gain substantial support; the revival of some forms of public participation; and the rise of new means of political communication. The reassertion of the political, as is shown here in the context of the UK, can create difficulties for the functioning of democracy. But my analysis suggests that it is not yet appropriate to conclude that this system of government is doomed, at least in the UK. Historical analysis shows that the belief that democracy is in peril is far from new. Such claims have repeatedly proved false – though this observation should not be a basis for complacency. Moreover, assessment of the past shows that the problems of the present have been identified or predicted previously, and that there are possible solutions to them that might be attempted. The challenges faced by the system are partly products of its own faults, rather than an external assault. Self-correction, which is within the hands of representative institutions, may therefore be of considerable assistance. There is some cause for optimism. The conclusions that follow explore the implications of this study for the UK, for Brexit, and its possible constitutional future. At the same time, they can be interpreted as a contribution to a broader debate about democracy in the developed world and beyond.

I. A LEGITIMATE PROCESS?

The referendum of 23 June 2016 was a startling exercise in political participation. The scale of the overall turnout was in itself impressive. So was the result in favour of leaving the EU, the far more radical option than remaining within it on renegotiated terms. Simply to dismiss this event would be to demean a collective act of more than 17 million people, who were asked for an opinion and provided it. That the views of the broadly less socially privileged and more numerous group which supported exiting the EU should prevail over the smaller number that voted to remain might be perceived as matter of fundamental democratic principle. The questioning of process, moreover, can suggest a lack of good health on the part of a polity. If losers do not accept defeat, the viability of the game is compromised. While certain campaign rules were violated, and the legal framework as a whole for referendums may not at present be wholly adequate, there are no credible claims that large-scale fraud took place. People who wanted to do so were able to vote, free of intimidation, and having done so, the ballot papers were counted properly, and results declared accurately. Further challenge is vulnerable to the charge of being a proxy for dislike of the outcome.

Nonetheless, despite all these reservations, and whatever the ultimate conclusions of the Brexit episode, it is necessary to recognise the serious constitutional problems raised by this experience. The mishandling of the process showed a lack of respect to all those who took part, on either side. These criticisms arise from the way in which the decision to leave was taken and implemented, and the consequences of that policy. It is necessary to recognise the difficulties not only as a retrospective judgement upon an unsatisfactory sequence of events – useful in itself – but as a means of informing future systemic reconfiguration. Such reform can be informed by and seek to avoid the repetition of past shortcomings. The charge that such views are in some way undemocratic, moreover, can be refuted, on the grounds that the connection between any supposed popular will expressed in the referendum and the approach adopted in response to it by the UK government was too tenuous to be credible. The meaning of 'leave' – which in any case only 37.4 per cent of those able to vote supported – was, partly unavoidably, partly because of bad practice, exceptionally vague. The vote was not a satisfactory basis for such drastic courses of action as stripping more than 60 million people of their present and future EU citizenship.

Rather than being a pure expression of direct public will, the referendum was embedded within the system of representative government. That it took place at all, and at the point that it did, and in the way it did, and the policies that followed, was the outcome of party and electoral politics. Public opinion – expressed through the referendum and other means – was important, but achieving influence, as inevitably it must, filtered through and in the context of the wider environment. Attempts to elevate the referendum and its result above the system of which they were a part attached an importance to them greater than they could rationally justify; and had the effect of destabilising the constitution as a whole. Yet this dysfunction was a product of the system and its internal imperatives – suggesting the existence of internal flaws that had produced the Brexit experience, and which it served to expose and aggravate in the process.

No constitution is perfect; and the UK system has many strengths. But these realisations should not prevent the identification and acknowledgement of faults, with a view to their possible correction. Some of the shortcomings that manifested themselves in relation to Brexit have – as this book has demonstrated – figured in past analysis of the UK system, suggesting that they are of an underlying and recurring nature (see, for instance, the analysis of JA Hobson, John H Humphreys, John St Loe Strachey and William Waldegrave). A feature common to a number of these accounts, confirmed by Brexit, is the idea of an internal imbalance: that one group, representing an assertive minority within a minority, can impose courses of action upon the whole, subject to inadequate constraint. Hobson, for instance, feared that the Commons might be subordinated to 'the pertinacious fanaticism of little organised groups representing a small minority of the electorate'.[1] It might seem curious to refer to such a scenario in the context of a decision that drew its claimed legitimacy from the outcome of a popular vote. That 17,410,742 people voted leave is inescapable. But not only was the choice so open-ended as to undermine the potential of the vote in itself to create a meaningful obligation. Further difficulties become apparent when certain prior questions are asked. Why was a referendum being held at this point, on this particular subject? The existence of overwhelming public demand for the vote on EU membership held in 2016 was never clearly demonstrated.

[1] JA Hobson, *The Crisis of Liberalism: New Issues of Democracy* (London, FS King & Son, 1909) 36.

Analysis of public opinion tracking carried out by MORI shows that, between June 2003 and February 2016, when respondents were asked to name 'the most important issue' and 'other important issues facing Britain today', the proportion mentioning the EU never reached 20 per cent; and most of the time was below 10 per cent (in June 2003 it was 26 per cent; in June 2005 it fell 1 per cent short of 20 per cent at 19 per cent; and in February 2016 it was 20 per cent). In May 2015, the month of the General Election that supposedly produced the mandate for holding the referendum, only 9 per cent named the EU as important. This figure was lower than those of crime, at 10 per cent; economy 36 per cent; education 21 per cent; housing 16 per cent; immigration 40 per cent; low pay 11 per cent; NHS 44 per cent; pensions 11 per cent; poverty 17 per cent; and unemployment 19 per cent. A referendum was held on none of these issues. However, perhaps some of those participating on 23 June 2016 had one or more of these topics of higher salience in mind when they voted. An increase in the perceived relevance for the EU was inspired from above. It was only with the referendum confirmed and looming that a sustained increase in the percentage of those naming the issue as important took place. By June 2016, when the vote was held, the total had reached 32. It has risen further thereafter. Throughout 2017 the figure exceeded 40 per cent.[2] Yet this surge represents a recognition of the reality that the referendum brought about. The existence of prior demand would be a far more dubious proposition to sustain.

Rather than the wishes of the wider public, it was a faction within the Conservative parliamentary party that provided the vital political impetus for the holding of the referendum. Having obtained a 'leave' victory, members of this group sought to deploy this result for their preferred purposes. Their approach enabled them to secure the acceptance of Brexit by a UK government, and obtain substantial concessions in the direction of the variant on this policy that they favoured (including early commitments from May to leaving both the Single Market and Customs Union). They clearly fit the description 'minority within a minority'. Most Conservative MPs had publicly supported 'remain' at the referendum[3] (as had a majority of all MPs[4]). The Conservative Party itself, though holding office in some form since 2010, did so while consistently accounting for well under half of participating voters: 36.1 per cent in

[2] The data, that run from 1974 onwards, can be found at: https://www.ipsos.com/ipsos-mori/en-uk/issues-index-2007-onwards last accessed 30 September 2018. I am grateful to Stuart Smedley, who is studying them as part of his forthcoming thesis on 'Public opinion and attitudes towards European integration in the United Kingdom, 1973–2016' for bringing this information to my attention.

[3] Philip Lynch and Richard Whitaker. 'All Brexiteers now? Brexit, the Conservatives and party change' (2018) 13(1) *British Politics* 31–47, p 33.

[4] 'EU vote: where the Cabinet and other MPs stand', *BBC*, 22 June 2016: https://www.bbc.co.uk/news/uk-politics-eu-referendum-35616946 last accessed 29 August 2018.

2010; 36.9 per cent in 2015; and 42.4 per cent in 2017.[5] This faction within the Conservatives did not have a precise composition, but nonetheless it represented a genuine current of thought within the party. If we are to estimate its size and composition, it is useful to consider the 81 Conservative MPs (79 and 2 tellers on a non-binding motion) who, on 24 October 2011 – despite a three-line whip to the contrary – supported a referendum that would offer the choice of leaving, remaining within, or renegotiating membership of the EU.[6] (It should be noted that not all of those who voted for the motion went on to support 'leave' in the referendum[7]). They were not operating in a vacuum. There was agreement with their position outside Parliament, especially among local activists who were or had been Conservative members and in sections of the traditional and online media. The rise in support for UKIP both encouraged and strengthened them. The debate in question took place in response to a public petition that had exceeded the set threshold of 100,000 signatories.[8] Further sympathisers within Parliament abstained on the motion, or reluctantly voted against (some of whom were ministers within the government). MPs from other parties also supported a popular vote, either rebelling against or in accordance with their party policy.[9] But the decisive force came from those most able to exert influence: Conservatives inside the Commons who were willing to defy their leadership and potentially inflict political damage on their own party and the government of which it was a part.[10]

This bloc was subsequently given various labels including the '81 Group',[11] operating within a party that had secured 306 MPs at the General Election of the previous year. In May 2013, 114 Conservative MPs supported a motion expressing regret that the Queen's Speech, setting out the legislative programme

[5] 'EU vote: where the Cabinet and other MPs stand', *BBC*, 22 June 2016: https://www.bbc.co.uk/news/uk-politics-eu-referendum-35616946 last accessed 29 August 2018.

[6] Hansard House of Commons (HC) Debates, 24 October 2011, col 46; 'Rebels: the full list', *New Statesman*, 25 October 2011: https://www.newstatesman.com/blogs/the-staggers/2011/10/north-mps-south-referendum last accessed 29 August 2018; Philip Cowley and Mark Stuart, 'The cambusters: The conservative European Union referendum rebellion of October 2011' (2012) 83(2) *The Political Quarterly* 402–06.

[7] Philip Lynch and Richard Whitaker. 'All Brexiteers now? Brexit, the Conservatives and party change' (2018) 13(1) *British Politics* 31–47, p 35.

[8] See 'Backbench business debate on the holding of an EU referendum': https://www.parliament.uk/business/committees/committees-a-z/commons-select/backbench-business-committee/news/eu-referendum-debate/ last accessed 29 August 2018.

[9] For further analysis, see: 'Rebels: the full list', *New Statesman*, 25 October 2011: https://www.newstatesman.com/blogs/the-staggers/2011/10/north-mps-south-referendum last accessed 29 August 2018.

[10] For an account of this group and its effectiveness see eg: Patrick Hennessy, 'David Cameron faces guerrilla war with Conservative MPs over Europe', *Telegraph*, 29 October 2011: https://www.telegraph.co.uk/news/politics/david-cameron/8857722/David-Cameron-faces-guerrilla-war-with-Conservative-MPs-over-Europe.html last accessed 29 August 2018.

[11] Andrew Grice, 'Exclusive: Tory rebels form new Eurosceptic group', *Independent*, 2 November 2011: https://www.independent.co.uk/news/uk/politics/exclusive-tory-rebels-form-new-eurosceptic-group-6255896.html last accessed 29 August 2018.

for the coming parliamentary session, did not contain reference to a referendum on continued EU membership. However, this vote was not subject to a whip;[12] therefore, though the episode was damaging to the government, not all of those taking part were necessarily part of the inner circle of the most resolute. It was the consistent pressure emerging from the most determined advocates of a referendum that eventually drove David Cameron to commit himself to the holding of a referendum.[13] He had initially attempted to placate this group and the forces it channelled – as he and previous Conservative leaders had already tried – through adopting a more Eurosceptic posture that fell short of allowing for the possibility of departure.[14] Eventually, with the Bloomberg Speech of 23 January 2013, Cameron (then Prime Minister in a coalition with the Liberal Democrats who were opposed to this policy) committed to a re-negotiation followed by a referendum on membership, should he secure a single-party majority at the next General Election.[15] Not content with this commitment, Conservative MPs then sought to secure more immediate steps to commence the process to which Cameron was pledged.[16]

After the referendum, concerted pressure on Cameron's successor, May, that the result must mean not merely exit but decisive dealignment from the EU came in particular from those connected with the 'European Research Group' (ERG).[17] In February 2018, a letter to the Prime Minister urging her to secure 'full regulatory autonomy' and the ability to enter into international trade agreements immediately after exit was signed by MPs reported to be associated with the ERG, totalling 62 (the Conservatives had 297 seats after the previous General Election).[18] Once more it must be stressed that the ERG were operating in a wider environment – albeit that it and those connected to it had helped generate – that was conducive to their actions. In particular, the referendum result could be seen by those who did not sympathise with the ERG cause as nonetheless strengthening their case. But persistent action of the type pursued

[12] Patrick Wintour and Nicholas Watt, 'EU referendum: Cameron snubbed by 114 Tory MPs over Queen's speech', *Guardian*: https://www.theguardian.com/politics/2013/may/16/cameron-snubbed-tory-eu-referendum last accessed 29 August 2018.

[13] See eg Mark D'Arcy 'How rebel MPs outfoxed Cameron to get an EU referendum', BBC, 29 December 2016: https://www.bbc.co.uk/news/uk-politics-parliaments-38402140 last accessed 29 August, 2018.

[14] See eg Ian Traynor, Nicholas Watt, David Gow and Patrick Wintour, 'David Cameron blocks EU treaty with veto, casting Britain adrift in Europe', *Guardian*, 9 December 2011: https://www.bbc.co.uk/news/uk-politics-parliaments-38402140 last accessed 29 August 2018.

[15] 'EU Speech at Bloomberg', 23 January 2018: https://www.gov.uk/government/speeches/eu-speech-at-bloomberg last accessed 29 August 2018.

[16] See eg 'Adam Afriyie pushes for vote on EU referendum before the election', *Guardian*, 6 October 2013: https://www.theguardian.com/politics/2013/oct/06/adam-afriyie-eu-vote-referendum-before-election last accessed 29 August 2018.

[17] Heather Stewart, '"We're the opposition", Rees-Mogg and his European Research Group', *Guardian*, 20 July 2018, *Guardian*: https://www.theguardian.com/politics/2018/jul/20/opposition-jacob-rees-mogg-european-research-group-profile last accessed 29 August 2018.

[18] Gordon Rayner, 'Jacob Rees-Mogg's Brexiteers lay down red lines in "ransom note" letter to Theresa May', *Telegraph*, 21 February 2018: https://www.telegraph.co.uk/politics/2018/02/20/eurosceptic-tory-mps-set-brexit-red-lines-letter-theresa-may/ last accessed 29 August 2018.

by the ERG was vital in reducing the chances of other options – such as not leaving, holding a second referendum at some point, or a less abrupt Brexit – being pursued. How successful the ERG will prove to be remains, as of the end of September 2018, uncertain. But its impact – and that of the group of MPs associated with it and their predecessors in earlier parliaments – has been on a scale out of proportion with its numbers.

But what specific features of the UK constitution facilitated this minority ascendancy? An appropriate starting point is the party system, that is crucial to the operation of representative democracy (and has some formal recognition, for instance through the Political Parties, Elections and Referendums Act 2000). Parties contest general elections on composite programmes. No-one person within a party is likely privately to support every policy item, but they are adopted on a basis of their aggregate acceptability. Conservative MPs who favoured a referendum on EU membership were able to force the referendum into the party programme because they prioritised this issue over party cohesion, while those who disagreed with them had a stronger aversion to damaging internal disruption than did advocates of a referendum. Similar principles applied in the post-referendum environment, with ERG associates displaying less qualms about entering into open dispute with fellow-Conservative MPs than others in the Party when contemplating rebelling.[19] Within the UK system, if a party secures an overall majority in a General Election – as did the Conservatives in 2015 – then the entirety of their programme is taken as having received an endorsement. There are some obvious problems with this principle such as electors not agreeing or being aware of every item proposed by the party for which they voted, and that parties are able to secure majorities in the Commons having received well under half of votes cast. Yet these defects have not yet led to a decisive revision of the theory of the mandate that they appear to undermine.

The UK party system also contributed to the Brexit episode in the sense in which it interacted with the controversy arising from UK participation in European integration. This issue has long been capable of dividing both the main parties, prompting sharp disagreements that the usual techniques of internal consensus building have struggled to resolve. Both the Labour and Conservative parties have resorted to the unusual measure of referendum pledges – implemented respectively in 1975 and 2016 – as the only apparent means of reconciling differences in this area. From this perspective, the 2016 referendum (like that of 1975) appears more as the product of party dysfunction that a means of securing direct public participation in a decision. It was an instrument by which a leadership could maintain a degree of unity, while on

[19] Heather Stewart, '"We're the opposition", Rees-Mogg and his European Research Group', *Guardian*, 20 July 2018: https://www.theguardian.com/politics/2018/jul/20/opposition-jacob-rees-mogg-european-research-group-profile last accessed 29 August 2018; 'Brexit deal: Tory rebel warns government could collapse', *BBC*, 17 June 2018: https://www.bbc.co.uk/news/uk-politics-44511969 last accessed 29 August 2018.

each side of the argument it was perceived either as a means of furthering, or halting, the cause of exiting the EU.

The regular party political system ceased to operate in another way in relation to Brexit. A key feature of parliamentary politics in the UK is their adversarial nature. Yet while Labour had not advocated a referendum in advance of the 2015 General Election, it reversed this position afterwards, supporting the European Union Referendum Bill in 2015. A likely reason for this decision was a desire to avoid being perceived as resistant to involving the people in settling an important matter. Some within Labour also anticipated with pleasure that the referendum would cause Conservative divisions. But for whatever reason, the official opposition failed to oppose. In the context of such a weighty decision, and given the adversarial premise on which the UK system traditionally rests, this absence is startling. Labour would presumably not have been able to prevent the passing of the legislation. But if it had maintained its previous stance it might have subjected the bill to more fundamental scrutiny than it did, challenging some of the premises on which the referendum was held. Both party leaders were therefore committed to the curious and problematic platform of the 'bluff-call' referendum, that was a key source of the difficulties that followed.

The absence of more regular party political contestation continued after the referendum. Conservative and Labour leaders accepted the result as necessitating an exit. In voting for the European Union (Notice of Withdrawal) Act 2017 Labour maintained acceptance of this principle, and that the executive should enjoy breadth of discretion in pursuing it. The parties offered voters what appeared to be broadly similar policies on the subject at the 2017 General Election. This coalescence between the two main parties (accompanied by continued – even intensifying – internal divisions) represented a serious restriction on the usual means by which the UK party system provides for choice, debate and scrutiny. Labour sought to find grounds on which it could criticise the government, but since 2015 would not challenge the overall basis of official policy.[20] Yet the parties had not disappeared. They had merely modified their behaviour. Throughout, the Brexit episode was shaped by party political concerns: their internal dynamics and competition with each-other and the anticipation that at some point familiar service might resume, and that they should be ready for it when it did. The way in which the parties colluded over aspects of Brexit suggests an important conclusion. Though it represented in large part a success for a minority faction of Conservative MPs and the particular tactics they deployed, the episode is attributable to a far wider group. Politicians across parties and on both sides of the campaign behaved in the way they did in pursuit of contradictory outcomes pertaining to the EU and the inter-party

[20] See eg John McTernan, 'Wanted: an opposition that will stand up to May on Brexit', *Financial Times*, 3 February 2018: https://www.ft.com/content/26d38726-081b-11e8-9e12-af73e8db3c71 last accessed 26 September 2018.

contest. Some were correct in their calculations, others were mistaken. Between them they created Brexit.

A second feature of the UK constitution that helped bring about the referendum and its aftermath was the parliamentary electoral system. The First-Past-the-Post method of determining the composition of the House of Commons has tended to create a considerable – though certainly not absolute – tendency in the direction of dominance by two parties. One of the consequences has been to deprive voters of a more meaningful choice between parties for whom a vote is not simply wasted (a defect of the 2017 General Election). Another is a strong incentive for the two main parties to avoid splitting, since the electoral consequences of doing so are likely to be grave. This tendency leads in turn to the presence within the parties of a range of views that are seemingly difficult or impossible to reconcile with one-another (including over the EU), as Keith Sutherland recognised.[21] It also creates the opportunity for particular factions to foist on the whole proposals (such as the EU referendum) that – though objectionable to many – are accepted because they are perceived as being preferable to fragmentation or at least prolonged internal conflict. The electoral system also contributed to Brexit through its propensity to reward parties that secure well under half of the popular vote with majorities in the Commons. The effect can be to magnify the importance of the given party and its internal dynamics. Thus in 2015, a referendum pledge forced on the Conservative Party by a minority of its MPs, which formed just one (admittedly prominent) part of a manifesto in an election at which the Conservatives received only 36.9 per cent of votes cast, could be deemed to be the subject of a democratic mandate, and could be implemented by a party that now had a Commons majority (with the official opposition, moreover, choosing to acquiesce in this policy).

A third aspect of the UK system requiring consideration involves the role of the executive. It appears as both weak and strong. On the one hand, through much of the period leading up to and following on from the EU referendum, it was, in this area of activity, subject to a potent outside influence: namely, that of the assertive faction within the Conservative Party (and forces aligned with it) discussed above. While it did not necessarily concede to every demand emanating from this source the executive operated within a general framework determined opponents of the EU within the Conservative Party had helped set. On the other hand, the executive was a powerful tool deployed in service of the objectives those nominally at its head decided – under duress or of their own volition – to pursue. Within Parliament, it introduces legislation and has priority over other business. With the support of the Civil Service, it is responsible for the formulation and conduct of policy, including diplomatic negotiations. The Article 50 case, though constitutionally significant, represented an obstacle

[21] See ch 8.

to the exercise of executive authority that was soon overcome. The European Union (Notice of Withdrawal) Act 2017 suggested acceptance by Parliament – and within it the Commons, including on the official opposition side – that the executive should be subject to minimal constraints. Those who sought the holding of a referendum, and then the enactment of Brexit in a particular way, were able to achieve progress towards their objectives primarily by imposing themselves on the executive, through their position of influence inside a party that from 2015 governed alone.

The various features of the UK constitution set out above – the party system, FPTP and the role of the executive – all contributed to a position in which the House of Commons was committed, first, to facilitating a referendum and, second, accepting the result as necessitating departure, led by the executive. Within the UK system, the will of the Commons – if sufficiently determined – can generally be decisive. As the analysis of various reform advocates discussed in this book has shown, this position became increasingly apparent during the nineteenth century and was given a degree of legal confirmation by the Parliament Act 1911. For a number of these observers, including JA Hobson, the ascendancy of the Commons – though an integral aspect of the coming of democracy – was a source of concern, creating an unchecked base of authority that might act contrary to the views of the public, or for malign ends, upon which there would be no effective limitation.

The contemporary House of Lords, particularly as a consequence of the removal of most of the hereditary peers under the House of Lords Act 1999, has become increasingly assertive and effective at securing amendments to bills, working in collaboration with the Commons.[22] However, there are limits on the extent to which it is willing to deploy even those powers it possesses. The Lords is reluctant to challenge the fundamentals of legislation, or to force the issue if the Commons is not receptive to amendments it has made. Yet received wisdom attributes to the Lords a loosely-defined role as a constitutional custodian.[23] It might be argued that changes to the underlying rules of a system should be subject to procedural requirements that are heightened relative to those involved in the introduction of more regular provisions. The attribution of a guardianship role to the Lords has the opposite effect, placing special responsibility for the constitution in a body of legally and practically circumscribed powers. However much expertise the Lords includes within it, its ability to act upon it is

[22] Meg Russell, 'A stronger second chamber? Assessing the impact of House of Lords reform in 1999 and the lessons for bicameralism' (2010) 58(5) *Political Studies* 866–85.

[23] Dawn Oliver, *Constitutional Guardians: the House of Lords* (London, The Constitution Society, 2015): https://consoc.org.uk/wp-content/uploads/2015/12/COSJ3942_Constitutional_guardians_WEB.pdf last accessed 26 September 2018; Lucy Atkinson, '*Talking to the Guardians*'*: The Constitutional Role of the House of Lords* (London, The Constitution Society, 2016): https://consoc.org.uk/wp-content/uploads/2016/10/House-of-Lords-PDF.pdf last accessed 26 September 2018.

limited by its lack of democratic legitimacy. In the case of Brexit, the Lords did not begin seriously addressing the constitutional issues until after the referendum had taken place. When it did, it did so as an entity the capacity of which to contest was constrained.

Beyond Parliament, the possibility for a meaningful challenge to the premises underlying Brexit was more limited still. The role of the courts was restricted. The importance of the successful legal challenge to the ability of the government to activate Article 50 of the Treaty on European Union under the Royal Prerogative should be recognised but also placed in perspective. It forced upon the legislature a power by which it seemed embarrassed. Parliament duly provided through statute the discretionary power that the executive had previously believed it already possessed under the prerogative. To be clear, the Article 50 ruling was of great significance in firmly asserting principles that are fundamental to democracy: that governments are subject to the law; that legal changes and alterations to individual rights must be conducted in accordance with established procedure; and that a referendum result does not in itself remove these requirements. That such maxims required defending was illustrative of the deleterious aspects of Brexit. But with or without the Article 50 judgement, the House of Commons possessed the power – in theory – to halt Brexit at any time, if necessary through installing a different government. Other forces discussed above, connected to the party and electoral systems, made such action unlikely (though at the time of writing, just within the scope of the plausible).

The Supreme Court majority, in its Article 50 judgement, sought expressly to preclude that it might become involved in ruling on whether the Sewel convention had been violated, despite this rule having recently been included in statute (for Scotland, and soon afterwards for Wales, but not yet Northern Ireland). Ultimately, any objections from devolved level regarding the approach the UK government took to Brexit had to be addressed politically. Negotiations were conducted on a basis that exit from the EU was a given. There were significant concessions at UK level, but ultimately the UK government proved willing to prevail upon the Westminster Parliament to legislate notwithstanding the withholding of consent from a devolved legislature – despite the constitutional understanding that it would not normally do so. The Westminster Parliament obliged the government and passed the European Union (Withdrawal) Act 2018. From the perspective of the Scottish executive, for the UK administration to operate in this way may have been a calculated outcome, and could help strengthen its case for a further independence referendum.[24]

In another country, particularly one with a federal constitution, the remits of all governmental institutions, including the central legislature, would probably

[24] For the deterioration in relations, see: Paris Gourtsoyan Nis, 'UK Government warning as SNP declares "guerrilla war" on Brexit', *Scotsman*, 15 June 2018: https://www.scotsman.com/news/politics/uk-government-warning-as-snp-declares-guerrilla-war-on-brexit-1-4755536 last accessed 26 September 2018.

be derived from a 'written' constitution, by which is generally meant a text of special legal, entrenched status, setting out the fundamental rules of the system. Limitations upon an equivalent body to the UK Parliament would therefore be determined by an adjudicatory entity – probably a court – based on its interpretation of the constitution. In the UK, the limits were derived from a convention that – even if included in an Act of Parliament – was seemingly not justiciable. If the UK government judged that it was proper to seek to legislate in a particular instance, then it could do so, subject only to the willingness of the Westminster Parliament to comply with it. The Supreme Court can rule on the extent of the remit of the devolved legislatures (as defined in Acts passed by the UK Parliament), but cannot determine in the same way limits on the UK Parliament.

As suggested previously, Brexit created an environment in which the Griffith dictum that whatever happens is constitutional appeared in some senses accurate. The limits and understandings of the system were being tested. Through the Article 50 case, the government, in its pursuit of Brexit, unexpectedly encountered a legal boundary. The judiciary held firm, at least in upholding the legislative supremacy of Parliament. Conventions, however, are of more amorphous quality than hard law and cannot be directly enforced in the courts. The UK government could not only unilaterally decide on a course of action in this area. It could also claim that it was acting in accordance with the convention, which included the difficult-to-define qualifying word 'normally'. There was no means by which the interpretation advanced and acted on by the UK administration could be definitively refuted (or verified).[25] In addition to the probing of existing constitutional arrangements, the referendum and the period that followed saw various players promoting creative views of the nature of the UK system. Thus, the devolved executives set out conceptions that had federal or even confederal qualities, in contrast to more traditional assertions of a unitary character. Furthermore, Theresa May, with her first October 2016 Conservative Party conference speech,[26] presented a view of the implications of the referendum result that, though she seemed to regard them as self-evident, lacked firm grounding in past constitutional thought or practice in the UK. Moreover, the member of her Cabinet with the Brexit brief, David Davis, who was therefore the primary custodian of the irresistible obligation she (and he) believed had been created, had previously advanced a position which appeared to contradict that to which she now cleaved. May did not achieve the exclusive executive control over Brexit that she demanded. Yet the basic principle that the referendum required departure, and in a form set out by her government, achieved a high level of adherence within the institution where it was needed if it was to prevail: the House of Commons. An area in which the Commons has applied significant pressure to the executive has been over having a 'meaningful vote', but at the end

[25] See: 'Statement on the Sewel Convention', 14 June 2018: https://www.gov.uk/government/news/statement-on-the-sewel-convention last accessed 30 August 2018.

[26] See ch1.

of the negotiation process. Even in this respect, what power exactly MPs have achieved for themselves, and what use they can and will make of it, remains unclear as I write.

The various tendencies and forces that drove, first, the holding of the referendum and, second, the response to the result were, therefore, able to find broad expression because of the strong position of the Commons within the constitution combined with the flexible nature of the system. Firm rules can be difficult to discern and enforce, militating in favour of the prevailing will within the elected chamber of Parliament. All of these circumstances made possible the conduct of a referendum on an exceptionally open-ended proposition that was subsequently accepted by the government and others as compelling a course of action far more specific than could have been discerned from the result. The policy of departure adopted implied major changes for the UK, including in its internal constitutional configuration. This transformation, to be legitimate, required a high level of democratic consent. Advocates of Brexit claimed that the referendum had provided a sufficient degree of approval. It did not. Closer scrutiny of the basis on which the vote was held and what followed reveals clear problems. Informed, considered, prior consideration and approval of the coming transformation, both by representatives and public, was not properly facilitated. Nor was the higher than usual level of consensus, that would ideally exist in such circumstances, obtained.

One of the arguments offered in favour of the use of referendums by their early advocates in the UK was that they would prevent the Commons, possibly under the influence of a determined minority within a minority, from imposing itself upon the Lords and implementing a measure that did not truly reflect the majority will of the public. Arguably, in the case of the Brexit episode, a referendum has been deployed to facilitate the very activity which it was hoped such a mechanism could prevent. Those most determined that the decision expressed in the 2016 referendum, as they saw it, be implemented were also the most opposed to the idea of the people being directly consulted again once a clearer idea of what leaving might mean had become possible. Even if one accepts the principle that a referendum on the EU was necessary, that it should be treated as binding and only reversible, if at all, by a further such vote, a more sophisticated approach than that adopted was available.

The debate of 2011 that ended with 81 Conservatives defying a three-line whip was on a three-option referendum, offering the choice of leaving, renegotiating or remaining. Implementing this method would be complicated in practice, but the Conservative MP Jacob Rees-Mogg – elected to the Commons the previous year, and who would go on to become the central figure in the ERG – addressed the criticism 'that a three-way referendum is confusing'. It was, he insisted 'not a problem because the motion calls for a Bill in the next Session, which can deal with any confusion. We can, in our wisdom, work out how to phrase a referendum – or series of referendums, if necessary – that will be understandable'. Moreover, Rees-Mogg held, 'we could have two referendums.

As it happens, it might make more sense to have the second referendum after the renegotiation is completed'.[27] This proposal should not be read as meaning that Rees-Mogg was at this point in effect endorsing a second referendum in the post-23 June 2016 circumstance.[28] However, it could be interpreted as suggesting that any popular decision to leave the EU should be founded in knowledge of the outcome, that an initial referendum decision to leave might not be sufficiently informed to be regarded as final, and therefore could be subject to reversal or confirmation by, in his scenario, a further vote.

II. THE CONSTITUTION AND THE FUTURE

An assessment of Brexit informed by specific historic reform proposals can, then, provide enhanced understanding of the nature of the process of leaving. How might it inform future approaches to the UK constitution, taking into account the Brexit episode but applicable regardless of its precise outcome? The following section proposes a series of principles that might usefully be applied. Some of them might be attained by changes in practice, others would require legislation, others still might require mechanisms unfamiliar within the context of the 'unwritten' UK constitution. Some of them may seem politically less viable than others. But now is a time of possibilities, both good and bad. It is appropriate in such a climate to expound ideas, not remain silent to avoid the charge of impracticability. Plans discarded in the past might be found useful at this later date.

First, regardless of the precise terms on which the UK leaves the EU (assuming it does depart at all), and of the nature of the post-Brexit relationship between the two, policy makers in this country should proceed in the knowledge that it is not possible fully to insulate the UK political system from the outside world. In this sense the objective of taking back control that was a prominent part of the 'leave' agenda is unattainable. Arguments about the relationship of the UK with the continent of which it is a part, and what it means for internal arrangements and policies, will persist. As Brendan Simms put it in a note – added in the wake of the EU referendum – to the paperback edition of his work *Britain's Europe: A Thousand Years of Conflict and Cooperation*, '[w]hat is certain is that departure from the European Union will not be the end either of the one-thousand year long dominance of Europe in British policy and politics, or of the profound role which the United Kingdom has played in determining the shape of the continent'.[29] Furthermore, the UK is likely to retain its

[27] Hansard House of Commons (HC) Debates, 24 October 2011, col 108.

[28] For Rees-Mogg on his earlier statement, see: Jacob Rees-Mogg to Lord Adonis, 5 September 2018: https://docs.wixstatic.com/ugd/fc5611_cb15b5bc1cd34cd0af41deae5e4e330e.pdf last accessed 28 September 2018.

[29] Brendan Simms, *Britain's Europe: A Thousand Years of Conflict and Cooperation* (London, Penguin, 2016) vi.

longstanding aspirations to be an influential force in the world. Achieving this impact unilaterally is not a serious proposition. The UK will need, therefore, to work with other states. The extent to which any such collaboration is effective will depend partly upon how far the participants within it – including the UK – are willing to pool their sovereignty, submitting themselves to the decisions of the whole. Helping to form, or perhaps joining, any such project will probably not be on the immediate agenda having left the EU. But the idea of participating in some kind of supranational or federal arrangement has a long history in UK thought. Whether considering the Empire, Europe, or the world as a larger unit, a great number of reform advocates discussed in this book – including Humphreys, Winston Churchill, Leonard Woolf, Friedrich Hayek, Ivor Jennings, JC Banks, John Pinder and Roy Pryce, and William Beveridge – all perceived the potential of some kind of incorporation into a larger entity. This idea will not vanish forever. In the meantime, UK central government will come under pressure to share the control that has supposedly been wrested from Brussels. At UK level, pressure for parliamentary input – a cause advanced by Arthur Ponsonby a century ago – is likely; and the devolved institutions will also press their case. The possibilities for fulfilling such expectations are discussed below.

Secondly, major referendums, if they are to be held in future, should generally involve governments (at devolved or UK level) seeking approval for clearly defined changes that they wish to implement. Ideally they should be post-legislative.[30] That is, as earlier advocates of referendums discussed in this book – Alex Thompson, J.A. Hobson and John St. Loe Strachey – proposed, they should be held on the basis of Acts of Parliament that come into force (or otherwise) after the referendum has taken place. The result in either direction should be binding within the terms of the Act. There is a strong case for considering means of refining such processes, to provide more meaningful, informed and consensual decisions. They include heightened requirements for a change option, such as thresholds and supermajorities – and possibly approval from two or perhaps three of Wales, Scotland, Northern Ireland, England. Another potential approach would be for England voting with one other to be sufficient (this result actually occurred in 2016, when England and Wales both produced 'leave' majorities). The prospect of just one of these four territories being able to veto all the others seems less desirable.

Thirdly, following on from this point, means must be found of binding together the territorial components of the UK, for so long as the UK exists in its current form, while maintaining their devolved autonomy. Most of the devolution debate in the UK has been about the transfer of power away from the centre: how extensive it should be, what functions precisely should be involved, what the limits and controls should be, the mechanisms used and the means

[30] For a contemporary view on these issues, see: Independent Commission on Referendums, *Report of the Independent Commission on Referendums* (London, Constitution Unit, 2018) 80–89.

by which devolution should be defined, and so on. Far less consideration has been afforded to possible means of ensuring that this dispersal of authority is accompanied by sustained cohesion. One of the drivers of devolution has been the fear of nationalism and possible secessions from the Union. However, in the case of Scotland in particular, it could be argued that such perceived dangers have not been averted by devolution and have even been made more real (in the case of Northern Ireland, the possibility of departure from the UK is built into the system in a way it is not for Wales and Scotland).

Aside from the position one takes on the continued existence or otherwise of the Union, while it exists it seems appropriate that steps should be taken to integrate the devolved territories more fully into the wider UK state, not through reducing their powers, but through providing them with a firmer role in the governance of the whole UK. Assuming departure from the EU is executed in some form and a substantial range of functions is transferred from the EU to the UK, there are a range of authorities that may have to be exercised in a uniform fashion to preserve the UK single market, but in which the devolved institutions have a proper interest. Furthermore, there are matters that are regarded as reserved to the centre, such as the negotiation and conclusion of international trade agreements, in which these entities should also be engaged, if they are to be provided with a full stake in the union. Current mechanisms for ensuring intra-UK consultation – most notably the Joint Ministerial Committee – are less than adequate for this purpose, as is widely recognised.[31]

A more satisfactory constitutional structure for the UK would provide for a clear territorial role in both policy formation and in the legislative process, as some of the authors of reform proposals discussed in this book, such as Ramsay Muir, recognised. It would also establish justiciable protections for the devolved areas against interference from the centre. The firmer the rights that were provided, the greater would be the break with existing constitutional understandings, and the more closely the UK would resemble a federal system. At this more ambitious end of the scale, a repetition of a scenario in which the UK government was able, through the Westminster Parliament, to legislate in a devolved area without consent from the legislature involved, would not be possible. Furthermore, UK level institutions would not be able unilaterally to enter into (or withdraw from) international treaties, and would require some degree of approval from devolved institutions or representatives. The dynamics of constitutional relations would change. One important consequence would be that major changes, such as those associated with Brexit, would have to be carefully considered and discussed with various interested parties in advance, and proceeded with on a basis of consensus.

[31] See eg *Devolution and the Joint Ministerial Committee* (London, Institute for Government, 2018): https://www.instituteforgovernment.org.uk/explainers/brexit-devolution-joint-ministerial-committee last accessed 30 September 2018.

The place for England in these arrangements is not yet clear. It is surely unsatisfactory for the majority of the UK population who live in England to enjoy neither more developed devolution, nor the enhanced territorial representation at the centre that new arrangements along the lines suggested above would entail. The most satisfactory remedy for this inequity would be the introduction of directly elected regional legislatures, out of which executives could be formed, across the whole of England (extending significantly upon the coverage and powers of the existing mayors). A model of this kind has had advocates including Churchill, Muir, John Mackintosh and Banks. Attainment of this goal might involve the people of England accepting the imposition from above of a set of geographical units that in some cases might appear arbitrary and artificial. As has been shown in this book, there is no one obvious model in this respect.[32] In any case, the present Conservative government has, in recent years, set a precedent for driving this kind of change from the centre, through the creation of devolution deals for local authorities in many parts of England, usually with directly elected mayors made a requirement. Moreover, once established, if provided with meaningful powers, these new English regional legislatures and executives could soon become firmly established within the territories they served, and on the UK stage. Welsh devolution, after all, was a divisive concept, rejected firmly by the people of Wales in a referendum in 1979, and only narrowly agreed to in the vote of 1997. Yet, after becoming a reality (with only delegated powers at first), it became increasingly embedded. There may be objections from within Wales, Scotland and Northern Ireland to the introduction of a system that implies the equivalence of these established territories to a newly devised set of English regions. Yet the alternative model – of a single English Parliament – would, as Churchill recognised, be destabilising, posing a threat to UK government, as well as the smaller components of the union.

A body that should play a central role in the inclusion of the territories at UK level is the fourth subject addressed here: the Parliament in Westminster. While Parliament has been active in seeking to scrutinise detailed aspects of Brexit in the period since the referendum, it did not properly address the issues at the crucial point: that is, when asked to provide for the referendum to be held. Nor, at the time of writing, has Parliament managed seriously to challenge the questionable interpretations placed by the UK government on the referendum, despite the outlook of majorities in both Houses. In the likely post-Brexit environment, it is reasonable to anticipate the legislative and policy workload of Parliament increasing. Taking into account already existing difficulties and the probability of increased strain, a range of potential reforms should be considered.

Proposals from earlier in the century – from the likes of Ivor Jennings and Bernard Crick – for a permanently functioning group of specialised Commons

[32] See ch 7.

committees, each overseeing the business of specific departments, have been realised up to a point. However, recommendations for such a system envisaged that they would oversee both policy and legislation. The system as it has developed has involved a focus on the former rather than the latter. Consequently, bills do not receive the quality of scrutiny that they might. Commons select committees might expand their size and role to take in a central place in the legislative process. Their attention should be directed not only to bills but also to statutory instruments, the anticipated use of which is already a controversial aspect of Brexit.

A strength of select committees is their ability to proceed by consensus, a quality that adds to their credibility. If they wish to expand their legitimacy further – and contribute to the model of a more inclusive constitution proposed here – they should consider ongoing collaboration with their equivalents in the devolved legislatures. Select committees may also wish to build upon existing experiments with the use of panels comprising members of the public to engage with policy issues.[33] Membership of such bodies can be determined by sortition, as described by, among others, Anthony Barnett and Peter Carty in their proposals for the second chamber, and Keith Sutherland. Involving randomly chosen individuals in the work of Parliament in this way could help address a complaint made by observers cited in this work, such as JFS Ross, that those elected to Parliament may represent the people, but they are not representative of them. It is possible through sortition to achieve a sample that is both random and constructed to include participants of various defined characteristics within it, if desired.

These panels, supported by expert advisers, might perform a useful role in such areas as considering legislative proposals before they are formally introduced to the House. Non-partisan scrutiny could be a means of identifying – and encouraging the correction of – faults that would otherwise go unaddressed. Perhaps such a process, if applied to what became the European Union (Referendum) Act 2015, would have drawn attention to some of the difficulties with it discussed in chapter two. Criticism from a group removed from the party political frontline might have been easier to act upon, or harder to ignore. Some might query the idea of placing a random group of members of the public in a position of authority. But this is a well-established feature of our legal system. I have served on a jury in criminal trials, and also attended a number of parliamentary committees charged with considering bills and statutory instruments. I found the former experience more reassuring as an effective process than the latter. On one occasion, I was fortunate enough to attend the Commons committee that considered the draft of the Human Rights Act (Amendment) Order 2004.

[33] For the work of Involve in this area, supporting the Housing, Communities and Local Government and the Health and Social Care committees in their investigation into adult social care, see: https://www.involve.org.uk/resources/blog/news/press-release-committees-hold-citizens-assembly-consider-best-way-funding-adult last accessed 26 September 2018.

This statutory instrument finally abolished the death penalty in all circumstances in the UK, in accordance with Protocol 13 of the European Convention on Human Rights, ratified by the UK the previous year. Few present in the room seemed aware of the significance of the moment, or even interested. The parliamentary process might benefit from the insertion of a less jaded element.

Beatrice and Sidney Webb proposed the creation of two elected parliaments covering different spheres of policy. If implemented in full, the bisection of government that this system would entail seems undesirable from the point of view both of effectiveness and accountability. However, their analysis has value in the contemporary environment in that they identified a growth in public business, and argued that to be able effectively to deal with it, Parliament had to expand its capacity, and broaden its legitimacy. The enhancements to Commons select committees suggested here could help achieve this purpose, though not in the precise way the Webbs advocated. An important characteristic of their model was that they envisaged the creation of a dual mandate differentiated according to functional purpose, rather than special territorial provision. Beatrice Webb did, however, concede that there might need to be some recognition of sub-UK national identity. In the intervening period pressure in this direction has grown, and found concrete expression in devolution in Scotland and Wales (it already existed in Northern Ireland at the time the Webbs wrote, and has been abolished, restored and suspended since). The need for fuller territorial integration at UK level discussed above might be met through reforms in another part of Parliament. Devolution proposals discussed in this book, including those of Ramsay Muir, held that a reformed second chamber could provide for this form of involvement. As with many of the general principles advanced here, there are a range of possibilities. Depending partly on other changes, they span from the incorporation of some additional Life Peers under the existing system, all the way to a full-blown federal House.

Whatever model is chosen, the Brexit experience suggests certain points of guidance. A second chamber is needed as a counterbalance to the Commons; and it should probably be more powerful than it presently is, in particular as a means of regulating changes of a constitutional nature. It could also be given a special role to which the Webbs alluded when describing the functions of their second Parliament: consideration of the future. Matters such as EU membership, alongside areas including environmental protection, have long term implications and will affect those not yet born, or at least not yet able to vote. Building the consideration of their rights into decision-making could be an important function for a renewed second chamber. A useful starting point would be an assessment of the recently initiated experiment in Wales with the establishment of a Future Generations Commissioner.[34]

[34] See: https://futuregenerations.wales last accessed 26 September 2018.

An augmentation of the authority of the Lords, however, requires enhancement to its legitimacy. This quality might be obtained through at least some of the composition being determined by direct or indirect election. The latter option could involve the incorporation of the devolved legislatures into the second chamber (a limited precedent for such a gathering is provided by the British-Irish Parliamentary Assembly). This modification, while it would provide more democratic legitimacy, would be less likely than direct elections to lead to the emergence of an entity able to usurp or seriously compromise the primacy of the Commons, an unhelpfully destabilising outcome. However, it would be more suited to providing the firm territorial input into the legislative process that was lacking in relation to Brexit; and generally in asserting itself with respect to matters of a constitutional nature. A more prominent role in these areas might be achieved without the need for the creation of new powers. The present Lords, though more confident than it once was, remains reluctant at present fully to deploy the mechanisms at its disposal (for instance, obstructing legislation until the government backs down or is able to use the Parliament Act; or vetoing statutory instruments). Much could change simply by enabling whoever occupied the second chamber to construe themselves and be perceived as entitled to behave more forcefully.

Any claim that the Lords is unsuited or impervious to radical change can be rebutted by reference to the history of the last century or so. It has had its powers twice restricted in law (1911 and 1949). Conventions have developed reducing its authority further. The Lords has admitted Life Peers, including women (under legislation passed in 1958) and the renunciation of Peerages and the admission of female hereditary peers has been permitted (1963). It opened itself to being regularly televised before the Commons (1985); and shifted from being a mainly hereditary to a mainly appointed chamber (1999). As a consequence of the latter measure, while the Conservative Party had previously possessed an inbuilt majority in the Lords, now no one party has this position of dominance. Once the site of the highest court in the UK, this aspect of the Lords came to an end in 2009 (under legislation passed in 2005), when the Supreme Court became operational. Further changes might be noted, such as developments in the Lords select committee system. The point is that the Lords can change, perhaps more rapidly and radically than the Commons. It could do so again (and need not necessarily change its name in the process).[35]

The main difficulty with the House of Lords is not so much the people who are members of it, but the means by which they came to be so. Changes to composition might, therefore, have an unfortunate consequence: the loss of the extensive knowledge and experience contained within it. In particular the disappearance of crossbenchers – that is Peers without party alignment – would, if it occurred, create a gap. For this reason, the various parliamentary

[35] Peter Dorey and Alexandra Kelso, *House of Lords reform since 1911: Must the Lords go?* (Basingstoke, Springer, 2011).

reforms discussed here should be accompanied by a concerted effort to incorporate experts, individually or in groups, into the work of Parliament, on a more sustained and deeper basis than is presently the case. They could work through the enhanced select committees proposed here, and other routes. The Churchill proposal for an expert sub-Parliament, perhaps taking a view on technical aspects of bills and statutory instruments, offers a useful starting point for consideration; as does the public advisory body envisaged by William Mckechnie. Some might object that the current climate is hostile to what the public might perceive as technocratic ideals. However, if such attitudes are powerful at present, they must be resisted. A rejuvenated Parliament could harness the contribution of academics and other specialists across different fields and demonstrate in public that they can work together with and to the benefit of democracy. Attaching these contributors to the legislature might provide them with an openness and legitimacy that their connection to the executive – as advocated by William Beveridge (followed by Richard Acland) with his 'Economic General Staff' model – would not (though experts will still clearly be needed in government). This proposal, like others set out in this work, could carry resource implications. But placed in perspective, they are not immense, certainly in comparison to the possible cost of the poor decisions they might help prevent. The money involved would certainly be of the quantity that can be obtained from public sources when to do so is judged a political priority. Parliament needs support if it is to perform its role satisfactorily. Rather than blaming MPs for shortcomings, we should help them. I return to a particular aspect of parliamentary oversight requiring augmentation subsequently.

A discussion of Parliament, its democratic legitimacy and the ways in which its composition is determined leads on to the fifth area of possible reform identified in this work: the voting system employed for the House of Commons. Earlier in this chapter I discussed negative aspects of FPTP as revealed by Brexit. Yet I have also shown that similar faults were being identified more than a century ago by the likes of Humphreys. There has been no change yet. Labour took office in 1997 pledged to holding a referendum on the adoption of a more proportional system, but did not do so. A referendum took place on the parliamentary voting system in 2011, under the Conservative-Liberal Democrat coalition. But the model on offer, the Alternative Vote, was not proportional and, in any case, the proposal was defeated. A variety of different and often more proportional systems have been introduced in the interim period, but not at Westminster level. The obvious explanation for the persistence of FPTP is that a shift away from it would require an initiative in this direction from a party – and its MPs – that had been successful through the existing system. However, at present, in as far as FPTP can be said to have contributed to Brexit, it has entailed a majority of MPs in the Commons as a whole and in both the main parties becoming committed to one of the most important decisions in the history of the UK against their wishes. Moreover, for different reasons, a substantial number of

MPs in the Conservatives and Labour are trapped – partly by FPTP – within a party controlled or at least under the heavy influence of forces inimical to them and their beliefs. While breaking with those whose outlook is incompatible with their own might seem sensible, the working of the electoral system substantially reduces the appeal of such a course of action. A solution to this dilemma could involve radical action, such as an alliance, if only of a temporary nature, between those across present divisions who find themselves in similar difficulties and have a shared interest in reform.

The sixth area of interest, that of the parties, follows naturally from the fifth. Historic narratives of the UK as a supposedly stable, internally peaceful country, in which democracy was able to emerge and flourish uninterrupted by authoritarian episodes, often focus on the idea of its avoidance of political extremism. In such scenarios, FPTP is presented as being an important contributory factor. Yet, at present, both parties are either led by (Labour) or subject to coercion from (Conservative) MPs of persuasions that do not fit this supposed pattern of moderation. Both these tendencies might be seen as populist in character in that they rely on appeals to mass constituencies beyond the elite – voters in the Labour leadership election, or in the EU referendum.[36] As I have suggested, that these parties have so far maintained their existence as single entities is partly attributable to FPTP. A move away from this system, on this analysis, could lessen the incentive for continued coexistence between otherwise incompatible groups (though a partisan realignment might also be a necessary precursor to such a reform). The existence of a wider selection of electorally viable parties would not prevent voters from supporting parties that might be regarded as extreme or populist, as they should be able to do in a democracy. But it would make a wider range of options available to the electorate. It might also help avoid a repetition of the Brexit-related phenomenon of a single party seeking to govern while divided to the point of dysfunction over an issue that was dominant at time, and one of the most important ever to have faced the UK. No variant on the party system will be perfect. Over many decades, various observers discussed in this work have identified problems with it that are likely to persist in some form. But no convincing and attractive replacement has been proposed. Some, such as that proposed by Brian Crozier, are of a sinister quality.

The seventh aspect of the constitution requiring attention in the wake of Brexit is the UK executive. Like other features of the representative system, its operating principles and role have been called into question by the episode. The principle of Cabinet collective responsibility has been strained: both in the lead up to the referendum, when it was formally suspended and – perhaps more seriously – in the period afterwards, when senior members of the government struggled to agree positions around which they could publicly unite (assuming

[36] See ch 5.

all of them were genuinely attempting to do so). Allowing ministers to promote the 'leave' option during the campaign, while denying them the full support of the Civil Service to this end, arguably confused the vital relationship of accountability between officials and individual political heads of departments, who in turn answer to Parliament. These difficulties epitomised the tension between direct and representative democracy. It became more pronounced because of particular aspects of the 2016 referendum including its open-ended quality, that the government did not want the radical change option of the two it offered, and that the 'leave' result it sought to avoid came about. Such was the impact of the referendum on the executive that its most senior political member, the Prime Minister David Cameron, resigned following his defeat. Pressure continued to exert itself, contributing to the decision of his successor, Theresa May, to seek an early General Election the following year.

The suggested principles that should apply to the future use of referendums might avoid some of these difficulties for the executive. Their disruptive potential will not be eradicated, nor should it be, since the purpose of constitutional reform should not be to create a system without tension. The 1979 popular vote on Scottish devolution was perhaps less flawed than that held on the EU in 2016 (though the 40 per cent threshold used was controversial). Yet it led to a no-confidence vote in the Commons that was carried, triggering a General Election and defeat for the Labour government. But, in contrast to the 2016 experience, the 1979 Scottish referendum did not bring about more than two years of internal conflict and paralysis, or the prospect of unprecedented changes that, though supposedly justified by the referendum result, were not presented as possible consequences of the vote at the time it took place.

Other reform principles presented in this chapter, if implemented, could reduce the chances of a scenario in which a government is subject to such powerful pressure from a minority group within a particular party as occurred with respect to Brexit. That the executive can be commandeered in this way is a particular concern given the prospect of an expansion in the discretionary power that will be available to it through delegated legislative powers. For this reason it is crucial that government activity is subject to measured scrutiny and control, for instance through committees within Parliament composed of a range of different viewpoints, rather than less representative self-convened factions. Furthermore, while recent years have seen governments (and within them, prime ministers) in relatively weak positions, this power balance is to a large extent politically derived. In earlier periods, for instance during the Margaret Thatcher (1979–90) and Tony Blair (1997–2007) administrations, at times the executive appeared dominant, partly because of large Commons majorities and favourable political circumstances.[37] In such circumstances, the need for limitations on its power – necessary at all times – is arguably even greater.

[37] See ch 8.

Within the UK constitution, formal checks upon the UK executive are not as great as they might be if, for instance, the second chamber were more powerful, or if the government did not rest on the confidence of the Commons and draw ministers from Parliament (as Graham Allen proposed), or were there a 'written' constitution setting out the respective powers of different institutions, enforced by a constitutional court or equivalent body. Therefore, given the discretion they possess, it is important that decision takers within the executive recognise those forms of behaviour that are supportive of democratic values, and that they should seek to act in accordance with them. The Brexit experience has provided examples of arguable failure in this self-regulatory mechanism. In some instances, the executive was prevented or dissuaded from following courses of action that might be seen as improper. But that it contemplated them at all was significant.

The exclusive role May asserted on behalf of her government as interpreter and implementer of the referendum result was a case of constitutional aggrandisement, partially but not fully checked by the judiciary (via the Article 50 case) and pressure from other sources, including Parliament. The European Union (Withdrawal) Bill as originally drafted was criticised for violating multiple constitutional standards, in areas such as the rule of law, the balance between executive and legislature, and the position of the devolved institutions. Again there was some dilution of the original government proposals, but the initial posture was nonetheless a source of concern regarding attitudes within the executive. The Act that eventually appeared, moreover, was passed – on the recommendation of the UK government – notwithstanding the denial of consent by the Scottish Parliament. Whether this event represented a violation of constitutional convention is a matter of opinion. Yet it demonstrated the willingness of the UK executive to assert itself constitutionally in a controversial way. Alongside action, inaction could prove contentious. The government was subject to criticism for failing robustly to defend the judiciary when attacked for its role in the Article 50 case. This reluctance could be seen, generally, as detrimental to the rule of law, within which the independence of proceedings is a crucial component. Furthermore, in this particular instance, it was the role of courts in scrutinising the legality of government action that was at issue. If declining sufficiently to rebut the attacks, the executive was arguably an accomplice in the diminution of means by which it might be restrained. Whether Brexit represents a temporary episode in which self-regulation became less effective as a containment device for the executive, or whether it marked the emergence of a longer lasting tendency, remains to be seen. Some of the other approaches to constitutional reform proposed here – in as far as they are effective at avoiding unearned single-party majorities in the Commons, or excessive influence on the part of organised minorities within parties – could reduce the chances of executive abuse.

An important operational principle of the executive that became subject to strain and doubt, already noted, was that of collective responsibility of Cabinet.

As with other norms and conventions that came into doubt in connection to Brexit, it is not clear whether it has been compromised in a more lasting sense, or if it will reassert itself in future. Difficulties in sustaining the principle of public unity among ministers around policy are a problem from the perspective of coherent government. They are also detrimental from a democratic standpoint. If the administration is not clear about what its own programme is, how can it be held to account for it? Prime ministers facing challenges in imposing the discipline of outward unanimity may respond by seeking to increase their control over government, perhaps through expansions in capacity at the centre, as has been advocated at various points, for instance by Michael Barber. But while a basic organising principle of government is the dispersal of legal and political responsibility between different secretaries of state (and their equivalents), for which they answer to Parliament, it will be difficult for a Prime Minister properly to supplant the authority of Cabinet and its members. A more radical change – not at the forefront of the political agenda at present, but used in various countries world-wide – would be to establish a directly elected presidency (or equivalent) in place of a premiership. Yet the holder of such a post might find their power restrained by a Parliament over which they lacked the levers of influence that prime ministers possess at present.

In fact, when we consider the problems that have arisen during the Brexit episode in relation to collective responsibility, it is better to regard their source as lying beyond the executive. They arose from tension within the Conservative Party that contributed first to a referendum and second to efforts, in response to the result, to bring about transformative change the nature and extent of which had not been defined in advance of the vote. A similar point can be made about Brexit and the Civil Service. It was subject to various stresses leading up to the referendum and afterwards. In the post-Brexit environment (assuming departure takes place, and in more than a cosmetic form) there will be a need for a permanent and substantial enhancement in the skills and capacity of Whitehall, to manage responsibilities being transferred from European to UK level. However, when discussing the need for reform, it is important to recognise that officials are ultimately subject to political imperatives determined by ministers. It was inevitable that a referendum on such a longstanding subject of controversy – especially since it bitterly divided the Cabinet and party of government – would create sensitivities for the Civil Service, as an impartial instrument of representative democracy. Disputes about how Whitehall should operate during this period were always likely. Moreover, following the referendum, the Civil Service faced a challenge of historic magnitude, for which it had not been allowed fully to prepare. An added difficulty was the failure of ministers to provide a clear policy framework within which officials could operate.

In the decades since the Fabian Society published *The Administrators* in 1964, innumerable government initiatives have replicated some of its main themes (that were prefigured by Harold Laski two decades beforehand). The instigators of these programmes, however, can seem unaware of their lack of originality. We can probably expect further such demands for change in future. No doubt there is always scope for improvement. But ministers calling for a more effective Civil Service should be aware that some of the greatest difficulties are generated by political imperatives. Reform of the wider constitution might channel some of these forces in a more satisfactory fashion, avoiding the creation of new indissoluble difficulties for Whitehall. One serious challenge to the Civil Service as currently configured could arise if the Brexit episode proves to be part of a more general transition towards polarisation in UK politics. An exceptional characteristic of the UK Civil Service in international comparison is its impartial, permanent nature, with a broad continuity of personnel across different administrations. While, since the 1960s, special advisers – temporary officials, appointed on ministerial patronage and exempt from Whitehall impartiality rules – have become a fixture of government, they have rarely exceeded 100 in total across the whole administration; and they are excluded from mainstream managerial roles. Alternation between radical Labour and Conservative governments, or some other form of violent oscillation, could create pressure for an augmentation of this component of the Civil Service.

Seventh, within the UK and internationally, Brexit has changed helped attract increased attention to and encourage changed perceptions of the Internet and connected technologies as tools for political campaigning. The accumulation and processing of personal data and the interaction between these practices and the use of social media are currently at the forefront of political debate, and frequently viewed in a negative sense. That it has created grounds for doubt about the integrity of a democratic process is in itself a problem. It is important to stress the uncertainty at work here. Assessing precisely the impact that online campaigning had upon the referendum result is a difficult task. Current concerns should not be a basis for hasty action. Any efforts to introduce new controls over content should be approached with extreme caution. They might well prove futile; and if not, they could be dangerous. Earlier calls for more balanced or truthful media, applied to the press, by the likes of Acland and Crozier[38] have not aged well. Some proposals currently attracting interest – such as measures to impose greater transparency on participants in campaigns[39] – seem reasonable in principle, though how well they would address some of the more serious concerns that have arisen lately remains to be seen. Rather than simply responding to and seeking to mitigate malign impacts associated with the Internet, the emphasis should be on positive intervention to promote an online environment that is democratically more healthy. The July 2018 interim report by the Commons Digital, Culture, Media and Sport

[38] See ch 5.

[39] See eg Independent Commission on Referendums, *Report of the Independent Commission on Referendums* (London, Constitution Unit, 2018) 178–90.

Committee as part of its inquiry into 'fake news' contained a sensible set of recommendations intended to contain problems and promote more favourable developments, including through public education.[40] We should not assume that proposals of the type Jay G Blumler and Stephen Coleman advocated in 2001, a more optimistic time from the perspective of digital engagement, are entirely precluded.[41] Changing the overall nature of the Internet is not realistic. However, the promotion of spaces in which more impartial discourse can develop might be more plausible. The use of public resources for such an end would be justified. Similarly, as Acland correctly argued,[42] journalism is worth paying for in some form.

The Internet and social media are part of a cluster of connected technologies that also includes Big Data, machine learning and AI. As shown in Chapter 9,[43] there are already a developed set of legal principles intended to ensure adherence to democratic norms in this field. They should be the starting point for action. Parliament should take on a central role in their promotion. It would focus principally on public sector activities, as well as considering how the overall environment can better be regulated. In September 2017 I submitted written evidence to the House of Lords Committee on Artificial Intelligence that addressed the possibility for new forms of parliamentary oversight. Identifying the difficulties raised by AI and machine learning from the point of view of ministerial accountability, I argued that:

> there could be value in adapting the approach taken by the Commons Committee of Public Accounts, supported by the National Audit Office. A parliamentary committee for Artificial Intelligence Oversight (AIO), or perhaps an agency reporting to Parliament, suitably resourced, could be established. Assuming it is a parliamentary committee, it might be a Joint Committee of both Houses, taking evidence and issuing reports to inform Parliament. The work of the AIO ought to focus on the implementation of policy, rather than its merits. It would be entrusted with monitoring across government whether artificial intelligence was operating in accordance with the policy objectives it was directed towards, and was doing so effectively, and in accordance with prescribed norms.[44]

In its report the Committee noted my recommendation for the establishment of 'a committee for artificial intelligence oversight, akin to the Commons Public Accounts Committee'. It concluded that '[w]hilst we do not intend to recommend the establishment of a permanent Parliamentary committee, we do agree

[40] House of Commons Digital, Culture, Media and Sport Committee, *Disinformation and 'fake news': Interim Report* (London, House of Commons, 2018) 64–73.

[41] See ch 9.

[42] See ch 5.

[43] See in particular ch 9 Appendices.

[44] Dr Andrew Blick – Written evidence (AIC0064), Evidence submission to House of Lord Select Committee on Artificial Intelligence: http://data.parliament.uk/writtenevidence/committeeevidence.svc/evidencedocument/artificial-intelligence-committee/artificial-intelligence/written/69503.html last accessed 26 September 2018.

with the sentiment that artificial intelligence policy must be scrutinised and the Ministers with responsibility held accountable'.[45] It called for annual reporting to Parliament on AI within government.[46] But the response from the Department for Business, Innovation and Skills to this particular point was barely comprehensible. It read:

> Governance of and reporting for the AI and Data Grand Challenge is based on the standard Industrial Strategy governance structures. As the Centre for Data Ethics and Innovation and the AI Council, composed of leaders from industry, academia, and the public sector, are stood up over the coming months, there may be a need to update these structures. Any such decision will be made through the existing Industrial Strategy decision framework. As the AI Council's secretariat, the Office for AI's responsibilities with respect to reporting will depend on the outcomes of these decisions.[47]

If present – broadly accepted – projections for the increased use of machine learning and AI within government (as elsewhere) are correct; and if other – also widely held – concerns about problems involving arbitrary outcomes and 'bias' prove accurate, then the government will need to provide a more coherent explanation of how accountability functions in this area. At some point I suspect new mechanisms, probably attached to Parliament in some way, will be needed. Ideally, they would be instigated before a major public scandal of some kind, but perhaps change tends to require such negative impetus.

The consideration above of the role of the Internet and the use of personal data in political campaigning gives rise to a concluding recommendation as to possible future constitutional models. If, for the sake of argument, a particular vote held on a specific question on a given day is potentially subject to improper manipulation, then an important constitutional observation – that could have been made long before the rise of the mass-use Internet – follows.[48] There are dangers in attaching excessive importance to any one process – whether it is a referendum, a division in the House of Commons, a General Election, a Cabinet conclusion, or a judicial decision. It is necessary to regulate, mediate and scrutinise each in its own way. Ultimately decisions have to be made, and one procedure or process may have to prevail over another. But balancing is vital, if the contrasting – and sometimes competing – elements that comprise democracy, such as majority decision-taking, respect for rights, and the seeking of consensus, are to be reconciled. A 'written' constitution can be one means

[45] House of Lords Select Committee on Artificial Intelligence, *AI in the UK: ready, willing and able?* (London, House of Lords, 2018) 116.

[46] ibid, 117.

[47] Secretary of State for Business, Innovation & Skills, *Government Response to House of Lords Artificial Intelligence Select Committee's Report on AI in the UK: ready, willing and able?* (London, Stationery Office, 2018) 36.

[48] Nat le Roux of The Constitution Society has made this point to me.

of imposing a structure through which this mediation takes place. Even it is subject to amendment, and judicial interpretations of the text can be subject to appeal.

I have explored extensively elsewhere the debate about whether or not the UK should create such an entity.[49] I support this course of action. In a sense, departure from the EU, if executed, will move the UK even further from this position than it is at present. As Vernon Bogdanor has argued, membership of the EU provided the UK with a body of higher, European law, that performed some of the functions of a 'written' constitution, taking precedence even over Acts of Parliament, that could be disapplied in as far as they were incompatible with it. From this point of view, he observes, withdrawal from the EU amounts to a transition from a written back to an unwritten constitution – a direction of travel no state in history has yet followed.[50] One of the consequences of this change will be that the protection for rights provided by the EU Charter of Fundamental Rights will be lost.[51] This change alone should be cause for alarm. As shown earlier in this work, prominent advocates of departure from the EU have regarded this action as part of a package of changes that included removal of protections associated with the European Convention on Human Rights (an instrument produced by the Council of Europe, not the EU) and promotion of the politicisation of justice and law enforcement.[52] Departure from the EU is not an end, but a beginning. If the tactics leading to Brexit were successful, then they may continue to be so for other purposes. Moreover, other minority groups may seek to pursue their objectives in the new political environment. It would seem appropriate, in the circumstances of a fresh start, to consider the possibility of creating a new body of rules that, like European law, have a special status, taking precedence over more regular policy, regulations, and even Acts of Parliament. The process leading to the creation of such a system might involve a convention, the membership of which could include members of the public chosen by sortition, the technique of random selection discussed above.

The idea of a written constitution has enjoyed advocacy across the political spectrum – but opposition also. During the 2010–15 Parliament, the House of Commons Political and Constitutional Reform Committee carried out the first ever official public inquiry into the subject of whether the UK should establish a 'codified' constitution (to which I was research fellow). In 2014 the Committee, while not making a firm recommendation as to whether it supported the idea,

[49] Andrew Blick, *Beyond Magna Carta: a constitution for the United Kingdom* (Oxford, Hart Publishing, Oxford, 2015).

[50] Vernon Bogdanor, *Brexit and our unprotected constitution* (London, The Constitution Society, 2018): https://consoc.org.uk/wp-content/uploads/2018/02/Brexit-and-our-unprotected-constitution-web.pdf last accessed 30 September 2018.

[51] See ch 8.

[52] See ch 3.

published three possible versions of such a text, drafted by Robert Blackburn.[53] Hard political impetus for the practical implementation of such a project was absent at the time. It is frequently claimed that a crisis of some description would be a necessary precursor to a written constitution. This argument often seems to be a convenient means of dismissing the idea as inappropriate for the UK, where serious disruptions supposedly do not occur. If Brexit helps discredit this premise, then at least some benefit will have been derived from the experience.

[53] The three texts and further details can be found at: https://www.parliament.uk/business/committees/committees-a-z/commons-select/political-and-constitutional-reform-committee/inquiries/parliament-2010/mapping-the-path-to-codifying---or-not-codifying---the-uks-constitution/report-a-new-magna-carta/ last accessed 28 September 2018.

Postscript

MEMORANDUM FOR COUNTRY CONTEMPLATING EXIT FROM THE EUROPEAN UNION

Dr Andrew Blick

Constitutional Issues

Departure from the European Union (EU) will have two main constitutional aspects to it:

a) The decision to leave
b) The implementation of the decision

The following memorandum deals with these concerns in turn.

A) Decision to leave

The taking of a decision as momentous as to exit from the EU should ideally rest on a high level of consent. With the importance of achieving this quality in mind, a number of possibilities should be considered:

Preferably, the government overseeing the process will be in favour of departure. It will therefore be comfortable with setting out in advance what are its objectives; and be committed to implementing them, should the necessary requirements of consent be met.

The decision could involve one or more referendums. In countries that do not make use of referendums, other methods may be used, akin to those used for purposes of constitutional amendment in the state concerned.

Decisions to leave (whether taken by referendums or other means) should seek to be founded in consensus, and should not rest on simple majority votes, but thresholds or supermajorities.

In countries with pronounced territorial differentiation (for instance in federations such as Spain and Belgium), there should be provision for the sub-components that make up the whole to have an input into the decision, perhaps with the possibility for a blocking minority, or even a unanimity requirement.

Ideally, there will be more than one decision-taking moment (involving referendums or other procedures): to instigate the process, and when the likely outcome becomes more apparent.

B) Implementation of the decision to leave

From a constitutional perspective, the process of exiting the EU is both challenging in itself and raises fundamental questions about the nature of the internal political system post-departure. Central areas of concern are likely to include:

The need to ensure that there is a clearly established legal power to trigger Article 50 before the process can begin.

The relative balance of responsibility for the exit process, between the central executive on the one hand, and the legislature (and perhaps sub-state territories) on the other hand.

The distribution of powers that may be repatriated from the EU between different tiers of governance; and the need to ensure that the departing state retains its own unified single market.

The legal consequences of leaving, including ensuring that a transition to a post-EU order is managed without excessive disruption.

The management of historically accumulated obligations and privileges, both internal and external, for which leaving the EU may create complications.

The constraints imposed by the 2-year limit prescribed by Article 50 of the Treaty on European Union. Agreeing the terms of exit might prove possible within this timeframe. But establishing a full set of arrangements for the post-exit relationship between the departing state and the EU, as well as with other countries and blocs, will be a greater challenge.

The constitutional implications of leaving will vary in accordance with the precise way in which the departing state leaves, an outcome that is itself subject to immense potential variation.

Constitutional Convention

Given the many systemic issues raised by a possible decision to leave the EU and its subsequent implementation, it is advisable to convene a constitutional convention – formed in accordance with democratic norms – to ensure an holistic, consensual approach is taken. Such a body should be formed and produce recommendations in advance of any decision to leave being taken.

Opinion on Challenging the Outcome of the 2016 Referendum

THE EU REFERENDUM result

OPINION

INTRODUCTION AND SUMMARY

1. We are asked to advise on whether the outcome of referendum held on 23 June 2016 on the United Kingdom's membership of the EU (**the Referendum**) may be challenged in light of the Electoral Commission's (**the Commission's**) recent report (**the Report**) into overspending by the certain pro-Leave campaign groups.
2. In summary, for reasons set out more fully below:
   (a) It is likely that at least some of the findings of the Report would (if upheld)[1] provide a sufficient basis to commence an election petition before the election court if the unlawful conduct had occurred in the context of a local or Parliamentary election. If breaches of the kind found by the Commission had been committed by the candidate for election – or his agent – the election would have been declared void. If those breaches had been committed by persons other than a candidate or his agent, the election court would then have had to consider whether they are likely to have affected the result. If so, the election could also have been declared void on that basis.
   (b) However, the law is clear that the election court has no jurisdiction to consider complaints about the conduct or result of the Referendum.
   (c) There is no other legal means by which the result of the Referendum may be challenged or set aside.
3. This may appear a surprising result. Although the Referendum was, in law, advisory only, it was (and still is) presented politically by some members of the Government as decisive and binding.[2] Yet there is no mechanism by

[1] It has been reported that the Commission's report may yet be the subject of judicial review proceedings.

[2] See e.g. *R (Miller) v Secretary of State for Exiting the European Union* [2018] 1 AC 61, [119].

which an authoritative ruling can be obtained from a court on the effect of the breaches found by the Commission or on the validity of the result.

BACKGROUND FACTS

4. The background facts are well known; we only set them out here in summary.
5. The Referendum was held on 23 June 2016. The question posed was: "*Should the United Kingdom remain a member of the European Union or leave the European Union?*" 51.89% of those polled voted in favour of leaving the European Union.
6. During the referendum campaign, Vote Leave Limited ("**Vote Leave**") was designated by the Commission as the lead campaign group in support of a vote to leave the EU. This had certain important consequences, including as to the level of spending it was entitled to incur during the campaign.
7. On 17 July 2018, the Commission published the Report, which set out the findings of its investigation into campaign funding and spending during the Referendum campaign. It found that Vote Leave, its senior leadership, and various other organisations and individuals that campaigned to leave the EU, had committed various offences under the Political Parties, Elections and Referendums Act 2000 ("**PPERA**"). In particular:
   (a) Vote Leave's "responsible person", David Halsall, had failed to deliver a complete campaign spending return, contrary to s. 122(4)(b) PPERA.
   (b) Vote Leave had exceeded the spending limited prescribed by PPERA. Both Mr Halsall and Vote Leave had thereby committed an offence under s. 118(2)(c)(i) & (ii) PPERA.
   (c) Mr Halsall had committed a further offence under s. 122(4)(b) PPERA by failing to include invoices and receipts for eight payments.
   (d) Vote Leave had failed to comply with an investigation notice and thereby committed an offence under para. 13(1) of Sch. 19B PPERA.
   (e) Certain payments made to Aggregate IQ and reported by Mr Darren Grimes (an individual associated with a body campaigning to leave the EU called BeLeave) should have been treated as incurred by Vote Leave.
   (f) Mr Grimes had incurred spending on behalf of BeLeave, a body that was not a permitted participant in the Referendum. Mr Grimes and BeLeave had thereby committed offences under s. 117(3) & (4) PPERA.
   (g) Mr Grimes had failed to deliver a spending return that complied with PPERA and had thereby committed an offence under s. 122(4)(b) PPERA.
   (h) Mr David Banks, the responsible person for a further body called Veterans for Britain, had delivered a spending return that contained an inaccurate donation report and had thereby committed an offence under s. 122(4)(b) PPERA.

QUESTION 1: WOULD THE ELECTORAL COMMISSION'S FINDINGS BE A SUFFICIENT BASIS TO AVOID AN ELECTION TO A LEGISLATIVE BODY?

8. Part VII of PPERA imposes a number of procedural and other requirements that govern the conduct of referendums in the United Kingdom. It also establishes a series of statutory offences, that might be committed during the course of a referendum campaign. Those include providing a false expenses declaration or publishing campaign material that does not comply with certain strict requirements (see ss. 125 and 126).
9. There is nothing on the face of PPERA to suggest that the commission of any of those offences might allow the result of the referendum to be declared void. This stands in contrast to the position under the Representation of the People Act 1983 ("**RPA**"), which provides a statutory mechanism by which the result of an election to a legislative body (such as Parliament or a local authority) may be challenged before an election court, which may set the election result aside.
10. In essence, those instructing want to know whether the offences identified in the Report would have provided a proper basis for an election petition – before an election court – to avoid the result of an election to a legislative body. We should make clear, however, that for the purposes of this Opinion we have assumed that the evidence before the Commission substantiates the conclusions drawn by that body (a matter which may be the subject of challenge in judicial review proceedings). We have not been asked to consider, and have not considered, whether that assumption is correct.

The Law Governing Challenges to Parliamentary and Local Elections

11. The right to challenge an election result – in the law of England – dates back to the mid-15th century.[3] In 1604 the House of Commons passed the "*The Form of Apology and Satisfaction*" and took over direct control of electoral challenges. The Form of Apology states that "*the House of Commons is the sole proper judge of return of all such writs and of the election of all such members as belong to it…*"[4]
12. The Parliamentary Elections Act 1868 passed the review of election results back to the courts. It established a statutory court – an election court – which could hear petitions complaining of an undue return or undue election of a Member.

[3] For a fuller discussion see O'Leary, *The Elimination of Corrupt Practices in British Elections 1868–1911* (Oxford, 1962), p. 7.

[4] See: *R (Woolas) v Parliamentary Election Court* [2010] EWHC 3169 (Admin) at §22.

13. The legislation now governing the right to challenge Parliamentary and local elections is the RPA. It consolidated various pieces of 19th and 20th Century legislation in this field. It provides that an election court has jurisdiction to hear challenges against the results of:

    (a) parliamentary elections (ss. 120ff);
    (b) local Government elections (ss. 127ff); and
    (c) parish and Community Council elections (s. 187).

14. The RPA establishes a number of electoral offences (termed corrupt or illegal practices). They include: incurring expenses above the maximum allowed (s. 76), bribery (s. 113), treating (s. 114) and undue influence (s. 115).
15. The RPA establishes a dual framework of liability. The same offences that give rise to criminal liability (via the jurisdiction of the criminal courts) may also provide the grounds for a petition before an election court. An election court is a civil court, which hears election petitions and determines them (albeit applying the criminal standard of proof).[5] If the election court finds that certain offences have been committed, the election result may be declared void. An election may be avoided on two bases:
16. First, s. 159(1) provides that:

> "If a candidate who has been elected is reported by an election court personally guilty or guilty by his agents of any corrupt or illegal practice his election shall be void."

17. Second, s. 164 provides that:

> "(1) Where on an election petition it is shown that corrupt or illegal practices or illegal payments, employments or hirings committed in reference to the election for the purpose of promoting or procuring the election of any person at that election have so extensively prevailed that they may be reasonably supposed to have affected the result—
>
> (a) his election, if he has been elected, shall be void, and
> (b) he shall be incapable of being elected to fill the vacancy or any of the vacancies for which the election was held.
>
> (2) An election shall not be liable to be avoided otherwise than under this section by reason of general corruption, bribery, treating or intimidation.
>
> (3) An election under the local government Act may be questioned on the ground that it is avoided under this section."

18. The function of s. 164 was explained by Mr Richard Mawrey QC in *Erlam v Rahman* [2015] EWHC 1215 (QB) as follows:

> "This section replaces what was once the common law rule relating to general corruption. In the past, particularly in the nineteenth century, it would happen

[5] For a discussion of the relationship between the criminal and civil regimes under the RPA, see the judgment of the Divisional Court in *R (Rahman) v Local Government Election Court* [2017] EWHC 1413 Admin.

that an election had been tainted with corruption or other illegal conduct but those seeking to set it aside could not prove any actual involvement in the wrongdoing by the candidate or his agents. Thus a body of law evolved to the effect that an election could be avoided on this ground but only if it could be shown that it was likely to have affected the result of the election."

The Conduct Identified by the Commission

19. We consider that some of the conduct identified by the Commission as having been committed during the Referendum could have met the test for corrupt and/or illegal practices under the RPA, if it had occurred during an election to a legislative post.
20. The clearest example of an offence identified by the Commission that is materially identical to an offence under the RPA is the offence of exceeding allowable expenses:
    (a) Section 76 RPA provides that it is an illegal practice for a candidate or election agent to incur expenses above the allowable threshold when they "*knew or ought to have known*" that threshold would be exceeded.
    (b) Section 118(2)(c) PPERA provides that both a responsible person and the organisation he represents will be guilty of an offence if he authorised expenses to be incurred above the threshold and he "*knew or ought to have known*" that the threshold would be exceeded. The Commission found that Vote Leave had exceeded the PPERA spending limit and that Mr Halsall and Vote Leave had committed an offence under s. 118(2)(c).
21. These two offences are sufficiently similar that we consider that the evidence relied on by the Commission, in reaching its conclusions, could also have been relied upon to find that an offence had been committed under s. 76 RPA (if the relevant conduct had occurred during an election campaign). We have not been asked to advise on whether, given the evidence before the Commission, a prosecution would be likely to succeed.
22. Much the same position emerges in respect of the offence under s. 122(4)(b) PPERA, of failing to deliver a compliant spending return (which the Commission found had been committed in the context of the Referendum).
    (a) Section 84 RPA (read together with ss. 81 and 86) makes it an offence to submit an election expenses return that does not comply with the relevant requirements. Section 86 provides that the offence may be excused if the failure to comply occurred "*by reason of inadvertence or any reasonable cause of a like nature.*"

(b) Section 122(4)(b) PPERA provides that an offence is committed if the requirements as to expenses returns (in ss. 120(2) and (3)) are not complied with "*without reasonable excuse*".

23. Once again, these two tests – though not identical – are similar. This means that the conduct relied on by the Commission would, if committed in the context of a Parliamentary or local election, be likely to have constituted the equivalent offence(s) under the RPA.
24. On the other hand, the liability thresholds for some of the other offences under PPERA are different from those under RPA:

(a) Section 82(6) RPA provides that it is an illegal practice "*knowingly*" to provide a false declaration as to election expenses.
(b) Section 123(4) PPERA provides that a responsible person commits and offence if he or she "*knowingly or recklessly*" makes a false declaration under that section. The Report states that the Commission had reasonable grounds to suspect that Mr Halsall and Mr Grimes committed this offence. These two offences are superficially similar, save that the threshold for liability under s. 123(4) PPERA is lower: the latter offence may be committed recklessly.

25. The offence of incurring expenses by or on behalf of a body that is not a permitted participant in s. 117(3) and (4) of PPERA does not have an obvious equivalent in RPA 1983.
26. Furthermore, the body or individual that commits the offence is not the same under the two regimes. As set out above, s. 159 RPA provides that an election will be void if the candidate or his agent is guilty of an offence. It is not necessary, in those circumstances, to show that it is likely that the result would have been different. Section 164 provides that the election may be void if other parties are guilty of an offence and it is likely that the offence would have changed the result of the election.
27. There is no 'candidate' seeking election in a referendum. On one view, the responsible person and a designated campaign group fulfil a similar function: they take legal responsibility for any false declarations in respect of an expenses return. Vote Leave, the designated lead campaign group, authorised expenses above the spending limit; had a candidate or his agent committed the equivalent offence in a Parliamentary election, the result would have been void under s. 159 RPA. However, the parallel is not exact; and if provision had been made for challenges to the result of the Referendum it is far from certain that the effect of a breach by the responsible person would have been to invalidate the result of the referendum.
28. The s. 164 RPA jurisdiction – to declare an election void if the conduct of third parties is likely to have affected the result – does not have an obvious analogy in the Referendum context. The Report does not make any finding of that kind; and any such finding would likely be highly contentious. As a result, it is difficult to say with confidence that the offences identified in the Report would be likely to 'translate' into a s. 164 finding by an election court.

Conclusion on Question 1

29. It is not possible to say with confidence that the findings of the Report could have provided the basis for an election petition, had the offences occurred in the context of a parliamentary election, rather than a referendum. The statutory regimes do not overlap seamlessly. However, it is clear that:
    (a) The offence of exceeding election expenses under s. 118(2)(c) PPERA is very similar – indeed materially identical – to the offence under s. 76 RPA. Some of the other offences identified in the EC Report are similar, though not identical, to offences under RPA.
    (b) Section 159(1) of RPA requires a candidate, or an election agent, to be liable for the offence. There is no exact equivalent position under PPERA.
    (c) However, if the conduct identified by the Commission as forming the basis for a criminal offence had been committed in the course of an election campaign, it could have formed the basis for an election petition. If the election court found that the candidate – or his agent – had committed the offences described above, the election would have been declared void. If the election court determined that the offence had been committed by other persons, and that breach was likely to have affected the result, the election result could have been declared void.

QUESTION 2: MIGHT THE REFERENDUM RESULT BE CHALLENGED BEFORE AN ELECTION COURT?

30. The short answer to this is "No". As set out above, PPERA provides no mechanism by which the results of a referendum might be set aside.
31. Furthermore, no such mechanism appears on the face of the Referendum Act 2015. It established the machinery for the Referendum. Section 4(b)(i) provided that:

> "the Minister may by regulations … (b) apply for the purposes of the referendum, with or without modifications – (i) any provision of the [RPA] 1983 Act, or (ii) any other enactment relating to elections or referendums, including provisions creating offences…"

32. The European Union Referendum (Conduct) Regulations 2016 (the "**2016 Regulations**") were made in the exercise of that power. Schedule 1 to the 2016 Regulations provided that certain provisions of the RPA should apply to the Referendum. Amongst the provisions of RPA that were to apply were: s. 113 RPA, which concerns bribery (para. 30 of Sch. 1) and s. 114 RPA, which concerns treating (para 31 of Sch. 1).
33. Paragraphs 37 and 38 incorporate various provisions of the RPA with the effect that breaching those provisions will be a criminal offence. However, there is nothing in Sch. 1 to the 2016 Regulations that incorporates the civil

jurisdiction of the election court to hear election petitions, or declare an election result void. On the contrary, various provisions in Sch. 1 exclude references to the election court, where it is referred to in RPA. For example, paragraph 36, which incorporates s. 167 RPA, specifically excludes the words "*or election court*" from s. 167, to the extent that it applies to the Referendum. Paragraph 43 does the same.

34. The only proper conclusion is that Parliament intended to exclude the jurisdiction of the election court to hear petitions seeking to challenge the outcome of the Referendum.
35. We have been asked to consider whether anything in EU law, or Convention case law might alter that result. Once again, the answer is "No".
36. In *Moohan v Lord Advocate* [2014] UKSC 67, the Supreme Court held that no claim could be brought in reliance on EU law by a group of convicted prisoners, who were not entitled to vote in the Scottish independence referendum. Lord Hodge led a unanimous Court in finding that: (i) the outcome of the referendum would not itself determine the citizenship of the petitioners or other people born in Scotland; and (ii) in any event EU law did not incorporate a general right to vote.[6]
37. The same reasoning would apply here. The outcome of the Referendum did not determine the citizenship rights of UK citizens: it was purely advisory and any interference with those rights only arose when the Article 50 notification was given.[7] Furthermore, just as EU law does not give rise to a general right to vote, so it does not recognise the existence of a general right to challenge the outcome of a referendum.
38. Article 3 Protocol 1 ("**A3P1**") of the European Convention on Human Rights provides:

> "The High Contracting Parties undertake to hold free elections at reasonable intervals by secret ballot, under conditions which will ensure the free expression of the opinion of the people in the choice of the legislature."

39. There is clear authority that referendums do not attract the protection of this provision. In *X v United Kingdom* (Application no. 7096/75; Admissibility decision of 3 October 1975) the European Commission of Human Rights (as it then was) held that the 1975 UK Referendum on EEC Membership fell outside the scope of A3P1:

> "The obligations of the High Contracting Parties under this provision are limited to the field of elections concerning the choice of legislature. The British referendum on EEC membership was not an election concerning the choice of the legislature: it was of a purely consultative character and there was no legal obligation to organise such a referendum. It did not, therefore, fall within the scope of Article 3 of Protocol No 1 to the Convention. It follows that a right to participate in the referendum could not be derived from that provision either."

[6] Relying on *R (Chester) v Secretary of State for Justice* [2014] AC 271.
[7] See the discussion in *Miller*, supra note 2.

40. That conclusion was reaffirmed by the First Section of the Strasbourg Court in *Moohan and Gillon v United Kingdom* (Application nos. 22962/15 and 23345/15; Judgment of 13 June 2017). The Court affirmed that "*the decisive factor was that the referendum was not 'an election concerning the choice of the legislature'*" (§42).

Conclusion on Question 2

41. In conclusion, the election court has no jurisdiction to hear a challenge to the Referendum result. None of PPERA, the Referendum Act 2015 or the 2016 Regulations, provide any basis for initiating proceedings before an election court, in order to avoid the outcome of the Referendum. Nor does EU law or the ECHR.

QUESTION 3: MIGHT THE REFERENDUM RESULT BE CHALLENGED BY ANY OTHER ROUTE?

42. Richard Mawrey QC – sitting as a Commissioner of the election court – said this in *Simmons v Khan* [2008] EWHC B4 (QB), at [28]:

> "It surely cannot be the intention of Parliament, when making a piece of electoral misconduct into a criminal offence, to ignore the effect of that misconduct on the election to which it relates. After all, the purpose of the misconduct must always be to affect the result of the election to which it relates. If a candidate's election has been procured by the commission of criminal offences, Parliament cannot be saying that his election should stand merely because Parliament has omitted to write into the sections creating those offences words saying 'these are also illegal practices'."

43. He concluded at [30] that:

> "where the 1983 Act or any related electoral statute makes conduct in relation to an election into a criminal offence, that conduct does amount to an illegal practice for the purposes of avoiding an election whether or not this is expressly spelled out in the section concerned."

44. However, those comments concerned conduct "*in relation to an election*", rather than a referendum. The contrast with the statutory regime governing referendums is clear: the latter establishes a number of criminal offences, but does not provide that <u>any</u> of those offences might form the basis of a civil claim – whether before an election court or otherwise – by which the result of the referendum may be challenged. We do not consider, therefore, that *Simmons v Khan* provides any real support for a challenge to the result of the Referendum.

Judicial Review

45. We consider that any challenge by way of judicial review, seeking a declaration that the Referendum result was unlawful, is bound to fail.
46. Paragraph 19 of Schedule 5 to the Referendum Act 2015 sets out a mechanism by which the number of ballots counted or votes cast in the Referendum might be challenged by way of judicial review:

> "19 – (1) No court may entertain any proceedings for questioning the number of ballot papers counted or votes cast in the referendum as certified by the Chief Counting Officer or a Regional Counting Officer or counting officer unless—
>
> (a) the proceedings are brought by a claim for judicial review, and
> (b) the claim form is filed before the end of the permitted period.
>
> (2) In sub-paragraph (1) "the permitted period" means the period of 6 weeks beginning with—
>
> (a) the day on which the officer in question gives a certificate as to the number of ballot papers counted and votes cast in the referendum, or
> (b) if the officer gives more than one such certificate, the day on which the last is given."

47. This establishes a statutory route by which "*the number of ballot papers counted or votes cast*" might be challenged. Any challenge to those certified figures by way of another route would be an abuse of process (as well as being well out of time). However, we do not consider that judicial review offers a viable route to challenge the Referendum result, on the basis of the facts disclosed in the Report.
48. Regulation 54 of the 2016 Regulations and s. 128(6) PPERA provide that the function of the Chief Counting Officer is to certify the number of ballots counted or votes cast. There is a bespoke statutory mechanism for challenging that certification. But in any event, it is not clear that the facts set out in the Report would provide a proper basis to challenge the certification of the Chief Counting Officer (who performs a purely arithmetical exercise). It is not his/her role to certify that the referendum was 'fair' and conducted in according with the relevant statutory requirements. We cannot identify an alternative appropriate defendant, who has taken a relevant, challengeable step in respect of the Referendum result. The legal regime does not provide for, or require, any such step. Instead, it leaves complaints about the fairness of the process to be dealt with by the political process.

Common Law

49. We have also considered whether there is any residual basis – at common law – that might allow the result to be set aside. A claim on that basis would need to show that:

(a) the conduct which is the subject of the Report would have been sufficient to avoid an election at common law;

(b) any common law cause of action and remedy has not been displaced by the statutory framework now established by Parliament; and
(c) the common law cause of action should apply equally to a referendum.

50. As to (a), it is certainly correct that the common law used to preserve the integrity of elections. Coke says, at 2 Inst. (1642), 168 – 169, that:

> "This act [West 1, 3 Ed, c. 5] briefly rehearseth the old rule of the common law (for elections out to be free) wherein both the said points are included; 1. It must be a due election, and 2. It must be a free election. "

51. In *Ashby v. White* (1703) 2 Ld. Raym. 938, Holt CJ referred with approval to Coke's statement that the protection of the freedom of elections by statute "*is only an inforcement of the common law*": see at p. 954.[8] In *Erlam v Rahman* [2015] EWHC 1215 (QB), Richard Mawrey QC stated at [36] that s. 164 of the RPA 1983 "replaces what was once the common law rule relating to general corruption" and at [136] that intimidation was undoubtedly a ground for questioning an election at common law (now found in section 115 of the RPA 1983).
52. As to (b), each of the above statements suggests that Parliament has now legislated in the relevant field, and so displaced the common law. This is not an auspicious basis for the suggestion that there subsists some common law cause of action whereby an election may be avoided.
53. As to (c), the earliest UK-wide referendum was the 1975 EEC Membership referendum. We are not aware of any authority to the effect that the 1975 referendum, any subsequent referendum or the Referendum were to be treated as elections to a legislative body, for the purposes of avoiding the result. On the contrary, as we have set out above, an analysis of the statutory scheme suggests the opposite.

Conclusion on Question 3

54. In the light of the above, we do not consider that the referendum result can be challenged via any other route (whether by way of judicial review or otherwise).
55. We have been asked to consider a Letter Before Action sent by Bindmans LLP to the Prime Minister on behalf of the Fair Vote Project. We note that Bindmans do not challenge the Referendum result (*see* §201), but rather challenge the Prime Minister's refusal to open a public inquiry into the

[8] The issue for the Court of the King's Bench was whether an action could be brought against the responsible officers in the courts, as opposed to in Parliament, for refusing to receive the claimant's vote. On that issue, Holt CJ dissented. Holt CJ said, at p. 954, that "it is a violation of that statute [West 1, 3 Ed, c 5], to disturb the plaintiff in this case in giving his vote at an election, and consequently actionable." The Court of King's Bench's decision was reversed by the House of Lords: (1703) 1 Brown 62.

circumstances surrounding the Referendum campaign. We consider that this approach affirms our conclusion, as set out above, that it is not possible to challenge the Referendum result. We do not express any views on the merits of the Fair Vote Project's challenge, which fall outside the scope of this advice.

56. We have also been asked to consider whether an application for permission to apply for judicial review, issued by Susan Wilson and others on 13 August 2018, alters the conclusions we have expressed above.[9] In their Grounds for Judicial Review, at §6(1)(a), the claimants sought a declaration that "*the Referendum result is vitiated by reason of corrupt and illegal practices*". However, in their Reply, they have clarified that they do not seek to challenge the outcome of the Referendum itself (§3).[10] It appears that this is because the claimants have reached the same conclusions as those we have set out above. They:
    (a) note that at least some of the findings of the Report would (if upheld) provide a possible basis for an election petition before an Election Court, if the unlawful conduct had occurred during a local of parliamentary election. However, they have not brought proceedings before an Election Court, presumably because they recognise that they cannot;
    (b) accept that no claim may be brought in reliance on paragraph 19 of Schedule 3 to the 2015 Act (Reply §12); and
    (c) do not rely on A3P1 as forming a part of their claim (Grounds for Reconsideration, §1).

57. Rather than impugning the outcome of the referendum itself, the Wilson claimants challenge:
    (a) the Prime Minister's decision that the UK should withdraw from the EU and the notification of that decision to the European Union; and
    (b) the Prime Minister's failure to take any steps in light of, amongst other things, the Commission's Report.

58. We consider that this approach also affirms our conclusions set out above. As with the Fair Vote Project's proposed challenge, we do not express any view on the merits of the Wilson claimants' case itself, which fall outside the scope of this advice.

MARTIN CHAMBERLAIN QC
TIM JOHNSTON
MATTHEW KENNEDY
26 OCTOBER 2018

[9] Permission was refused on the papers by Supperstone J on 21 September 2018. The claimants renewed their application for permission on 28 September 2018.

[10] "*This is not a challenge to the outcome of the Referendum.*"

Bibliography

Graham Allen, *The Last Prime Minister: Being Honest About the UK Presidency* (London, Graham Allen, 2001)

JC Banks, *Federal Britain?* (London, George G Harap & Co, 1971)

Michael Barber, *Instruction to Deliver: Tony Blair, Public Services and the Challenge of Achieving Targets* (London, Politico's/Methuen, 2007)

Anthony Barnett and Peter Carty, *The Athenian Option: radical reform for the House of Lords* (Exeter, Imprint Academic, 2008)

Tony Benn, 'Developing a Participating Democracy', speech to the Annual Conference of the Welsh Council of Labour given at the Winter Garden Pavillion, Llandudno in Joan Bedington (ed), *Speeches by Tony Benn* (Nottingham, Spokesman Books, 1974)

Tony Benn and Andrew Hood, *Common Sense: A New Constitution for Britain* (London, Random House, 1993)

William Beveridge, 'An Economic General Staff', 5 March 1935, in Sir William Beveridge, *Planning under Socialism and other addresses* (London, Longmans, 1936)

Lord Beveridge, *for World Government* (London, Crusade for World Government, 1948)

Jay G Blumler and Stephen Coleman, *Realising Democracy Online: A Civic Commons in Cyberspace* (London, ippr/Citizens Online, 2001)

Douglas Carswell and Daniel Hannan, *The Plan: Twelve months to renew Britain* (Douglas Carswell and Daniel Hannan, 2008)

Winston L Spencer-Churchill, *Parliamentary Government and the Economic Problem* (Oxford, Clarendon Press, 1930)

Winston Churchill speech on federalism, 'Local Parliaments For England', *The Times*, Friday 13 September, p 4, Issue 40003

Robert Colville, *Politics, Policy and the Internet* (London, Centre for Policy Studies, 2008)

Bernard Crick, *Reform of the Commons* (London, Fabian Society, 1959)

Sir Stafford Cripps, 'Democracy and Dictatorship: The Issue for the Labour Party' (1933) IV(4) *The Political Quarterly* October–December, 467–81

Brian Crozier, *The Minimum State: Beyond Party Politics* (London, Hamish Hamilton, 1979)

Hugh Dalton, 'The Labour Party's Proposals for the Reform of Parliamentary Procedure' (1934) V(4) *The Political Quarterly* October–December, 469–79

Editors of the Ecologist, *A Blueprint for Survival* (London, Penguin, 1972)

Edward Goldsmith, 'What of the Future?' in Edward Goldsmith (ed), *Can Britain Survive?* (London, Tom Stacey, 1971)

'Group of Conservatives', *Some Proposals for Constitutional Reform: Being the Recommendations of a Group of Conservatives* (London, Eyre & Spotiswoode, 1946)

Friedrich A Hayek 'The Economic Conditions of Interstate Federalism', reproduced in Friedrich A Hayek, *Individualism and Economic Order* (London, Routledge & Kegan Paul Ltd, 1949)

JA Hobson, *The Crisis of Liberalism: New Issues of Democracy* (London, FS King & Son, 1909)

John H Humphreys, *Proportional Representation: A Study in Methods of Election* (Whitefish, Kessinger Publishing, 2004)

W Ivor Jennings, *A Federation For Western Europe* (Cambridge, University Press, 1940)

W Ivor Jennings, *Parliamentary Reform* (London, Victor Gollancz for the New Fabian Research Bureau, 1934)

Harold J Laski, 'Introduction' to *'Passed to you, please': Britain's red-tape machine at war* (London, Victor Gollancz, 1942)

JP Mackintosh, *The Devolution of Power: Local democracy, regionalism and nationalism* (Harmondsworth, Penguin, 1968)

William Sharp McKechnie, *The New Democracy and the Constitution* (London, John Murray, 1912)

Ramsay Muir, *How Britain is Governed: A critical analysis of modern developments in the British system of government* (New York, Richard R Smith, 1930)

John Pinder and Roy Pryce, *Europe After De Gaulle: Towards a United States of Europe* (Harmondsworth, Penguin, 1969)

Arthur Ponsonby, *Parliament and Foreign Policy* (London, Union of Democratic Control, 1914)

Julian Roche, *On-line Government* (London, Bow Group, 1995)

JFS Ross, *Parliamentary Representation* (London, Eyre & Spottiswoode, 1948)

EF Schumacher, *Small Is Beautiful: Economics as if People Mattered* (New York Harper Perennial 2010 reprint, first published 1973)

John St Loe Strachey, *The Referendum: A Handbook to the Poll of the People, Referendum, or Democratic Right of Veto on Legislation* (London, T Fisher Unwin, 1924)

John Strachey and CEM Joad, 'Parliamentary Reform: the New Party's Proposals' (1931) II(1–4) *The Political Quarterly* (London, Macmillan, 1931)

Keith Sutherland, *The Party's Over: Blueprint for a Very English Revolution* (Exeter, Imprint Academic, 2004)

Alex M. Thompson, *The Only Way to Democracy* (London, Clarion Newspaper Co, 1900)

William Waldegrave, *The Binding of Leviathan: Conservatism & the Future* (London, Hamish Hamilton, 1978)

HG Wells, *World Brain* (New Delhi, Isha Books, 2013)

Mrs Sidney Webb, 'A Reform Bill for 1932' (1931) II(1–4) *The Political Quarterly*, (London, Macmillan, 1931)

Sidney and Beatrice Webb, *A Constitution for the Socialist Commonwealth of Great Britain* (Cambridge and London, London School of Economics and Political Science/Cambridge University Press, 1975)

LS Woolf, *International Government* (London, Fabian Society, 1916)

Index

INTRODUCTORY NOTE

References such as "178–79" indicate (not necessarily continuous) discussion of a topic across a range of pages. Wherever possible in the case of topics with many references, these have either been divided into sub-topics or only the most significant discussions of the topic are listed. Because the entire work is about 'Brexit' and the related 'referendum', the use of this term and certain others which occur constantly throughout the book as entry points has been minimized. Information will be found under the corresponding detailed topics.